# The MOSAIC of CHRISTIAN BELIEF

## Twenty Centuries of Unity & Diversity

## ROGER E. OLSON

**InterVarsity Press**
Downers Grove, Illinois

Apollos
Leicester, England

InterVarsity Press
P.O. Box 1400, Downers Grove, IL 60515-1426
World Wide Web: www.ivpress.com
E-mail: mail@ivpress.com
APOLLOS (an imprint of Inter-Varsity Press, England)
38 De Montfort Street, Leicester LE1 7GP, England
Website: www.ivpbooks.com
E-mail: ivp@uccf.org.uk

InterVarsity Press® is the book-publishing division of InterVarsity Christian Fellowship/USA®, a student
movement active on campus at hundreds of universities, colleges and schools of nursing in the United States of
America, and a member movement of the International Fellowship of Evangelical Students. For information
about local and regional activities, write Public Relations Dept., InterVarsity Christian Fellowship/USA, 6400
Schroeder Rd., P.O. Box 7895, Madison, WI 53707-7895, or visit the IVCF website at <www.ivcf.org>.

Cover photograph: Erich Lessing / Art Resource, N.Y.

USA ISBN 0-8308-2695-5
UK IBN 0-85111-782-1

Printed in the United States of America ∞

Library of Congress Cataloging-in-Publication Data

Olson, Roger E.
  The mosaic of Christian belief: twenty centuries of unity and
diversity / Roger E. Olson.
    p. cm.
Includes bibliographical references and indexes.
  ISBN 0-8308-2695-5 (cloth: alk. paper)
  1. Theology, Doctrinal—Popular works. 2. Evangelicalism. I. Title.
  BT77 .O28 2002
  230—dc21
                                                                                        2002007426

British Library Cataloguing in Publication Data

A catalogue record for this book is available from the British Library.

| P | 18 | 17 | 16 | 15 | 14 | 13 | 12 | 11 | 10 | 9 | 8 | 7 | 6 | 5 | 4 | 3 | 2 |
| Y | 16 | 15 | 14 | 13 | 12 | 11 | 10 | 09 | 08 | 07 | 06 | 05 | | | | | |

*Dedicated to*
*Al Glenn,*
*Model, Mentor, Friend*

# CONTENTS

# PREFACE

This book was born out of nearly twenty years of teaching introductory courses in Christian doctrine and theology in university, college and seminary. During those years I used many different one-volume textbooks and asked students to read them carefully and critically. While my students and I benefited from each book I used and we read and discussed together, none of them seemed entirely satisfactory for our purposes. My students and I together decided that what was needed was a very basic, relatively comprehensive, nontechnical, nonspeculative one-volume introduction to Christian belief. I felt the need to write such a book, and thus the present volume came into existence. Much more about it and about me—the author—is presented in the introduction. I hope that this handbook will glorify God, edify the church, inform and stimulate students, and answer people's questions about Christian beliefs, while misleading readers as little as possible.

I would like to thank my fine friends at InterVarsity Press who helped plan the book and guided it to fruition. I would also like to thank my wife Becky and daughters Amanda and Sonja for their patience with my writing obsession. I thank Stanley Grenz and Gregory Boyd for their (entirely independent) friendships and years of good listening and giving advice.

I dedicate this book to my theological mentor and model of twenty-five years Alfred (Al) Glenn, without whose faithful support, encouragement and prayers I would not have become a theologian. Al is my model of an irenic evangelical as well as my friend, colleague and advisor.

Throughout this volume the abbreviations *ANF* and *NPNF* will be used for texts that may be found in the multivolume sets *The Ante-Nicene Fathers: Translations of the Writings of the Fathers Down to A.D. 325*, ed. Alexander Roberts and James Donaldson, 10 vols. (Grand Rapids, Mich.: Eerdmans, 1988) and *A Select Library of the Nicene and Post-Nicene Fathers of the Christian Church,* ed. Philip Schaff, 14 vols. (Grand Rapids, Mich.: Eerdmans, 1984). (Identical multivolume sets are also published by Hendrickson Publishing of Peabody, Mass.) These are generally available in most church-related college and university libraries as well as in most seminary libraries. Many public libraries keep them in reference collections. They are also available in the collection known as the *Christian Classics Ethereal Library (CCEL),* which is on the Internet (ccel.org) and available on compact disc from the publisher (see the website for more information). The edition of John Calvin's *Institutes of the Christian Religion* used throughout is the one found in The Library of Christian Classics published by Westminster Press (now Westminster John Knox), 1960, edited by John T. McNiell and translated by Ford Lewis Battles.

# INTRODUCTION
## The Need for a *"Both-And"* Theology

Numerous fine volumes expounding Christian belief have been published in recent decades and many of them are still in print and readily available to readers interested in understanding what Christianity has to say about God, humanity, salvation, the church, life after death, the end of the world and a variety of other religious subjects. Why another one? What distinguishes this volume from those already written by Christian theologians?

### Unapologetic Apology for Yet Another Handbook of Christian Doctrine

While there may be nothing totally new under the sun, this handbook of Christian belief is intended to fill a perceived gap in the shelf of expositions of Christian teachings. Like most of them, it aims at being *thoroughly biblical* and *both faithful to the Great Tradition of Christianity as well as contemporary in its restatement of what Christians have always believed*. It also intends, however, to provide a *mediating theological perspective within the broad tradition of evangelical Protestant Christianity*. A mediating theology is one that attempts to bridge unnecessary and unfortunate gulfs between perspectives and interpretations within a single religion—in this case Christianity. Such an approach values unity as well as truth and assumes that at times it is necessary for equally committed Christians to agree to disagree about secondary matters and come together on common ground. One way in which this may be accomplished is by a rediscovery and new valuing of our common Christian heritage of belief—what will here be called the Great Tradition of Christian teaching. Other terms for the same stock of commonly held Christian beliefs include "consensual Christian tradition" and "mere Christianity." Some have used the less felicitous label "generic Christianity" for this common ground of belief shared by most Christians down through the ages since the early church. This concept of common Christian ground of belief will be explored in the first chapter. This volume seeks to explain to uninitiated readers what that common tradition includes in terms of unity, what it allows in terms of diversity and what it excludes in terms of heresies—beliefs generally considered completely incompatible with Christianity even thought they appear from time to time wearing the "Christian" label.

While a mediating theology emphasizes unity of belief and common ground shared by different groups of Christians, another way in which a mediating approach to Christian belief may be partially achieved is by showing that within that general common area of shared Christian belief there exists room for real diversity. Too many Christians identify "authentic Christian belief" with one narrow slice of Christian thought. Part of the process of Christian maturation is recognizing legitimate diversity and even disagreement within larger unity and agreement. In spite of important differences of interpretation and opinion, for example, Christians in the Eastern Orthodox, Roman Catholic, Presbyterian, Methodist, Baptist and Pentecostal traditions share a common faith—insofar as they stand within their own *Christian* denominational heritages and have not succumbed to radical sectarianism or liberalized theology. That is to say, for example, the Westminster Confession of Faith of the Presbyterian tradition and the Methodist Articles of Religion share much common ground even though they diverge significantly at secondary points. They are both expressions of Christian belief and not of secularism, paganism, Hinduism or Buddhism. The same could be said for many other traditions within the Great Tradition. Even historic Eastern Orthodoxy, Roman Catholicism and Protestantism—the three broad branches of the Christian religion—share much in common when compared with other world religions, spiritual philosophies and worldviews. This book's title is a metaphor for this mediating approach that seeks to emphasize *both* Christian unity *and* Christian diversity in terms of beliefs. A mosaic melds multiformity and rich diversity of colors with harmony and complexity into a pattern that conveys a unified image without sacrificing variety. Great Tradition Christianity holds both unity and diversity together. Christians can be and, at their best, are "of one mind" about the most important matters related to God, but they also contribute richness to that single worldview with their various perspectives. One major goal of this volume is to portray Christian belief in all its glorious harmony and rich diversity.

Equally important to the goal of presenting a mediating approach to Christian belief is this volume's goal of expressing the best of *evangelical Christianity* in terms of that tradition's beliefs. The concept *evangelical* is a much disputed and perhaps essentially contested one. In its broadest possible sense it is synonymous with *Christian* in that Christianity is gospel-centered more than law-centered. *Evangelical* comes from a Greek word for the gospel or good news proclaimed by the apostles following Jesus Christ's death and resurrection. The gospel is the apostolic message of full and free salvation through Jesus Christ and by God's grace through faith in him. Thus, any church, organization or person who proclaims that gospel faithfully is evangelical.

Throughout history, however, movements have adopted the evangelical label in a more specific way to describe themselves. In Europe to this day *evangelical* is virtually synonymous with *Protestant* and designates a form of Christianity (e.g., a church or denomination) that is not Roman Catholic or Eastern Orthodox but stands in the reforming heritage of Martin Luther and John Calvin and the English Reformation led by Thomas Cranmer. In Great Britain *evangelical* was a term used to describe revivalistic movements led by John and Charles Wesley and their friend George Whitefield in the eighteenth century. In the United States *evangelical* and *Evangelicalism* have come to describe especially that form of (mostly) Protestant Christianity that crosses denominational boundaries and is generally conservative in theology, conversionist and evangelistic, biblicist, and focused on Jesus Christ as God incarnate, crucified Savior, risen Lord, and returning king. Evangelicals stand out from other Christians by their emphasis on the importance of a "personal relationship with Jesus Christ" through an experience of conversion involving repentance and faith and a daily life of discipleship to Christ that involves prayer, Scripture reading and seeking by God's help to emulate the Savior. In the second half of the twentieth century a loose coalition of moderately conservative, evangelical Christian individuals, denominations and groups came together to support one another and promote their common evangelical ethos.[1]

---

[1]For those unfamiliar with this evangelical coalition and its unity and diversity, see Jon R. Stone, *On the Boundaries of American Evangelicalism: The Postwar Evangelical Coalition* (New York: St. Martin's Press, 1997); Gary Dorrien, *The Remaking of Evangelical Theology* (Louisville, Ky.: Westminster John Knox, 1998); and Donald W. Dayton and Robert K. Johnston, eds., *The Variety of American Evangelicalism* (Downers Grove, Ill.: InterVarsity Press, 1991).

This volume speaks about Christian belief broadly and generally out of this evangelical tradition rooted as it is in the historic Protestant heritage. It seeks also, however, to speak on behalf of all Christian traditions including Eastern Orthodoxy, Roman Catholicism, and nonevangelical varieties of Protestantism that remain faithful to the Great Tradition of Christian teaching and belief. As will become clear, however, it does not speak for but against those modern manifestations of Christianity that are more counterfeit than authentic. It does not assume that everything labeled *Christian* is authentically Christian, and it will attempt to articulate the differences between Great Tradition Christianity in all its varieties and counterfeit Christianity that promotes a different gospel or includes a strong element of teaching and belief that is incompatible with the gospel of Jesus Christ and the Great Tradition of Christianity.

Besides attempting to present Christian belief in a mediating manner from within a broadly evangelical perspective, this handbook of basic theology will strive to be irenic in spirit and tone as opposed to polemical in approach. Many books of belief are dogmatic and argumentative. Here every attempt will be made to draw Christians together without sacrificing essential truths of divine revelation or the great heritage of Christian doctrine. *Irenic* comes from a Greek word for peace and means "of a peaceable spirit." An irenic approach to expounding Christian beliefs is one that attempts always to understand opposing viewpoints before disagreeing, and when it is necessary to disagree does so respectfully and in love. An irenic approach to doctrine seeks common ground and values unity within diversity and diversity within unity. An irenic approach does not imply relativism or disregard for truth, but it does seek to live by the motto "in essentials unity, in nonessentials liberty, in all things charity."

Even though this volume is written from an Arminian perspective (believing in human persons' God-given free will), it seeks to treat Reformed theology (Calvinism) and all other branches of authentic Christian theology with respect and in a spirit of love. The purpose here is not to win a victory for any particular theological orientation within Christianity, but to provide a mediating exposition of common Christian belief that acknowledges and respects diverse Christian traditions and interpretations. This volume may interpret the Great Tradition of Christian belief more from an Arminian perspective than from a Reformed/Calvinist point of view, but that does not imply any antipathy or hostility to

Reformed theology.[2] In fact, this is a test case of this book's distinctive approach to expounding Christian belief: It seeks to be fair to all the major theological orientations within Great Tradition Christianity, taking seriously their distinctive contributions, without sacrificing or hiding the author's own particular theological orientation.

In addition to *mediating, evangelical* and *irenic,* this volume strives to present Christian belief in a *nonspeculative way.* In this writer's opinion and in the emphatically expressed opinions of many of his students, far too many published expositions of Christian doctrine fly too often into unwarranted speculation about matters having to do with the attributes of God and eternal inner workings of the Trinity (God in himself), the precise nature of the incarnation of God in Jesus Christ, the reasons for and effects of Christ's atoning death, and the details of biblical eschatology (the future return of Christ and end of the world). This writer has frequently heard college and seminary students as well as laypeople in churches' adult forums ask impatiently, how do you know that the Holy Spirit is the "bond of love" between the Father and the Son? And, why are you so sure that Jesus could not have sinned? These and other quite traditional interpretations of biblical revelation have arisen and been taken for granted in Christian theology for hundreds of years, and yet astute and perceptive novices in theology often regard them as sheer speculation. Even the most strenuous explanations and defenses fail to satisfy this quest for justification of theological claims in something other than flights of speculative fancy. The examples regarding the doctrines of the Trinity and the person of Jesus Christ (Christology) above are only two possible examples. There are many others: the precise nature of God's eternity in relation to time, the details of the consummation of God's plan and purpose for human history in the future, the precise location of those who have died before their resurrection and judgment, and "the furniture of heaven and temperature of hell."

While holding opinions about such matters is perfectly normal and acceptable, can anyone really claim to *know* answers to such questions or have reasonable and justified models of these realities? Speculation is not necessarily wrong. There is such a phenomenon as "reverent and reasonable

---

[2]Readers unfamiliar with the categories Reformed/Calvinist and free will/Arminian in Christian theology (also known as "monergist" and "synergist") may wish to consult Alan P. F. Sell, *The Great Debate: Calvinism, Arminianism, and Salvation* (Grand Rapids, Mich.: Baker, 1982).

speculation," and it is probably unavoidable in any attempt to give answers to questions that go beyond what is clearly stated in Christianity's basic sources. However, this writer—like most of his students—believes that one pitfall of much well-intentioned Christian theology has been unwarranted speculation. Granted, it helps keep theologians employed. On the other hand, it often undermines and even discredits Christianity when Christians claim to know more than it is possible to know given Christianity's sources and norms. Unwarranted speculation appears in any affirmation that simply has no solid basis in the sources and norms with which one is working and yet claims to be something more than mere guesswork. The purpose of this book is not to provide new and unheard-of answers to difficult questions, but to describe the rough unity and colorful diversity of Christian belief. Where speculation seems to lie behind and within Christian belief, that will be duly noted and this writer will strive to avoid adding to the problem.

Finally, this presentation of Christian belief will strive for *simplicity without oversimplification*. Far too many introductory books of Christian doctrine and theology claim to be written for relatively educated and intellectually curious beginners (e.g., students beyond high school) but are actually written for other scholars. This is an almost irresistible temptation for authors of such books. This writer knows, for example, that other scholars and professors will examine this book and it is tempting to include subtleties, nuances and academic digressions to avoid their criticisms. Inevitably, however, giving in to that temptation leads to confusing the uninitiated readers. This volume will make every attempt to avoid use of theological jargon except when certain technical terms are crucial to understanding its content, and then they will be explained immediately in the context where they first appear. Similarly, this volume will avoid delving into subtle scholarly disputes and shades of interpretation that go beyond what any theological novice needs to know to move beyond that status into initiation in basic Christian theology. At the same time, however, oversimplification will be avoided here. Readers will be challenged to learn and stretch as they read. This book will not avoid important historical theological concepts and terms such as "hypostatic union," but it will explain immediately (at least once) that this is a technical term in Christian theology for the doctrine of the incarnation of God in Christ by means of a union of two natures: human and divine.

These, then, are the distinguishing characteristics of this contribution to the shelf of books already published about Christian belief: *mediating (both-and as opposed to either-or whenever possible), evangelical, irenic in spirit and tone, nonspeculative* and *relatively simple for the uninitiated.* Each chapter will examine and expound a particular locus (issue, set of questions) of Christian theology. The scope and sequence will be traditional, progressing after introductory questions about theology's method (sources and norms) to the loci of divine revelation, nature and attributes of God, Trinity, and so on. The final chapter will deal with Christian beliefs about the ultimate future and what Christians hope for and confidently expect at the end of world history. Each major chapter (after the first one dealing with unity and diversity that substitutes for the traditional "prolegomenon" or "foundations and methods" chapter) will follow a uniform outline: a statement of the underlying issues and questions of the doctrine, followed by a brief description of the consensus of Christian teaching about it, followed by an exposition of the major alternative beliefs outside of the consensus (heresies), followed by treatment of the main diverse interpretations of the doctrine within the broad Christian consensus and concluding with some suggestions for a unitive view that emphasizes "both-and" rather than "either-or."

## Both-And Rather Than Either-Or Theology

The perceptive peruser or mere casual reader of this volume may have noticed that so far little has been said about the nature or necessity of either *belief* or *theology* in Christianity, let alone the meaning of *both-and rather than either-or* as an approach to them. Careful, detailed explanation of all of that will appear in chapter one, but for persons simply trying to decide whether to buy or borrow this book to read, a preliminary description and defense of these ideas will be offered here. As much as professional theologians and theologically-minded pastors may deplore it, it is a fact that today many persons who are committed personally to Jesus Christ and to Christianity as a way of life have little use for anything approaching formal doctrine or theology. *Belief* is for many of them slightly more acceptable than *doctrine,* but *theology* often sends shivers down the spines of Christians who are convinced—rightly or wrongly—that much of what is wrong with Christianity, and especially Western Christianity, has arisen through formal theological reflection. A favorite slogan of many experiential Christians is "Jesus unites; doctrine divides." The "Jesus movement" of the early 1970s has left a profoundly anti-intellectual stamp upon much of North American Christianity and especially on the evangelical movement. So have the charismatic movements and the many independent churches and ministries that have attracted millions of people into their memberships and orbits of influence.

Some sociologists of religion have suggested that contemporary Christianity—especially in North America—is in danger of devolving into a "folk religion." One of the characteristics of a folk religion is lack of reflection on the intellectual implications of revelatory experiences and failure to integrate these experiences with other spheres of life. Folk religions often flourish in a compartmentalized, largely privatized sphere of life such as small cell groups of people with similar experiences who network with each other so long as they find support. Feelings tend to take precedence over intellect, and clichés and slogans (often put to music) take the place of coherent and developed doctrinal affirmations. Folk religions generally resist critical reflection and formal confession of belief in favor of subjective experiences and pragmatic methods of problem-solving in the spiritual realms of existence. An example of such a folk religion in North America is the so-called New Age movement that arose around 1970 as a new manifestation of some very ancient beliefs and practices. Although a few new agers have attempted to provide this extremely diverse spiritual phenomenon with some intellectual moorings, they have been largely ignored by grassroots spiritual seekers who most certainly read books about paranormal experiences and invisible spiritual realities but by and large resist coherent explanations as too confining and dogmatic. Astrology—believed by almost all new agers—may be popular but has little or no influence on communities religious or secular.

Is Christianity becoming a folk religion somewhat like the New Age movement? Is Christian belief in, for example, petitionary prayer becoming something like new age belief in astrology? The pressures put upon Christianity by secular society to privatize its beliefs and practices militates in this direction. Impulses within Christian movements contribute to the process of reducing Christianity to a set of subjective experiences and feel-good clichés. What "feels good" and "provides comfort" is often the main criterion by which grassroots Christians decide what to believe and how to practice their spirituality. The church becomes a support group rather than the communal bearer of a tradition that values truth. This may seem like a dismal analysis of the present condition of Christianity in North America. To be sure there are many Christian churches and organizations as well as individual writers and publications that protest the trend toward folk religion. Small pockets and outposts of "confessional Christians" who value the intellectual and theological heritage of Christianity crop up and flourish here and there. Jeremiads are published decrying the problem of truncated and reduced Christianity with titles such as *No Place for Truth* and *The Scandal of the Evangelical Mind*. How much impact these have on the problem is debatable. Scholars pay attention and professors mumble qualified agreement, but the average North American Christian often misses the message altogether because his or her spiritual sustenance comes more from Christian television and small spiritual support groups than anything written or taught by scholars.

The problem with a folk religion, of course, is that it has little or no public impact and tends over time to lose its shape and become compatible with anything and everything. Folk religions are porous and fluid. Feelings—on which they thrive—are notoriously indistinguishable. Pollsters report that approximately twenty-two percent of adult Americans believe in reincarnation, and that must include many people who consider themselves committed Christians. When queried about how they reconcile belief in reincarnation with traditional Christian belief in the bodily resurrection (clearly communicated in the New Testament and defended by all major church fathers and Reformers) many such persons simply appear puzzled by the question. Anyone who has attempted to teach Christian doctrine or theology to young adult Christians has experienced this odd eclecticism in which completely incompatible notions are combined in a soup of experiential spirituality.

Out of this postmodern, relativistic cultural milieu and because of disillusionment with heated arguments over seemingly minor points of biblical and doctrinal interpretation that have divided entire denominations unnecessarily, a deep antipathy has arisen toward formal theology as intellectual reflection on an objectively given deposit of divine revelation. Even greater aversion has arisen to beliefs and practices labeled traditional. Many sincere, devout Christians' attitude toward the entire realm of doctrine and theology is active disinterest if not hostility. And yet most maturing Christians are well aware that somehow *believing* plays a necessary role in being Christian. Few, if any, Christians actually reject beliefs in favor of a wholly subjective, feeling-oriented spirituality. After all, does not the New Testament itself encourage believing and confessing such things as "Jesus is Lord"? Finding the right balance between *believing* and *experiencing* seems too difficult for many postmodern Christians and little help is forthcoming from pulpits and lecterns in their churches. On the one hand, some evangelical ministers and teachers emphasize believing as if it were the be-all and end-all of authentic Christianity. On the other hand, many more emphasize "experiencing God" or "doing what Jesus would do" as the be-all and end-all of authentic Christianity. What is an ordinary Christian to think and do?

This book aims at making a modest contribution to overcoming a part of the problem described above. Folk religion is a poor substitute for historic Christianity; formal, academic, intellectual "head knowledge" is an equally poor substitute for personal transformation through a relationship with the triune God. But the greater threat at the present moment—in this postmodern, highly individualistic and experience-oriented culture—is folk religion. This writer, like many other theologians of various Christian traditions, is profoundly disturbed by the decline these past twenty years in the average Christian's awareness of *basic Christian beliefs*. This writer is also deeply impressed by the hunger many young Christians have for an exposition of Christian beliefs that respects their autonomy as persons created in God's image and endowed by God with intellectual powers of discovery and discernment. They have inquiring minds and want to be presented with historic Christian beliefs in all their unity and diversity and given permission to decide for themselves under God and together with a faith community what they should believe. The day is gone forever when most people will accept a doctrine just because it is traditional and they are told (as in the old German saying) "Eat up, little birdies, or die!" But a new day is here when many Christians want to know what the historic Christian faith includes in terms of beliefs about God and themselves and why there are so many varieties of interpretation within Christianity and how to handle all of that. This book is aimed at giving such critical, inquiring Christian minds something to start with: *a fresh exposition of the old Christian faith in its unity and diversity.* Hopefully this will provide a stepping stone out of the swamp of folk religion and onto a more intellectually rigorous path toward truth.

This is a book about *doctrine* and *theology,* which are both about *beliefs.* It would be appropriate here to explain what these terms mean and how they relate to each other. *Belief* is simply the assent of the mind to a proposition or set of propositions. A proposition is a truth claim. Not all propositions are straightforward, directly factual claims to truth. Some are metaphorical and aim at saying something about reality indirectly by making a comparison or evoking a response. One might well argue that there are other senses of belief. For example, a person might believe in another person without being able to translate that into assent to a proposition. While that is true, surely everyone recognizes that without some propositional content such as "John is a good person" believing in a person is hardly distinguishable from liking him or her. Without digressing into a philosophical discussion of the nature of *belief* and *believing,* suffice it to say here that one sense is that they involve giving assent to propositions or truth claims. Try to empty Christianity of all truth claims and it becomes a very vacuous phenomenon. There is then nothing to believe or disbelieve. Christians have always believed certain propositions and disbelieved other ones. This is embedded in the biblical witness itself and is evident from the earliest Christian writings after the New Testament where early church fathers found it necessary to summarize essential Christian beliefs in sets of propositions to which converts gave their assent.

*Doctrine* is a relatively complex religious belief. Of course, the term is often used as a synonym for a religious belief. But consider the common statement "I believe in the doctrine of the Trinity." Ordinary language indicates that we often recognize a distinction between a simple belief and a doctrine, although the two go hand-in-hand in many cases. A doctrine develops out of beliefs and is a belief or set of beliefs examined, reflected upon, and affirmed as true in a formal way by an organized community of believers. "I believe in God the Father Almighty, maker of heaven and earth" begins the Apostles' Creed. In one sense this does express a doctrine. On the other hand, it does not. The doctrine of the Trinity was developed by the early church to explain and protect the beliefs confessed in the Apostles' Creed. It is somewhat more complex and also secondary—a step removed in terms of reflection—to the confession of belief in God the Father Almighty and his Son Jesus Christ and the Holy Spirit. An analogy might be helpful. In United States jurisprudence a person believes in and confesses religious freedom on the basis of the Constitution's Bill of Rights. Separation of church and state is a judicial doctrine developed by judges who have to interpret and apply the First Amendment to the Constitution where that Bill of Rights—including freedom of religion—appears. It evolved through a process of reflection on the guarantee of religious freedom and is more complex than that. Yet it would be quite difficult for anyone to confess belief in religious freedom in the United States without accepting some version of separation of church and state. Some may try, but after two hundred years it appears impossible. The doctrine of separation of church and state—although hotly debated as to its details and its application—is now part and parcel of freedom of religion in the context of American society. And yet, belief in religious freedom is one thing; belief in separation of church and state is something else—a distinction with hardly a difference.

*Theology* is the process of examination and reflection that leads to the construction and reconstruction of doctrines. Of course, sometimes the word *theology* is simply used as a synonym for *doctrine* as in, "our theology is thoroughly trinitarian," or, "her theology of the end times is premillennial." This is an informal way of speaking. More correctly and precisely, theology is the process rather than the product. The product is doctrine. Sticking to our earlier analogy, we might say that theology is similar to the process of judicial examination and judgment in United States courts when a law is challenged. Often this process leads to "doctrines" that become somewhat set in stone as authoritative precedents that later judges must take almost as seriously as the Constitution itself. Over a period of time cases coming to the Supreme Court of the United States led to the judicial doctrine of separation of church and state, which is not actually (contrary to what most people believe) clearly articulated in the Constitution itself. As late as 1819 some states used religious tests for candidacy for public office. Only members of certain approved denominations could serve in the state assemblies or legislatures. The Supreme Court gradually struck down these religious tests on the basis that they were inconsistent with the guarantee of religious liberty in the Bill of Rights. Thus evolved the doctrine of church-state separation. A similar process led the undivided early church of the Roman Empire to develop the doctrine of the triunity of God (Trinity). Theology is the process of reflecting reasonably on divine revelation and on consensus beliefs about it. The nature of theological reflection will be a subject of chapter three.

Theology gives rise to construction and reconstruction of doctrine. Doctrines are highly developed, relatively complex expressions of beliefs of tradition-communities such as the early Christian churches or later denominations. Often doctrines are developed defensively; they arise out of concern to protect certain beliefs about God, Jesus Christ, salvation and so forth from erosion, distortion or outright rejection. Sometimes Christian communities overreact to perceived heresies. (A *heresy* is a wrong belief—one that seriously undermines some crucial dimension of the gospel itself and must be denied and rejected.) The pendulum swings one way and then another in the process of theological reflection that leads to doctrinal construction and reconstruction. For example, many Christian theologians—especially Protestants and Eastern Orthodox—believe that the Roman Catholic Church overreacted to modernism in its ranks in the nineteenth century by making papal infallibility a dogma. (A *dogma* is a required doctrine which cannot be questioned without serious repercussions.) Even some progressive Catholic theologians have suggested as much. Similarly, some Protestant groups have overreacted to the perceived threat of modernism by developing a doctrine of strict biblical inerrancy. Often such overreactions give rise to opposite overreactions. Some liberal theologians who value modernity as a source and norm for Christian theology have denied not only infallibility and inerrancy but also the entire "house of authority" in Christian thought so that there is no absolute norm of truth above the individual.

The result of this pendulum swing effect of theology is "either-or" theology. In other words, people begin to accept without question a series of false alternatives: *either* papal infallibility *or* doctrinal chaos; *either* biblical inerrancy *or* relativism; *either* tear down the "house of authority" *or* live under oppression, and so on. Manifestations of either-or thinking in Christianity are everywhere. Either God is three or God is one. Either God is absolutely all-determining or he is not God. Either human beings are totally depraved from birth or there is no need of God's grace for salvation. Either people are unconditionally predestined by God or salvation is not a free gift. Either grace is conveyed through sacraments or the sacraments are "merely symbolic." Either the resurrection is physical or it is not real. On and on it goes.

What is unfortunately often unnoticed is the possibility of "both-and" in many cases of doctrinal divisions and controversies. Could it be that God is *both* three *and* one? Could it be that God is both self-limiting (in order to allow creatures room for some self-determination) and sovereign? Could it be that salvation is completely of grace alone even though humans are genuinely free and must decide freely (apart from any determination) for or against it? Could it be that sacraments such as baptism and the Lord's Supper are more than "mere symbols" even though they do not convey grace automatically? Perhaps many of the doctrinal divisions that have arisen are due to unnecessary bifurcations—false alternatives. Either-or thinking becomes a habit. People fail to look for the combinations, the truth in both sides. What if instead Christians began to focus on synthesis rather than analysis? Instead of focusing obsessively on differences as if they could never be reconciled, what if God's people looked long and hard for the truth in seemingly irreconcilable but equally biblically supported beliefs and doctrines? This is not to suggest that every belief has some important truth that should be discovered and combined with the truth in its opposite. For example, belief in reincarnation seems simply incompatible with what Christians have always regarded as their ultimate source and norm for belief—Jesus Christ and the inspired Word of God that testifies of him. Christ did not come back as another person. He was incarnate only once and rose from death as the same person he was before he was born and before he died. Resurrection and reincarnation cannot be combined. However, different ideas of resurrection may both contain elements of truth. In fact, this is exactly what the apostle Paul seems to be doing in 1 Corinthians 15 when he calls the resurrection body a *sōma pneumatikos,* a "spiritual body." Some have claimed that Jesus' risen body was and is fleshly in a materialistic way. That Paul denies. But he does not deny that it was and is a body and not a nonsubstantial entity like a ghost. Both-and; not either-or. Both body and spiritual; not one or the other.

Certainly the idea of looking for the element of truth in conflicting beliefs and doctrines and seeking to transcend false alternatives in syntheses of the truth in both sides is not new. The nineteenth-century German philosopher G. W. F. Hegel advocated such an approach to philosophy and many of the nineteenth-century mediating theologians of Germany, Great Britain and North America attempted to apply his dialectical thinking of synthesis out of thesis and antithesis to problems of theology. Unfortunately, all too often Hegelian-inspired mediating theology resulted in watered down, rationalistic philosophical theologies. The nineteenth-century Danish Christian thinker Søren Kierkegaard protested against Hegelian synthesis because he believed it detracted from the majesty and mystery of God and God's self-revelation, which could only be grasped in paradoxes. Once again a false either-or developed in theology: either theological truth is expressed in paradoxes or it is open to rationalistic synthesis that leaves little or no room for mystery. This writer does not agree with either Hegel—who seemed to believe the human mind is capable of thinking God's thoughts after him and grasping ultimate reality in rationally coherent concepts and systems—or Kierkegaard, who overreacted to Hegel by reveling in the "absolute paradox" of Christianity such that human reason is believed to be incapable of making any progress in understanding divine revelation coherently.

One of theology's tasks is to construct relatively coherent, workable models of the transcendent realities revealed by God in Jesus Christ and the inspired record and interpretation of him that we know as Scripture. Part of that task is to reconstruct older models insofar as they are partial and distorted due to overreaction to other models. (Here *model* refers not to a scale model that actually depicts a larger figure but to a disclosure model or analogue model that represents something else that cannot be literally depicted. A model of an atom is a disclosure or analogue model. The Trinity is such a model of the three-in-oneness of God as that is revealed in Jesus Christ and Scripture.) Sometimes, this writer is convinced, the very best reasonable and faithful reflection on divine revelation fails to construct or reconstruct a single model that does justice to all that is revealed about a particular reality. Many authors have pointed out that this is the case even in physics where models of light as particle-like and wave-like must be used in a complementary way without being combined. And yet in both physics and theology inquiring minds struggle to discover single models that synthesize the seemingly conflicting truths in alternative and complementary but uncombined models. Both-and theology does not automatically exclude either-or; it does not automatically rush to synthesis. But it looks at twin truths of divine revelation and seeks to do justice to both in the best way possible. Sometimes that means affirming as true two seemingly incompatible models of reality. Sometimes it means constructing new models that do more justice to the whole of what is revealed by God than older models.

Historical theology yields many examples of false either-or thinking about beliefs and falsely opposed alternative doctrines that harden into exclusive models causing unnecessary division in the Christian community. The infamous debate between Martin Luther and Catholic reformer Desiderius Erasmus over free will and divine determination is a case study. Wishing to emphasize the gratuity of grace and depravity of humans, Luther argued that the human person is a mule ridden by either God or the devil without any self-determination in spiritual matters. Wishing to emphasize the responsibility of human beings, Erasmus argued that they are relatively free and self-determining within limits. Luther did not deny human responsibility and Erasmus did not deny human fallenness and dependence on grace. In the heat of argument, however, their models of divine-human interaction and roles in salvation fell into absolute antithesis to one another with negative results for Catholic-Protestant relations afterward. Luther's lieutenant in the Protestant Reformation, Philipp Melanchthon, tried to work out a synthesis of Erasmian and Lutheran perspectives but failed—largely due to lack of cooperation by followers of the two Reformers. The task remains for Christian theologians to discover and, if possible, combine the truths in both models. Some will reject such a project due to unalterable commitments to one or the other model. However, it seems to many Christians that scriptural support for both models can be found and equally committed Christians believe in human self-determination and divine determination. Can the two be combined in a synthesis? Perhaps not. But at the very least both beliefs can be recognized as authentically Christian insofar as they neither violate the sovereignty of God nor the responsibility of human persons.

Why is both-and theology important? This writer's conviction is that forced false alternatives of doctrine and their resulting divisions within the church universal undermine the credibility of Christian witness in the world. The incessant quarreling and cold indifference between God-fearing, Bible-believing, Jesus-loving Christians is scandalous to the secular world—as it should be scandalous to Christians. They also serve to convince many Christians that theology and doctrine are detrimental to Christianity. They see that under the guise of "passion for truth" many Christian theologians carry on a crusade for their own pet one-sided doctrines, and they flee from the specter of inquisitions into the equally dangerous territory of folk religion. Once again we see a false either-or at work. Subjective folk religion devoid of all rigorous doctrinal examination and affirmation is not the only alternative to rigid, one-sided, inquisitorial dogmatism. Development and affirmation of doctrines is compatible with continuing quests for new and greater light, and Christian experience of God is compatible with intellectual wrestling with theological issues.

The approach to these issues and tasks taken in this book is a very modest one. No goal of achieving synthesis of all truth is even envisioned. Rather, in each doctrinal locus the problem of false alternatives will be described, the underlying consensus of Christian belief will be expounded, the alternatives to the overwhelming consensus of the Christian church's teaching will be explained, the legitimate diversity of opinion and interpretation within Christian thought will be explored, and some possible unitive viewpoints that have the potential for reuniting Christians (especially evangelical Protestants) will be proposed. Of course, all of this will inevitably reflect this writer's perspective in spite of his best attempts to speak on behalf of the evangelical Christian community as a whole.

The writer's own theological perspective is shaped by several influences, and the reader (or prospective reader) deserves to know what these are. First, the writer is a Baptist who stands within the broader evangelical free-church tradition that includes many denominations that do not call themselves "Baptist." The writer grew up in and was spiritually and theological nurtured by Pentecostals and then later Pietists. Both emphasize a personal relationship with Jesus Christ as the primary element of vital, authentic Christianity. On the other hand, the writer has come to value the wider catholic tradition that transcends any denomination and embraces the common teachings of the early church fathers, Reformers and modern conservative and evangelical theologians. The writer strives to be progressive in his evangelical approach to theology while respecting the Great Tradition of Christian teaching. He strives to be ecumenical while faithfully valuing his own tradition's distinctives. Finally, the writer is deeply committed to the authority and freedom that is found only in Jesus Christ through the indwelling of the Holy Spirit by faith. These few sentences do not say very much about the writer's own perspective and approach, but hopefully they say enough to communicate something of their distinctive flavor. The writer promises to do his best to prevent his own private and confessional biases from getting in the way of expounding Christian belief faithfully, but no claim to God-like objectivity is made. Nor should such be expected from any theologian.

# CHAPTER 1

# CHRISTIAN BELIEF

## Unity *and* Diversity

Should all Christians share certain beliefs in common? Is there a necessary common ground of "mere Christianity" that defines authentic Christianity in terms of its belief content? Or may everyone claim to be equally authentically Christian and yet believe whatever his or her mind and will find acceptable? These are profound questions and many modern and postmodern people would prefer to avoid answering them. If we say that everyone who claims to be Christian must hold to certain beliefs in order to make that claim stick, so to speak, then we risk imposing a kind of uniformity that smacks of authoritarianism and seems not to respect individualities of peoples and cultures. On the other hand, if we say that each Christian may legitimately create his or her own recipe of beliefs and expect others to acknowledge him or her as Christian regardless of conformity of beliefs with historic Christian teachings, we risk emptying the term *Christian* of all meaning. Is every individual and group that claims to be Christian automatically to be recognized by others as truly Christian? Or are there certain minimal standards of belief (and perhaps behavior as well) that must mark authentic Christian existence and validate claims to Christianity?

The problems embedded in these questions are profound and tackling them is risky business. Inevitably one will be accused of either intolerant dogmatism or vacuous relativism or both! Nevertheless, these are questions that beg answers of some kind—however tentative those answers may be. That is because we live in an age and culture in which religion tends to be polarized by shrill and inflexible fundamentalisms that allow little or no diversity of belief—and by lazy individualism and relativism that acknowledge little or no authority outside the self. The greater the perceived threat of one becomes, the more its opposite asserts itself, and the cycle becomes vicious. Is there a way out of this either-or situation of false alternatives between, on the one hand, completely shapeless, individualized Christianity with no absolute center (let alone boundaries) in which all claims to being Christian must be acknowledged and, on the other hand, dogmatic, exclusive, intolerant fundamentalist Christianity that tends to define authentic Christianity in terms of mental assent to a detailed, comprehensive system of doctrinal assertions? Here I will propose one possible approach—the way of affirming a strong central core of identifiable Christian belief drawn from Christian sources including the consensus of Christian teaching about God, Jesus Christ and salvation down through the centuries. Before making such a proposal, however, it will be useful to examine in some more detail the need for a unifying set of beliefs and what may provide them.

## The Necessity of Unity and the Great Tradition That Unifies

People who think that Christianity does not need to be defined even partially in terms of common beliefs may not have thought about the issues in sufficient depth. People who think that all Christians must believe exactly alike about virtually everything also may have failed to consider the issues deeply enough. The great seventeenth-century French Christian philosopher Blaise Pascal commented, "a plurality that cannot be integrated into unity is chaos; unity unrelated to plurality is tyranny." Another way of expressing the first half the axiom is to point out what should be obvious: *something that is compatible with anything and everything is nothing in particular.* If "Christianity" is compatible with any and every truth claim, it is meaningless. It would then be indistinguishable from, say, Buddhism or atheism. Truly it would be chaotic, shapeless and devoid of identity. Christian thinkers and leaders have always recognized this and have sought to identify a core of essential Christian beliefs that all mature, capable Christians must affirm in order to be considered truly Christian.

We see this in the New Testament itself where the writer of the first epistle of John avers that anyone who says that Christ has not come in the flesh (i.e., that Jesus Christ was not truly human) is to be considered anathema (excluded). The early church of the first and second centuries was plagued by people claiming to be Christian but teaching "another gospel" known to historical theologians as Gnosticism. The Gnostics considered matter evil and denied the real incarnation and bodily resurrection of the Son of God. Their teachings about creation, Christ and salvation were so utterly contrary to what the apostles preached and the church fathers after them taught that the Christian churches of the Roman Empire developed baptismal confessions of right belief to be affirmed by all persons joining the churches. The early Christian leaders rightly recognized that a "Christianity" that included both adherents of the gospel proclaimed by the apostles such as Paul and John and Gnostics would be meaningless because it would be compatible with too much, if not everything.

The same situation exists today as it always has existed in some form. Today Gnosticism appears under the guise of "esoteric Christianity." Some individuals and groups that embrace and promote Gnostic ideas still claim to be Christian. Examples may include the Church of Christ, Scientist (Christian Science), and other New Thought groups and churches that make a strong distinction between "Jesus" and "Christ" and deny any real, unique ontological incarnation of God in the man Jesus. Some churches that claim to be authentically Christian promote belief in reincarnation, practices such as trance channeling and other psychic experiences, and teach a view of God that is essentially pantheistic (i.e., an essential identity between God and the world). Many such self-identified Christian groups appeal to a hidden meaning of Scripture to support their beliefs, and one even publishes a "metaphysical Bible dictionary" that is more or less necessary in order to understand Scripture's allegorically expressed "deeper truths." The early church fathers after the apostles had to distinguish between those truth claims that were legitimately Christian and those that were not, and in order to do this they could not merely repeat words of apostles in the circulating gospels and epistles. The Gnostics and other promoters of alternative visions of Christianity appealed to the same writings and to a supposed secret, unwritten tradition of additional teachings handed down to them from the apostles. In the face of such pluralism of conflicting truth claims and messages about authentic Christianity the leaders of Christian churches and Christian thinkers of the second and third centuries simply had to develop doctrines. This was the beginning of what I am calling variously the Great Tradition, the consensual tradition and the interpretive consensus of Christianity.

The core of beliefs insisted upon by the majority of the early church fathers (as distinct from some of the peripheral notions that individual church fathers developed and promoted as their own) was taken up again by the Protestant Reformers in the sixteenth century and has become over two millennia something like the tradition of historic precedents laid down by U.S. Supreme Court decisions over two centuries. Neither one is infallible; both are open to reconsideration and possible revision in light of their respective original and ultimate authoritative sources (divine revelation itself in the case of Christianity and the U.S. Constitution in the case of the U.S. Supreme Court). And yet, both are highly regarded as secondary authorities whose guidance is to be sought by every new generation of Christians and by each new high court of the United States. To a certain extent, then, the core of apostolic and post-apostolic teachings that form the common consensus of the teaching of Christianity defines what it means to be authentically Christian in terms of beliefs. Without that unifying core of ideas anyone and everyone who claimed the label *Christian* and appealed to Jesus Christ and the Bible would have to be accepted as truly and equally Christian. But history has proven that to be impossible. Jehovah's Witnesses appeal to the Bible (or at least their version and interpretation of it) to deny and reject the deity of Jesus Christ and the triunity God. Christian Scientists and Mormons appeal to the Bible and Jesus Christ (as well as their own additional sources) to promote their own distinctive denials of God's transcendence (wholly and holy otherness). Unless we are willing to empty the category *Christian* of all recognizable meaning, we will have to embrace the importance of beliefs no matter how intolerant or exclusive that may seem.

On the other hand, those who overemphasize the importance of beliefs for defining authentic Christianity sometimes explicitly or implicitly reject all diversity and plurality. This is one of the hallmarks of religious fundamentalism. While *fundamentalism* has various possible meanings, one generally agreed-upon characteristic is militantly enforced doctrinal uniformity. To be sure, the same problem appears among Christians who do not call themselves fundamentalists. It is not so much the word as the phenomenon with which we are here concerned. What if each and every major landmark decision of the U.S. Supreme Court was treated as equally authoritative with the Constitution itself? What if no diversity of interpretation of the Constitution was allowed and citizenship was defined as necessarily including full agreement without mental reservation with every Supreme Court decision?

There are those dogmatic Christians who seem to overdefine Christianity such that being authentically Christian includes (for them) firm adherence to a detailed set of extrabiblical beliefs, some of which are quite alien even to the Great Tradition itself. For example, some conservative Christian groups insist that belief in a "premillennial return of Christ" (that Jesus Christ will return to earth to rule and reign for one thousand years at the end of history) is an essential Christian belief for all Christians. While it is true that Revelation 20 may provide support for premillennialism and some early church fathers and Reformers were premillennial, an objective view of the whole of Scripture and the entire sweep of Christian history does not support the claim that this is part of the core of essential Christian teachings that make up the consensual tradition of the church universal. Individual Christian churches and groups may make such specific beliefs part of their own doctrinal statements, but within the wider and larger historical Christian tradition itself diversity on this and many other matters has been the norm.

All of this is simply to say that for Christianity *beliefs matter but not all beliefs matter equally*. The Great Tradition of the Christian church's unified teachings stretching from the second century into the twentieth century (but especially formulated in the crucial stages of the first few centuries and the sixteenth century when the reformations took place) help us determine which beliefs matter the most and which are secondary or even further removed from the heart of Christian faith itself. Without knowledge and recognition of that consensual tradition each generation of Christians is left to reinvent extremely complex solutions to old problems by itself. Knowing the Great Tradition simply provides another guidance mechanism for interpreting and applying divine revelation to questions and issues that arise, and it helps distinguish counterfeit forms of Christianity such as the cults from groups and movements that differ from each other in secondary ways but equally affirm the core of apostolic Christian ideas.

What is the Great Tradition? Where is it found? What does it include? Unfortunately there are no absolute answers to these questions. The Great Tradition is a relatively nebulous phenomenon. Eastern Orthodox Christians will present it in one way; Roman Catholics will present it in another way; various Protestant groups will describe it in their own ways. Most of these, however, can at least agree that it is to be found in the common ideas expressed as essential beliefs handed down from the apostles themselves to the early church fathers. Eastern Orthodox theologians may add "as these came to be expressed in the decrees of the first seven ecumenical councils." Roman Catholic theologians may add "as they have been received and authoritatively interpreted by the hierarchy of the church in fellowship with the bishop of Rome." Most Protestants will want to say "as they were rediscovered and taught by the Reformers of the sixteenth century." The early Christian writer Vincent of Lérins (died around 450) proposed a rule of thumb for identifying the Great Tradition that has come to be known as the "Vincentian Canon": *What has been believed by everyone (Christians) everywhere at all times.* Whether such universality of belief has ever existed is debatable, but if we substitute for "everyone" "most Christian leaders and teachers" we may find in Vincent's canon a useable criterion.

In recent decades some Christian theologians have explored the consensual tradition in dialogues between Eastern Orthodox, Roman Catholic and various Protestant theologians and discovered significant common ground. Methodist theologian Thomas Oden has pulled together from the early church fathers and Reformers a great deal of material that he believes forms such a Great Tradition and based on that published a three-volume system of Christian theology titled simply *Systematic Theology* (San Francisco: Harper & Row, 1987-1992). Some Protestant theologians look to the Protestant Reformers' retrieval of the patristic doctrinal consensus of the first three or four centuries of Christianity. Luther, for example, held to both *sola scriptura* (Scripture alone as the ultimate source and norm for faith and practice) and the relative authority of the first four ecumenical (universal) councils of the undivided church (Nicea, Constantinople, Ephesus and Chalcedon). Calvin generally agreed with this. The more radical Reformers, the Anabaptists, respected and often quoted from the early church fathers, although their retrieval and regard for the councils and creeds of the early church were more qualified.[1] The great Anglican lay theologian and apologist C. S. Lewis

---

[1]For details regarding the Reformers' views of the Christian consensual tradition and for a strong recommendation of the Great Tradition of Christian thought for evangelical theology, see D. H. Williams, *Retrieving the Tradition & Renewing Evangelicalism* (Grand Rapids, Mich.: Eerdmans, 1999). For dialogue between Eastern Orthodox, Roman Catholic and Protestant theologians about the Great Tradition and its retrieval, see James S. Cutsinger, ed., *Reclaiming the Great Tradition: Evangelicals, Catholics & Orthodox in Dialogue* (Downers Grove, Ill.: InterVarsity Press, 1997).

attempted to describe and recommend his own version of Christianity's essential consensus of belief in *Mere Christianity*, which originated as a series of radio addresses on the British Broadcasting Corporation during World War II. Many other Christian authors have set forth their own statements of this consensual tradition and recommended it as a guide for Christian stability in modern and postmodern times.

Appeal to "Scripture alone!" and declarations such as "Ain't nobody but Jesus going to tell me what to believe!" sound good when presented in a context of rigid, either-or, reactionary fundamentalism that rules out all individual freedom of thought and attempts to enforce secondary doctrines as essential Christian beliefs. But in the wider context of secular and pagan culture in which not only boundaries but the very core of Christianity is threatened by all kinds of cults and ideologies and alternative gospels—many parading as Christian or compatible with Christianity—these simplistic appeals to Scripture alone and individualistic soul liberty are inadequate. Christians need an interpretive tradition and communities that value it as second only to Scripture itself in order to define what "authentic Christianity" believes. Although there will always be disagreement even among scholars about exactly what is included in that Great Tradition, it is apparent that most Christian theologians of all major branches of Christianity—including evangelical Protestants of many denominational backgrounds—agree that it includes those basic assumptions and declarations agreed on by most if not all of the church fathers of the second through the fourth centuries (and perhaps into the fifth century ending with the great Council of Chalcedon's definition concerning the person of Christ).

For most Protestants it will also include the rediscovery of the doctrines of grace by the major Protestant Reformers of the sixteenth century (Luther, Zwingli, Bucer, Cranmer, Menno Simons). The latter may or may not be found in the early church fathers. Many of the Reformers believed "justification by grace through faith alone" *(sola gratia et fides)* could be found implicit in Augustine's later writings. In any case, the Reformers and their faithful heirs among the post-Reformation Protestant theologians and Reformers respected the early church consensus of teaching while wishing to add the dimension of salvation as a sheer gift of grace received by faith alone which may have been muted somewhat in the writings of the church fathers.

Here the Christian consensus or Great Tradition will be treated as a minimal set of core beliefs generally agreed upon by all or most of the church fathers plus the sixteenth-century Reformers. I believe that it existed as well in the medieval Catholic and Orthodox churches even though it was overlaid with numerous nonessential human traditions derived more from specula- tion and popular piety than from divine revelation or the apostolic witness. For example, I regard the basic contours of the doctrine of the Trinity—the eternal substantial equality of three distinct persons revealed as Father, Son and Holy Spirit—as part of the Christian consensual tradition, while I do not regard the medieval conclusions drawn about the precise relations of the three persons in the eternal triune life as part of that Great Tradition. The Eastern churches rejected the idea that the Holy Spirit proceeds eternally from the Father *and* the Son *(filioque)* while the Western (Catholic and most Protestant) churches adopted that idea as part of the Nicene faith in the Trinity. Neither view is necessary for the Great Tradition and both are judged to be speculative.

The same could be said about specific branches of Christianity's distinc- tive beliefs about icons (Eastern Orthodoxy especially holds them in rever- ence), Mary (the Roman Catholic Church has developed a detailed set of beliefs about her), sacraments (Protestants have always been divided over the nature of Christ's presence in the Lord's Supper), and the end times (evan- gelical Protestants have disagreed much about the details of Christ's return and earthly reign). Neither *monergism* (belief that God is exhaustively all- determining and the sole final cause of every event including human deci- sions and actions) nor *synergism* (belief that humans have free will and must freely cooperate with God for God's perfect will to be done—especially in individual salvation) is essential to the Great Tradition. The Christian con- sensus is divided over so-called predestination as well as over free human par- ticipation in salvation. Erasmus and Luther—who argued vehemently over those issues—are both judged here to be players in and contributors to the Great Tradition. Unfortunately, their disagreement over that issue overshad- owed their much greater agreement about the Trinity and deity of Christ, salvation as a gift of grace and not of works, and God's final and ultimate sovereign triumph over the flesh, the world and the devil.

As nebulous and amorphous as the Great Tradition of Christian belief may seem at this point—until we fill it in with greater detail in each chap- ter—it is not an empty concept any more than is the concept of court prece- dents in U.S. constitutional law and judicial process. In the year 2000 the U.S. Supreme Court handed down a series of seemingly contradictory rulings about the implications of the Constitution for matters such as student-led prayer in public school settings, late-term abortions, public funding for parochial schools' equipment used for special-needs students, and so on. Many journalists and even scholars were left scratching their heads. But others pointed out that the Supreme Court was not seeking perfect consistency between all of its rulings but rather general consistency with precedent rulings on the same subjects. Of course, the nine justices would declare that their rulings are drawn from the Constitution of the United States, but if pressed they (and certainly the law professors who have to explain them and their decisions) would admit that in many cases they cannot simply "go by the Constitution alone." The Constitution does not address many of the pressing questions that come before them. So they draw on constitutional *principles* in part, at least, *as these are found in a pattern of court rulings between the constitution and today.* Some experts have dubbed this a penumbra (like an aura) of the Constitution. For example, separation of church and state and especially the so-called wall of separation between them is not explicitly declared in the Constitution, but it has become part of the penumbra of the Constitution. While that bare interpretive tradition of precedents does not settle every matter, it provides guidance. To be sure, individual precedents and the whole interpretive tradition or penumbra may be wrong in some cases. Supreme Courts are free to say so, but they rarely do and then only when they believe the clear meaning of the principles in the Constitution itself demand it.

Christians should know their religious heritage including the Great Tradition or consensus of basic Christian belief as well as they know their Bibles. In fact, one might go so far as to say that it is like a Third Testament although clearly not as inspired or inspired in the same supernatural way as the New Testament is in Christians' eyes. The Great Tradition is something like a canon outside the canon and, to switch metaphors, a map or a compass. So where may this consensual tradition be found? Can a Christian lay his or her hands on it? Does it exist between the covers of a book? Unfortunately not. And that may go far toward explaining why it is so little known by Christians. Many denominations of Christianity have tried to encapsulate its bare essentials by including early Christian creeds and denominational confessions of faith in their official worship books and books of discipline and doctrine. The so-called Apostles' Creed is one very brief statement of the Great Tradition of Christian belief. The Nicene Creed expands on the beliefs expressed in the Apostles' Creed, and the Chalcedonian Definition affirms an expansion and interpretation of the Nicene Creed. The misnamed Athanasian Creed is a longer, much more detailed summary of basic Christian beliefs and one that most Protestants do not embrace as heartily as they have the Apostles' Creed and Nicene Creed.[2]

The writings of the early church fathers often contain versions of what was known to them as the "Rule of Faith" or simply the "Apostolic Teaching." Second, third- and fourth-century church fathers (some of whom were also bishops—overseers of groups of churches) Irenaeus, Tertullian, Origen, Cyprian, Athanasius, Basil of Caesarea, Gregory of Nazianzus and Gregory of Nyssa especially expressed the unity of Christian belief as a relatively brief "Rule" (canon, standard) with various expressions. These usually centered around and stayed very close to the incarnation of God in Jesus Christ (against the Gnostics) and later the equality of Father, Son and Holy Spirit (against Arians who denied the full and true deity of both the Son and the Holy Spirit). They also emphasized the resurrection, return of Christ and unity of Christ's body the church. The details of interpretation of the Rule of Faith varied from one church father to another. But the common ground found among the church fathers' expressions of basic, essential Christian belief is striking.

The Reformers wrote their own updated rules of faith that often included affirmation of the Apostles' Creed and the Nicene Creed and newer statements of faith and catechisms (usually in the form of questions and answers) that were used to teach Protestant children and converts both the unifying doctrines of Christianity and the distinctives of the particular Protestant denomination. Luther and his lieutenant Melanchthon wrote the *Augsburg Confession* (also known as the *Augustana*). Calvinists wrote the *Heidelberg Catechism,* and the Presbyterians in Great Britain wrote the *Westminster Confession* and *Catechisms.* Almost every Protestant statement of faith— including those of the free churches that claim not to have creeds and binding confessions—affirm certain basic unifying beliefs shared by all Christians

---

[2]The creeds and many confessions of faith as well as their historical backgrounds may be found in John H. Leith, ed., *Creeds of the Churches: A Reader in Christian Doctrine from the Bible to the Present,* rev. ed. (Richmond, Va.: John Knox Press, 1973); and Ted A. Campbell, *Christian Confessions: A Historical Introduction* (Louisville, Ky.: Westminster John Knox, 1996. For scholarly treatments of the early Christian creeds and their development, see J. N. D. Kelly's two volumes *Early Christian Doctrines* (San Francisco: Harper & Row, 1978) and *Early Christian Creeds* (London: Longmans, 1960).

down through the ages except those of Gnostic or other radically alternative gospels and modern theological liberals and "Christian cults."

All of that is to say that what is called the Great Tradition or Christian consensus is not found in one place but must be distilled from the various sources of Christian teaching—especially the formational sources of the undivided early church and the sixteenth-century Protestant Reformers. While it may not be the case that all Christians ever believed all the same things everywhere (Vincentian Canon) one can find great implicit and explicit agreement about the basic shape of Christianity in terms of beliefs about God, the universe, human existence, redemption, etc. In this book I will do my best faithfully to present that agreement in contemporary language and then show that it is also compatible with limited diversity.

## Orthodoxy and Heresy: The Authority of the Great Tradition

A Christian is a person who affirms basic Christian beliefs—otherwise known as orthodoxy. That may sound exclusive and intolerant to many readers. Don't slam this book shut and put it back on the shelf (or do worse with it!) just yet. Let me explain. To be sure, there are other legitimate definitions of *Christian*. A Christian is a Christ-follower. A Christian is a member of a Christian church. A Christian is a person transformed by the Spirit of God into a living witness to Jesus Christ and his gospel. A Christian is someone baptized in the name of Father, Son and Holy Spirit (or perhaps in Jesus' name) who continues to claim and affirm that baptism. I could go on, but let us return to our first statement of the meaning of *Christian* above. *Orthodoxy* simply means "right belief" or "doctrinal correctness." In that sense it may be used broadly or narrowly. Lutheran orthodoxy is correct Lutheran belief. Who decides what that is? That's problematic, but almost nobody rejects the concept itself simply because it is difficult to settle its exact identity in practice. If being Lutheran were compatible with anything and everything, then being Lutheran would have no meaning. The same could be said (and must be said!) with regard to any tradition-community and of Christianity itself.

Many people shudder at the sound of *orthodoxy* because it wrongly connotes to them religious fundamentalism. To others it is a negative concept because it conveys the idea of a static worship and spirituality with no life and no contemporary expression. Perhaps both reactions are subconsciously adding *dead* to *orthodoxy* and thinking of all orthodoxy as "dead orthodoxy." But what if we retrieved and brushed off and refurbished the concept whether we use the word or not? (What other word could we use?) Orthodoxy is really—in the broadest and most generous sense—"mere Christianity." It is that core of essential beliefs denial of which results in serious distortion of the Christian message of the gospel and Christian mission such that "Christianity" becomes unrecognizable.

To be sure, there are people who deserve acknowledgment as Christian who do not yet (and may never) fully grasp, confess and understand the whole consensus of Christian belief. There are simple Christian folks who sing of the Trinity without ever studying the doctrine of the Trinity and may be incapable for a variety of reasons of grasping or affirming it intellectually. There are highly educated, sophisticated Christian academics who have come to hold doubts and reservations about certain essential Christian beliefs—even after and perhaps as a result of studying them—but who pray "Lord, I believe; help Thou my unbelief!" and they are Christians too. All kinds of qualifications of an equation of Christian with orthodox belief are in order. But in the whole and in the main, being a Christian includes seeking to understand and affirm those beliefs that identify Christianity's view of God, the world, sin and redemption. By no means is that the same as declaring anyone who does not hold orthodox Christian beliefs unsaved or destined for hell. God's justice and mercy decide the eternal destinies of individuals, and while right belief may play a crucial role in how that falls out, the final decision is God's and God's alone. We should be extremely wary of declaring other persons' spiritual status as reconciled with God or not reconciled with God, destined for heaven or destined for hell. These are matters best left up to God alone. However, we must at times make decisions about who is Christian and who is not and what organizations are truly Christian and which are not. In such cases, what they believe comes into play very significantly in any right judgment.

*Heresy* is the counterpart to *orthodoxy*. A heresy is a belief (usually when it is taught) that contradicts orthodoxy significantly. To follow our earlier analogy: A heresy within a Lutheran context is a belief taught by someone claiming to be Lutheran that is significantly contrary to essential Lutheran beliefs and teachings (Lutheran orthodoxy). For example, most Lutherans have always considered and Lutheran doctrinal confessions declare that Christ's risen and glorified human body is "in, with and under" the elements of bread and wine in faithful celebration of the Lord's Supper. This view of "real presence" in the sacrament is sometimes known as "consubstantiation" to distinguish it from the Catholic doctrine of "transubstantiation." A Lutheran who taught either transubstantiation (that the elements of bread and wine cease to be those and become wholly body and blood) or that Christ's presence is entirely nonbodily and only indirect through the Holy Spirit or that the Lord's Supper is only symbolic would be teaching heresy within a Lutheran context. What may be done about that varies from one Lutheran context to another. *Heresy* does not necessarily imply loss of salvation or an inquisition or excommunication.

Should we retain or retrieve the concept *heresy* for Christianity in general today? Many Christians become very uncomfortable with that. They wrongly assume the worst—that any talk of *heresy* automatically leads to trials and sanctions and exclusions. That the state churches in cooperation with secular governments once persecuted those judged heretics does not mean that the concept of heresy itself is dispensable. If we don't use the term *heresy*, we will have to invent a new term for those beliefs that radically contradict the core of the Christian consensus (especially when they are taught as truth for all Christians). (Remember that by "Christian consensus" here I *do not mean* "whatever most Christians happen to have believed for a very long time." I mean a more specific set of beliefs and teachings that have been judged by nearly all Christians from earliest times to be faithful, necessary expressions of the divine revelation and the apostolic teachings found in the New Testament.) Not every minority opinion or novel idea counts as heresy in this broader Christian sense. Rather, a Christian heresy would only be a belief that clearly and quite radically opposes the heart of the Christian matter—"mere Christianity"—the identity of Christianity. As will become clear throughout this primer, recognition of heresy does not exclude recognition of diversity of interpretation. There is room for widely varying interpretations of basic Christian beliefs, but not every interpretation that claims to be authentically Christian should be accepted as valid.

One problem that very seriously obstructs acceptance of the concepts *orthodoxy* and *heresy* is a prevalent confusion between *their legitimacy as concepts* and *having a precise way of identifying and handling them.* This writer believes those are two very different matters. Especially for free-church Christians (such as Baptists) there is no clean, neat, unambiguous way to divide orthodoxy from heresy. That is because free-church Christians—unlike the Roman Catholic Church and some so-called magisterial Protestant denomi-

nations—do not have elaborate processes in place for judging beliefs. The
Roman Catholic Church has an informal and formal magisterium—a set of
rules (canon law) and courts for investigating and judging beliefs and teachings. Ultimately, the pope in concert with a court in Rome can decide that a
particular belief is heretical and exclude it. This has led even in very recent
years to silencing of theologians and a few excommunications.

Free-church Protestants generally handle matters in a much less structured
way and often controversies over beliefs and teachings lead to schisms because
there is no clear way to decide what is orthodoxy and what is heresy. That does
not make these categories and concepts invalid for free-church Protestants,
however. Individual congregations and individual Christians must sometimes
decide about these things. Denominations must sometimes become involved
and vote in general assemblies or conventions. Often these decisions take the
form of resolutions. The process is often long, imprecise and more a matter of
muddling through to a rough consensus than coming to a clear and clean
decision. Often people deplore these processes and ask, why can't we all just
get along and get on with the business of worshiping God and winning lost
souls to Christ? Sometimes that would be better. But none of this can displace
entirely the ambiguous reality of categories such as orthodoxy and heresy.
Whether the terms are used and whether there is a precise process for distinguishing between them—the phenomena must be real. The alternative is utter
chaos. Those churches and denominations that have attempted to abolish anything like orthodoxy and heresy as distinct categories have always ended up
constructing their own similar categories with different labels.

Imagine that you move to an unfamiliar city and state—far away from
where you have ever lived before. You want to find a church to join and so
you dig the yellow pages and look up the category Churches. You notice
that the list of Christian churches is long and complex—divided into numerous denominational categories including a long listing of "Independent
Churches." Sociologists of religion tell us that two things have happened in
the last decades of the twentieth century that complicate this matter of
choosing a church. First, many people have such little familiarity with or
concern for beliefs that they don't even know what to look for other than
clues to how churches worship. Many people base their decisions about
churches more on worship styles or programs for children, youth or adults
than on what the churches believe. And yet every church has beliefs. Finding
out what they are is not as easy as it used to be, and many church hunters

don't have any idea what questions to ask or what clues to look for. Denominational titles don't help as much as they used to, and the list of nondenominational churches (many of which actually do have a denominational affiliation but wish to hide it) is getting longer every year. Second, many and perhaps most churches have seriously downplayed theology and doctrine in the second half of the twentieth century. It is very difficult to find out exactly what a church believes and whether or not it actually takes the beliefs it says it holds seriously. Unless you are committed to a denomination already and find that there is a church of that denomination in your new city, you may be in for some very tough church searching. All kinds of churches call themselves Christian, and some that really are Christian do not use that label because it is so ambiguous. How will you narrow the range of possibilities? What questions will you ask when you call the church? What will you look for in its advertising, literature, Internet home page, worship service, preaching and teaching? Without a clear sense of what is orthodox in the broad sense you could find yourself in a church that advertises itself as Christian but denies the Trinity, the deity of Christ, salvation by grace alone, and a host of basic Christian beliefs.

I could continue here with other illustrations to support the argument for the importance and inevitability of the categories orthodoxy and heresy. Anyone who has ever found himself or herself charged with leading an interdenominational effort of some kind or helping start a new church or denomination already knows the issues. A "Christian" effort that includes all comers on an equal basis regardless of beliefs is fated to fail. Creed or chaos; orthodoxy or anarchy. A place to begin in distinguishing between basic Christian orthodoxy and serious heresy that must be avoided and excluded is the Great Tradition—that core consensual tradition of fundamental beliefs shared in common by nearly all Christians down through the church's history. Its authority is that of a guide. Its authority does not stand independent of and certainly not higher than Scripture's authority. But it is a secondary, relative authority that deserves great respect and should be ignored only with fear and trembling.

## Preserving Unity While Allowing Diversity

If one major task of theology is to identify Christian orthodoxy, an equally important one is discerning the difference between those essential core beliefs of Christianity and the secondary beliefs that Christian individuals and groups value and promote but that are not crucial to the very identity of Christianity itself. Christianity has always included and allowed such a distinction—except when it has been dysfunctionally distracted into extreme forms that tolerate no dissent or diversity. During the Reformation of the sixteenth century a Greek term was appropriated by Protestants to describe secondary and tertiary beliefs: *adiaphora,* which may be translated "things indifferent" or "matters about which Christians may disagree and still be equally Christians." This concept has been juxtaposed in contrast to *status confessionis,* which indicates a belief that is essential and the denial of which constitutes heresy if not apostasy (departure from Christianity altogether).

A well-balanced Christianity recognizes that some beliefs matter more than others; some truths are worth dividing over if necessary and others are not. With regard to the former Luther declared, "peace if possible, but truth at any cost!" Among the latter the early church fathers and the Reformers placed opinions about "the furniture of heaven and the temperature of hell" (to borrow a phrase from Reinhold Niebuhr). In other words, while belief in life after death and a real distinction between two everlasting destinies known as heaven and hell is part of the consensus of Christian belief, their exact natures is not.

I find it helpful to distinguish between three categories of true Christian beliefs in order to strike the right balanced approach to preserving orthodoxy for the sake of Christian identity and unity, and at the same time avoiding uniformity and a narrow, dogmatic, all-or-nothing Christianity. By "true beliefs" is meant beliefs any particular individual Christian or group of Christians accepts as true (corresponding with reality). Most of the time we find reasonable Christians treating some of these truths as essential to Christianity itself—Christian orthodoxy. Denials of these would constitute rank heresy if not outright apostasy. Christian identity is at stake with these. I will call these *dogmas.* Likewise, reasonable Christians usually recognize a secondary category of beliefs that are important to a particular tradition-community of Christians (e.g., a denomination in the broad or narrow sense) but are not essential to Christianity itself. I will call this category *doctrines* in a more narrow and technical sense than "doctrine as any belief." Finally, almost all reasonable and reflective Christians recognize that some religious beliefs are mere opinions because there is no Christian consensus about them, they are not clearly taught in Scripture, and they do not touch on the gospel itself. Often they are of a speculative nature—mere guesswork without strong justification. For lack of a better label I will call these *opinions.* In one sense the middle category is *adiaphora* in that these beliefs are not crucial to Christianity itself. But for a specific denomination they may be important enough to not be adiaphora within its ranks. The third category includes adiaphora in every sense.

Placing beliefs in their proper categories is no easy task, and Christians have quarreled over it for centuries. It is one reason for the many denominations of Protestants. Filling the middle category are all kinds of beliefs about the sacraments or ordinances. Baptists, for example, usually agree with Eastern Orthodox, Roman Catholic and other Protestant Christians that Jesus Christ is God incarnate, the second person of the Trinity. They consider this an essential Christian belief. However, they believe that even other Christians are not baptizing correctly and that this is no small matter. Only believers who are old enough to understand their confession of faith in Jesus Christ after repenting of their sins may be truly baptized, and Christian baptism should always be by immersion rather than pouring or sprinkling. This is a Baptist doctrine, but it is not dogma for identifying Christianity itself. Every denomination has such distinctive doctrines as well as some recognition of dogmas that form the common ground beneath their feet and other Christians' feet. Pentecostals hold as doctrine but not dogma that "baptism of the Holy Spirit" is an experience for all Christians subsequent to conversion and is always accompanied by the phenomenon of speaking in tongues.

Contrary to many people's misconception, Eastern Orthodox and Roman Catholic Christians recognize Protestants as Christians if they share the basic dogmas of historic, orthodox-catholic Christianity with them. But they have their own distinctive doctrines that they regard as very important and require adherents to share. Eastern Orthodoxy venerates icons in worship and devotion. (This is very different from worshiping them. They are used as "points of contact" for prayer and meditation.) That is not optional for being Eastern Orthodox. Roman Catholics hold as doctrine that Mary was born without inherited sin (immaculate conception). They may call this a *dogma,* but in fact it is a doctrine in our scheme because they do not insist that one must believe it in order to be Christian. Most forms of Christianity regard as mere opinion beliefs about intelligent life on other planets, the age of the earth and the exact details of the events of the end times such as the identity of the antichrist. These examples are chosen because Christians have written speculative articles and books about them and one can hear sermons about them on Christian television. But hardly any denomination elevates these beliefs—whatever they may be—to important or essential status.

So who decides which Christian beliefs belong in which categories? As the reader may have guessed, that is a very controverted question. The Eastern Orthodox family of churches says that this process is in the hands of the faithful people of God as their bishops interpret and apply their common voice. What that really means, of course, is that the bishops decide and, at their best, do so by carefully listening to the voice of God and to the voices of their people. Scripture, tradition, reason, and experience no doubt play a role as well. For the most part, Eastern Orthodox would say that this has already been settled long ago—in the councils of the church that met and promulgated decrees and canons about doctrine and practice in the first eight centuries of Christian history. The Roman Catholic Church has its magisterium that decides these categories and their contents. Occasionally the bishops gather to advise the pope and together they elevate what has been held as opinion to a higher status of dogma or doctrine. Protestant groups have no definite process for placing true beliefs in their right categories. It is an ongoing, messy process of debating, holding meetings, voting at annual conventions, and writing and rewriting doctrinal statements. In the year 2000 the Southern Baptist Convention revised its "Baptist Faith and Message" to include as doctrine some beliefs that previously had been left to individual judgment. Among other things, they forbade the ordination of women as senior pastors and proclaimed God's exhaustive foreknowledge of future free decisions of creatures.

I will look to the Great Tradition to help distinguish between those beliefs that should be dogma, those that should be doctrine, and those that may be left to opinion. Generally speaking, the touchstone for making such distinctions within the Great Tradition has been Christ and the gospel of free salvation through his death and resurrection. This is the Christological touchstone. Jesus Christ is the heart of the whole matter: "What think ye of Christ?" Placed in the dogma category have been beliefs that are judged essential to confessing Jesus Christ as unsurpassable Lord and Savior, including confession of him as God incarnate and the sacrifice for the sins of the world. Other essential beliefs have been placed in the dogma category to protect the gospel of Jesus Christ. The Trinity is an example of such a belief.

"What saith Scripture?" is the touchstone of the doctrine category. Beliefs that seem to be clearly revealed in the biblical witness but not essential to belief in Christ are placed there. Speculation is the touchstone of the opinion category. Beliefs that cannot be strongly supported by the Christological touchstone or the Scriptural touchstone and whose only justification is very indirect inference from other beliefs or speculative interpretations of obscure passages of Scripture belong in that category. Still, none of this makes preserving unity and allowing diversity easy or scientific. There is no consensus among Christians about how this works and what belongs in which category. Here, then, I will simply admit to taking a venture and risk strong disagreement as I go about describing what I think constitutes the essential core of Christian beliefs. Most of the time that is synonymous with the Great Tradition.

One way to preserve unity and respect diversity within the broad Christian community is to identify essential Christian beliefs—dogmas—and distinguish them from secondary beliefs and mere opinions. "In essentials unity, in nonessentials liberty, in all things charity." Another way, closely related to that project, is to identify the center and boundaries of Christianity in terms of its cognitive implications for believing. Two major models have arisen in modern Christianity and have perhaps been latent for centuries. They are the model of thinking of authentic Christianity as a "bounded set category" and the model of thinking of Christianity as a "centered set category." Is it necessary to assume that a person or organization is *either* completely Christian *or* not at all Christian? Is being Christian—even in terms of beliefs—a black-and-white situation? The bounded set category model indicates that at least for mature Christians and organizations claiming to be Christian it is. They are *either* Christian *or* not Christian. For persons who embrace such a model, *boundary identification and maintenance* becomes very important, and *excluding people* is a way of demonstrating that Christianity has boundaries and therefore has identity. Christian orthodoxy is inside the boundaries and heresy is outside the boundaries.

The centered set model views Christianity as a fluid and flexible force field held together by a strong, magnetic center. The boundaries are not as important as the center that identifies authentic Christianity, and all are recognized as truly Christian who are held in, as it were, by the center and are not moving away from it. This model does not reject all boundaries, but it does reject any absolute boundaries other than the center itself, and it allows that perhaps no Christian is perfectly centered. People and organizations can be more or less Christian according to their relationship to the core of Christian experience and beliefs, which is conversion and commitment to Jesus

Christ and the basic message about him proclaimed by the apostles and preserved by the early church fathers and Reformers.

Both models have their flaws, but this writer judges the bounded set
model as less viable for preserving unity and diversity than the centered set
model. The bounded set model ends up allowing little or no distinction
between the center (the gospel) and the boundaries (orthodoxy). It also
leads inevitably to obsessive boundary maintenance and inquisitorial judgments about whether persons and groups are Christian or not. It is too rigid
and absolutistic. The centered set model may have the weakness of ambiguity, but it allows for genuine diversity of interpretation without relativism.
One can be authentically Christian while being wrong about certain beliefs.
In this model, Christian orthodoxy is defined as a set of beliefs, the form of
which varies according to culture and generation, that remains relatively
faithful to the gospel message itself. One can be and usually is more or less
orthodox. However, one can fall into heresy by rejecting a belief that is
intrinsic to the gospel and spinning off into another solar system, as it were,
revolving around some other gospel than the Jesus gospel. Even in the centered set model some beliefs and the persons who hold and promote them
are beyond the pale, so to speak, and no longer Christian. Some beliefs and
persons who hold them are within the pale (i.e., held by the center in the
force field) even if they are far out.

As we move through our discussions of particular loci of Christian doctrine we will begin in each case with the center and its penumbra—Christian
orthodoxy. What have faithful Christian church fathers and Reformers generally agreed on in this area? This is our focus on unity. In order to understand it better, we will look at its alternatives—heresies—which are beliefs
generally judged to be beyond the pale, away from the center of gravity of
Christianity entirely. These are usually beliefs of a theological nature that
have been or are held by teachers of Christians, not beliefs of non-Christian
religions and philosophies except insofar as these have been promoted by
Christians to other Christians. Then we will examine diverse Christian beliefs
within the pale of Christian orthodoxy. These are often points of significant
controversy between Christians who are equally committed to the center and
doing their best to interpret it faithfully even if they cannot all be correct.
Finally, I will make some suggestions about how major points of diversity
and disagreement within Christianity might be interpreted so as to bring
diversity closer toward unity.

# CHAPTER 2

# SOURCES AND NORMS
# OF CHRISTIAN BELIEF

## One *and* Many

C hristians believe many things for a wide variety of reasons. Our question here is not, what do Christians believe and why? so much as, what are proper Christian beliefs and how are they constructed and reconstructed? The first question may be a merely descriptive one; the second question is meant to be more prescriptive. The difference lies in "what is" versus "what should be." Imagine that one day all Christians worldwide awoke believing in reincarnation. Would reincarnation automatically be a Christian belief that day? In one sense, yes. In our sense here, no. In other words, we are looking for *proper Christian beliefs,* not merely *beliefs held by most Christians.* Sociologists of religion focus their research on what adherents of particular religious movements and groups do believe and why. Theologians focus more on what beliefs are *true to the essence of their own religion.*

### Issues and Polarities of Christian Belief About Sources and Norms

Do most Christians believe in the resurrection of the body or in the immortality of souls? Who knows? Many teachers of Christian theology of all branches of Christianity complain that many Christians seem to believe more in ethereal, immortal, nonbodily existence forever after death in heaven (or, for those who die completely apart from Christ and his grace, in hell). But most of them will say that this view of life after death is more Greek (Hellenistic) than biblical and Christian. When we are trying to determine proper Christian beliefs polls do not count for very much. What does count? That is the basic question of this chapter and, as the reader might suspect, again there is no simple, straightforward answer. Some might expect the answer to be, simply, the Bible! Others—perhaps of Eastern Orthodox and Roman Catholic persuasions—might want the answer to be, just as simply, what the church has always taught! Some charismatics may prefer the answer, spiritual experience! But none of these are the answers all by themselves.

There is no more basic, foundational issue of Christian theology (or perhaps any religion's theology) than the issue of this chapter: *What counts as authoritative sources and norms for determining proper Christian beliefs?* What are the right and true sources and canons (norms, standards) for deciding which beliefs are orthodox and which are heretical? What guides and provides stability as Christians continue the tasks of examining and constructing (or reconstructing) Christian beliefs? Why is this belief (e.g., bodily resurrection) more appropriately Christian—more orthodox—than that belief (e.g., immortality of souls or reincarnation)? Any answer automatically presupposes some authoritative sources and norms. Mere personal preference or even the preference of a group hardly counts. As soon as the question arises, why is that preference better than another preference? some higher standard must come into play or else preference (taste, arbitrary choice) becomes the ultimate standard and Christianity becomes folk religion disconnected from objective truth.

Unfortunately, however, for much of its existence as a distinct religion Christianity has not been able to speak with a unified voice about appropriate sources and norms for handling beliefs. Matters would be so much simpler if all Christians—or even a majority—agreed on sources and norms. Don't all agree that the Bible is the ultimate source and norm for Christian beliefs? Certainly most agree that the Bible is one major source and norm, and perhaps most would also agree that it is the highest source and norm, but then questions arise such as, what does it mean? and what should Christians do when there is strong disagreement among Christians about the Bible's meaning? Then other sources and norms come into play such as *tradition, reason* and *experience*. Some branches of Christianity have developed magisteria outside the Bible by which they determine right interpretations of the Bible. The Eastern Orthodox family of churches tends to regard the Bible as one (perhaps the major) part of a greater phenomenon known simply as Tradition.

Tradition, in this sense, is the consensus of Christians (especially magisterial leaders such as bishops and emperors and doctors or teachers of the church) during the first approximately nine centuries of Christianity. The Bible was selected and the canon determined within this authoritative and divinely inspired process of Tradition. So were beliefs and practices not explicitly taught in the Bible (although none of them, so Orthodox people claim, conflicts with the Bible). Roman Catholic Christians may appeal to Scripture *and* Tradition together and recognize an authoritative interpretive role of the church hierarchy. Protestants traditionally have appealed to the written Word (Bible) and the Holy Spirit who inspired it and illumines its meaning to faithful readers as the "pattern of authority" for Christian belief. But when push comes to shove in debates over matters of doctrine many Protestants appeal to creeds and confessional statements of the Great Tradition (especially the early church and sixteenth-century Reformation movements) as penultimately authoritative.

In this complex and often confusing situation in which there is no precise scientific means of determining orthodoxy and separating it from heresy, many Christians prefer to fly by the seat of their pants and go with whatever beliefs seem both reasonable and comforting. Or they simply accept what a favorite preacher, writer or Christian teacher says. Not uncommon is the (not-so-methodical) method of simply watching and listening to several religious television or radio programs and accepting what is heard—even if elements contradict each other and have little to do with what Christians have always generally believed. Sometimes Christians even draw their beliefs as much or more from secular or religious movies and network television programs than from historical Christian sources. The result is a blooming, buzzing confusion of beliefs all wearing the label *Christian*. Into this situation occasionally come some Christian authorities loudly proclaiming the need to bring uniformity and order out of pluralism and chaos, and to achieve this end they promote "back to the Bible" or "return to tradition" or "the rule of reason," hoping that elevating one source and norm as absolute and excluding the rest will unify Christianity and recover its identity. Some of these voices are those of fundamentalists who usually promote "Bible only"

while attempting to impose a certain set of traditional doctrines as dogmas
for everyone to believe.

One major polarizing issue in Christian theology, then, is whether there
exists *one source and norm* for Christian belief or *several sources and norms.*
To be sure, there are other polarities and unresolved questions related to this
locus of theology's method. However, no controversy could possibly be
more fundamental and pressing than proper sources and norms. It consumed much of the energy of the early Christians after the apostles when the
Gnostics claimed the ultimate source and norm to be a secret, oral tradition
handed down to them from Jesus and an inner circle of his disciples as well as
their own confirming "gnosis" or "esoteric wisdom" from "on high." Other
early Christian leaders such as Montanus (mid-second century) insisted that
the ultimate source and norm for Christian belief was his own prophecies as
they were directly dictated to him by the Holy Spirit.

During the Reformation of the sixteenth century, the Reformers faced
claims of ultimate sources and norms for Christian belief from the official
church of Rome and from fanatics (extreme radical reformers), some of
whom rejected Scripture and tradition entirely in favor of private revelations
and inner messages of the Spirit. Certain rationalists of that time and afterwards claimed to be Christians but elevated universal human reason to a status of ultimate authority even for doctrine. The early church fathers and the
Reformers especially had to face these challenges and develop as unified a
vision of proper Christian sources and norms as possible. Is there some basic
core of agreement about this in the Great Tradition of Christianity? Is it possible to identify the main Christian sources and norms and separate them
from secondary or false sources and norms that have wrongly been elevated
to ultimacy?

### The Christian Consensus About Sources and Norms

We must admit up front that any identification of proper Christian sources
and norms for right Christian belief is a risky venture. The New Testament
itself uses and appeals to several sources: God's Son Jesus (Heb 1), the
Hebrew Scriptures (i.e., Old Testament) (2 Tim 3:16), the gospel proclaimed by the apostles (Rom 1:16-17), the Spirit of God (Jn 16:13), and
the letters of apostles (2 Pet 3:15-16). Prophets uttered messages from God
in the early churches and the disciples and apostles handed down a tradition
of teaching to younger men and women who led the churches they estab-

lished. Paul quotes non-Christian poets and philosophers. Jesus seemed to side with certain Jewish teachers against other ones. Is there a discernible pattern in all of this? Probably none that is incontrovertible. The earliest Christian churches had several sources to use in developing their beliefs and judging between contrary beliefs. They lacked a specifically Christian canon such as the Jewish leaders (e.g., Pharisees) had for Jews in synagogues. They had apostles, however, and the teachings of men and women recognized as apostles seemed to carry great weight within and among most Christian churches of the first century.

If you were to travel back in time to a Christian house church in Rome in the mid-first century you would probably hear people appealing to Hebrew prophets such as Isaiah and reading from their scrolls. You also would probably hear one or two Christian prophets stand and give messages from the Spirit of God to the congregation. You may hear someone read from a circular letter by an apostle such as Paul or Barnabas, and you may hear a member of the congregation give a report on a conversation with one of Jesus' disciples that took place during a visit to Jerusalem. You would almost certainly hear an elder of the congregation (similar to a priest or pastor in later centuries) give an exhortation to the members and visitors based on what he or she understood the Hebrew Scriptures to mean combined with an understanding of the combined teachings of the apostles. The focus would be on the death and resurrection of Jesus Christ and how God was in him and in those events reconciling and transforming the world. What you would not notice is a "New Testament" such as developed later.

As doctrinal controversies arose and especially as people claiming to be Christian teachers and prophets moved around among the Christians of the Roman Empire urging them to believe various things, certain men began to pick up the fallen torches of the apostles (the last of whom died around A.D. 90) and claim to have some measure of their authority because they knew them and were taught by them. These "apostolic fathers" and "teachers of the churches" gathered the apostles' writings and began to develop an authoritative set of sources and norms for determining which of the contradictory teachings of the many roaming Christian ministers were truly Christian. These early church fathers whose claim to apostolic succession stuck, as it were, often appealed to three main sources and norms in arguing against heretics and their teachings and for what they considered to be correct Christian beliefs: *the Rule of Faith, the writings of the apostles* and *the Hebrew prophets.*

The Rule of Faith is shorthand for the basic content of Christian belief that church fathers preserved, interpreted and applied. Over time it was distilled into brief baptismal formulas and eventually into what came to be known as the Apostles Creed. Church fathers such as Irenaeus, Tertullian, Origen, Cyprian and Athanasius did not claim merely to have learned it and memorized it. They could point to various apostolic writings and quote from them to support their claims that this Rule or Tradition of apostolic teaching was the norm for Christian belief. So, alongside the norm was the written source which eventually evolved into the New Testament (officially agreed upon in the Western churches in the last decade of the fourth century). Well before there was a formal canon of Christian Scriptures (and its precise extent and limits were never quite fully agreed on) there was an informal consensus that whatever had been written by an apostle or widely read with spiritual benefit among the churches held special divine authority. But when heretics appealed to the same writings, the church fathers turned to the Rule as the authoritative distillation of Christian teachings to create and preserve unity and exclude false teachers. It became the center of the core of Christian teaching and belief—the ultimate norm drawn out of Scripture itself.

Over a period of approximately one hundred and fifty years, four crucial ecumenical councils were held to settle major doctrinal disputes among Christians and write definitive statements about the implications of the apostles' teachings and the Rule for Christian belief. These ecumenical councils and their creeds and definitions of faithful belief were received as semi-authoritative by the sixteenth-century Protestant Reformers. They became a "canon outside the canon" just as the Reformers (especially Luther) recognized a "canon within the canon" of Scriptures. Luther and then later Reformers dropped the so-called Apocrypha (thirteen Jewish books that were not part of the Hebrew Bible but had been accepted into the Christian canon by Eastern Orthodox and Roman Catholic Church leaders) and insisted that the Rule of Faith expressed in creeds and confessional statements is secondary in authority to the inspired Scriptures—the sixty-six books of the Bible.

The principle *sola scriptura* or "Scripture alone as ultimate source and norm" for Christian faith and practice came to be part and parcel of Protestantism. In practice, however, the Reformers and most of their followers accepted "highs" and "lows" in Scripture itself in terms of directness of witness to Jesus Christ, and Luther called the Bible "the cradle that holds the

Christ." They also accepted writings outside the Bible—especially the Apostles' Creed, Nicene Creed, Chalcedonian Definition, Athanasian Creed and the writings of the early church doctors and teachers (such as those church fathers mentioned above)—as part of an authoritative interpretive tradition or informal magisterium. The authority of the latter, the Reformers would claim, is like the light of the moon compared to that of the sun—reflected glory.

To sum up to this point, a rough consensus developed among the various branches and churches of Christianity during the formative periods of the first four centuries and the sixteenth century that *God's revelation to the Hebrew prophets and in the apostolic witness to Jesus Christ as carried forth in God's written, inspired Word, the Bible, and as distilled in the essence of the Rule of Faith is Christianity's ultimate source and final norm for faith and life.* The Eastern Orthodox churches link this closely with Tradition and argue that it is the broader category to encompass all of the sources and norms of Christianity including the Bible, creeds, unwritten teachings of the churches in liturgy (forms of worship), prayer and devotional life (using icons), etc. This authoritative Tradition was complete, the Eastern Orthodox say, with the seventh ecumenical council in the eighth century. The Roman Catholic Church largely agrees about Tradition while leaving it open-ended. New councils may meet as necessary to formulate doctrine, revise canon law, solve disputes and so on. Whatever a council determines has always been faithfully believed by the people of God whether it has ever been written or not becomes part of the church's orthodoxy. Scripture is not the repository of all truth, but for both Eastern Orthodox and Roman Catholic Christians it is the special touchstone of truth above all others. Protestant Christians and especially those who call themselves evangelicals elevate Scripture above Tradition and use the consensual tradition respectfully but critically.

By now the reader may wonder how there can be any hope for Christian unity or even identity of authentic Christianity when there is no uniform agreement about Christianity's sources and norms. That would be a natural response. But the reader is urged to look at the common ground among the various branches of Christianity. All regard special divine revelation from God as their ultimate source and norm. All agree that Scripture is the written form of that revelation and has as its main purpose and function to reveal Christ to people who no longer walk the same soil he does. That is, contemporary people are not able to interview Jesus or his disciples or the apostles. All view something variously called the Rule of Faith or the Creed or the Gospel Tradition as the special distillation of divine revelation that serves as a touchstone for guiding Christian belief and distinguishing between false versions of Christianity and those that may legitimately lay claim to the title *Christian*.

Compared to all the other possibilities this is not insignificant common ground. The Great Tradition elevates Scripture to a special status of authority for determining who God is and what God wants with people. But just as salvation may be by faith alone without faith ever being alone (i.e., it is accompanied by resulting good works), so Scripture may be the sole supreme source and norm for Christian belief, but it is never alone. In it is Jesus Christ and that which promotes him as a canon within the canon. Outside it is the Rule of Faith expressed in many different brief versions and the basic consensual tradition that serves as a history of interpretation that guides people through the maze of possible interpretations (or misinterpretations) of Scripture. There is, then, a *pattern of authority* down through the Christian centuries that serves Christians well even if imperfectly as they seek to determine what is proper Christian belief and to construct and reconstruct doctrine and discern orthodoxy.

While there is no uniform agreement about the sources and norms of Christian theology for Christian belief, a rough consensus has developed (with significant dissent here and there throughout Christianity) that there are *four main specific sources and norms* properly used by Christian theologians, and these together have come to be known as the "Wesleyan Quadrilateral." The Wesleyan Quadrilateral is not unique to John Wesley, the founder of the Methodist movement and the Great Awakening revivalist of the eighteenth century, but predates him in various forms. The great Church of England theologian Richard Hooker developed his own earlier version of it in the latter part of the sixteenth century. Twentieth-century American Methodist theologian Albert Outler coined the phrase "Wesleyan Quadrilateral." In actuality, however, some version of it is ancient and common among Christian thinkers. The Wesleyan Quadrilateral (henceforth simply the Quadrilateral) regards proper Christian belief as shaped by four main sources and norms: *Scripture, tradition, reason* and *experience*. (Hooker had neglected the last element and therefore his version before Wesley was more of a triangle or three-legged stool than a quadrilateral.) No claim is being made here that one can find this precise pattern of authority and method for theology throughout Christian history except implicitly. Most Christian thinkers from the second-century church through the twentieth century have used these four deep wells and guidance mechanisms in determining sound doctrine.

By *Scripture* most church fathers and Reformers would mean the written form of divine revelation—the writings of the Hebrew prophets and early Christian apostles. Disagreement may exist about the parameters of the canon of Christian Scriptures (primarily over inclusion or exclusion of the Apocrypha), but that does not undermine the general agreement about the Bible's special authority for giving rise to and shaping correct Christian belief. Can the Bible's special authority be proven? Can the U.S. Constitution's special authority be proven? The answer in both cases is *no*. Both are foundational authorities accepted by all or nearly all in the tradition-communities shaped by them. By *tradition* most church fathers and Reformers of Christianity would mean what we have here been calling the Great Tradition of "mere Christianity"—the consensus beliefs held in common by the early church fathers and the Reformers of the sixteenth century as expressed in common by the ecumenical creeds and Reformation confessions of faith. By *reason* most would mean logic—especially the rule of non-contradiction that forbids equal affirmation of opposite propositions. In Christian belief as in every other area of life the search for coherence and intelligibility is essential. *Reason* does not necessarily or usually include any highly developed, complex philosophy, although philosophy has always been theology's conversation partner. By *experience* most Christian thinkers would mean not private, personal experience but human experience and especially the religious experience of God's people in the community of faith. To be sure, different Christian thinkers and communities would appropriate and use these four sources and norms in different ways. Wesley (and Hooker before him) saw them as a continuing conversation between themselves with Scripture having primary place of dignity and authority.[1] In spite of varying receptions and uses of this Quadrilateral it can be found assumed and operative to some extent in many Christian thinkers throughout church history.

---

[1]For a more detailed description and analysis of the Quadrilateral, see Donald A. D. Thorsen, *The Wesleyan Quadrilateral: Scripture, Tradition, Reason and Experience as a Model of Evangelical Theology* (Grand Rapids, Mich.: Zondervan, 1990).

## Alternative Views of Sources and Norms

One of the best ways to understand the Christian consensus on any subject
of belief is to examine its alternatives. Some wag has commented that "heresy is the mother of orthodoxy" and "orthodoxy owes more to heresy than it
cares to admit." Indeed. To a very large extent Christian belief after the early
era of the first century developed in dialectical relationship with beliefs put
forth as Christian that were judged to be contrary to the very identity of
Christianity. Throughout later church history other views have arisen within
Christian communities and on the margins of Christianity that have been
judged by most Christian leaders and thinkers to be completely inconsistent
with the gospel as well as incompatible with the Great Tradition. Often these
views have begun somewhere outside of the Christian community and crept
in. Occasionally they arose within the Christian community as ministers,
theologians and lay thinkers attempted to solve theological problems and
reconstructed beliefs in inappropriate ways.

One of the earliest and most threatening alternative views of Christian
sources and norms for belief arose among those Christians who came to be
called Gnostics. Legend says that this movement—which became pluralistic
in the second century—began with a single source: Simon Magus (Simon
the Magician) of Samaria, whose confrontation with the apostles is
recounted in the Book of Acts. In any case, by the second century Gnostic
sects, schools and communities flourished on the margins of Christianity
throughout the Roman Empire.[2] Even after Gnosticism was driven underground by Christian emperors and bishops it existed and reappeared time
and again throughout history. In twentieth-century Western culture it
appears in various forms of esoteric Christian movements and New Thought
groups. The term *Gnosticism* comes from the Gnostics' common view of the
ultimate source and norm for Christian belief: *gnosis,* which may be translated from Greek as "wisdom" or "higher knowledge." The Gnostics
claimed (and teachers of esoteric Christianity claim) that they possess a special spiritual capacity and knowledge that eludes ordinary Christians who
must depend on written and human authorities. Gnostics follow leaders who
impart to them special knowledge that transcends normal understanding and
is usually considered secret. In ancient Christianity this secret spiritual

---

[2]One excellent source of information on Gnosticism is Giovanni Filoramo, *A History of Gnosticism,* trans. Anthony Alcock (Oxford: Basil Blackwell, 1991).

knowledge included the ideas that "Christ" is someone other than the man "Jesus," that "Christ" indwelt "Jesus" but never really fully identified with him, and that human souls or spirits are sparks of the divine fullness.

In its broadest sense, Gnosticism is any religious reliance on special insight and wisdom that is not available to the uninitiated and those unprepared for it. The early church fathers rejected this claim of Gnosticism to possess special knowledge not even known fully to all of the apostles and not available to all Christians. Christian fathers and Reformers have steadfastly opposed all forms of Gnosticism in favor of belief in the objectivity, universality and availability of divine revelation. Of course, some Christian leaders have accused others of falling into forms of Gnosticism unwittingly. This seemed to be the case with certain medieval mystical groups and Reformation radical sects that emphasized an "inner light" that rivaled Scripture in terms of authority. In contrast to all such claims, at the heart of Christianity stands a public, objective and open revelation of Godself in Jesus Christ and Scripture.

A phenomenon in some ways similar to Gnosticism and yet different as well was Montanism. This also arose in the early Christian community in the mid-second century and flourished in parts of the Roman Empire for over a century. It has modern forms as well. Montanus—for whom the movement is known—claimed that the Holy Spirit used his vocal chords as an instrument of direct communication and that his prophecies were as inspired as those of the Hebrew prophets and Christian apostles. This "New Prophecy" movement (as it was known in the second century) posed a serious challenge to the stability of Christianity, and the leading bishops of the area where Montanism was strongest rose up against it and condemned it because of its claim that one man's prophecies were equal with the apostles' teachings and writings. Unfortunately, the official church leaders may have overreacted to Montanism. It appears that the reaction against it inadvertently led to a decrease and eventual cessation of the gifts of the Spirit among Christians.

Throughout church history Montanist-like movements have arisen and claimed their own prophecies (whatever form these took) as equal with Scripture even where they went far beyond Scripture and contradicted the Great Tradition of Christian teaching. The Church of Jesus Christ of Latter-Day Saints (Mormon) has been viewed as a modern Montanist movement because, while claiming to be Christian, it considers the writings of Joseph Smith and other prophets and presidents of the church equally authoritative with original divine revelation and Scripture. Certain charismatic movements of the twentieth century are widely criticized as Montanist-like insofar as they offer new doctrines out of prophecies given by individuals.

During the 1970s a new Christian movement arose along the fringes of the American Jesus People movement that called itself a "Holy Order" and claimed to possess both Gnostic-like higher wisdom and Montanist-like prophetic messages. The group's robed ministers roamed the streets of cities across North America spreading their gospel that included reincarnation, psychic powers, and a strong distinction between "Christ" (a spiritual consciousness in everyone) and "Jesus" (the master of Christ-consciousness). This eclectic movement of esoteric Christianity also considered certain writings of a spiritual prophet-leader divinely inspired and authoritative alongside Scripture. This writer had several confrontations with members of that group as they attempted to infiltrate a Jesus People coffeehouse. Many young, impressionable Jesus People were taken in by their passion, compassion and claim to superior spiritual knowledge and wisdom. Fortunately, when the Holy Order sought membership in the local Christian ministerial association their application was turned down because even the more liberal Protestant ministers and pastors recognized that this gospel was something different from the authentic Christian gospel even though the young emissaries of the Holy Order talked about Jesus Christ and love and salvation and community, etc. A major reason for resistance to the group's claims to be "just a new form of Christianity" was its use of new, authoritative sources and norms for determining what Christians ought to believe and how they ought to worship and carry out their lives of devotion and discipleship.

In the eighteenth century a new movement arose among intellectual Christians that came to be known as Deism or natural religion. These "enlightened" Christians insisted that all divine revelation—including Scripture—and especially the Great Tradition of Christian teaching and belief had to be judged by the canons of modern philosophical and scientific knowledge. The British philosopher John Locke was a precursor of natural religion insofar as his book *The Reasonableness of Christianity* (1695) judged divine revelation itself by modern, secular standards of inquiry and knowledge. Locke's Jesus was reduced to "The Messiah"—a kind of ethical prophet and spiritual leader who helped humanity rise to a newer and higher level. (Locke did not, however, deny any of the dogmas of Christianity. He simply neglected them.) Deism and natural religion proper actually began with

Locke's disciple John Toland and then came to its purest form in Matthew Tyndal, both of whom argued that enlightenment reason must be the ultimate source and norm even for Christian belief. Other Deists and natural religionists who considered themselves Christians in some sense of the word included Thomas Jefferson and Benjamin Franklin. In Europe a form of Deism and natural religion flourished among the intellectual elite and found organizational form in the Unitarian movement that began in London and spread to the United States in the last decade of the eighteenth century. The great German philosopher Immanuel Kant wrote *Religion Within the Limits of Reason Alone* (1793), which represents a deistic and natural religion approach to Christianity.[3]

All of the Deists and natural religionists—most of whom considered themselves Christians—would agree with syndicated columnist Sidney Harris that "God gives no insider tips." In other words, the true source and norm for determining correct Christian beliefs is the same source and norm for all human investigation and thought: natural reason. The Deists believed quite optimistically that natural human reason functioning at its best leads all reasonable, reflective people to certain core beliefs about God, moral duty, life after death, etc. Where does Jesus Christ fit in? According to them, he was simply the greatest human prophet of moral wisdom who ever lived. Kant called Jesus "the ideal of humanity well-pleasing to God." This expresses very well the common view of Jesus among these Enlightenment thinkers.

A fourth and final alternative view of sources and norms for Christian belief is liberal theology which, generally speaking, arose out of (or under the influence of) Deism and natural religion while incorporating elements of idealism into it. Liberal theology drew heavily on the philosophies of Kant and another nineteenth-century Christian thinker, G. W. F. Hegel. Without reducing Christian sources and norms to natural reason or general revelation in nature or philosophy, liberal Christian thinkers did tend to elevate "the best of modern thought and human experience" to the status of a source and norm of Christian belief equal in weight with special divine revelation in Scripture. One of the most representative liberal theologians of the modern world was German church historian Adolf Harnack, who gave a series of lec-

---

[3]An excellent secondary source on Deism and natural religion is James M. Byrne, *Religion and the Enlightenment from Descartes to Kant* (Louisville, Ky.: Westminster John Knox, 1996).

tures in Berlin in 1900 that were published as *What Is Christianity?* in 1901. Harnack viewed authentic Christianity as a simple message about God and his kingdom (as an ethical social order within history) brought especially by Jesus but wholly consistent with reason and experience. A careful reading of his and other volumes of classical liberal theology, however, reveals that their true touchstone for determining what beliefs are essential to Christianity was general human reason and experience and especially ethical experience in the call to duty. Many of the central beliefs of Christianity's consensual tradition were easily ignored or dismissed. Among these were the deity of Jesus Christ (especially his preexistence) and the Trinity. One particularly popular form of liberal theology in the twentieth century has been process theology, which uses a secular philosophy known as process thought (developed largely by philosophers Alfred North Whitehead and Charles Hartshorne) as a source and norm for Christian belief implicitly equal with Scripture itself.

A helpful, simple definition of "liberal Christian theology" that applies to Deism and natural religion as well is "maximal acknowledgment of the claims of modernity" in constructing and reconstructing Christian beliefs. Modern reason and investigation—including science, philosophy and sociology—play determinative roles in natural religion and liberal theology. They are not merely advisory; they are regulative. In response to both Deism/natural religion and liberal theology, more traditional Christian thinkers have appealed to the supremacy of special divine revelation—God's Word—as expressed in divinely inspired Scripture as the ultimate source and norm for Christian belief. By no means does this mean discarding reason or experience, and very often it does mean a new emphasis on the Great Tradition to show that these new forms of Christianity undermine the very essence of Christianity by neglecting or rejecting crucial dogmas of Christianity such as the incarnation and the Trinity.

One major conservative Christian response to Deism and liberal theology has been to assert a hierarchy among the elements of the Quadrilateral: Scripture first, tradition second, reason third, and experience a distant fourth. Some reactionary Christian critics have even wanted to take away experience as any norm at all and reduce the role played by reason. Fundamentalism has arisen as one fairly extreme response to natural religion and liberal theology. It's motto is "the Bible only!" and fundamentalists insist on isolating the Bible as the sole source and norm for Christian belief. Other, less extreme Christian critics of liberal theology and natural religion have suggested that a return to the Quadrilateral as it was originally intended and used is the best response.

## Diverse Christian Views of Sources and Norms

Now that we have delineated the Christian consensus regarding the sources and norms for proper Christian belief (construction and reconstruction) and its major alternatives, what are some main differences of interpretation within Christian orthodoxy? What is the range of diversity about this foundational issue within Christianity? Of course, some Christian groups and theologians are uncomfortable with diversity and would respond, "none!" or "very little!" Yet an honest and objective look at the Great Tradition and the wide world of contemporary Christians who are generally accepted by other Christians as authentically Christian, even if mistaken about some foundations and beliefs, observes that diversity does exist. Equally God-fearing, Bible-believing, Jesus-loving Christians can and do disagree about the *proportion* of authority given to the sources and norms of the Quadrilateral.

Some Christian thinkers elevate *tradition* as the overarching source and norm (under God himself, of course). For many and perhaps most Eastern Orthodox and Roman Catholic theologians, the Great Tradition of Christianity is a work of God in revelation such that Scripture is regarded as part of tradition, even if one with its own special dignity and authority. The Roman Catholic Church has stated quite clearly in some of its councils (e.g., Trent, Vatican I and Vatican II) that Scripture and tradition cannot be separated and that Scripture is the God-inspired creation of the church as it was led to select the canonical books by the Holy Spirit. Tradition is, then, the entire process of God's Spirit speaking to and within the church—first through the apostles and then through the bishops who succeeded them and through the councils of the church and through Scripture and through the faithful people of God in prayer, worship and witness.[4] The Catholic Church makes a distinction between this Tradition and traditions, which include customs of the church, canon laws and rules for regulating church life, particular enduring practices and patterns of devotion and worship, liturgy and so forth. Tradition (with a capital T) is

---

[4]For a contemporary statement of the Catholic view of tradition and Scripture, see *The Church's Confession of Faith: A Catholic Catechism for Adults* (San Francisco: Ignatius Press, 1987), pp. 44-48.

the whole that is greater than the sum of its parts (traditions). According to Catholic thought—and Eastern Orthodoxy would not be very different except in details—God maintains the Christian (Catholic) church in truth such that Tradition cannot fundamentally err.

The Catholic Church has from time to time elevated some portion of tradition to the status of required dogma (essential belief for being Catholic if not Christian) even when the belief is not found clearly expressed anywhere in Scripture. This is only done when it is judged by the bishops "with the consent of the faithful" (or occasionally unilaterally by the pope speaking for the faithful people of God) that this portion of tradition (e.g., Mary's conception without the taint of original sin) is ancient, universal, and worthy of all acceptance beyond debate. The Catholic Church and its theologians use Scripture, reason (including Aristotle's philosophy), and experience within the context of the Great Tradition (as it interprets that) to formulate dogma and doctrine.

Traditionally, Protestants emphasize *Scripture over tradition* and over every other source and norm of theology, but they do so in varying degrees. Against the traditions of the Roman Catholic Church of his day, Martin Luther emphasized *sola scriptura* ("Scripture alone" or "Scripture above all") in discussing theology's foundational sources and norms. Most other Protestant and radical Reformers followed him in that. However, the picture is not as simple as often thought. Luther did not reject any and all authoritative tradition, he only rejected any equality of tradition (with a big *T* or small *t*) with Scripture, and even within Scripture itself Luther found a "canon within the canon" in the phrase *"Was Christum treibt"* (what promotes Christ). For Luther (and to some extent most other Reformers), Scripture may be the sole, ultimate source and norm for all Christian faith and practice, but it is to be interpreted using Jesus Christ as criterion and the Great Tradition (early church consensus and major ecumenical creeds) as guide to interpretation. *"Was Christum treibt"* was for Luther the canon within the canon, and the Great Tradition (e.g., Apostles' Creed) was for him a kind of canon outside the canon.

Other Protestant Reformers emphasized Scripture over all other sources and norms in their own ways, some receiving the consensual tradition as a relative authority more or less and others tending to ignore it except when it served their polemical purposes to quote from church fathers. All of the Reformers used tradition, reason and experience critically in developing their accounts of Christian belief. They were wary of these secondary sources and norms precisely because they had been misused by medieval Catholic theologians and sometimes by mystics and fanatics.

The role of *reason* in theology has been debated since the early church period. Church father Tertullian argued (using reason!) against Christians' following reason to determine their beliefs. Of the incarnation of God in Jesus Christ he said, "I believe it because it is absurd!" This was almost certainly hyperbole, but other Christian theologians after him have also tended to denigrate the role of reason. Blaise Pascal asked, "Do you love by reason?" He was countering the supreme role given to enlightenment rationalism even within religion by the Deists.

Some Christians have placed a high value on reason and rationality, however. This is true even within Christian orthodoxy and not only among Deists and natural religionists who hold reason supreme. Second-century church father Justin Martyr was a philosopher before he converted to Christianity and afterwards continued to wear his special philosopher's robe. He and Clement of Alexandria (third century) claimed that Christianity is the true philosophy and perfectly consistent with the best of Greek metaphysical thought. In the Middle Ages, Catholic thinker Thomas Aquinas attempted to integrate Aristotle's philosophy with biblical revelation, and in his massive system of theology entitled *Summa Theologiae* the "angelic doctor" (Thomas) often quoted from "the philosopher" (Aristotle) as if his authority were almost equal with that of divine revelation. Later medieval theologians were often also philosophers and vice versa.

Perhaps the best example of a Christian thinker in the modern world who has appropriated reason as a major source and norm for Christian belief is German Protestant theologian Wolfhart Pannenberg. In volumes such as *Theology and the Philosophy of Science* (1976) Pannenberg argued that Christianity is true precisely because it is rationally coherent and claimed that this can be demonstrated quite apart from appeal to any existential experience of encounter with God or "faith." To be sure, neither Pannenberg in the twentieth century nor Justin Martyr in the second century nor any orthodox Christian thinker in between believed that reason is the sole or even primary source and norm for Christian belief, but many did and still do rely heavily on reason and philosophy not only to defend the truth claims of Christianity but also to construct and reconstruct doctrines.

*Experience* is a most ambiguous concept. Few, if any, Christian theologians have emphasized it over Scripture, tradition or reason. Many have neglected it altogether as a source or norm for Christian belief. After all, as Luther commented sarcastically against the fanatics of his day, "experience is a wax nose any knave can twist to suit his own countenance." In other words, experience is not very useful for determining what one ought to believe because it is so subjective. On the other hand, some Christian movements and groups throughout history have relied heavily on mystical experiences or shared community experiences for discerning truths about God. Pietism is a movement within Protestantism that wished to recover a "heart Christianity" out of the dry bones of "head religion" or mere "historical faith." Seventeenth- and eighteenth-century Pietists such as Philip Spener, August Francke and Count von Zinzendorf had a profound influence on John and Charles Wesley and the great revivals known as the Great Awakenings. They emphasized personal encounter and relationship with God as equally important as doctrinal knowledge and understanding in identifying and developing authentic Christianity.[5] In the twentieth century, orthodox Christian movements as different as Pentecostalism and neo-orthodoxy stressed experience in their own ways. For all of these Christian movements, *experience* is not so much a vehicle of doctrinal information as it is a confirming factor in providing guidance and discernment. For them, as for Pascal, "the heart has reasons the reason knows not of."

The real watershed of diversity within orthodox Christianity with regard to sources and norms lies between those Christians who emphasize *tradition* over or as including Scripture and those who emphasize *Scripture* over or even to the neglect of tradition. Both sides of that watershed make some uses of reason and experience in identifying and determining Christian belief. Even this watershed is not absolute, however: because Scripture is always being interpreted, tradition usually plays some normative role in that interpretive process. At the same time, tradition is so broad and vague that it needs Scripture as the compass within it.

## A Unitive Christian View of Theology's Sources and Norms
In spite of what some Christian thinkers and leaders may claim, many

---

[5]An excellent source on Pietism is Ted A. Campbell, *The Religion of the Heart: A Study of European Religious Life in the Seventeenth and Eighteenth Centuries* (Columbia: University of South Carolina Press, 1991).

sources and norms inevitably come into play whenever a group of Christians attempts to determine what exactly proper Christian belief is. *Sola scriptura* is a wonderful ideal principle. It rightly expresses the conviction that the Bible is the norming norm *(norma normans)* and most important source for determining right belief in all matters of Christian faith and practice. However, Scripture is never uninterpreted except when being quoted and even then, unless the quotation is from the Hebrew, Aramaic or Greek, the translation reflects some element of interpretation. The Quadrilateral is inevitable and highly valuable as a pattern for determining Christian belief and for constructing and reconstructing Christian doctrines. However, the Quadrilateral is not an equilateral. Tradition, reason and experience are not sources and norms in the same way or on the same level with Scripture, which itself reflects to the Christian tradition community the very mind of God in an accommodated way.

As we will see in a later chapter, Scripture is an authority of mediated immediacy. God's Word itself is mediated to us through the multifaceted text of inspired Scripture which is *theopneustos,* "God-breathed" or inspired. What this means in practical terms is that in the process of examining and determining proper Christian belief no appeal can be made *against Scripture*. Anyone who says, "Scripture teaches that such-and-such is true, but I disagree and urge that Christians believe something contrary to Scripture" is departing from foundational Christian thinking in precisely the same way that a United States judge would be departing from American jurisprudence and his or her own oath by saying "The Constitution holds that such-and-such is a basic principle and right, but I disagree and rule against the Constitution." That is unthinkable.

Scripture is our ultimate authority for Christian faith and practice because it is inspired by God (a doctrine we will explore in a later chapter) and because it is that constituting text that creates Christian identity in terms of belief. As one twentieth-century theologian has said, "the text [Bible] absorbs the world." In other words, *for Christians* the biblical narrative and witness as a whole is the lens through which we view experience and reality. There is no question of the Bible being wrong about ultimate reality—the deepest questions and answers of life. For Christians, the biblical narrative and witness is that which shapes our view of the world, our own lives, the past and future, right and wrong, and the meaning of history. But Scripture must be interpreted. And interpretation—especially for purposes of establishing shared belief within Christianity and Christian communities—must start with the biblical materials and proceed inward and outward in an ongoing process of reflection. Within Scripture there is a touchstone: *"Was Christum treibt."* That means incidental references and comments that have nothing directly to do with Christ and his mission are not as directly relevant to establishing essential Christian belief as those portions of Scripture that promote that.

From outside Scripture we look to the Great Tradition as earlier described (the basic common beliefs held by early church fathers and sixteenth-century Reformers) as a *norma normata* (normed norm) that guides and directs Christian reflection without controlling it. Also from beyond Scripture itself we use basic rules of logic such as the norm or rule of non-contradiction. Any two propositions that absolutely contradict each other (which is not always easy to prove or disprove) cannot both be affirmed as true by any reasonable person. Even within Christian doctrine and belief we must not embrace unintelligible nonsense, which is what a true contradiction always is. Finally, experience should come into play in somewhat the same way as reason—not as a major source or controlling norm that regulates belief, but as a guide to attention. Shared Christian experience can and inevitably does serve as something of a compass in reflecting on Scripture's meaning, but it is quite dangerous if separated from or elevated above tradition and reason.

Christian belief develops and is regulated within a continuing communal conversation within the churches, and that conversation appeals primarily to Scripture (understood as witness to Jesus Christ) and secondarily to the Great Tradition of Christian thought (especially in the patristic era and sixteenth-century Reformations), and it uses fundamental laws of reason (above all the law of non-contradiction) and shared Christian experience to guide and direct the conversation that unfolds without controlling it. A Christian belief, then, is one that arises out of Scripture and points to Jesus Christ, is generally consistent with the consensual tradition of Christian thought, and is logically coherent with other Christian beliefs and illumines the shared experience of Christians. One always has to be open to the possibility, however, that fresh elucidation of Scripture's meaning may force reform (revision) in some part of tradition. It is possible that aspects of the Great Tradition of early Christian thought and Reformation belief may be wrong, but it is highly unlikely that the whole of the Great Tradition would be mistaken, as some restorationists or primitivists seem to claim.[6]

We should all simply admit that this process of using Christian sources and norms to determine proper Christian belief is not in any way scientific.[7] If it is a science at all, it is a hermeneutical science that involves a great deal of interpretation in which "horizons" (perspectives, sets of experiences) are brought together and fused as much as possible. It involves a great deal of judgment and therefore risk. Nevertheless in spite of all that messiness, the task of establishing proper Christian belief is not like choosing based on mere preference or taste. The process has sources and norms and involves an on-going conversation between them.

---

[6]Some Christian movements—especially certain radical, sectarian Protestant ones—claim that the church, including Christian belief and practice, fell into apostasy almost immediately after the first century. These "restorationists" seek now to restore the "primitive" or original New Testament faith and order and they generally tend to ignore two thousand years of tradition.

[7]This is contrary to certain "scholastics" in Catholic and Protestant theology who have regarded the process as scientific. Nineteenth-century Reformed (Calvinist) scholastic theologian Charles Hodge and the entire "Princeton School" of theology he represented seemed to think of theology as very objective and linear—much like natural science was thought to be. Hodge thought of Scripture to theology as nature is to science and considered theology little more than studying Scripture and placing its revealed doctrines in proper order within a system.

# CHAPTER 3

# DIVINE REVELATION

## Universal *and* Particular

The previous chapter virtually equated Scripture with revelation while noting that some Christians have distinguished between them. For Eastern Orthodox and Roman Catholic Christian thinkers, Tradition (as opposed to traditions) is a vehicle of divine revelation, and Scripture is one part of that larger revelational phenomenon. Luther tended to distinguish between revelation of God in Jesus Christ and Scripture as a secondary, written revelation. In the twentieth century, Karl Barth, a leading Swiss neo-orthodox theologian, strongly distinguished between God's revelation as self-disclosure in Jesus Christ and witness to that self-disclosure in Scripture. In other ways Christians have linked and yet distinguished revelation and Scripture. Yet nearly all Christian thinkers throughout history—unless one counts modern liberal theologians as "Christian thinkers"—have considered the canonical Scriptures to be the unique source and norm for determining proper Christian belief. On the other hand, they have at the same time usually acknowledged that Scripture is not all there is of divine revelation and that it is a form of or witness to revelation even though it is that form and witness that is uniquely relevant to and authoritative for determination of right Christian belief.

## Issues and Polarities of Christian Belief About Divine Revelation

What is divine revelation? In the broadest possible sense it is any way in which God communicates himself or something about himself to others. In a narrower sense it is God's self-disclosure to creatures for the sake of their redemptive transformation. Many definitions may be offered, but the essence of them all is that revelation is God's message by whatever means that transcends what creatures can know by themselves. Philosophers have long talked of "man's search for God" and many books have been written by philosophical theologians attempting to use autonomous (unaided) reason to establish God's existence and nature.[1] In response to this project that attempts to go around divine revelation and know God apart from any divine self-disclosure, Pascal asserted that "the God of the philosophers is not the God of Abraham, Isaac and Jacob." In other words, according to Pascal and many other Christians, one may discover or construct a concept of God through unaided reason, but such a "God" is never identical with the God that "people of the book" (Christians and Jews) have known and worshiped. Much debate swirls around that issue even among Christians. Some disagree very strongly with Pascal while acknowledging that at its best such a natural knowledge of God (apart from special divine revelation and using unaided reason alone) is vague and not redemptive. At best it can be a bridge between unbelief and belief.

Where and how has God revealed himself and what does that revelation do in terms of yielding knowledge of God? Christians have always assumed—as have Jewish believers—that God reveals himself. Divine revelation is one of Christianity's givens. That does not mean belief in divine revelation is arbitrary; many presuppositions are more than arbitrary. It means that the assumption of divine revelation in Scripture and tradition that is consistent with logic and shared human and Christian experience is basic to Christianity. The same kind of legitimate assuming is found in the United States Declaration of Independence: "We find these truths to be self-evident." An assumption is something "found to be self-evident" even though it is confirmed by continuing experience and consistent with reason. That all persons are created equal is self-evident within American tradition. It is foundational—a properly basic belief that needs no proof. So it is with divine rev-

---

[1]One example of such a purely rational search for God that claims success is Mortimer Adler, *How to Think About God: A Guide for the 20th-Century Pagan* (New York: Collier Books, 1991).

elation. Christianity assumes it even though most Christians believe good reasons can be given for it. *Apologetics* is the process of providing those reasons. Beyond assuming that God has revealed himself and that this revelation is available, Christians have developed a minimal consensual tradition that forms a small but stable plot of common ground. This consensus will be explained in the next section of this chapter.

Many issues have arisen within Christian tradition that have led to diverse beliefs about divine revelation. Often a pendulum swing effect has come into play leading to Christian theologians and groups going to extremes against each other. One polarity within the broad Christian consensus tradition about divine revelation is over *general (universal) revelation versus special (particular) revelation.* This includes the issue of a possible natural knowledge of God based on general revelation and reason. Another polarity within Christian belief has to do with the issue of the nature of special, supernatural, particular revelation: Is it *primarily personal or propositional?* Finally, some Christians have assumed that *revelation is completed while others have argued that revelation continues to unfold.* These differences of interpretation have led to great diversity and even at times hostility within Christianity between groups of Christian teachers and their followers. Sometimes this manifests a false "either-or" mentality and the search for a "both-and" approach is badly needed.

### The Christian Consensus About Divine Revelation

If there is any one belief that unites all Christians it is that Jesus Christ is God's unique and unsurpassable self-disclosure. The apostle who wrote a letter to the Hebrews said it best in Hebrews 1:1-2: "In the past God spoke to our forefathers through the prophets at many times and in various ways, but in these last days he has spoken to us by his Son, whom he appointed heir of all things, and through whom he made the universe." One of the earliest Christian writings outside of those included in the New Testament is the anonymously written *Epistle to Diognetus.* The unknown second-century Christian author expressed very well the Christian consensus when he wrote of Jesus Christ ("God's Child" and "the Word"), "what man had any knowledge of what God was, before he came?"[2] The early church fathers' writings

---

[2]Quoted in *The Apostolic Fathers,* trans. J. B. Lightfoot and J. R. Harmer, ed. and rev. by Michael W. Holmes, 2nd ed. (Grand Rapids, Mich.: Baker, 1989), p. 301.

make clear that they did not reject any and all revelation of God or knowledge of God before Jesus Christ, so this question no doubt includes an element of hyperbole. Nevertheless, the church fathers and Reformers never tired of emphasizing the uniqueness and unsurpassability of the revelation of God in Christ. The great fourth-century church father and bishop Athanasius based his defense of the full deity of the Son of God who became human in Jesus Christ, against those who would demote him to a second god unequal in substance with the Father, in part on the fullness of revelation of God in him.

Luther adamantly insisted that there is no true knowledge of God apart from Jesus Christ and that whatever is true of God's being outside of Christ is not meant for us to know. In modern theology Karl Barth has developed a thoroughly Christocentric (if not Christomonistic) system of theology called *Church Dogmatics* that begins with and is thoroughly pervaded by the idea that Jesus Christ is God's self-revelation to humanity in a unique and unsurpassable sense. Reformer John Calvin, who produced the first true Protestant systematic theology (coherent summary of beliefs), summed up this consensus well when he wrote that although God is revealed in the natural order, because of humanity's fall into sin "no one now experiences God either as Father or as Author of salvation, or favorable in any way, until Christ the Mediator comes forward to reconcile him to us."[3] The consensus of Christian belief, then, is that God is specially revealed in Jesus Christ and that this surpasses other revelations of God that may exist.

A second point of general agreement among Christians with regard to divine revelation is that God is revealed in some manner, although imperfectly and impersonally, in the natural world and history as a whole. Karl Barth seemed to deny this in a curt response to another Swiss theologian named Emil Brunner. Their famous (or infamous) debate during the 1930s had to do with whether or not God is revealed in nature—including human nature. Some have argued that Barth, in his response, *Nein!* (No!), rejected any general revelation of God and restricted divine self-disclosure to Jesus Christ. That is debatable. What is beyond debate is that the argument between Barth and Brunner[4] was primarily over whether a "point of con-

---

[3]John Calvin *Institutes of the Christian Religion* 1.2.1, p. 40.
[4]For the relevant essays, see Karl Barth and Emil Brunner, *Natural Theology*, trans. Peter Fraenkel (London: Geoffrey Bles, Centenary Press, 1946).

tact" for the gospel may be found in human existence. In the process of rejecting such, Barth seemed to reject any knowledge of God outside of Jesus Christ and perhaps even any revelation of God outside of Jesus Christ and the Word of God that testifies to him (viz., special revelation). (In latter volumes of his *Church Dogmatics* Barth seemed to allow some natural knowledge of God, but he always resisted any normative role for general revelation or natural theology in Christian theological reflection.)

With the possible exception of Barth and a few other modern neo-orthodox theologians, the vast majority of Christians have always believed that God is revealed, however vaguely, in the natural order that he created, including human existence itself. The great medieval Catholic thinker Thomas Aquinas developed a "natural theology"—knowledge of God through evidences and reason alone—based on the existence and order of the world and on human conscience. He admitted that such knowledge of God is insufficient for salvation and for knowing God as loving person, but he believed (and the Catholic church accepts) that God's existence is manifest in nature and that human reason is fully capable—in spite of sin—of grasping that. Among Protestant Reformers, John Calvin especially worked on this belief in a general revelation of God and argued in his *Institutes of the Christian Religion* that were it not for sin clouding humans' minds, the revelation of God in nature would yield a true knowledge of God. Luther believed and taught that all human beings have a bare knowledge of God's existence through nature. The early church fathers everywhere assumed such a revelation of God while at the same time asserting its inadequacy for redemption. The apostle Paul seemed to outline such a view of God's revelation in nature in Romans 1 and the psalmist extolled the evidences of God in the heavens that declare God's glory (Ps 19).

Everywhere and at all times Christians have agreed (with very few exceptions such as possibly Karl Barth) that there is a bare true knowledge of God—perhaps only that God exists—possible through God's revelation in nature. The overwhelming emphasis in Christian belief about divine revelation, however, has come down on the nature of God's higher, clearer and fuller revelation in Jesus Christ. But how do those who have lived after Jesus' resurrection and ascension know about him? And what about those who lived before his life on earth? Christians have generally agreed that God prepared the world for his unique self-revelation in Christ through the Hebrew prophets and their writings and continued that revelation after Christ's departure via Christian apostles and their writings. Thus, Christians have accepted the existence of spoken and written revelation alongside of Jesus Christ insofar as it points to and centers around him. The writings of the Hebrew prophets were treated as God's Word by Jesus (who often quoted Moses, for example, as speaking on behalf of God) and the apostles. Scattered throughout the apostolic writings are references to special revelation to and through prophets and their writings (e.g., 2 Tim 3:16 and 2 Pet 1:20-21). The majority of the early church fathers quoted from Hebrew prophets as well as from apostolic writings as if all of them were vehicles of special divine revelation.

The process of determining a Christian canon (closed list) of inspired books began with the second-century Christians' response to a Christian teacher in Rome named Marcion who, among other heresies, believed the Hebrew religion—Judaism—was not a precursor to Christianity and attempted to expunge Jewish influences from Christianity. Marcion attempted to limit Christian recognition of inspired writings to only a few portions of the apostles' writings that he considered Gentile (e.g., Luke, portions of Acts and portions of ten Pauline epistles). The church responded by affirming the Hebrew canon as its own (later known as the Old Testament) and by beginning to add to it equally inspired writings of apostles (later known as the New Testament) beyond Marcion's truncated canon. Slight differences of judgment about several books held back a united Christian canon until late in the fourth century. By the end of the second century and beginning of the third century, however, one finds church fathers Irenaeus, Tertullian and Origen agreeing on most candidates for inclusion in the Christians' "Testament" of inspired works. The Bible, then, came to be regarded by all Christians as a form of special divine revelation—above nature but below Jesus Christ himself.

The great twentieth-century theologian Karl Barth provided a relatively sound summation of the Christian consensus about divine revelation in his *Church Dogmatics*. In the first volume of this massive thirteen-volume summa of Christian thought Barth explicated a threefold, hierarchical structure of divine revelation and its main forms.[5] To be sure, not all Christian

---

[5]Karl Barth, *Church Dogmatics* 1/1: *The Doctrine of the Word of God*, part 1, ed. G. W. Bromiley and T. F. Torrance, trans. G. W. Bromiley (Edinburgh: T & T Clark, 1975), chap. 1, part 4, "The Word of God in Its Threefold Form," pp. 88-124.

thinkers throughout the ages or in the twentieth century would agree completely with Barth's description of divine revelation, and most would want to add to it something more about *general revelation of God in nature*. Barth almost totally neglects the latter. It has never played a great role in Christian belief, however, and most Christian reflection on divine revelation has focused on *special revelation of God*. *That* God is revealed in nature—including creation itself, human conscience and possibly history as a whole (universal history)—has seldom been denied and almost always assumed. But *the benefit* of that general revelation of God has always been questioned. Barth's explication of the threefold nature of divine revelation rightly focused on special revelation that aims at redemption.

For Barth, special revelation appears in three interrelated forms: *God's Word revealed* (God's personal self-disclosure in Jesus Christ), *God's Word written* (inspired, canonical Scripture) and *God's Word preached* (the gospel proclaimed by the church in all ages). While there may be room for debate between Christians about the exact nature and extent of these forms of divine revelation, and not all would agree with Barth's delineations of them, *that God is specially revealed* in Jesus Christ (revelation itself) and in Scripture (inspired witness to revelation itself) and in the proclamation and testimony of the faithful people of God, the church has generally accepted and agreed on. The Eastern Orthodox churches want to emphasize that its Great Tradition of worship (liturgy) is included in the third form of divine revelation and by no means less than Scripture itself. Conservative Protestants tend to emphasize the role of Scripture as God's Word often to the neglect of the third form of divine revelation. Most Pentecostals and charismatics wish to view the third form of revelation as a continuing work of God the Holy Spirit in testifying to Jesus Christ and guiding God's people into all truth. Nevertheless, the threefold form of God's Word—divine revelation—provides significant common ground, that is, a consensual tradition, for Christians down through the ages and today.

## Alternatives to Christian Belief About Divine Revelation

We have already seen that some who call themselves Christians have challenged the Christian consensus or even propelled the development and formation of that consensus. Marcion of Rome was one such person. Throughout Christian history others on the fringes of the church have raised proposals about divine revelation that have been rejected by Christians in general. What alternative views—heresies—would Eastern Orthodox, Roman Catholic and most Protestants reject as beyond the pale of Christian belief?

One alternative to Christian belief in this area of divine revelation is that *divine revelation may surpass Jesus Christ and Scripture* in the sense that new revelation may supersede and replace them. As strange as it may seem, some Christians have embraced such new and allegedly superior revelations without rejecting as completely irrelevant the older, allegedly inferior revelations of God in Jesus and through the apostles. This is why Barth's third form of divine revelation is often downplayed if not ignored in standard, conservative accounts of Christian theology. Conservative theologians often fear that including the words and deeds of the church after Jesus Christ and the apostles opens up a Pandora's box of potential new revelations surpassing original divine revelation. In Germany in the 1930s the National Socialist Party (the Nazis) promoted German culture and even Hitler and the party as bearers of a new and higher revelation of God, and some German Christians accepted this. The response by more traditional and faithful Christians was the "Barmen Declaration" of the Confessing Church movement that declared Jesus Christ as sole Lord for Christians and rejected any belief in a new savior and lord or a superseding revelation of God in culture. The Unification Church of Rev. Sun Myung Moon of Korea believes in a "Lord of the Second Advent" who will appear from Asia and deliver a more complete revelation and salvation than Jesus brought. The book *The Divine Principle* is believed by many Unificationists to be a more complete and surpassing revelation than that of the canonical Bible. Many sects and cults on the fringes of Christianity have produced or identified new revelations that stand in contrast to original revelation given by God in Jesus and through the prophets and apostles.

Another alternative to historic, consensual Christian belief is that *general, universal revelation—because it is available to reason apart from faith—is greater than special divine revelation.* This heresy usually takes the form of a claim that special divine revelation in Jesus Christ, Scripture, and the preaching of the church merely re-presents what is generally revealed and available to universal reason. Some philosophical theologians have held this view of divine revelation. Most notable among them is the German idealist philosopher G. W. F. Hegel, who believed that the best of philosophy (human thought and culture) is divine revelation, and that reason itself—without any special, supernatural aid or faith—can discover whatever is of any importance communicated through the symbols of special revelation. For him, Jesus Christ was merely the re-presentation within history of a rational truth that is timeless and universal—the union of God (Absolute Spirit) and humanity. The death of Jesus on the cross is re-presentation in concrete, historical form of a "speculative Good Friday" as God's eternal self-alienation and self-actualization on the "cross" of creation.[6] To a lesser extent, or in a less radical way, many philosophically-minded Christian thinkers have repeated Hegel's basic perspective on divine revelation. There exists a revelation of "The Real" everywhere, certain self-proclaimed religious pluralists argue, and every religion has its own form of it. Jesus Christ and Scripture are simply Christianity's apprehension of that noumenal (beyond the senses), idealistic and transcendental "Real" which is God or the divine. All major religions have their own, equally valid apprehensions of it.

A third and final alternative to Christian belief about divine revelation suggests that *the highest and best form of divine revelation is completely interior and mystical.* Some Christians have rejected objective, outer divine revelation as ultimate and embraced a personal (i.e., individual) revelation of God in an "inner light" or "existential awareness" as greater than the historical revelation of God in Jesus Christ and Scripture. Such Christians do not reject Jesus Christ or Scripture, but they tend to listen for Christ within and read Scripture for the purpose of hearing God speak to them personally through it. On the more liberal theological side this approach to divine revelation emphasizes the "Christ of faith" over the "Jesus of history." Twentieth-century German theologian and New Testament scholar Rudolf Bultmann tended to reduce divine revelation to a new self-understanding in encounter with Christ through the message of the cross. He taught that for Christian existence the Christ of faith who is known inwardly by faith is more important than the historical Jesus. Of course, even Bultmann would not drive too wide a wedge between them. For him, the Christ of faith is connected with the word of the cross preached in the church about the self-sacrificing death of the Jesus of history. Nevertheless, the focus on revelation as the subjective encounter-experience is widely interpreted by more tradi-

---

[6]Hegel's philosophical theology is best expressed in relation to Christianity in his *Lectures on the Philosophy of Religion*, trans. E. B. Speirs and J. Burden Sanderson, ed. E. B. Speirs (New York: Humanities Press, 1962).

tional Christians as lessening the importance of the objective revelation of God outside the faith of the individual.

On the more conservative theological side this approach to divine revelation emphasizes the "inner light of Christ" within each person and encourages Christians to listen to that more than to the "dead letter" of a book (the Bible). Finding historical examples of this mystical approach is somewhat difficult as most of the people who hold this view of divine revelation do not write about it, but one possible historical example is the early Quaker or Friends movement. George Fox and other Quakers of the seventeenth century tended to locate revelation within the heart of every individual, and belief in this "inner light" of Christ became a distinctive teaching of Quakerism. Many Quakers or Friends in the twentieth century have adopted a more traditional Christian view of divine revelation without giving up the idea that Christ illumines Christian minds and hearts in a special way.

The Christian churches and their leaders and theologians have rejected these three views of divine revelation as too far from the center of Christianity to be considered orthodox. Each one has its own unique danger and denies something believed by most Christians to be essential to the gospel of Jesus Christ and the essence of the Christian identity. The idea that new divine revelations may supercede even Jesus Christ and surpass even canonical Scripture denies the uniqueness of Jesus Christ as God's self-revelation in person and opens the door to all kinds of new messiahs and incarnations. If such claims and expectations were allowed at all, it would be impossible to maintain any stable identity of Christianity or message of the gospel. Where such openness to new revelation surpassing Jesus Christ and Scripture has been taken seriously, Christianity has been transformed into a cult.

The idea that general revelation grasped by reason is greater than special revelation and in some way rules over it or judges it fails to take seriously enough the noetic effects of sin (the fallenness of the human intellect) and undermines the very necessity of Jesus Christ and Scripture. If general revelation is greater than special revelation, then it is difficult to see why special revelation is necessary. This approach also tends to focus attention more on a generic religiousness and a spirituality transcending the gospel of Christ than on that gospel. Christianity, then, is in danger of becoming merely a symbolic re-presentation of philosophy just as Hegel believed.

Belief that the highest form of revelation is individual and inward very seriously undermines the objectivity of God's Word in divine revelation. If there is no higher, clearer and more authoritative revelation than one's inner experiences or inner light, then each person is free to establish his or her own Christian beliefs that best fit his or her inward spiritual feelings or messages. There is no escape, then, from folk religion and no outward test by which to judge inner revelations. Relativism is the dangerous and nearly inevitable outcome of such a view of divine revelation. That is not to denigrate experience of God and of Jesus Christ within one's own heart and mind. In fact, this truth does not detract from the reality of God speaking inwardly. It only says that these messages and experiences of God cannot be acknowledged as the highest source and norm for proper Christian belief. Unless something transcends inner experience it becomes the ultimate authority and then everyone is free to believe whatever seems right in his or her own heart. The consequence of that would be chaos.

## Diverse Christian Beliefs About Divine Revelation

The minimal Christian consensus regarding divine revelation leaves much room for diversity of interpretation and opinion and, in fact, orthodox Christianity does include within itself great variety of belief on the subject. Three areas of discussion, disagreement and even debate are worthy of consideration here. First, Christians who agree about the core doctrine of divine revelation often disagree vigorously about *natural knowledge of God*. Second, within modern Christian theology significant debate has swirled around *the nature of special revelation as primarily personal or primarily propositional*. Third, *differing beliefs about continuing revelation—especially the "gift of prophecy"*—give rise to divisions and sometimes arguments.

Some Christians and churches believe very strongly in *rational, philosophical knowledge of God* that does not draw on special revelation or faith but relies solely on the evidences of God in nature and reason. The Roman Catholic Church officially holds as doctrine that God can be known as Creator in this way. In order to know God as redeemer, the church affirms, one must possess a special revelation and have faith in it. The great medieval Archbishop of Canterbury Anselm developed purely rational arguments for many Christian beliefs and taught that God's existence and nature can be proven logically. He developed what came to be known as the "ontological argument" for the existence of God and deduced from God's necessary existence many of God's necessary attributes. According to Anselm, the Bible says that "the fool says in his heart, 'There is no God'" (Ps 14:1) because denial of

God's existence is a logical fallacy. The definition of God is "the being greater than which none can be conceived," and since existing outside the mind in reality is greater than existing only in the mind, anyone who says "the being greater than which none can be conceived does not exist except as an idea in my own mind" contradicts himself.[7] Thus, God's existence is part of the very definition of God (and only of the definition of God), and so long as a person can hold the right thought of God in his or her mind, proving God's existence to that person is simple.

Two centuries later Catholic thinker Thomas Aquinas developed other arguments for the existence of God that relied less on pure logic and more on evidences of nature. According to Thomas, there are five ways of proving God's existence and all begin with observation of the world or human existence. The best known of these is the "cosmological argument," which deduces God's necessary existence from the contingent (nonnecessary) existence of the cosmos. This is popularly known as the "first cause argument" because it attempts to prove that in order for the finite, contingent world of causes and effects to exist at all, it must have an uncaused, first cause as its source.

Various forms of natural theology have flourished among Christians since the second-century church fathers known as the Apologists used evidence, reason and philosophy to demonstrate the reasonableness of Christianity. Anselm and Thomas are just two of the best known and most influential theologians in Christian history to rely heavily on general revelation and reason to construct a natural theology. Neither one believed that general revelation and unaided reason are capable of yielding redemptive knowledge of God; both believed in divine special revelation as the remedy for the ignorance of God brought about by sin. However, like most other rational theologians who emphasize natural theology, they viewed it as a kind of vestibule through which one could gradually introduce open-minded inquirers to the higher revelation of God in Christ and Scripture. In modern theology certain Protestant theologians such as Wolfhart Pannenberg have used anthropology (in the broad, philosophical sense of the study of human existence) as a tool of natural or "fundamental" theology. Twentieth-century theologian Paul Tillich looked to and used existentialist philosophy as a

---

[7]Anselm, "Proslogium," in *Saint Anselm: Basic Writings,* trans. S. N. Deane (La Salle, Ill.: Open Court, 1962).

tool for leading persons into awareness of special revelation.

Many Christian theologians have been quite uncomfortable with emphasis on general revelation and natural theology. Karl Barth, for example, recognized no positive, true knowledge of God outside of Jesus Christ and argued that to look for revelation of God elsewhere is to move toward idolatry. Many Protestant theologians have affirmed a bare knowledge of God through general revelation while denying any "natural knowledge of God" in the sense of a true knowledge of *who God is* and *what God is like* through nature alone. Luther and Calvin both expressed grave reservations about any positive role for general revelation or natural theology, and Calvin averred that even though God is revealed in nature, sin has so blinded fallen humans that unless they encounter God through Christ and the Scriptures they will only construct idols from that revelation. There is, then, no true knowledge of God gained from nature, and natural theology should play no normative role in constructing or reconstructing Christian belief. So, on the one hand, Catholic theology and some Protestant thinkers regard universal revelation of God in nature in a very positive light, while on the other hand, many Protestant Reformers and theologians set universal revelation aside as of little or no value and focus all attention on God's particular revelation in Jesus Christ, Scripture and (possibly) the church's proclamation of the Word of God.

The second major flash point of controversy and cause of diversity over divine revelation among Christians has to do with *the nature of revelation as primarily personal or primarily propositional.* Although this debate has ancient antecedents it is primarily modern. Many twentieth-century Christian theologians argue that divine revelation is *God's self-communication* and not *communication of information about God.* Scottish Protestant theologian John Baillie explained revelation as the "mighty acts of God in history" in *The Idea of Revelation in Recent Thought,* a book that drew heavily on the theological approaches of Barth and Brunner. According to Baillie, "the revelation of which the Bible speaks is always such as has place within a personal relationship. It is not the revelation of an object to a subject, but a revelation from subject to subject, a revelation of mind to mind."[8] The manner or mode of this revelation as self-disclosure is event and not proposition. Baillie,

---

[8]John Baillie, *The Idea of Revelation in Recent Thought* (New York: Columbia University Press, 1956), p. 24.

like Barth and Brunner, admits that there are propositional statements that are rightly drawn from divine revelation; there are propositions appropriate to divine revelation, but there are no "revealed propositions." Behind this view of revelation lie commitments to God's transcendence above and beyond all human language and the desire to affirm the personal nature of God and the redemptive purpose of revelation. Ultimately, the theologians who view revelation as personal (i.e., having the nature of event within relationship) wish to retrieve a supposed *relational ontology* (philosophy of being that places highest value on persons and their relationships) of the Bible. Some critics regard this as an influence of existential philosophy within theology.

Against the view of revelation as exclusively personal or eventful is the idea of *revelation as primarily propositional.* In other words, according to many conservative Protestant theologians, in revelation God communicates information about himself in factual statements or in language the meaning of which can be expressed in factual statements. One of the best known proponents of such a view is conservative twentieth-century evangelical thinker Carl F. H. Henry, who criticized Barth's, Brunner's and Baillie's views of revelation as inevitably leading to a diminution of doctrine. How does one derive doctrine from nonpropositional revelation? Perhaps the most consistently propositional view of divine revelation is that proposed by British evangelical theologian and philosopher Paul Helm in *The Divine Revelation.* A major thesis of Helm's is that "actions without propositions are dumb."[9] In other words, Helm argues, if God's self-disclosure or revelation were exclusively personal, eventful and not at all communicative of information there would be no way to know anything objectively true about God. Revelation is communication of meaning or it does not really reveal anything, and meaning is a function of factual truth claims (propositions).

Neither Helm nor Henry deny that God acts or that God's acts have something to do with divine revelation, but they agree that apart from divinely communicated interpretation those acts would be useless for yielding knowledge of God. "Revelation," then, is a pattern of act plus interpretation, and that interpretation must be given by God or we have no reason to think it is true. In spite of their inclusion of "event" and "act" in the pattern of divine revelation, Henry and Helm seem to place the most value on

---

[9]Paul Helm, *The Divine Revelation* (Westchester, Ill.: Crossway, 1982), p. 4.

the divinely communicated propositional content of revelation. The main purpose of revelation, so it would seem, is to communicate correct doctrine so that we humans will think the right thoughts about God.

The third and final main subject of disagreement among orthodox Christians with regard to divine revelation relates to *its nature as complete or continuing*. Whether revelation is primarily personal event or communication of information, the question still arises whether there is any more of it or whether it stopped sometime in the past. We have already seen that all orthodox Christians agree that there is a certain complete and unsurpassable quality to revelation in Jesus Christ and Scripture. But what about Barth's third form of revelation—the preaching of the church? Might God have new truths to communicate through prophecy? All orthodox Christians agree that if such continuing revelation exists it must be measured by Jesus Christ and Scripture. But what about truths that are not already communicated there? Does prophecy within the church exist today and, if so, do prophetic messages count as divine revelation? Some Christians believe that all true divine revelation is summed up in Jesus Christ, Scripture and the faithful proclamation of the gospel of Jesus Christ in the church. These "cessationists" believe the completion of the canon of Scripture brought to an end the "utterance gifts of the Spirit" mentioned by Paul in 1 Corinthians 12 such as prophecy, speaking in tongues, interpretation of tongues, word of wisdom and word of knowledge. Prophetic messages were meant only for the infancy of the early church when it had no inspired collection of authoritative Christian Scriptures.

Most Pentecostal and charismatic Christians, on the other hand, believe that God may and sometimes does continue to communicate non-doctrinal truths through prophetic messages in the church. Pentecostal-charismatic healing evangelist and educator Oral Roberts encouraged such openness to new revelation from God throughout the second half of the twentieth century, as did many other similar evangelists and preachers. Evangelical theologian Wayne A. Grudem reopened the subject with his volume on prophecy titled *The Gift of Prophecy in the New Testament and Today* (Crossway, 2000). More conservative Protestants have generally feared that any belief in or practice of continuing revelations from God might lead into cultish aberrations such as the unusual beliefs held by certain sects on the fringes of Christianity that are based largely on "new prophecies" delivered by modern religious leaders breaking out of the mainstream of traditional Christianity.

These three controversial subjects related to divine revelation provide much diversity within Christianity. Some particularly narrow-minded Christian leaders and thinkers may object to including persons who hold opposite views from their own on these topics within orthodox Christianity. However, Christian men and women who embrace the Great Tradition of Christian belief and teaching about God, Christ, salvation and so on, stand on different sides of these debates. The Swiss theologians Barth and Brunner vehemently disagreed about the possibility of natural knowledge of God and possibly even about general revelation itself. And yet they agreed about the major doctrines of Christianity such as the deity and humanity of Christ and salvation by grace alone. They were both Reformed evangelical theologians in spite of their disagreement about universal revelation. John Baillie and many other modern Protestants who reject propositional revelation agree with the church fathers and Reformers and conservative evangelical and Catholic Christian thinkers about the great beliefs of the consensual tradition. Wayne Grudem, who promotes belief in continuing revelation through modern-day prophecies, is a staunch defender of classical Christian doctrines as are the cessationists, who disagree with him about that particular subject.

## A Unitive Christian Vision of Divine Revelation
Perhaps the divisions between equally classical Christians over divine revelation are examples of false polarities—unnecessary either-or thinking. As is often the case, those who emphatically emphasize one side to the exclusion of the other are overreacting to a danger out of fear of what might happen if that view is taken to an extreme. For example, Barth worried much that any openness to natural knowledge of God—however minimal—might lead to "culture Christianity," a religion that is not so much Christian as it is a prop for a particular culture's values. He worked out his mature theology in the context of the Nazification of the German churches in the 1930s. Even the volumes of his *Church Dogmatics* written after that were influenced by what Barth thought he observed then and there: a tendency to use openness to revelation of God outside of Jesus Christ and Scripture to support a false religion under the guise of "German Christianity." In reaction to this, Barth threw the baby of general revelation and natural knowledge of God's existence out with the bathwater of "culture Protestantism." On the other hand, some proponents of natural theology (sometimes called "foundational" or "fundamental theology") tend to spend so much time and energy exploring

common ground between Christianity and non-Christian philosophies that, in spite of good intentions, secular sources and reasoning come to play a normative role in their Christian reflections.

What if we assume that divine revelation is both-and rather than either-or? That is, what if we assume that a universal, general revelation of God does exist and is available for everyone everywhere at all times (as Paul seems to say in Romans 1) and that our controlling source and norm for Christian belief is God's particular, special revelation in Jesus Christ, Scripture and the preaching of the church? For example, even though there is no natural knowledge of God in the sense of a positive content of true belief about God drawn from nature and reason alone (as Paul also seems to argue in Romans 1), perhaps we could say that a reasonable examination of nature always raises certain *questions of transcendence*—questions about God and life after death, etc.—that find their most satisfying answers in particular divine revelation. There do seem to be certain perennial, transcultural issues and concerns that we might label life's ultimate questions. What is our purpose for living? What is "the good life"? Is there some life beyond bodily death? Where did the universe come from? Why does it exist? These and many other questions may be seen by Christians as arising out of universal revelation and pointing toward particular revelation of God.

The answers, Christians say, are found in God's Word in person (Jesus Christ) and in inspired Scripture. The church's preaching draws out those answers and fits them to the questions. The danger in such a "method of correlation," of course, is allowing the questions to control the answers. This is what Paul Tillich seemed to do. But another danger is rejecting the questions and the questioners in favor of an exclusive focus on the answers. But what are answers without questions? To some critics, that seemed to be Karl Barth's error. The both-and perspective, then, with regard to divine revelation, may be to view universal revelation as consisting of questions about existence (naturally arising out of nature as God's handiwork) and particular revelation as God's special communication that provides the answers to those questions. Of course, our Christian beliefs are shaped more by the answers than by the questions.

A similar reconciling process may be applied to the division between personal and propositional accounts of divine revelation. In its extreme forms, at least, these are false alternatives. Even Christian thinkers who have gained notoriety for promoting ideas of revelation as exclusively personal (i.e., having the character of act or event within relationship of self-disclosure) or exclusively propositional (i.e., having the character of communication of factual information) almost always pay some lip service to the necessity of the other aspect as well. Once again, these extremes are surely overreactions to perceptions of dangers lying in too much stress on the opposite view. The pendulum swings. What if we view divine revelation as *both* personal *and* propositional in a more balanced way? Evangelical Protestant theologian Bernard Ramm raised this suggestion in writings such as *Special Revelation and the Word of God,* where he wrote, "the disjunction presented so frequently in modern theology between revelation as either 'information' or 'encounter' is false. . . . The structure of special revelation calls for a hard event and a hard word of interpretation."[10] Without revealed interpretations in language, in other words, the revealing events would be unrevealing.

Finally, and once again, the either-or problem of false alternatives appears in the division between finished revelation and continuing revelation. So long as we give primacy and normativity to original revelation in Jesus Christ and Scripture, there is no great danger (although there may be some risk which is not bad) in acknowledging a certain kind of continuing revelation. While God does not reveal new truths of a doctrinal nature that are necessary for salvation or even for sound Christian discipleship, God may and probably does speak today. What sense does it make to argue that God does not speak through anything like prophets and prophecies (whatever they may be labeled now) if we believe that God will reveal himself in a new way (not as someone else) in the future? In other words, even cessationists believe that God will make a new appearance in the consummation of history when Christ returns. God will "speak" and "appear" in a way that is not now happening. What principle, then, forbids belief that God may speak and appear (metaphorically speaking) through special utterances, messages and miracles now? There does not seem to be any good reason to say that such cannot happen. On the other hand, there does seem to be very good reason for disbelieving any new revelations that contradict or surpass the truths of salvation so adequately revealed in original divine revelation.

---

[10]Bernard Ramm, *Special Revelation and the Word of God* (Grand Rapids, Mich.: Eerdmans, 1961), p. 158.

# CHAPTER 4

# CHRISTIAN SCRIPTURE

## Divine Word *and* Human Words

Some Christians view the Bible as "that manuscript from heaven," and others view the Bible as uniquely inspiring literature—divine ideas communicated through human literature. Could it be both? We have already noted the special role of Scripture in the pattern of Christian authority for belief. Very early in the history of the church its *fathers* (leading thinkers and overseers) began to quote *prophets* and *apostles* as special authorities and eventually this led to the formation of the Christian canon of Scripture. Just as many Hebrew scholars and theologians considered the prophets and their writings specially inspired and even dictated by God, so many of the early church fathers treated the apostles' writings as uniquely inspired if not dictated by the Holy Spirit.

### Issues and Polarities of Christian Belief About Scripture

Despite the early recognition of some writings as specially inspired by God, there was no universal agreement about the extent of the canon of these writings. Jewish scholars and rabbis tended to limit their Scriptures to twenty-two inspired books (which are divided into thirty-nine in most Christian Bibles). However, the Greek translation of the Hebrew prophets known as the Septuagint included thirteen historical books and books of wisdom that came to be known among Protestants as the Apocrypha. Eastern Orthodox and Roman Catholic traditions have included them as inspired books of the Old Testament. Until the middle of the fourth century, debates over the details of the Christian canon (New Testament) continued in Christian churches of the Roman Empire. Some early Christians had little or no use for 3 John or Revelation. Others did not seem to know of Hebrews or questioned its authorship and therefore canonicity. Clearly, then, Scripture was not dropped out of heaven as depicted on the cover of one book about the Bible that calls it *That Manuscript from Heaven*. Humans played a role in writing Scripture, selecting and closing the canon, and interpreting the Bible. On the other hand, as we will see, the consensual tradition of Christian thought and teaching has always regarded Scripture as uniquely inspired and authoritative for determining what Christians should believe as well as how they should live. The alternative divine *or* human applied to the Bible is a false one that has led to unnecessary and unfortunate polarities of belief about Scripture.

### The Christian Consensus About the Bible

On the surface there may seem little or no unity among Christians with regard to the Bible. The book *What Christians Believe About the Bible* describes in detail twelve major ancient and modern Christian interpretations of the nature of Scripture—from Roman Catholic to feminist theology.[1] Books such as *The Battle for the Bible* and *Why Christians Fight over the Bible* survey the fields of conflict between and within Christian communities.[2] Most attention in recent decades has gone to arguments over the Bible and all too little has focused on the common ground shared by most Christians who believe that the Bible is uniquely God's Word in written form.

The New Testament speaks of the Hebrew Scriptures as God's Word and treats them as having special status and authority even within the early Christian communities. Second Timothy 3:16 and 2 Peter 1:20-21, both of which exalt Scripture, both almost certainly refer to the writings that came to be

---

[1]Donald K. McKim, *What Christians Believe About the Bible* (Nashville: Thomas Nelson, 1985).
[2]Harold Lindsell, *The Battle for the Bible* (Grand Rapids, Mich.: Zondervan, 1976); John P. Newport and William Cannon, *Why Christians Fight over the Bible* (Nashville: Thomas Nelson, 1974).

known among Christians as the Old Testament. The Jewish prophets and their writings were regarded by early Christians as "oracles of God," even if they felt the need to interpret them differently from the ways in which the Jewish leaders of the first century interpreted them. When the Roman Christian teacher Marcion attempted to vilify the Hebrew writings among Christians and to demean the apostolic writings that were too Jewish (e.g., Matthew and James), the second-century Christian leaders harshly criticized him and asserted the authority of those writings for Christians. Church father Tertullian spoke for most of the leaders of the late second-century and early third-century Christian communities when he condemned Marcion's truncation of the canon in *The Five Books Against Marcion* (or simply, *Against Marcion*). Tertullian argued for the authority of the Hebrew Scriptures and the entire collection of apostolic writings (Gospels and Epistles) on the basis of their divine origin, ancient dignity, and unity. Several early church fathers refer to the prophets' and apostles' writings as "oracles of God" and use them to refute the teachings of those they consider heretics. The great church father Origen placed the divine origin and authority of the Scriptures near the beginning of his *On First Principles*, which was written around A.D. 200 and is considered by many the first truly systematic treatment of Christian belief by a Christian thinker. There Origen asserted that the Hebrew prophets and Christian apostles were inspired by the same Holy Spirit and that "the Scriptures were written by the Spirit of God."[3]

The Roman Catholic Church throughout the centuries has consistently affirmed the divine origin and authority of the canonical books of the Bible that were first conclusively identified by Pope (bishop of Rome) Damasus I in a council or synod of bishops at Rome in 382 and by Alexandrian bishop and church father Athanasius in his Easter Letter of 367. Councils of bishops in Hippo and Carthage in North Africa affirmed the canon in 393 and 397. The Catholic Church's bishops and popes again declared God the author of the sacred canonical writings at councils in Florence in the fifteenth century and Trent in the sixteenth century. The First Vatican Council (1870) decreed canonical Scripture to be sacred, inspired, authoritative and without error. Pope Leo XIII explained what the church believes about the divine nature of Scripture in 1893 and used the phrase "dictation of the Holy Spirit" to define Scripture's inspiration. The Second Vatican Council (1962-

---

[3]Origen *On First Principles (De Principiis)*, Preface, para. 4 and 5, *ANF* 4:240.

1965), however, softened the nineteenth century's emphasis on the divine side of Scripture by including the human aspect: "To compose the sacred books, God chose certain men who, all the while he employed them in this task, made full use of their powers and faculties so that, though he acts in them and by them, it was as true authors that they consigned to writing whatever he wanted written, and no more."[4] Of course, alongside its affirmations of Scripture as divinely inspired and authoritative, the Roman Catholic Church has also consistently elevated tradition to a status of an authoritative source of teaching and belief. The Second Vatican Council made clear that of the two sources—which are not in conflict with each other—Scripture has the primacy.

The sixteenth-century Protestant Reformers rejected the Catholic Church's teaching about tradition as an authoritative source of correct Christian belief alongside of Scripture and elevated the Bible over and above all other sources and norms for determining proper Christian belief and practice. They also excluded the so-called Apocrypha and limited the canon of Scripture to the books recognized by the Jewish religious leaders (Genesis through Malachi) as inspired and the New Testament (Matthew through Revelation). Luther considered the Bible the "cradle that holds the Christ" and affirmed its divine origin while recognizing higher and lower levels of relevance if not authority within it. He often referred to the Bible as "the Holy Spirit's book" and never tired of asserting its complete divine origin and authority. At times the German Reformer went so far as to claim that the Bible was wholly and entirely dictated by the Holy Spirit to the human authors and that even grammatical errors, trifles and historical trivia in Scripture are from the Holy Spirit. At the same time, however, Luther urged Christians to read all of Scripture in the light of Christ and especially the cross of Christ. He toyed with the idea that the epistle of James might have entered the canon by mistake, but he never suggested excluding it from Protestant Bibles. He did, however, tell Protestant ministers who looked to him for guidance to avoid preaching out of certain books of the Bible—especially Revelation because no one knows what it means.

John Calvin and his followers in the Reformed branch of Protestantism also held Scripture to be divine in origin though written by men. Calvin wrote in his *Institutes of the Christian Religion* about the intrinsic connec-

---

[4]In McKim, *What Christians Believe*, p. 17.

tion between the Holy Spirit and the written Word of God in Scripture and argued that only dogs deny that the Holy Spirit came down upon the apostles as they wrote heavenly mysteries as they were instructed by the Spirit.[5] Nowhere in his writings does Calvin even attempt to explain how divine inspiration worked in the production of Scripture, but he clearly attributes the ideas if not the words to God. The Reformed confessions of faith stress the divine quality of Scripture and its consequent infallibility and authority for all matters of Christian faith and practice. John Wesley held Scripture in high esteem as the rule for testing all beliefs and guiding all faith and practice. According to him, "the Scriptures are the touchstone whereby Christians examine all, real or supposed, revelations"[6] because "all Scripture is inspired of God—the Spirit of God not only once inspired those who wrote it, but continually inspires, supernaturally assists, those that read it with earnest prayer."[7] While Wesley admitted a human element of Scripture such as grammar and writing style, some of the more conservative Reformed and Lutheran orthodox theologians of that post-Reformation, early modern period averred that even the vowel points of the Hebrew in the Old Testament texts were inspired by God.

Few if any of the great thinkers of the Christian tradition denied the human element of Scripture. The overwhelming emphasis, however, was on the divine aspect of Scripture for much of the church's history. As already seen, both the Catholic Church and Luther (if not other Protestants) at times went so far as to suggest that the Holy Spirit dictated the very words of Scripture to the human authors. Modern Christian thought brought a sea change. Even among orthodox Christian thinkers there arose a new sense of the humanity of Scripture. (We leave aside for the time being the Deists and liberal thinkers who tended to reduce the divine side of Scripture to a nonsupernatural illumination of the human authors' minds.) One of the most highly regarded conservative Reformed theologians of the nineteenth and early twentieth centuries was Benjamin Breckinridge Warfield, who taught theology at Princeton Theological Seminary for many years. Although he held a very high view of Scripture that stressed the divine "verbal inspiration" (i.e., not the authors but the very words were the objects of the pro-

---

[5]John Calvin *Institutes of the Christian Religion* 1.8.11, p. 91.
[6]In Thomas Oden, *John Wesley's Scriptural Christianity* (Grand Rapids, Mich.: Zondervan, 1994), p. 58.
[7]Quoted in ibid., pp. 56-57.

cess known as inspiration *[theopneustos]*), Warfield acknowledged a human element in Scripture and denied inspiration as "dictation."[8]

The vast majority of twentieth-century Christian thinkers—Catholic and Protestant alike—have moved away from a dictation model of inspiration in order to do greater justice to the phenomenon of Scripture itself. Modern biblical scholarship has pointed out the individualities of the authors as true authors. Paul's epistles display a personality and style quite different from John's and Peter's. Questions have been raised as well about the composition of Old Testament and New Testament books, with many conservative scholars believing that Isaiah was actually written by two (if not three) entirely distinct persons and that 2 Corinthians is actually two or more of Paul's letters edited into one. In light of some "assured results" of biblical criticism, more than a few mainstream Christian scholars have lowered their view of Scripture so that it appears to be little more than a great Christian classic composed not by God but by men (and possibly women) of profound religious insight and wisdom.

Such Christian thinkers have shifted the focus of the doctrine of the Bible from its divinity to its humanity and tried to discover some way in which it can have unique authority as a fully human book chosen and used but not authored by God. More conservative Christian scholars have tried to balance the divine and human aspects of Scripture by developing theories of *verbal inspiration without dictation* and *dynamic, concurrent inspiration*. These will be discussed further under the section of this chapter that deals with diversity in Christian belief about the Bible. Suffice it to say here that the consensus that Scripture has a divine origin and possesses divine authority because of its unique inspiration continues to unite faithful Christians of many traditions and denominations.

### Alternatives to the Christian Consensus About Scripture

Often the best way to understand the Christian consensus is to examine its alternatives—those views that radically deviate from and challenge the generally accepted belief of the Great Tradition. What views of the Bible lie so far from the Christian center that they must be judged heretical in the sense that they are completely incompatible with authentic Christianity? Here we must

---

[8]Benjamin Breckinridge Warfield, *The Inspiration and Authority of the Bible* (Philadelphia: Presbyterian and Reformed, 1948), pp. 152-153.

make an honest admission. Such judgments must be made with all humility and recognition that in a context of freedom of religion and separation of church and state they do not carry the same connotation of coercion that they used to carry. That is all to the good. Some branches of Christianity may very well judge this writer's view of Scripture un-Christian or sub-Christian. Some views this writer judges heretical are held by men and women who consider themselves authentically Christian. By no means does criticism of a belief as heretical imply a judgment about a person's spiritual condition before God (only God is the judge of that) or his or her worth as a person, citizen, community member and so on. The heresies or alternatives described here are simply beliefs that have at times been claimed as Christian by Christians and yet seem to this writer, as well as to other Christians, seriously defective to the point of being contrary to the very spirit of the gospel and the essence of true Christianity. To the extent they are accepted, in other words, they alter the very identity of Christianity, distorting it beyond recognition.

One such alternative with regard to Scripture is belief that it is *nothing more than a (or the) Christian classic and not at all supernaturally inspired by God*. Finding this heresy within Christianity before the modern era began is a challenge. Throughout much of the church's history it would have been illegal to pronounce such an opinion against the accepted doctrine of the Bible. A few skeptics here and there may have suggested such, but they were usually not Christians. The great seventeenth-century French writer Voltaire sometimes disparaged official Catholic doctrines including the church's traditional view of Scripture, but more often than not he was aiming his barbs not so much at the Bible itself as at the church's official dogmas and the folk religion of uneducated clergy and peasants. Certainly Thomas Jefferson and other Deists considered themselves Christians of some kind, and they hardly considered the Bible supernaturally inspired or wholly authoritative. They did not, however, reject it as uninspired. Jefferson valued the Bible's moral teachings and produced a truncated New Testament commonly known as "Jefferson's Bible" which left out most of the supernatural stories and apocalyptic literature. It consists almost exclusively of the moral teachings of Jesus and the apostles.

The skeptics and Deists of the Age of Enlightenment were precursors of liberal theology and its offshoots. Friedrich Schleiermacher, nineteenth-century father of modern theology, was also the founder of the entire liberal approach to Christian belief. He was a very influential German scholar, preacher and cultural figure who attempted to reconstruct Christian theology for its "cultured despisers."[9] Schleiermacher and later liberal theologians within Protestant Christian churches and institutions relativized the authority of Scripture by elevating universal human experience (a "religious a priori") and reason (often a particular philosophy) to a status equal with the Bible in determining proper Christian belief.

A twentieth-century liberal Protestant thinker named Harold DeWolf expressed this liberal approach to the Bible best: "The Bible as a whole was accomplished by an extraordinary stimulation and elevation of the powers of men who devoutly yielded themselves to God's will, and sought, often with success unparalleled elsewhere, to convey truth useful to the salvation of men and nations."[10] According to liberal theologians, the biblical writers were religious geniuses who cooperated with the divine Spirit (or self-expressive activity of God) so completely that their writings achieve an inspiring quality and effect seldom if ever noticed elsewhere. However, for these thinkers, there is nothing supernatural, completely unique, or absolutely authoritative about the Bible. They prefer to say that the Bible is inspired insofar as it is inspiring. It's unique quality lies in its function. For Christians down through the ages and for many others, the Bible serves as the Christian classic that, though flawed and full of errors, shapes the Christian identity. Liberal theologian Gordon Kaufman describes Scripture as special only because it "contains glorious literature, important historical documents, exalted ethical teachings."[11]

The liberal approach to Scripture is heretical because it ultimately denies or completely undermines Scripture's unique authority. The problem is not that liberal thinkers wish to do justice to the human quality of Scripture but that their model of Scripture's inspiration cannot do justice to the Bible's divine quality. In their hands the Bible becomes a historical novel or a powerful work of fiction that shapes manners and morals by creating a world to inhabit. For many liberal thinkers, the objective truth of the Bible as correspondence with reality is relatively irrelevant. What really matters is that it

---

[9]Perhaps the most well-known of Schleiermacher's works in English translation is *On Religion: Speeches to Its Cultured Despisers,* trans. John Oman (New York: Harper, 1958).

[10]L. Harold DeWolf, *A Theology of the Living Church,* rev. ed. (New York: Harper & Row, 1960), p. 76.

[11]Gordon Kaufman, "What Shall We Do with the Bible?" *Interpretation* 25, no. 1 (1971): 96.

transforms people's lives for the better. The focus is not as much on the authorship of Scripture—divine or human—as on Scripture's authorship of readers and their responses.[12]

But the question naturally arises: if God is not in some special and even supernatural way the ultimate author of Scripture, why believe it is unique or even special? Why could not some other book effect spiritual and personal transformation just as effectively? Many liberal theologians, in fact, will readily admit that other great classics of world religions may serve their readers in the same way that Scripture serves Christian readers. Liberal theology's diminution of Scripture's supernatural divine origin and authority stands in stark contrast to the overwhelming testimony about and submission to Scripture in the Great Tradition of Christian thought. It inevitably leads to adoption of some other authority for determining proper Christian belief because there is no escaping belief within communities. Even a church that rejects all dogma and doctrine has at least affirmed one belief: no dogma or doctrine. One might legitimately ask why? A Christian community without acknowledgment of the Bible's unique and supreme authority is like a United States without the Constitution. Furthermore, Jesus and the early church of the apostles appealed to Scripture as having authority from God.

If liberal theology's "illumination theory" of Scripture's inspiration (as expressed in DeWolf's comment quoted above) and its consequent denial of Scripture's unique, objective truth and authority constitutes one alternative to Christian belief about the Bible, its opposite is fundamentalism's implicit bibliolatry or worship of the Bible as somehow sharing in the divine nature and authority of God himself. Here we arrive at a heresy promoted by few published theologians. It is very difficult to find a Christian theologian or teacher of Christians who openly professes this heresy. Rather, it is a false view of Scripture that often appears in folk Christianity and is occasionally hinted at in magazine articles and popular books and, of course, sermons. The great Swiss theologian Emil Brunner complained that many conservative Protestants treated the Bible as a "paper pope." In a sense, of course, the entire Great Tradition of the church and especially the Protestant Reformers elevated Scripture to a position higher in authority than any bishop's includ-

---

[12]For firsthand expressions of this liberal view of Scripture and conservative and moderate views as well, see *Conservative, Moderate, Liberal: The Biblical Authority Debate*, ed. Charles R. Blaisdell (St. Louis: CBP Press, 1990).

ing the pope's. However, what Brunner meant was the view under consideration here—that Scripture is not only inspired by God and authoritative for Christian faith and practice and infallible in communicating the will and way of God for salvation, but also literally, technically inerrant in everything upon which it touches, including matters of history and cosmology.

In most cases this unorthodox view of Scripture includes belief in inspiration as mechanical dictation in which the human authors played only the role of secretaries of the Holy Spirit. The Bible, then, becomes for many fundamentalists the Christian equivalent of the Muslim Qur'an which is believed to exist in heaven, written by Allah, dictated to Muhammed and certain of his colleagues and incapable of being translated. (Translations of the Qur'an are considered by orthodox Muslims as commentaries rather than true Qur'ans.) This may be orthodox Islam, but the same view of the Bible denies its human aspect and risks idolatry. One of the few Christian writers who has expressed a view something like this is fundamentalist evangelist and publisher John R. Rice, who argued for inspiration of the Bible as "dictation" and treated the human authors as mere penmen of the Holy Spirit.[13]

While it may seem harsh to call the fundamentalist view of Scripture heresy, the reader must remember that such a judgment is not a reflection on a person's salvation. It is only to say that *the belief in question is beyond the pale of acceptable Christian belief and teaching.* It is something that ought not to be taught or believed among Christians because it is scandalous to the gospel of God delivered in Jesus Christ and handed down in the Great Tradition of the church. And yet we have already seen that some Christian church fathers and Reformers came close to holding a dictation model of divine inspiration of Scripture. Indeed. At times we must use principles of divine revelation and the consensual tradition against elements of the Great Tradition itself. Insofar as any church father or Reformer actually did believe in and teach a mechanical dictation of Scripture to prophets and apostles such that they were not fully personal, conscious contributors to the process, he fell short of upholding the full and unique authority of God and the humanness of Scripture and risked idolatry of the Bible (bibliolatry).

Even Calvin, who emphasized the divine authorship of Scripture, readily admitted a human and historical element in the Bible that in no way detracted from its delegated authority from God over the church. Calvin

---

[13]See McKim, *What Christians Believe,* p. 57.

taught that the Bible is inspired by the Holy Spirit but also accommodated to human capacities for understanding and, in contrast to dictation theories of Scripture's origin, he implied that only the ideas and not the actual words originated in heaven and were implanted in the human author's minds.[14] One modern evangelical theologian cautioned fundamentalists tempted by "maximal conservatism" to remember that "it is as possible to sin to the right as to the left." In other words, overemphasis on the divinity of Scripture can be just as wrong as overemphasis on the humanity of Scripture. The Bible is a *mediated* authority because God is above Scripture and Scripture is culturally conditioned—accommodated to the authors' personalities and readers' capacities. It is not direct divine speech, as it were, but a collection of pieces of literature fully displaying marks of human culture, language and authorship *as well as* divine influence and authority.

## Diverse Christian Beliefs About the Bible

Within Great Tradition Christianity—the orbit of orthodoxy—there is room for wide diversity of opinion about the exact nature of Scripture's inspiration, authority and infallibility. All faithful Christians view Scripture as *both* divine (in origin and inspiration) *and* human (in form and style) and authoritative for determining proper Christian belief. But they disagree about two major issues related to the Bible: *What is the relationship between Scripture and tradition?* and *What is the precise nature of inspiration?* Included in the second issue is the question of *infallibility* or *inerrancy*. Does divine inspiration necessarily imply preservation from all error? Might the Bible be supernaturally inspired and authoritative for matters of salvation but not entirely without error? Debates over these issues and questions divide Christians— perhaps unnecessarily.

Eastern Orthodox and Roman Catholic Christians generally affirm an intrinsic interdependence of Scripture and tradition such that a choice between them is not only unnecessary but also dangerous. Protestants, on the other hand, generally elevate Scripture above both Tradition and traditions with the Reformation motto *sola scriptura*—Scripture alone as God's authoritative Word for determining proper doctrine and practice. For Protestants, the Bible is the highest court of appeal or, to change metaphors, the constitution of the church, when it comes to determining right beliefs and

---

[14]See Calvin's *Institutes* 1.6.

excluding wrong beliefs. Eastern Orthodox and Catholic thinkers argue that this is impossible. There cannot be one highest authority under God because Scripture always needs to be interpreted. When Scripture is unclear, who determines its meaning or what Christians should believe and how they should live? How? Is it possible that everything important for Christian discipleship and church life is crammed into one book or collection of books? Some Protestants go part way with Eastern Orthodoxy and Roman Catholic belief and argue that the Great Tradition of the early church is also authoritative for proper interpretation of Scripture and confession of faithful belief about certain matters not clearly stated in Scripture.[15] Most Protestants, however, respond that as important as the Great Tradition of the early church's teaching may be, when push comes to shove and one must make a choice between Scripture and tradition, the former trumps the latter every time because it is uniquely inspired as God's Word in written form and the special bearer of Jesus Christ and the gospel. The Eastern Church and Roman Catholics respond that this push-coming-to-shove situation simply does not happen if one properly identifies the Great Tradition of the church's teaching.[16]

According to the Roman Catholic tradition of Christianity, Scripture, though uniquely inspired and even infallible, is dependent on the church and its tradition because the same Holy Spirit that inspired the prophets and apostles as they wrote also inspired the early church as it selected the writings and identified the canon. Contrary to what many Protestants have thought, the Catholic Church does not elevate Tradition over Scripture, but it does see them as inseparably united. One expression of this in a contemporary Catholic catechism for adults states, "holy Scripture contains the whole faith in substance, but the faith can be grasped in its totality and fullness only in the light of Tradition."[17] The Second Vatican Council, which went far

---

[15]For a Protestant example, see D. H. Williams, *Retrieving the Tradition & Renewing Evangelicalism* (Grand Rapids, Mich.: Eerdmans, 1999).

[16]Of course, Eastern Orthodox and Roman Catholic communions do not share a common understanding of the Great Tradition. The former regards the first seven ecumenical councils of the church as a kind of closed canon of tradition. The latter believes that all truth important for salvation and Christian discipleship is already implicit in the tradition of the people of God but that some of it is yet to be fully identified and brought out as authoritative for Christian belief. They also disagree about the wording of the all-important Nicene Creed of 381.

[17]*The Church's Confession of Faith: A Catholic Catechism for Adults* (San Francisco: Ignatius Press, 1987), p. 47.

toward healing the worst evidences of the Catholic-Protestant breach, affirmed that "The Church does not draw her certainty about all revealed truths from the holy Scriptures alone."[18] Thus, Scripture is not complete or supreme in terms of authority for Christian faith and practice. Nothing stands over or against it, but without the Great Tradition of Christian teaching and belief—as identified by the magisterium of the church (i.e., the bishops representing the faithful people of God)—Scripture is often obscure and many truths not contained in Scripture would be lost. Examples of these dogmas outside of Scripture are the immaculate conception of Mary and Mary's bodily assumption into heaven.

Generally speaking, magisterial Protestants (those within mainstream Protestant groups such as Lutherans, Episcopalians and Presbyterians that recognize creeds and confessions of faith) believe that the Great Tradition helps Christians hold on to faithfully accepted Christian beliefs insofar as they are consistent with Scripture, but all traditions are subject to Scripture's authority. An early Lutheran statement of faith authored by Luther himself declared "God's Word should set the articles of faith and no one else, not even an angel" (Smalcaldian Articles, article 2 [The Mass]). That is to say, Christians should abide by articles of faith (dogmas, doctrines), but these must be clearly derived from Scripture and must not be created or "set" (determined) by some extrabiblical tradition. The issue between Eastern Orthodox and Roman Catholic churches and Protestants, then, is not so much whether the Great Tradition can be valued and affirmed as whether Scripture is *sufficient* and *supreme* when it comes to deciding what proper Christian belief should be. Protestants agree that it is, even while they use other sources and norms as aids to interpret it and as tools for shaping Christian beliefs judged to be biblical. The Eastern and Roman churches agree that it is not sufficient, even while they claim that Tradition (as opposed to traditions) never contradicts Scripture.

The second controversy about Scripture that causes diversity among Christians relates to the questions of *biblical inspiration, authority* and *infallibility* (or *inerrancy*). As we have already seen, the Christian consensual tradition affirms the canonical Scriptures of the Old and New Testaments as uniquely, supernaturally inspired, specially authoritative and trustworthy in all matters of faith and practice. Most simply put, according to classical

---

[18]Ibid.

Christianity, the Bible is God's Word written in human words by human authors. Theologians have endlessly speculated and argued about the precise nature of the Word of God in Scripture. What does *inspiration* mean if not *dictation* or *illumination?* About what is the Bible authoritative? To what areas of interest and concern does its trustworthiness extend? Is it inerrant in everything it affirms including all reports of historical events, speeches, chronologies and so on? These questions may not seem important, but many Christian thinkers have judged them significant to the Bible's role in determining proper Christian belief. If the Bible contains errors of reporting of historical events, for example, how can anyone be certain of its accuracy in matters pertaining to salvation?

Although a vast range of opinions exists about these matters, here we must limit discussion to only a few major proposals. Some conservative theologians affirm what they call "plenary verbal inspiration" (*plenary* means "full, complete, entire") of Scripture and insist that the Greek word *theopneustos* ("God-breathed") in 2 Timothy 3:16 refers to the very words of Scripture and not only or even primarily to the human authors. They also believe that all of the words of Scripture (i.e., all of the Bible's affirmations) are inspired. Other conservative theologians believe and teach that *inspiration* refers not to words or propositions but to authors. The authors were inspired as they wrote. The wording of the Greek in the crucial passage is unclear. It can be interpreted either way. Those who regard the authors and not the words or propositions of Scripture as inspired by God also tend to regard the process of inspiration as indirect and the words of Scripture as more the human authors' than the Holy Spirit's. This view is sometimes known as "dynamic inspiration." Most who hold it also believe that inspiration is "plenary"—true of all of canonical Scripture and not just some portion of it.

Plenary verbal inspiration implies that the human authors of Scripture were not mere secretaries of the Holy Spirit, and the process of divine authorship through them was not mechanical. Instead the authors were guided by the Spirit of God to the very words they freely chose to use. Conservative evangelical theologian Millard Erickson expresses this model of inspiration well and in a manner consistent with earlier proponents such as Benjamin Warfield and Carl F. H. Henry:

> It is our suggestion here that what the Spirit may do is to direct the thoughts

of the Scripture writer. The direction effected by the Spirit, however, is quite precise. God being omniscient, it is not gratuitous to assume that his thoughts are precise, more so than ours. This being the case, there will be, within the vocabulary of the writer, one word that will most aptly communicate the thought God is conveying (although that word in itself may be inadequate). By creating the thought and stimulating the understanding of the Scripture writer, the Spirit will lead him in effect to use one particular word rather than any other.[19]

Erickson denies that this account of inspiration as verbal and plenary amounts to divine dictation. Even though the human authors could (or would) not have chosen any other words than the ones preferred by the Holy Spirit and to which the Spirit inexorably led them, they were not coerced or overwhelmed in the process. Their full personal powers of consciousness and will were operative. Erickson illustrates this process with an analogy of a student and mentor and with another analogy of a secretary and employer. In both cases, he argues, the student and secretary may write exactly what the mentor and the employer wanted written without any dictation. This is only because they have worked under and with them so long and know them so well. So, according to this view, the human authors were so compliant to God's guidance and supervision and so yielded to the Holy Spirit that they freely chose the very words God wanted to use. Any other view, proponents of plenary verbal inspiration aver, simply cannot do justice to the divine and human authorship of the Bible and inevitably ends up in either mechanical dictation—a form of bibliolatry—or else mere illumination, a relativization of the Bible. Unless the very words of the original manuscripts were words selected by God and at the same time freely chosen by the human authors, the Bible is not God's authoritative written Word in human words.

The major alternative orthodox view of inspiration is "dynamic inspiration" and has found champions among conservative Protestant thinkers such as James Orr in the late nineteenth century and early twentieth century (a friend of Benjamin Warfield's who disagreed with him about this issue) and I. Howard Marshall. Contemporary evangelical theologian Clark Pinnock has also promoted it in his important book *The Scripture Principle*. According to this view *inspiration* refers primarily to the writers and not primarily

---

[19]Millard J. Erickson, *Christian Theology* (Grand Rapids, Mich.: Baker, 1983), 1:215.

(only secondarily) to the writings. The exact words are not especially in view as objects of inspiration. Its proponents point to 2 Peter 1:20-21, which does not use *theopneustos* but appears to be referring to the same process as 2 Timothy 3:16. In the 1 Peter passage it is men who are moved by God and who spoke from God. The dynamic model of inspiration sees the human authors as receiving divine thoughts and communicating them in their own words using their own styles and expressions. This was not a "punctilinear" event (to use Pinnock's wording) but rather a process through which the Spirit of God prepared the human authors and led them up to the point where they freely wrote in their own words truths God wanted communicated.[20] Theologians who hold this view believe it alone does justice to the divinity and humanity of Scripture and that any other view—including plenary verbal inspiration—falls into either too great an emphasis on divine authorship to the exclusion of real human contribution or too great an emphasis on human authorship such that the divine authority of Scripture is relativized. These theologians simply cannot see how plenary verbal inspiration differs from dictation. The dynamic model has the advantage of accounting for the very different styles of the authors as well as for the many idioms, cultural forms and trivial asides one finds in Scripture. It is difficult to see how plenary verbal inspiration accounts for Paul's poor grammar, including unfinished sentences!

It will come as little or no surprise to most readers that those Christian thinkers who affirm plenary verbal inspiration tend also to affirm strict inerrancy of Scripture. That is, because the Bible is God's Word written and was produced by a process in which the Holy Spirit chose the very words (even if the human authors also chose them in some sense), every report and affirmation of Scripture must be without error in every way possible. That is certainly not to suggest that all of Scripture must be taken literally. Proponents of verbal inspiration readily admit that the Bible contains various kinds of literature and that some of it is meant to be figurative. A parable, for example, is not to be interpreted literally even though it is verbally inspired. The Holy Spirit is a great storyteller. But when it comes to biblical assertions of fact— whether historical, cosmological or metaphysical (having to do with ultimate

---

[20]For descriptions of the dynamic model of inspiration, see Clark Pinnock, *The Scripture Principle* (San Francisco: Harper & Row, 1984), pp. 63-64; and I. Howard Marshall, *Biblical Inspiration* (Grand Rapids, Mich.: Eerdmans, 1982), pp. 31-47.

reality)—verbal inspiration theorists usually insist that they are all completely accurate. Any errors are either only apparent or crept into manuscripts through copyist errors after the original autographs (original manuscripts) were penned. A major champion of biblical inerrancy is Carl F. H. Henry, who argues in his multivolume work *God, Revelation, and Authority* (Waco, Tex.: Word, 1976-1983) that inerrancy is a direct implication of inspiration and a requirement for authority.

Other classical Christians, especially those who hold to a more dynamic view of inspiration, argue that Scripture can be inspired and authoritative without being inerrant. One such thinker is Dewey Beegle. In his book *Scripture, Tradition and Infallibility* (Grand Rapids, Mich.: Eerdmans, 1973) he argued that the Bible can be truly and fully inspired and authoritative as God's Word even if it is not inerrant. He examined many alleged discrepancies and factual errors in the Bible and concluded that some are indeed errors—at least by today's standards—and that appealing to the nonexistent original autographs as the only inerrant writings is fallacious. However, Beegle insisted that the Bible is nevertheless wholly inspired and God's Word authoritative for all Christian faith and practice even though it contains minor errors. He appealed to a commonsense distinction between essentials and nonessentials within the biblical witness and insisted that while the former—mostly matters of spiritual significance for salvation and discipleship—must be inerrant and in fact are inerrant, the latter are not and need not be. Beegle's book created a fire storm of controversy among conservative Protestant theologians and contributed to a wholly unnecessary and debilitating "Battle for the Bible" that continues into the twenty-first century.

### A Unitive Christian View of Scripture

It is very unlikely that one person can point the way out of or beyond some of the controversies about the Bible within contemporary orthodox Christianity. However, following our thesis that many polarities of belief are unnecessary because they represent false alternatives and radical swings of the pendulum in overreaction, suggested next are some concepts about Scripture that may begin to combine the essential truths in both sides of some debates over the Bible. With regard to *Scripture and its relation with tradition* it might be helpful to think of the Great Tradition (not all traditions) as analogous to the history of supreme court precedents and of Scripture as analogous to the U.S. Constitution. With regard to *inspiration and trustworthiness of Scripture* it might be helpful to view Scripture *sacramentally* (as sacrament of God's Word) and *functionally* (as infallibly directing readers to God and salvation). Space here permits only a few cursory remarks along these lines. Fuller treatments of similar ideas about the Bible may be found in the writings of G. C. Berkouwer and Donald G. Bloesch.[21]

Evangelical theologian Bloesch attempts to resolve some of the conflicts over the nature of the Bible by rising to a higher perspective—above the minutiae of Scripture and arguments over its detailed accuracy—where Scripture is seen as "authoritative because it is penetrated and filled with the Holy Spirit."[22] In other words, whatever its exact mode of inspiration and whether or not it is strictly inerrant, Scripture is the vehicle of God's grace to humans and is indwelt by the Spirit of God and used by God's Spirit to transform lives. The Bible is the sacrament of God's Word because, although in one aspect it is a human book of human words and sentences, it is also a material channel of God's grace and is uniquely used by God to bring people into transforming encounter with God that informs and changes them. Because the Bible becomes God's Word it always already is God's Word. Because the Bible already always is God's Word it becomes God's Word. The Holy Spirit is the change agent in this "becoming."

Apart from the Holy Spirit—even as Calvin affirmed—the Bible would be to the sinner a dead book. But in the "hands" of the Spirit of God the Bible has always again and again become the unique instrument that shapes the identity of God's people and transforms their lives. Because God chose it to be this unique instrument and witness, it has always been since its inception a unique authority to which Christians turn for guidance and correction, and by which they measure all truth claims about God and salvation. The Bible is the book of the church, its constitution both in the sense that it forms its supreme norm for faith and life and in the sense that it constitutes the church's identity. The church of Jesus Christ lives from and according to the Bible without treating it as a dead rule book or mere book of information.

---

[21]See G. C. Berkouwer, *Holy Scripture*, trans. Jack B. Rogers (Grand Rapids, Mich.: Eerdmans, 1975). Donald G. Bloesch's writings are a major inspiration behind this writer's views and this book. For the latest word from Bloesch about Christian theology, see his unfolding series Christian Foundations (Downers Grove, Ill.: InterVarsity Press) which will be complete in seven volumes when finished sometime in the first few years of the twenty-first century.

[22]Donald G. Bloesch, *Holy Scripture: Revelation, Inspiration & Interpretation*, Christian Foundations 2 (Downers Grove, Ill.: InterVarsity Press, 1994), p. 129.

The Bible is not like a phone book or science textbook. It is a witness to God and channel of God's transforming presence. It is a living book.

How should the Bible's unique character as authoritative witness be understood in relation to the Great Tradition of its interpretation in the early church and Reformation? The tradition both gives rise to the canon as a limited collection of divinely inspired writings and the Bible gives rise to the tradition. There is a sense in which the Bible precedes the tradition even though the precise and final identification of the extent of the canon took place as part of the Great Tradition. The prophets and apostles and their testimonies to God were already there. The tradition only recognized them and, under the influence of the Holy Spirit, put them together and closed the collection. And yet, that is not insignificant. What ties Scripture and church tradition (i.e., the Great Tradition) together is the Holy Spirit who is the divine personal force behind and within both. One cannot dismiss tradition as unimportant or totally lacking in authority because Scripture came to be as canon within tradition.

One must also avoid elevating tradition alongside or above Scripture because the Holy Spirit through tradition led the church to identify the canon of inspired prophetic and apostolic writings as uniquely authoritative for the church's faith and practice. Otherwise, tradition alone would be sufficient. Why would the church need a canon of Scriptures if tradition were as authoritative or more authoritative? All of these questions and the answers they point toward lead to the conclusion that the Holy Spirit of God is the sacramental authorizing agent of the Bible and that the Bible's special quality is as unique instrument of encounter with and knowledge of God. Thus, Scripture is above tradition—including the Great Tradition—but not independent of it. The same Spirit who worked in and through the consensual tradition of the early church also inspired the prophets and apostles as they wrote. The analogy of the U.S. Constitution and the history of high court precedent decisions is apt although far from perfect. Today as Christians look into Scripture for true belief about God and salvation we must not disregard the Great Tradition in which Scripture as canon was born. That tradition helps us understand Scripture as the book of the people of God. But when and if there is ever a choice between what Scripture says and what tradition says, Scripture is the higher authority. Both have their authority only from the Holy Spirit.

Donald Bloesch helpfully defines inspiration of Scripture as *both* verbal *and* dynamic-personal: "The writers [of the Bible] are assisted and led by the Spirit of God rather than being the pens of the Spirit, who alone is the actual author of Scripture. . . . Inspiration is the divine election and superintendence of particular writers and writings in order to ensure a trustworthy and potent witness to the truth."[23] Bloesch argues that divine inspiration is ultimately a mystery to which no theory can do justice. The most we can say is that in this process "the words of human beings are adopted to serve the purposes of God."[24] Thus, it is appropriate to say that *both* the words are inspired *and* that the human authors were inspired—although in different ways. What ties them together is the purpose and power of the Holy Spirit who initiated, guided, superintended and assures the effectiveness of the process. Because of the Spirit's role in Scripture it is a sacrament of God's presence to the church and the individual reader.

*Infallibility* rather than *inerrancy* is our preferred term for describing inspired Scripture's accuracy and trustworthiness. Inerrancy inevitably tends to imply technical, detailed, scientific accuracy that is foreign to much of the literary genre of Scripture and to the cultures within which it was written. To demand such perfection of Scripture is to impose a modern standard on an ancient writing. It also ignores or distorts the plain phenomenon of Scripture which contains many minor flaws, inconsistencies and inaccuracies by standards of technical perfection. For example, in 1 Corinthians 10 Paul warns his readers to avoid making the same immoral and idolatrous mistakes as the Hebrew people did in the wilderness when "in one day twenty-three thousand of them died" (1 Cor 10:8). The parallel passage in the Old Testament—Numbers 25:9—reports that twenty-four thousand died in that incident. Which is correct? To insist that this kind of minor inconsistency did not exist in the original manuscript (either of Numbers or 1 Corinthians) is completely unnecessary. Scripture's authority does not depend on freedom from such minor discrepancies which—given the culture and the type of literature and the author's intent—should probably not be called errors. Rather, Scripture's authority depends on the authorship, presence and power of the Holy Spirit communicating spiritual life and truth through it. Bloesch writes that "scriptural inerrancy can be affirmed if it means the conformity of what is written to the dictates of the Spirit regarding the will and purpose of

---

[23]Ibid., p. 119.
[24]Ibid., p. 120.

God. But it cannot be held if it is taken to mean the conformity of everything that is written to the facts of world history and science."[25]

Surely a better term than *inerrancy* would be *infallibility* because it better
describes the power of Scripture never to fail in its main purpose, which is to
teach people about God and transform them in encounter with him. Swiss
theologian Emil Brunner used a homely illustration for this divine and
human quality of Scripture in which the Bible is the Christian's inspired and
infallible authority for all matters of faith and practice while at the same time
flawed with regard to nonspiritual matters. The old logo of RCA Victrola
record players (still used on some RCA equipment) was a dog listening
intently to a large lily-shaped megaphone of an old 78-RPM record player.
The motto that always accompanied the logo was "His Master's Voice."
Brunner suggested that this is how it is with the Christian and the Bible. In
spite of all the scratches and bumps and distortion of the needle and ampli-
fier the dog recognizes and listens intently to his master's voice on the
record; the Christian hears the voice of God speaking through the very
human words of the Bible with all the cultural conditioning and minor flaws
in the text. Bloesch, who agrees fully with Brunner, rightly concludes, "The
paramount question is not whether the Bible is true in the sense of being
fully accurate in everything it reports, but whether the Bible leads us into
truth, whether the Bible brings us truth. But the Bible could not lead us into
truth unless its central claims were true, unless its overall witness were reliable and dependable."[26]

---

[25]Ibid., p. 107.
[26]Ibid., p. 299.

# CHAPTER 5

# GOD

## Great *and* Good

C hristians believe that God is revealed uniquely in Jesus Christ and that Scripture—the Bible—is the uniquely inspired witness to Jesus Christ and therefore to God. We find our clues for thinking about God in Scripture and we regard Jesus Christ as the heart of the matter. The church's faithful preaching and teaching and worshiping down through the centuries is a third revelatory witness to Jesus Christ, and its sense of who God is as expressed in the faithful devotion of God's people over centuries and across cultures strengthens the overwhelming and undeniable impression from Scripture that the God of Israel, Jesus Christ, the prophets and apostles is *both* great *and* good. From Jesus' prayer opening, "our Father who art in heaven" to the child's prayer opening, "God is great; God is good," to the various hymns mature Christians sing, everything in divine revelation and Christian devotion points together to this duality: Our God is both *glorious beyond our understanding* (transcendent) and *perfectly good beyond any creaturely goodness.*

### Issues and Polarities of Christian Belief About God
Throughout the history of Christian thought about God's nature and

attributes the pendulum has swung between emphasis on God's *greatness* and emphasis on God's *goodness*. All Christians of the Great Tradition have acknowledged both aspects of God and sought to do justice to both equally. However, in many cases specific theologians and groups of Christians have overemphasized one side of God's revealed nature to the neglect if not outright denial of the other side. In fact, it is no overstatement to say theologians and Christian traditions have almost always tended to begin with one of these two poles and relativize the other one in its light. This is not a conscious impulse or effort, but a result of concern with some previous or contemporary Christian theology or spirituality that is perceived as going too far in the other direction. If ever in any locus of Christian belief a false polarity is noticeable it is here. It even exists in the writings of single theologians of the tradition. Luther is a good example. When he was responding to what he considered a weakening of God's greatness in late medieval Catholic thought and spirituality (e.g., in Erasmus's theology which asserted human freedom), the German Reformer strove mightily to protect and promote God's majesty to the point that he proposed a hidden aspect of God in which God is absolute freedom, power and will and may do and be whatever he chooses. The hidden God is completely free from creatures and may damn them without reason if he chooses. That he does not do so, but rather chooses to save some, is as great a mystery for Luther as that God might destroy every creature and creation itself with absolute impunity. When Luther was responding to philosophers who tended to overemphasize God's greatness so as to make any real incarnation in humanity impossible, he responded by asserting God's goodness in Jesus Christ. The God who could exert judgment and wrath and destroy everyone and everything in spite of his promises is also the God revealed with a face of love, mercy and grace in Jesus Christ and his cross. Luther cautioned Christians not to speculate about the dark, hidden God but to look to God in Jesus and simply trust him to keep his promises as he will.

Many Christian theologians and Christian communities have not been as prepared to embrace paradox as Luther was. They have attempted to provide a more rational, intelligible account of God's nature and discover ways to bring together God's infinite greatness and God's infinite goodness. Twentieth-century Reformed theologian Karl Barth defined God as "he who loves in freedom" in *Church Dogmatics* 2/1. For Barth, God's greatness is best expressed as his absolute freedom. God is not bound by anything other than his own Word. But at the same time, God's goodness is best expressed as his perfect love which, though free in relation to creatures, also binds God according to his Word. Barth attempted to reorient the problem of God's greatness and goodness by arguing that they are not at all in conflict or even tension *if* we abandon all thoughts of projection (i.e., projecting our own human experiences of greatness and goodness onto God) and instead learn from God in Christ what these mean.

Some theologians of the Christian tradition seem obsessed with God's absolute greatness and find great difficulty doing justice to God's true goodness. For thinkers like Anselm of Canterbury, God's goodness is his greatness; God is so great that whatever God thinks or does is automatically good, and what humans ordinarily think of as good—even at its best—is not true of God in himself insofar as it suggests suffering or passibility (i.e., ability to be affected by what is outside himself). Even compassion is not truly an attribute of God, Anselm wrote, but only a feeling we humans have when we contemplate God's great mercy. Even God's mercy, of course, is not in any way drawn forth by creatures and their plight but determined by God for his sake alone. Such overwhelming emphasis on God's greatness finds its Christian roots in the thought of the church father Augustine, who pictured God both as "the One" of (Neo) Platonic thought and as the cosmic emperor. Not only Christian theologians, however, but also ordinary laypeople often prefer to sing hymns extolling God's majesty and absolute sovereignty and with resignation assign God's will as the cause of everything that happens.

Other theologians and lay Christians within orthodoxy seem to place the strongest emphasis on God's love and goodness—that is, on God's personal being and relationality. From medieval mystics to post-Reformation Pietists to modern "open theists," many orthodox Christians begin with God revealed in Jesus Christ and Scripture as "our Father" and "Abba"—a supreme being of perfect relational love and kindness—and relativize God's greatness in light of that aspect. While they may gladly sing "Immortal, Invisible, God Only Wise," they often prefer hymns with great lyrics extolling "love divine, all loves excelling," if not popular gospel songs such as "Sweet Hour of Prayer" or "In the Garden."

John Wesley was a theologian of the Great Tradition who focused much on the personal nature of God and God's goodness. Never did he deny or intentionally neglect the greatness of God, but he seemed to believe that side of God's being had already been stressed enough in Protestant churches. His own Methodist movement was greatly influenced by the German romantic-Pietist Count Nicholas Ludwig von Zinzendorf who, like other near-mystical Pietist Protestants, talked and wrote often about God as humanity's and especially the Christian's lover and friend. Especially for these theologians—and to a lesser extent for Erasmus and others in the Catholic tradition—Jesus Christ is the perfect clue to God's being. Of course there is more to God than Jesus, and Jesus is God under the veil of humanity, but they believe that Jesus is the sufficient clue to God's character as genuine love, care, compassion and patience. God's self-sacrificing love shown in Jesus' parables (e.g., of the prodigal son and waiting father) and in Jesus' death for sinners is more important than God's absolute transcendence and dark sovereignty.

Hopefully enough has been said in this admittedly lengthy introduction to impress on readers the problem for Christian belief in this area. Yes, Christians could simply embrace a complete paradox and claim that God is *both* wholly other (infinitely great) in immeasurable and incomprehensible power, glory and majesty *and* near, self-sacrificing, involved, kind and caring, compassionate lover and friend. But the question continually pressing itself upon all inquiring minds who seek to *discover a rationally intelligible account of Christian belief* is, how is our God who is one divine being (not a Janus-like, two-faced god) both *great* in the greatest sense possible and *good* in the best sense imaginable? Goodness within relationship *seems* to imply need or at least genuine reciprocity if not interdependency. Greatness *seems* to imply independence and self-sufficiency. How can God be *both* self-sufficient, limitless power, the all-determining reality determined by nothing and no one *and* at the same time Savior of the world who is patient, compassionate, longsuffering and kind?

## The Christian Consensus About God

Perhaps no set of issues related to Christian belief has consumed so much time, attention and energy among Christian theologians as *the nature and attributes of God*. Churches have felt a need to get it right when it comes to thinking about God. No doubt that has to do with the biblical warnings about idolatry. It may also have to do with the ambiguities within divine revelation itself with regard to God's nature. According to both the Hebrew prophets' and the Christian apostles' writings in canonical Scripture, God is a *holy* God. Holiness is not so much a moral quality (although it is also used to describe God's righteousness and righteous expectations) when applied to God in divine revelation as it is a quality of being superior in every way. A more metaphysical term for the same quality of being is *transcendent*. Christian theologians from the early church fathers through modern theology and representing all major branches of Christianity emphasize that the God of the Bible is transcendent or "wholly other"—holy. This theme pervades Scripture. Paul spoke about the God of Christians in his sermon to the Athenians recorded in Acts 17:22-33 and stated that this God has no need of anything and is not like the idols carved out of wood or stone and worshiped by so many people (Acts 17:24-26).

God's heavenly majesty, creatorship of all, sovereign lordship and freedom from need are all manifestly revealed in Scripture and embraced in the Great Tradition of Christian thought. In the history of theology this aspect of God is generally labeled God's transcendence or "incommunicable nature and attributes." That is, this side of God represents his independence over against creation and creatures and his glorious completeness and power. The attributes or characteristics of God associated with it are those expressed in divine revelation that are unique to God and not communicated to or shared with humans even if humans possess as part of the image of God certain features that dimly reflect something of these glorious attributes.

Equally important in both Scripture and tradition is God's aspect of being personally present and relational, involved in creation and history. This is God's *immanence* and it is expressed throughout divine revelation alongside God's transcendence. In Acts 17 Paul is reported as not only stressing God's freedom from need and God's uniqueness but also the fact that "in him we live and move and have our being" (Acts 17:28). Scripture portrays God's Spirit as intimately present sustaining all things, and God's guidance and direction of history points up his presence and nearness. The God of the prophets and apostles is never far away and always involved with his people. The psalmist affirms that it is impossible to escape God's presence because God is everywhere (Ps 139:7-12). While this may be and is often considered an affirmation of a metaphysical quality of God's greatness (omnipresence) it may just as well be interpreted as a praise to God for his universal presence with love and care. God's immanence is not merely his being everywhere or in all things as their sustainer. Rather, it is even more God's loving presence around all things drawing them to himself and luring them to his goals for them.

God's personal presence, concern and care for creation and creatures is a theme equal with God's holiness and transcendence in divine revelation. Jesus' modes of address to God—"Father" and "Abba"—suggest this aspect of God. It is quite traditional in Christian theology to distinguish this side of God from his holy and transcendent (incommunicable) side not as a different nature of God but as a second aspect of God's being in relation to creation: God's goodness. *God is good as well as great; great as well as good.* God is immanent-personal-benevolently involved as well as holy-transcendent-perfectly free and self-sufficient. These two sides or aspects may seem to stand in some tension. They are certainly not identical in human thought. It seems we must distinguish them even as we hold them together.

Both sides of God's being have been acknowledged throughout the history of Christian belief. Denial of either side would amount to heresy. Neglect of one side in favor of the other, however, is common within orthodox Christianity and leads to all kinds of problems. Here our goal will be to elucidate the common affirmation of these two aspects of God as part of the Great Tradition, and then we will turn to alternatives to such an affirmation, then to variety and diversity within it, and finally to some suggestions for moving beyond the tendency of Christians to emphasize one side to the neglect of the other.

Most of the early church fathers addressed belief about God because of the need to distinguish the God believed in and worshiped by Christians from the gods of the pagan religions and the divine being(s) of the philosophical schools. Most of this reflection and debate took place in the Roman Empire and in the context of Hellenistic and Roman culture rather than in Palestine or the context of Hebrew thought. By and large, the early Christians thought of the God they believed in as the God of the Hebrew prophets even if more fully revealed. At times they borrowed heavily from Greek and Roman philosophies to describe God. Paul set the precedent for that in his sermon in Athens, where he quoted Greek poets and philosophers positively (Acts 17:28). According to the Greek and Latin fathers of early Christianity, God is *transcendently great* and *immanently good*. This dialectical description of God was affirmed also by the medieval Orthodox and Catholic theologians and by the Reformers of the sixteenth century.

Second-century church father and Christian apologist Athenagoras wrote *A Plea for the Christians* around 177 in which he countered the common rumor that Christians were atheists (because they did not believe in all the gods) by asserting:

we are not atheists, therefore, seeing that we acknowledge one God, uncreated, eternal, invisible, impassible, incomprehensible, illimitable, who is apprehended by the understanding only and the reason, who is encompassed by light, and beauty, and spirit, and power ineffable, by whom the universe has been created through His Logos, and set in order, and is kept in being.[1]

Later in his "Plea" Athenagoras adds to this strong statement of God's greatness an affirmation of God's goodness in contrast to the gods who are capricious, arbitrary and at times evil: "But God, being perfectly good, is eternally doing good."[2] Around the same time another Greek church father and bishop named Irenaeus (born in Greek Asia Minor but living in Latin Gaul) wrote about the goodness of God as well as God's greatness against the Gnostic heretics. In his *Five Books Against Heresies,* Irenaeus argued that God is "long-suffering" and full of "kindness and transcendent power."[3]

The fourth- and fifth-century church father Augustine, generally considered one of the greatest and most influential thinkers of the Great Tradition of Christianity, also frequently combined God's greatness and goodness. In *Enchiridion (Faith, Hope and Charity)*—a small handbook for instruction in Christian belief—the North African bishop and church father wrote:

> For the Christian it is enough to believe that the cause of all created things, in heaven and on earth, visible or invisible, is none other than the goodness of the Creator, who is the one and true God: that there is no being whatsoever but God Himself or what comes from Him. . . . As even the infidels admit, the omnipotent God, primal Power of the world, being Himself supremely good, could not permit anything evil in His works, were He not so all-powerful and good as to be able to bring good even out of evil.[4]

The great medieval Catholic theologian Thomas Aquinas equated God's greatness (as infinity and metaphysical perfection) with God's goodness. For him, fullness of being—which belongs to God alone—is necessarily the greatest good as well. God is both being itself, the source of all that has being, and perfect goodness itself. For Thomas, this implied that God is also

---

[1]Athenagoras *A Plea for the Christians* 10, *ANF* 2:133.
[2]Ibid., chap. 26, p. 143.
[3]Irenaeus *Against Heresies* 3.20, *ANF* 1:449-50.
[4]Augustine *Faith, Hope and Charity (Enchiridion)*, trans. Louis A. Arand (Westminster, Md.: Newman, 1955), pp. 17-18.

omnipotent (all powerful) and immutable (unchangeable) and also perfectly benevolent and merciful.

The Protestant Reformers also affirmed the duality of God's greatness and goodness. The Swiss Reformer Ulrich Zwingli wrote *An Exposition of the Christian Faith* (1531) in which he expressed belief, together with all the Protestants, that God is both supremely powerful and supremely good. He referred to God as "the eternal, infinite, and uncreated Good" (chapter 1) and asserted that God, who is the "Source and Creator of all things" is also goodness itself in justice, mercy, righteousness and gentleness. He asked, "who could worthily extol the greatness of this divine goodness and generosity?"[5] The radical Reformers (Anabaptists) and post-Reformation Pietists and revivalists (Wesley, Edwards) all equally affirmed the greatness and majesty of God—God's transcendence—and God's goodness and love, his personal presence or immanence.

Many modern people are familiar with the great Puritan preacher and theologian Jonathan Edwards only through his sermon "Sinners in the Hands of an Angry God," and they have the impression that this eighteenth-century preacher did not believe in a good God but only in a wrathful God. To be sure, Edwards extolled the transcendence of God as God's infinite superiority of being over and above all creatures, and he emphasized God's holiness and human dependence and sinfulness, but in concert with the Great Tradition of Christian belief about God, Edwards also affirmed God's essential goodness. In his essay "God Glorified in Man's Dependence," the Puritan divine wrote of God as that being and power upon whom everything depends for its very being and goodness itself. In *The Nature of True Virtue*, Edwards explained that God's goodness lies in his "virtue," which is "benevolence toward being," that is, love. God's overflowing love within the Godhead (Trinity) is the fountainhead of all virtue, and thus creaturely benevolence has its source in God's perfect goodness. John Wesley, contemporary of Edwards, also extolled the goodness of God and preached and wrote tirelessly about God's love without ever qualifying God's transcendent power.

Twentieth-century theologian Karl Barth attempted to update the Great Tradition of Christian teaching and reflection on God's nature by describing

---

[5]Ulrich Zwingli, "Exposition of the Christian Faith," chap. 1 in *On Providence and Other Essays,* edited for Samuel Macauley Jackson by William John Hinke (Durham, N.C.: Labyrinth, 1983), p. 243.

the two aspects as "perfections of freedom" and "perfections of love" (thus, describing God as "he who loves in freedom"). According to Barth, God's transcendence is his freedom, which is more than absence of limits; it is being grounded in his own being, being determined and moved by himself.[6] God's immanence or personal presence is his love, which is more than sympathetic feeling; it is seeking and creating fellowship; it is grace.[7] God, Barth avers, is equally both—total freedom and perfect love. In freedom God stands apart; in love God comes near. God is not at one time one and at another time the other, but rather always both.

The consensus of Christian belief about God, then, has always been that God is *both* transcendent in the sense of possessing a superior quality of being such that everything depends on God for its existence, *and* immanent in the sense of being graciously present in love with his creation. Throughout history Christian thinkers have attempted to distill from divine revelation those essential attributes of God that express God's unique transcendence and God's immanent goodness and personal presence. Commonly listed among the attributes of God's transcendence are *self-sufficiency (aseity), eternality, omnipresence, omnipotence,* and *omniscience.* Some theologians add *immutability* and *impassibility* (defined below). To be sure, the list of attributes can be very long, but here we are attempting to list those most commonly mentioned within the Great Tradition of Christian thought about God and only those that are not reducible to something else. Among the commonly listed attributes of God's immanence or personal presence are *love, faithfulness, mercy, justice* and *wisdom.* Again, more than these may be listed and often are. Some books of systematic theology and some statements of doctrine include long lists of divine attributes, but it seems these sufficiently express the basic, common attributes of God in the Christian consensus.

God's self-sufficiency (aseity) is his quality of being the source of his own being. Nowhere does Scripture state this explicitly, but it is implied in testimonies to God as the Creator of all things (Is 44:24). Perhaps the clearest witness to this facet of God's greatness is Paul's declaration to the Athenians that God "is not served by human hands, as if he needed anything, because he himself gives all men life and breath and everything else" (Acts 17:25).

---

[6]Karl Barth, *Church Dogmatics* 2/1: *The Doctrine of God* (first half volume), ed. G. W. Bromiley and T. F. Torrance, trans. T. H. L. Parker et al. (Edinburgh: T & T Clark, 1957), p. 301.
[7]Ibid., p. 353.

God's eternality is his quality of being without beginning or end and free from the constraints of time (Ps 90:2). God's omnipresence is his freedom from spatial limitations and positive presence throughout his creation (Ps 139:7-10). God's omnipotence is his ability to do anything consistent with his nature (Mk 10:27), and God's omniscience is his knowledge of everything actual as actual and possible as possible (Heb 4:13). Many theologians of the Great Tradition of Christian thought add the attribute of immutability, which means God's unchangeableness (Ps 102:27; Mal 3:6). The same usually include impassability, which means God is incapable of suffering or being affected by anything. Impassability is usually alleged to be a necessary implication of self-sufficiency and immutability. (The Scripture passages selected above are only representative; each attribute draws on many portions of Scripture.)

God is great in all these ways and in each way God is qualitatively superior in being beyond any creature and the whole creation itself. Each attribute is subject to interpretation and great debate has often surrounded the precise meanings. Some theologians have argued that God's omnipotence means he can do absolutely anything that is not a logical contradiction. Luther seems to have held that strong view of God's omnipotence. Others, like Barth, have argued that God's omnipotence means he can do whatever is consistent with his own nature. All have agreed, however, that God is powerful beyond human comprehension and not limited by any weakness or inability.

God's personal presence as immanent goodness is expressed in attributes such as love, which means that God is benevolent, gracious and affectionate and seeks the good of all (1 Jn 4). God is also faithful in that he is constant, consistent, truthful and reliable (Jas 1:17). For some Christian theologians, God's faithfulness sufficiently expresses God's unchangeableness. Immutability is adequately stated as faithfulness because God is a person and not a timeless truth or a changeless object. God's mercy is his compassion and patience (Neh 9:17; Ps 103:8). His justice is his perfect equity and righteousness in all his ways (Deut 32:4), and his wisdom is his perfect insight into the right and good course of action (Rom 11:33).

These attributes of God highlight his personal nature; the attributes of God's greatness and transcendence highlight the fact that he is not a *human* person. In divine revelation and the Christian consensual tradition, God is personal in that he is relational, knowing, thinking and willing. God is not a thing or a force but a personal being. At the same time, God is not a creature or a human being (although he took on humanity in Jesus Christ), but almighty being itself, beyond finite limitations.

## Alternatives to the Christian Consensus About God

During two millennia of Christianity many ideas of God and God's relationship with the world have arisen within and around the margins of Christian communities. Here our concern is not with ideas of God or the divine or gods outside of Christianity; we will only examine those that have been proposed within Christianity as authentically Christian but that have been judged beyond the pale of orthodoxy by the vast majority of a broad spectrum of Christian leaders and thinkers. In other words, we are not interested here in, say, Muslim beliefs about God—even though most or all of them would be in some sense alternatives to the Christian consensus—but in beliefs about God that have been seriously claimed as Christian and accepted by some Christians, and yet are inconsistent with divine revelation and the Christian consensual tradition. In order to keep matters relatively simple or merely manageable we will focus attention on two main alternative views of God: *Deism* that overemphasizes God's transcendence to the detriment of God's immanent presence and loving involvement, and *panentheism* that overemphasizes God's immanence to the detriment of God's transcendence.

*Deism* is a term that may designate either a specific religious movement among intellectuals of the Enlightenment era (especially the eighteenth century) or a view of God that often played a significant role in that movement but is distinct from it. Deism in the second sense is our concern here; roughly speaking, it is any view of God that portrays him as both Creator of the cosmos and relatively uninvolved if not uncaring. God, according to Deism, is the architect of the universe and its moral governor but not intimately involved in its day-to-day operations. Some wag has described the deist God as an absentee landlord. In this view, God is the almighty, supreme being who rules providentially over all precisely by creating the natural laws that govern events, but he does not normally intervene either in overt or hidden ways in the course of those events or the laws that determine them. There have really been very few consistent Deists in this sense; even the great religious thinkers of the enlightenment "age of reason" found it difficult to hold steadily to this doctrine of God.

One who came close and whose influence has been lasting was the eighteenth-century French thinker Voltaire who, though an ardent opponent of

the Roman Catholic hierarchy, did consider himself a free-thinking Christian. He espoused a rational, scientific belief in God that he labeled merely
"theism." According to Voltaire, a theist is "a man firmly persuaded of the
existence of a supreme being, just as good as he is powerful, who has formed
all the extended, vegetative, sentient, and reflective beings; who perpetuates
their species, who punishes crimes without cruelty, and rewards virtuous
actions with kindness."[8] Voltaire's God exercises only a general providence
through the natural laws he created, however, and as a general rule does not
exercise special providence. (The concept of providence has to do with
God's beneficent control over all that happens and will be discussed in chapter eight. General providence directs all of nature and history; special providence is God's special intervention on behalf of individual nations and
people.) Specific events in nature and history are not God's actions or caused
by God except insofar as God is the author of the natural laws that brought
them about. Voltaire and other Deists tended to neglect the issue of miracles
or special actions of God in response to prayer and left the impression that
such belief is superstitious if not blasphemous. Deism has entered the fabric
of American popular religion through the so-called founding fathers of the
American republic, many of whom were Deists of some kind. Consistent
Deism would be a heresy because the God of revelation is immanently
involved and responsive to human prayer and does at least occasionally act
miraculously. The God of revelation exercises special providence as well as
general providence; he is not only a remote and distant power and principle
of creation, but also the subject and author of history, redeemer and covenant partner.

  *Panentheism* is any view of God that places too much emphasis on God's
immanence (or the immanence of the world in God) and neglects God's
self-sufficient transcendence. The term itself is an alteration of *pantheism*
which has never been espoused in any significant way by any Christians. Pantheism identifies God with the cosmos and is typical of ideas of God held in
both Hinduism (especially Vedanta) and certain forms of Western rationalism (e.g., the enlightenment thinker Spinoza). Panentheism is more dialectical than pantheism or theism in that it suggests that God and the cosmos
(universe, world, nature) are mutually interdependent but not identical. In
the words of one of its most famous theorists, the nineteenth-century philos-

---

[8]Quoted in James Collins, *God in Modern Philosophy* (Chicago: Henry Regnery, 1959), p. 150.

opher Hegel, panentheism means that "without the world God is not God." Many modern Christian thinkers have developed and promoted panentheistic concepts of God in which God is in some way dependent on the world and the world is dependent on God.

Twentieth-century process theology is a school of thought within liberal Christianity that views God as eternally evolving along with the universe. According to one of the main philosophers who inspired process theology, Alfred North Whitehead, "it is as true to say that the world creates God as that God creates the world." Process theology comes in many forms and flavors, but all share a common belief that the God of divine revelation, though eternal (i.e., everlasting), is not self-sufficient but dependent on the world for the content of his life experience. The world is immanent in the life of God and God is immanent in the life of the world, but God does not possess "prior actuality" to the world process. Many twentieth-century liberal theologians adopted some form of panentheism because it absolves God of responsibility for the horrors of that genocidal century. For panentheists God is not omnipotent or absolutely sovereign because the world forms a limit, as it were, to his being. God is the "fellow-sufferer who understands"[9] but not the holy and transcendent God who is free and powerful and able to control his creation.

Classical Christians of many stripes reject both Deism and panentheism as beyond the pale of orthodoxy because both views of God deny something essential to the biblical witness and gospel proclaimed by the prophets and apostles. Deism denies God's personal presence and intimate involvement in creation and history and reduces God to an original Creator and moral governor who is not religiously available. How such a God who may be watching us from a distance enters into covenant relationships with people or responds mercifully to their needs is difficult to discern. Such a God may be a necessary postulate of reason, as Kant claimed, but that is a far cry from the personal God of divine revelation. Panentheism denies God's holy transcendence and reduces God to a persuasive force in the creative process who cannot bring about significant change in the world without agreement and cooperation from creatures. How such a God who may suffer with suffering people rescues them or brings history to a final victory of good over evil is difficult to

---

[9]Alfred North Whitehead, *Process and Reality: An Essay in Cosmology* (New York: Free Press, 1929), p. 532.

discern. Such a God may be the fulfillment of a rational need or moral desire, but that is a far cry from the all-powerful God of divine revelation.

## Diversity Within Christian Belief About God

Much of the variety and diversity within Christian thinking about God arises from the duality of God's greatness and goodness. Within orthodox Christian thought the duality is always preserved in intention if not in reality. That is, proper Christian belief that is faithful to divine revelation and the Great Tradition confesses that God is both perfectly good and unsurpassably great. However, some theologians and groups of Christians have developed views of God that they believe are true to revelation and the consensus of Christian thought during the patristic age and the Reformation but that emphasize either God's transcendence or God's personal presence and goodness in a special way. Often this arises from a concern with some previous approach to God's being that is perceived as one-sided. The pendulum swings.

Some Christian theologians have sought to do justice to God's greatness by positing a "hiddenness of God" in which God is said to be governed by nothing—not even his own nature. Luther especially appealed to this idea and was no doubt influenced by a strain of medieval philosophy known as *nominalism*. Nominalism denied the objective reality of universals such as "human nature" and believed that only particulars such as actual human individuals exist. The main philosophical alternative to nominalism (with regard to universals) is *realism,* which holds that universals are more than terms—as nominalism claimed—and actually have some ontological status. That is, human nature exists in a sense apart from the particular human beings who instantiate it. Nominalists viewed God as absolute, unconditioned, self-determining will without any limits other than those imposed on our thought by logic itself (because we cannot even think or talk intelligibly without the laws of logic). God, nominalists believe, is completely free. Even his attributes of goodness do not govern his will. An act is good because God declares it so; he does not declare it so because it is intrinsically good. Luther found in nominalism an ally in his sixteenth-century attempt to exalt the greatness of God over what he perceived to be a captivity of God to the medieval Catholic church's theological and ecclesiastical systems such as scholasticism and sacramentalism. But what about revelation of God's love and goodness? Luther posited a "hidden God" behind the face of God in revelation, but warned Christians not to speculate about what the hidden

God may be like. He urged them to look on God in Jesus Christ where he is revealed as perfectly good, while remembering that God can be anything God chooses to be and can do whatever he wants to do. This *deus abscondi-tus* (hidden God) concept of Luther bled into many other forms of Protestant theology such that it became common for both Lutheran and Reformed theologians in many different Protestant traditions to speak of God as the all-determining reality who is good in some sense beyond our comprehension and whose ways are hidden when it comes to evil.

Twentieth-century Protestant theologian Karl Barth reacted against this hidden God proposal and argued that the God of Christianity is the God of Jesus Christ and none other. There is no God lurking, as it were, behind the God who loves in freedom and who reveals his greatness precisely in lowering himself without losing himself in the incarnation and cross. Barth's alleged "Christomonism" (Christ-only) was a reaction to any explicit or implicit thought of God hidden behind Christ. Two hundred years before Barth, John Wesley also rejected the idea of the hidden God in favor of a God of perfect love revealed truly in Jesus Christ. Lutherans and some in the Reformed tradition affirm the hiddenness of God in order to protect and preserve God's greatness. Wesley and most in the Methodist tradition (and its numerous offshoots) as well as Barth (who was Reformed) affirm the non-hiddenness of God and God's real self-revelation in Jesus Christ in order to protect and preserve God's goodness.

Another area of debate and controversy about the nature of God within orthodox Christianity has to do with the attribute of God's greatness known as *immutability*. Most simply put, the question is, can God change?[10] Classical Christian theism has usually responded to the question negatively, while offering some qualifications such as "except in the incarnation in another— the humanity of Christ." In other words, much of the Great Tradition of Christian thought has affirmed God's essential immutability such that God's nature cannot and does not undergo any alteration whatever except in being united with humanity in the incarnation. Even then, the incarnation is said not to have changed God but only to have added to the divine life the human nature of Jesus Christ. The subtleties of the doctrine of God's essential immutability are truly difficult to grasp and far beyond the scope of this

---

[10]For a survey of various Christian views on this issue, see Catholic theologian Thomas G. Weinandy, *Does God Change?* (Still River, Mass.: St. Bede's Publications, 1985).

chapter. However, informed Christians and inquirers into Christian belief should know that while all orthodox Christians have always affirmed that God is not subject to being changed by any power against his nature or will, they have not always agreed on whether God can alter his own will and ways in relation to creation.

There are at least two main views regarding God's ability (or inability) to change: "strong immutability" (including impassibility—inability to suffer) and "weak immutability" (excluding impassibility and affirming ability to suffer). Medieval Christian bishop and theologian Anselm of Canterbury affirmed the strong sense of divine immutability. For him, as for most other medieval scholastic Catholic thinkers, God is metaphysically and morally perfect and any change in God at all would be a change to something less than perfection. There is, then, no potentiality in God at any time; God is always perfect actuality—the "being greater than which none can be conceived." God is fullness of being. Any being that changes cannot be already metaphysically and morally perfect. So, Anselm denied that God "feels" anything in response to creation. For him, God's compassion is not really a feeling that God has in response to our misery but only a kind of projection onto God of our own feelings when we contemplate his greatness and mercy. For most classical Christian theists (including many Protestants in the Reformed tradition), God is great beyond ability to change; any change whatever—including responsive feelings—must be a sign of imperfection and therefore cannot be true of God. Any change in God is only change according to our finite perception.

Other Christian theists—unimpressed by the logic of perfection in Christian scholasticism—affirm a weaker sense of immutability and argue that God can and does change in response to creatures while remaining identically himself in nature and character. Both the nineteenth-century German mediating theologian I. A. Dorner and twentieth-century Karl Barth affirmed the weaker sense of immutability—although they did not think of it as "weaker" than the more traditional scholastic view.[11] Barth, relying heavily on Dorner, argued that the older view of God's immutability does not do justice to God's

---

[11]For Dorner's treatment of immutability, see the exposition in Claude Welch, *Protestant Thought in the Nineteenth Century* (New Haven, Conn.: Yale University Press, 1972), 1:278-82. Karl Barth writes, "Those who know [Dorner's] essay will recognise as they read this [Barth's] sub-section how much I owe to Dorner's inspiration" *Church Dogmatics* 2/1: *The Doctrine of God,* ed. G. W. Bromiley and T. F. Torrance, trans. T. H. L. Parker et al. (Edinburgh: T & T Clark, 1957), p. 493.

freedom, love and life. In fact, the Swiss theologian preferred *constancy* over *immutability* to describe God's changelessness. For him, God is revealed in Jesus Christ and God's Word to be a living God who remains himself even as he goes out of himself to have a real history with the world he has created.[12] God is life and movement and not Aristotle's "unmoved mover" who is also "thought thinking itself." God is not altered or changed by his history with the world, but neither is he immobile or static.

While Barth leaves unclear exactly to what extent God opens his own life to being affected by creatures in the history he has with them, some of his followers and interpreters have drawn out implications of Barth's view of God's immutability as constancy-through-history. Dutch theologian Hendrikus Berkhof calls God's immutability his "changeable faithfulness" and emphasizes God's covenant partnership with humanity. German theologian Jürgen Moltmann emphasizes both God's futurity in relation to the world and the suffering of God based on God's self-limitation *(kenosis)*. All of these theologians affirm that God is not changed by anything outside himself and that he is constant and faithful. However, drawing on Dorner and Barth, they go much further than the scholastic Catholic and Protestant theologians did in seeing God as personal and therefore open to some kind of change.

There are as many points of disagreement and reasons for diversity within Christian orthodoxy about the doctrine of God as there are attributes of God. Each attribute requires interpretation. What does it mean to say that God is eternal? Since Augustine in the fifth century and Boethius in the sixth century, many Christians have insisted that God's eternality is his freedom from duration and succession of time—i.e., timelessness. "Eternal now" is one view of God's eternality. But other theologians have argued that God's eternity is to be understood not as timelessness or simultaneity with all times but as everlastingness.[13] That is, God has no beginning and no end, but he does endure through time and experiences temporal succession. Thus, for these thinkers, God's eternality is consistent with temporality. Similar differences of opinion and interpretation may be found within the literature of Christian theology dealing with each and every divine attribute.

---

[12]Barth, *CD* 2/1, pp. 503ff.
[13]See Nicholas Wolterstorff, "God Everlasting," in *God and the Good,* ed. Clifton J. Orlebeke and Lewis S. Smedes (Grand Rapids, Mich.: Eerdmans, 1975), pp. 181-203.

## A Unitive Proposal for Christian Belief About God's Nature

If there is anything that all Christians have always agreed about regarding God (beyond God's existence) it is that God is *both* great *and* good. As we have seen, Christians have not always agreed on the exact nature of God's greatness and goodness. We have barely scratched the surface of controversy among Christians about this matter because at its most basic level that controversy comes down to the tension expressed in the question, *how is it possible for God to be great beyond creaturely greatness and at the same time good in some sense that is meaningful in terms of human goodness?*

No orthodox Christian wants God to be merely a great human being projected into heaven. According to the biblical witness and the consensual tradition and perhaps logic itself for God to be God he must be incomparably great—transcendent, holy and majestic. This seems to be the import of Isaiah's vision of God in Isaiah 6 and of many other portions of Isaiah. The Danish philosopher-theologian Søren Kierkegaard described God as "wholly other" in order to exalt God above the immanent World-Spirit of the German philosopher-theologian G. W. F. Hegel. From the early church fathers through the Reformers to modern Christian thinkers a consensus has developed that God is, in Anselm of Canterbury's terms, "the being greater than which none can be conceived." Even the founding liberal Protestant theologian Friedrich Schleiermacher regarded God as the being upon which all creatures are utterly dependent and who is not dependent upon anything outside of himself. On the other hand—sometimes in stark contrast with this emphasis on God's greatness—stands the counterpoint of God's immanent personal presence and goodness. The tension between these two truths has sometimes been so severe as to break apart. Nowhere is that better illustrated than in Luther's concept of God hidden and revealed.

Perhaps the wisest approach to this tension is to let it be. That is, with dialectical thinkers who embrace paradox, we might simply say that the God of Christianity is both wholly other and personally present in a loving and relational way and refuse to speculate about how both can be true. But inquiring minds want to know if there is a way out of sheer contradiction. So long as Christians seem to embrace paradox comfortably without attempting to resolve the element of apparent contradiction—that is, relieve the paradox so far as possible—inquiring minds both inside and outside of Christianity will wonder if Christian belief is possible without a sacrifice of the intellect.

The task of making Christian belief intelligible includes relieving paradoxes insofar as possible. The danger in such a project lies in sacrificing one side of the truth to the other, which has happened repeatedly throughout Christian history. One looks in vain for any meaningful goodness of God in some systems of Christian belief. One looks in vain for any meaningful greatness of God in others. Is there a way forward toward unity in this field of Christian belief? Can God's transcendent greatness be affirmed together with God's personal and good presence and vice versa?

What follows here is this writer's tentative proposal. It is not intended to constitute a dogmatic answer for all Christians everywhere. However, this proposal represents an approach to a Christian doctrine of God that this writer finds helpful. Two crucial concepts combined lie at the center of this approach. First, *insofar as possible we should avoid speculation about God's inner life apart from creation.* We know God only as God reveals himself to us, and mystification appears as soon as we begin to speculate about God apart from his self-disclosure and relationship with the world. Luther and especially his right-hand man, Philipp Melanchthon, emphasized the importance of avoiding speculation in theology. Melanchthon argued that we know God only in his effects (i.e., works) and not at all "in himself." One can take this approach too far, of course, because God's revelation does intend to tell us something about his eternal nature and person(s). However, often speculation about God's being within himself before and apart from creation leads to a kind of philosophical theism that makes it exceedingly difficult to affirm any real loving relationship between God and creation.

The second principal concept is *in his greatness God is capable of self-limitation.* While this may seem self-evident to some novices in the study of Christian theology, it is actually quite controversial among Christian theologians. All Christian thinkers have affirmed that in spite of or because of his greatness there are some things God cannot do. God cannot obliterate himself. All Christians have affirmed this (in spite of a few radical theologians of the 1960s). Many classical theist Christians also affirm that God cannot limit himself. If God is the being greater than which none can be conceived, he cannot be anything less than absolutely unconditioned, timelessly eternal, all-determining and fully actualized, with no potential for change of any kind. We have already touched on this with regard to the debate about God's immutability. The problem is that such a view of God creates tremendous problems for affirming God's personal nearness and relationality with the world that he has created. How can a metaphysically absolute God—one who is always and forever fully actualized in every conceivable sense and cannot open himself up to any element of change—truly relate to anything or anyone outside of himself? Such a God inevitably ends up looking very much like Greek philosopher Aristotle's "Thought Thinking Itself," who created the world without even knowing it. To say that God cannot limit himself—that is, open himself up to real interaction with creatures such that they have an effect on him—seems not only contrary to divine revelation in which God is constantly interacting (to the point of being "grieved") but also illogical. A God who is so great that he cannot in any way limit himself is not so great after all and turns out to be more like a timeless principle than a relational person.

Two concepts, then, might begin to point the way toward a unitive Christian vision of God as both truly transcendent and genuinely personal, present and good. First, we only know God in relation to the world through his self-revelation; second, God can limit himself in ways that preserve his intrinsic, eternal nature. One theologian of the Great Tradition, a well-known orthodox Protestant thinker, who affirms God's self-limitation is Thomas F. Torrance of Scotland. Torrance built his reputation as one of the twentieth century's great theologians by being ecumenical and mediating. That is, he constantly appealed to the Great Tradition of Christian thought to bring Eastern Orthodox, Roman Catholic and Protestant Christians to the table of dialogue, and he was a bridge-builder between seemingly conflicting schools of Christian belief. In *Space, Time and Incarnation*, this Scottish theologian wrote about the God-world relationship:

> The world, then, is made open to God through its intersection in the axis of Creation-Incarnation. Its space-time structures are so organized in relation to God that we who are set within them may think in and through them to their transcendent ground in God Himself. Jesus Christ constitutes the actual centre in space and time where that may be done. But what of the same relationship the other way round, in the *openness of God* for the world that He has made? Does the intersection of His reality with our this-worldly reality in Jesus mean anything for God? . . . it means that space and time are affirmed as real for God in the actuality of His relations with us, which binds us to space and time, so that neither we nor God can contract out of them. Does this not mean that God has so opened Himself to our world that our this-worldly experiences

have import for Him in such a way, for example, that we must think of Him as taking our hurt and pain into Himself? . . . If God is merely impassible He has not made room for Himself in our agonied existence, and if he is merely immutable He has neither place nor time for frail evanescent creatures in His unchanging existence. But the God who has revealed Himself in Jesus Christ as sharing our lot is the God who is really free to make Himself poor, that we through His poverty might be made rich, the God invariant in love but not impassible, constant in faithfulness but not immutable.[14]

By no means is Torrance or this writer encouraging belief among Christians that God so changes in relationship with the world that he ceases to be God. Certain radical theologians who used the labels "Christian atheism" and "death of God" in the 1960s gave the idea of divine self-limitation a bad name. Rather, Torrance is simply affirming that in his greatness and out of his goodness God freely chooses to be God for the world in such a way that he allows himself to be affected by it.

An analogy may help illustrate and elucidate this proposal for reconciling God's greatness and goodness. A person who marries faces a wonderful and sometimes terrifying decision about having children. The potential father or mother is not less than who he or she is without a child. Many young adults who marry choose never to become parents. They remain who they are and have been. But if they chose to become a parents they also remain who they have been while undergoing a kind of change that can be described as both self-limitation and self-actualization. Anyone who has experienced becoming a parent knows what this means. Some of the freedom of not being a parent is gone the moment one becomes a parent. A certain limitation of responsibility and love intrudes into life. One opens oneself up to vulnerability. A new kind of pain becomes possible and inevitable—the pain of being rejected by one's offspring and the pain of watching helplessly as the beloved child makes terrible mistakes as he or she matures. What is wrong with seeing God-in-relation with us in a similar light? Does it detract at all from God's transcendent greatness to think of God as voluntarily undergoing such change that does not affect his existence or essence? Neither Torrance nor this writer believes so. While

---

[14]Thomas F. Torrance, *Space, Time and Incarnation* (New York: Oxford University Press, 1969), pp. 74-75. For an examination of the revelational evidence for the point of view expressed by Torrance, see Joseph M. Hallman, *The Descent of God: Divine Suffering in History and Theology* (Minneapolis: Fortress, 1991).

remaining who and what he has been from all eternity, God undergoes a change of mode of existence in creation and incarnation that may best be described as a divine *kenosis* (from the Greek for self-emptying). God sovereignly restricts his unrestricted, all-determining power and blissful, triune joy and risks the pain of rejection, loss and death on the cross.

# CHAPTER 6

# GOD

## Three *and* One

The Christian belief in the Trinity—God as three persons and yet one God—is often shrugged off even by Christians as just a mystery. Here perhaps more than anywhere else Christians have often appealed to paradox to justify what they are supposed to believe. "God is one in three, three in one" is what many say when expressing what *Trinity* means.

### Issues and Polarities of Christian Belief About Triunity

Inquiring minds—both Christian and non-Christian—can hardly be blamed for wondering, three *what* and one *what?* and is this a contradiction? Then there is the problem that the words *Trinity* and *triunity* cannot be found in Scripture. Nor can the whole concept be found explicitly spelled out in the Bible. And to compound the problem, the trinitarian doctrine (as contrasted with belief in God as triune) took decades, almost a century, to carve out and perhaps never was completely settled. Unfortunately, some Christians have become so exasperated by the seeming confusion surrounding belief in the Trinity—that God is one divine being eternally existing as three distinct persons—that they have functionally given up on it. They may be members of a church with the word *Trinity* in its name; they may pay lip service to belief in something called Trinity if asked; they may sing a hymn about God's triunity now and then in worship. But fewer and fewer Christians seem actually to embrace the belief known throughout Christian history as *Trinity*. As one modern Catholic thinker has said, modern Christians tend to be functionally unitarian.

And yet, at the same time, there is a revival of the doctrine of the Trinity in late twentieth-century and early twenty-first-century Christian theology. Numerous scholarly and popular books have poured forth explaining and exploring this seemingly arcane concept. Reflective Christians who drink somewhat deeply at the wells of Christian sources ask questions about the Trinity. The search for Christian identity often leads back to affirmation of this uniquely Christian concept. Here our purpose is only to scratch the surface of this all-important Christian doctrine, setting forth first what it essentially means and why there is tension over it within Christian belief. Then we will explore the consensus of Christian belief and some alternatives to it, then examine the major points of diversity within orthodox Christian belief about the Trinity, and conclude with a few remarks about a contemporary unitive view.

As we will see in the next section of this chapter, this belief is nearly unique in that the undivided early Christian church set forth a unifying creed that was meant to serve as a definitive but not exhaustive statement. This is known as the Nicene Creed, more technically correctly called the Nicene-Constantinopolitan Creed. It was formulated in two universal councils of the Christian churches' leaders in the Roman Empire: the Council of Nicea (325) and the Council of Constantinople (381). If one wants to know what the Christian consensus—the Great Tradition—says about *who God is*, that creed is the convenient and right place to look. All three major branches of Christianity—Eastern Orthodox, Roman Catholic and Protestant—affirm the faith of Nicea, which is another way of saying they affirm the Trinity. Some Protestant churches officially affirm the Nicene Creed and others only implicitly affirm it in that they are functionally Nicene. That is, many noncreedal Protestant churches such as Baptists and other free churches believe in the essence of the doctrine of the Trinity without using the Nicene Creed as a touchstone of orthodoxy.

In spite of this great agreement among Christians that God is both truly three (persons) and one (divine being), tensions and polarities have given rise to debate and controversy within Christianity. Some orthodox Christians within the Great Tradition have emphasized the three and downplayed the one in this field of Christian belief. That is, occasionally a tendency has arisen to think of the Trinity as a divine committee or even family with a hierarchical structure. On the other hand, some orthodox Christians within the Great Tradition have emphasized the one and downplayed the three by thinking of the Trinity as a single person with three dimensions or manifestations (roles, masks). Other points of tension and debate have arisen within the Great Tradition in spite of overwhelming agreement about God as Trinity. One of these—the so-called *filioque* controversy—contributed greatly to the enduring division between Eastern and Western Christian churches.

Christian belief in God as triune did not arise in the fourth century with Roman emperor Constantine and the Christian bishops that he dominated. Belief that it arose then as part of a vague paganizing or Hellenizing of Christianity is a caricature often promoted by anti-trinitarian cults and sects. All one has to do is read second- and third-century church fathers such as Athenagoras, Tertullian, Irenaeus, Origen or Cyprian to see immediately that Christians believed in the Trinity long before Constantine called all the Christian bishops to the first ecumenical council at Nicea in 325. Their belief may have been somewhat inchoate before the fourth century when it became necessary to establish a unifying doctrine because of denials of the Trinity. But once that unifying doctrine was formulated and promulgated it reflected what had already been believed by nearly all Christians for centuries. Here our approach will be to begin with an explanation of the Nicene doctrine of the Trinity that has served for most of Christian history as the official statement of orthodox Christian belief about God. In many ways this statement—encapsulated in a creed—has served as the doctrinal identity of authentic, orthodox Christianity for many centuries. Then we will back up from there and examine its roots in divine revelation. Why did the Christian leaders feel justified in affirming this doctrine? Was it a matter of speculation or an expression and protection of the God revealed in Jesus Christ? Finally, we will look at agreement about the Trinity after the New Testament among church fathers and Reformers. The task is to set forth, as briefly and simply as possible, the Christian consensus about this very important and uniquely Christian belief.

## The Christian Consensus About the Trinity
The early Christian Rule of Faith centered around the person of Jesus Christ

as the eternal, divine Son of God who become incarnate for the salvation of humanity. Similar statements of basic Christian belief—creeds—may be found in second- and third-century Christian writings by teachers of the churches such as Justin Martyr, Irenaeus, Tertullian, Origen and Cyprian. Against the Gnostics and other false teachers, bishop Irenaeus wrote about the unified teaching and belief of the Christians handed down from the apostles. Irenaeus was himself a disciple of Polycarp, bishop of Smyrna, who was a disciple of John the disciple of Jesus. Of the common faith of the churches, Irenaeus wrote around A.D. 177:

> The Church, though dispersed throughout the whole world, even to the ends of the earth, has received from the apostles and their disciples this faith: [She believes] in one God, the Father Almighty, Maker of heaven, and earth, and the sea, and all things that are in them; and in one Christ Jesus, the Son of God, who became incarnate for our salvation; and in the Holy Spirit, who proclaimed through the prophets the dispensations of God, and the advents, and the birth from a virgin, and the passion, and the resurrection from the dead, and the ascension into heaven and His [future] manifestation from heaven in the glory of the Father "to gather all things in one," and to raise up anew all flesh of the whole human race, in order that to Christ Jesus, our Lord, and God, and Saviour, and King, according to the will of the invisible Father, "every knee should bow, of things in heaven, and things in earth, and things under the earth, and that every tongue should confess" to Him, and that He should execute just judgment towards all.[1]

Similar statements of the faith of Christians about God and Jesus Christ may be found in most of the second- and third-century church fathers. Occasionally one even finds one of them declaring Jesus Christ to be God. Origen, one of the greatest teachers of the early third-century Christians in the Eastern part of the Roman Empire, declared the equality of God the Father and the Son of God who became incarnate as Jesus Christ: "Whatever, therefore, is a property of bodies, cannot be predicated either of the Father or of the Son; but what belongs to the nature of deity is common to the Father and the Son."[2] He continues in the same vein with regard to the Holy Spirit and affirms the equality of all three: "Moreover, nothing in the Trinity can be called greater or less, since the fountain of divinity alone con-

[1]Irenaeus *Against Heresies* 1.10, *ANF* 1:330-31.
[2]Origen *De Principiis (On First Principles)* 1.1.8, *ANF* 4:245.

tains all things by His word and reason, and by the Spirit of His mouth sanctifies all things which are worthy of sanctification."[3] Around the same time, a Roman critic of Christianity named Celsus confirmed (in case there is any doubt) that Christians worshiped Jesus as God. Writing around A.D. 177—about the same time as Irenaeus and before Origen—Celsus attempted to ridicule Christianity by pointing out their worship of only one God combined with worship of Jesus as God.[4]

In the early fourth century a powerful challenge to the Christian consensus about God and Jesus Christ and the Holy Spirit arose in Alexandria, Egypt. A Christian leader and theologian named Arius argued that the *Logos* (Word)—the Son of God—is not equal with the Father but a great creature. His concern was to protect monotheism—belief in one God—as well as belief in God's immutability. Arius treated belief in God's triunity—which had never yet been spelled out in any formal way by the church as a whole—as folk theology. He wanted to correct the widespread impression both inside and outside of Christianity that Christians believed in three gods or three distinct divine persons. The resulting furor led to six decades of struggle to define the doctrine of the Trinity. The ins and outs of that struggle cannot be recounted here. Numerous books have already provided the details of the great Arian controversy and the achievement of the unifying doctrine of the Trinity brought about by it.[5] Suffice it to say that the first self-identified Christian emperor, Constantine, waffled back and forth between Arian theology, which denied the Trinity, and Athanasian theology (named after Athanasius, the bishop of Alexandria who championed belief in the Trinity) that affirmed it. Christian bishops who gathered in two great ecumenical councils in 325 (Nicea) and 381 (Constantinople) articulated a unifying creed for all Christians everywhere. It is known simply as the Nicene Creed:

> We believe in one God, the Father All Governing, creator of heaven and earth, of all things visible and invisible. And in one Lord Jesus Christ, the only-begotten Son of God, begotten from the Father before all time, Light from

---

[3]Ibid., 1.3.7, p. 255.

[4]Celsus *On the True Doctrine: A Discourse Against the Christians,* trans. R. Joseph Hoffmann (New York: Oxford University Press, 1987), p. 116.

[5]One book that explains this controversy and provides the significant primary sources in a short collection is William G. Rusch, trans. and ed., *The Trinitarian Controversy,* Sources of Early Christian Thought (Philadelphia: Fortress, 1980).

Light, true God from true God, begotten not created, of the same essence as the Father *[homoousion tō patri]*, through Whom all things came into being, Who for us men and because of our salvation came down from heaven and was incarnate by the Holy Spirit and the Virgin Mary and became human. He was crucified for us under Pontius Pilate, and suffered and was buried, and rose on the third day, according to the Scriptures, and ascended to heaven, and sits on the right hand of the Father, and will come again with glory to judge the living and dead. His Kingdom shall have no end. And in the Holy Spirit, the Lord and life-giver, Who proceeds from the Father, Who is worshiped and glorified together with the Father and the Son,[6] Who spoke through the prophets; and in one, holy, catholic, and apostolic Church. We confess one baptism for the remission of sins. We look forward to the resurrection of the dead and the life of the world to come. Amen.[7]

The upshot of the two councils of the fourth century and the Nicene Creed they promulgated for all Christians was and is a virtual consensus among Christians that the God worshiped is three persons *(hypostaseis)* and one substance *(ousia)* or being. God is one—monotheism—by virtue of the common essence or substance, and three by virtue of the distinction of persons within this Godhead.

After the fourth century, Christian emperors, bishops and theologians generally agreed that in spite of its essential mysteriousness the Trinity is the essential dogma of authentic Christian belief. Church fathers of both the Greek-speaking East and Latin-speaking West equally affirmed it in spite of some arguments over details. The medieval theologians speculated about it but embraced it nevertheless. The majority of the Protestant Reformers took no exception with it and usually warmly endorsed and promoted it. Only a few radical Reformers became non-trinitarian, and they were generally rejected as false reformers by Luther and Calvin and the other mainline and radical Reformers. The confessions of faith of the major branches of Protestantism all affirmed the doctrine of the Trinity, and most of the worship books of Protestant churches included the Nicene Creed. Even the non-creedal churches that spun off the radical Reformation such as the various

---

[6]The phrase "and the Son"—*filioque* in Latin—was added to the Nicene Creed in the West later and has become a traditional part of the creed in Roman Catholic and most Protestant traditions. The Eastern Orthodox churches reject it as it was not included in the original form of the creed in A.D. 381.

[7]Taken from John H. Leith, ed., *Creeds of the Churches: A Reader in Christian Doctrine from the Bible to the Present*, rev. ed. (Richmond, Va.: John Knox, 1973), p. 33.

Anabaptist and free church groups seldom took exception to trinitarianism. A few Baptist and Congregational churches broke from trinitarian faith in the later eighteenth and early nineteenth centuries and helped form the anti-trinitarian Unitarian movement. In the early twentieth century some Pentecostal congregations formed the Oneness movement that denies any essential distinction between the three persons of the Godhead. Some cults and sects on the fringes of Christianity have also rejected the Trinity, but for the most part the doctrine of the Trinity has remained for two thousand years an essential part of the Great Tradition of Christian belief. Denominations and organizations that deny it completely (as opposed to holding an eccentric interpretation of it) have generally been relegated by other Christians to the status of cults. Why? What is so important about this model of God?

What is it about the basic doctrine of the Trinity—as expressed by the early church fathers and by the Nicene Creed and most Christian leaders and theologians since—that makes it so crucial? The answer lies in a fundamental Christian intuition that is rooted in divine revelation and Christian experience: *the intuition that Jesus is God but not all of God.* The same could be said about the Holy Spirit: *the Holy Spirit is God but not all of God.* There is one more element to this basic Christian intuition: *"Hear, O Israel: The LORD our God, the LORD is one!"* (Deut 6:4). In other words, the dogma of the Trinity arises as the only protection of a mystery that lies at the very heart of Christian identity: *the mystery of monotheism—that God is one being—combined with worship of three distinct entities as equally God.* This intuition of mystery is expressed in Scripture itself indirectly in John 1, Colossians 1, Hebrews 1 and John 14-17 (among many passages). While it is true that no passage of Scripture spells out the doctrine of the Trinity, it is also true that the whole of Scripture's witness to who God is and who Jesus Christ and the Holy Spirit are makes no sense at all without the model of Trinity and that all alternative concepts end up doing violence to some essential aspect of revelation, Christian experience and possibly even reason itself.[8]

Can the Christian consensus about the Trinity be summed up in a few brief phrases? We have already seen that this is exactly what the early church

---

[8]There is an ancient tradition of philosophical reflection on the question whether God can be absolutely one without community and still be fully God. That is, if God is personal and love would he not need the world as object of his self-realization? Would not the world become necessary for God? Among others, British philosopher of religion Richard Swinburne has taken this approach to defending the doctrine of the Trinity philosophically.

fathers tried to do in the two fourth-century councils that produced the Nicene Creed. Another way of summing up the trinitarian belief about God is by way of an acrostic that contains the first letters of six statements about the Trinity elaborated by Christian theologian Augustus Hopkins Strong (d. 1923): TRIUNE.[9]

> Three recognized as God;
> Regarded as three distinct persons;
> Immanent and eternal, not merely economical or temporal;
> United in essence;
> No inequality;
> Explains all other doctrines yet itself inscrutable.

Strong is correct that since the earliest days of postapostolic Christianity Christians have recognized a threeness in God: Father, Son and Holy Spirit. Matthew 28:19 contains the triune formula for Christian baptism and this is quoted by the writer of the *Didache* or *Teaching of the Twelve Apostles*—perhaps the earliest extant Christian writing after the New Testament itself. The apostle Paul used the triune formula in benedictions toward the ends of some of his epistles; the second-century bishop and church father Ignatius of Antioch (d. 112) used colorful triune language in his letter to the Ephesians: "you are stones of a temple, prepared beforehand for the building of God the Father, hoisted up to the heights by the crane of Jesus Christ, which is the cross, using as a rope the Holy Spirit; your faith is what lifts you up, and love is the way that leads up to God."[10]

The distinction of three persons was expressed by use of the Greek word *hypostaseis* (subsistences) by the late fourth-century Cappadocian fathers, Basil, Gregory of Nazianzus and Gregory of Nyssa who, together with Alexandrian bishop Athanasius, were instrumental in bringing the entire church to embrace the Nicene faith. This Greek word does not carry the same individualistic emphasis of selfhood so often denoted by modern use of the term *person*, but it does nevertheless connote distinction-in-relationship. The early Christians and medieval theologians emphasized that God's triunity—three-

---

[9]The six statements are elaborated by Strong in *Systematic Theology: A Compendium* (Valley Forge, Penn.: Judson Press, 1907), pp. 304-52. This writer learned the acrostic from his own theology professor Dr. Ralph Powell of North American Baptist Seminary.

[10]Ignatius "To the Ephesians" (paragraph 9), in *The Apostolic Fathers*, trans. J. B. Lightfoot and J. R. Harmer, ed. and rev. by Michael W. Holmes, 2nd ed. (Grand Rapids, Mich.: Baker, 1989), p. 89.

ness in unity—is not only true of God in relation with the world, but also true within God himself from all eternity. If otherwise, Jesus Christ would not be affirmed as God and yet someone distinct from the Father and the Holy Spirit. The phrase "immanent Trinity" refers to the eternal triunity of God within himself; the "economic Trinity" refers to the triunity of God in salvation history and in divine revelation—God for us. The key to the doctrine of the Trinity that holds it together with monotheism ("dynamic monotheism") is the confession that there is no inequality of being—all three persons share all essential divine attributes. The doctrine of the Trinity, Strong rightly argued, is crucial for understanding other Christian beliefs for without it they are changed beyond recognition.

Although not without controversy, the dogma of the Trinity has become the unifying and identifying belief of Christianity throughout the centuries. Some version of it—and there is room for diversity within orthodox confession of the Trinity—has nearly always been held and affirmed by every major Christian church father and Reformer as well as by all major Christian traditions and denominations. Without it and apart from it Christianity becomes just another monotheistic religion. It loses its unique identity as gospel because belief in the saving incarnation and divine triunity go together. In the words of twentieth-century theologian Catherine LaCugna, the Trinity is the "mystery of salvation."[11] It is not speculation or cosmic numerology or mere dogma but the expression of "God for us." Anyone who takes seriously the incarnation of God in Jesus Christ for the salvation of the world *and* the supremacy of God in and above all things—God as "He who loves in freedom"[12]—must grasp and confess the mystery of the Trinity. The authentic church spread throughout ages, cultures and denominations has always done so.

### Alternatives to the Christian Consensus About the Godhead

Of course there are numerous non-trinitarian concepts of God in world religions and philosophical theologies. Here, however, our focus will be on those alternatives to the Nicene faith of the churches that exist within Christianity. That is, under consideration here are only those views of God that are non-trinitarian or even anti-trinitarian and yet embraced and promoted

---

[11]Catherine Mowry LaCugna, *God For Us: The Trinity and Christian Life* (San Francisco: HarperSanFrancisco, 1991).
[12]Karl Barth, *The Doctrine of God, Church Dogmatics,* 2/1, trans. T. H. L. Parker et al. (Edinburgh: T & T Clark, 1957), pp. 257-321.

by people and groups identifying themselves as Christians. Three such heresies about the Godhead have challenged belief in and confession of the Trinity: *modalism* (also known as *Sabellianism*), *subordinationism* (known in two forms as *Arianism* and *adoptionism*), and *tritheism*. Each one attempts in some way radically different from the orthodox consensus of the church—Nicene trinitarianism—to explain the pattern of divine revelation of God as three and yet one, one and yet three. All existed in some form in the early church after the apostles, and their increasing power and popularity among Christians forced the church to promulgate and enforce (at least on bishops) the Nicene Creed. All three (or four—as there are two distinct forms of subordinationism) have reappeared within Christendom from time to time. All three appear in Christian folk theology as well as occasionally among trained theologians and church leaders. All three do violence to the identity of Christianity, although some of them are more dangerous than others.

The first major alternative to trinitarian belief about God is *modalism*. It is also sometimes known as *Sabellianism* after Sabellius, one of the early Christian teachers who promoted the view. Modalism is the idea that Father, Son and Holy Spirit are not three distinct persons—*hypostaseis*—but merely three distinct modes of revelation or manifestations of the single person who is God. In this view, God is by nature a simple being with no internal distinctions. Modalism begins with the truth of monotheism and then attempts to fit the revelation of Father, Son and Holy Spirit into that without seriously adjusting classical monotheism. According to it, the "persons" of Father, Son and Holy Spirit are merely masks worn by God—as a single actor in Greek theater played more than one role in a play by coming on stage wearing different masks. Modalism, then, denies any immanent threeness in God—the immanent Trinity (in God himself)—and opts only for an economic triunity (God's interaction with creation). God sometimes appears as Father, sometimes as Son and sometimes as Holy Spirit, but in himself in eternity God is one being and one person not identical with any of the three revealed modes.

The problems with modalism should be fairly obvious to anyone who is biblically literate and believes that in divine revelation God truly reveals who he is and not who he is not. The modalist model of the Godhead simply cannot be made consistent with several events recorded in the New Testament: the baptism of Jesus during which the Father's voice spoke and the Holy Spirit descended upon him in the form of a dove; Jesus' prayer in John 17 in which he petitioned to Father to make his disciples one even as he and the

Father were one (Jn 17:20-23); and Jesus' request in the Garden of Gethse-mane that the Father take the cup of suffering from him and concluded, "not my will, but yours be done" (Lk 22:42). Clearly Jesus and the Father are two distinct personal identities and not merely distinct modes or manifes-tations of a single person. The same can be said of the Holy Spirit and modalism. Jesus referred to the Holy Spirit as "another Advocate" or "another Counselor" *(paraklētos)* to be sent "by the Father" or "from the Father" (Jn 14:16, 26). Clearly the Spirit is not merely another mode or manifestation of the Father and the Son. Also, if modalism is true, then the implication is unavoidable that in revelation God hides himself rather than reveals himself. The question inevitably arises, who is God behind the masks of Father, Son and Holy Spirit? Or, which one of these is the true face of God? In either case modalism leaves us wondering who God really is. Some-thing like the modalist view is believed by members of several Pentecostal denominations that are together known as "Jesus Only" (because they affirm that Jesus is all of God and baptize only in Jesus' name) and "Oneness Pen-tecostals" (because they hold to the essential oneness of the Godhead and deny any immanent threeness).

The second major alternative to trinitarianism among self-identified Christians is *subordinationism,* which appears in two forms: *adoptionism* and *Arianism.* Subordinationism also begins with strict, undifferentiated mono-theism and then tries to explain how three can be "one God." Both forms of subordinationism identify God with the Father and subordinate the Son and the Holy Spirit to God. They are lesser beings who are nevertheless some-how also divine. Adoptionism was first taught by a second-century Christian bishop of Syria named Paul of Samosata, who was deposed by a synod of Christian bishops around the middle of the third century. His teaching was that Jesus Christ was a great prophet and messiah raised up by God the Father and "adopted" as his special Son. But the Syrian bishop denied any essential threeness in God himself. He reduced the Son of God to a human prophet and virtually ignored the Holy Spirit except as a force of divine power and presence in the world. The Unitarian movement—founded in the late eighteenth century by rationalist Christians—promoted a form of adop-tionism as its alternative to trinitarian belief. Some modern liberal theolo-gians also teach a form of adoptionism in which Jesus Christ is nothing more than a "fully God-conscious man," the "human face of God," or "God's representative among men."

The second form of subordinationism is Arianism—named after the early fourth-century Alexandrian Christian leader Arius, who sparked the great controversy over the Trinity that gave rise to the Nicene Creed. Arius argued that the Son of God—the Word (Logos)—preexisted the man Jesus and became incarnate in him. Thus, Jesus was not merely a human prophet or messiah. But Arius denied that the heavenly Son of God is God or equal with God; according to him Jesus Christ is the incarnation of God's first and greatest creature who is a secondary god and not at all equal with the Father. Arian subordinationism has reappeared since the fourth century several times; in the twentieth century it appeared as the official doctrine (without the name of Arius acknowledged or attached) of the Watchtower Bible and Tract Society (Jehovah's Witnesses) and several sects closely related to it. According to the Watchtower organization, Jesus Christ is not God or equal with God but the incarnation of the archangel Michael who is God's first and greatest creature. While Arius did not propose such an identity for the preincarnate Word and Son of God, they share the same basic concept of who and what Jesus Christ is.

The problems with subordinationism of both varieties are fairly obvious to anyone who takes seriously the revelational witness to Jesus Christ and the Holy Spirit and the incarnational model of redemption. As the early church fathers never tired of emphasizing, *we are only saved by God, and if Jesus Christ is not God we are not saved.* The great fourth-century opponent of Arianism, bishop Athanasius of Alexandria, wrote the classic treatise *On the Incarnation of the Word (De Incarnatione)* to promote that fundamental Christian belief—that human salvation depends entirely on the truth that Jesus Christ, who accomplished it, is truly God and truly human. Luther made the same point in the sixteenth century. Both Athanasius and Luther faced down subordinationist opponents who would destroy the gospel itself by reducing Jesus Christ to a prophet or exalted creature and salvation to following his example. According to both the early church father and the sixteenth-century Reformer and the entire Great Tradition of Christian teaching, Jesus Christ is God deeply sunk in the flesh and he accomplishes salvation by joining humanity with deity in his own person and destiny—death and resurrection. Subordinationism inevitably reduces salvation to moralism if not legalism.

The third alternative to trinitarian belief among Christians is *tritheism*—implicit (hardly ever explicit) belief in Father, Son and Holy Spirit as three separate divine beings or gods. While several theologians have been accused of promoting tritheism, few if any have ever actually admitted that they believed in three gods. Tritheism appears most often in Christian folk religion and folk theology as uninformed and untutored Christians describe the Trinity as if the Godhead were a committee. Certain analogies used in teaching children about the Trinity border on tritheism as they describe it in terms of a piece of fruit or an egg: one object made up of three parts. Both the committee analogy ("eternal councils of the Godhead") and the edible object analogy (apple, egg) fall short of the monotheistic element in Christian trinitarianism. The doctrine of the Trinity is not that God is one object made up of three separable parts; it is that God is one perfectly unified being made up of three inseparable and wholly equal persons who—as several theologians have said—interpenetrate one another eternally *(perichoresis)*. Some theologians have so stressed the community aspect of the Trinity that, while avoiding blatant tritheism or even the implicit tritheism of folk theology, they have implied too great a difference and distance between the Father, Son and Holy Spirit. The medieval mystical theologian Joachim of Fiore (d. 1202) verged on tritheism in his account of the ages of history tied to persons of the Trinity, but even he did not intend to teach that there are three gods.

The only alternative to the beliefs delineated above seems to be the orthodox doctrine of the Trinity. If modalism is wrong as it must be, then either subordinationism or tritheism or trinitarianism must be right. If subordinationism is wrong as it must be, then either modalism or tritheism or trinitarianism must be right. One could go on. The model with the least problems in terms of revelation, reason, tradition and experience is the basic doctrine of the Trinity—as mysterious as it is. How one being can be three persons and how three persons can be one being seems beyond comprehension. The great British Christian writer C. S. Lewis acknowledged and celebrated this in *Mere Christianity*. He drew on the story of the "Flatlanders" who lived in a two dimensional world and could conceive of lines and fields but not depth and cubes to illustrate our own human situation facing the mystery of the Trinity. We cannot conceive how a single, perfectly unified being can also be three distinct persons, but that does not mean it is incoherent or impossible. There must be a missing dimension, and no doubt when we arrive at our final destination that dimension will be revealed to us and we will be able to comprehend the Trinity.

How important is belief in the Trinity? Was the fifth-century North African church father Augustine right that "whoever denies the Trinity is in danger of losing his salvation; whoever tries to understand the Trinity is in danger of losing his mind?" Today the popular mind—even the popular Christian mind—often has an antipathy to any connection between salvation and belief. We prefer to say that sincerity is what really matters to God. But is that true? Does God really not care how we think of him? Does it matter to God—from a Christian perspective—whether mature, responsible Christians believe that Jesus Christ is God incarnate? Is it "okay with God" for such persons to believe that Jesus Christ is merely a prophet or an angel? Is there any problem with believing that Jesus is the Father and the Son and the Holy Spirit? What about confessing God as three beings—three gods?

While it is true that God does not judge people primarily by their beliefs about him but by their trust in him, might it also be true that trusting God in a mature and effective way might depend at least in part on coming to know who God is and thinking rightly about God and that believing the wrongs things about God is detrimental to a mature and transforming relationship with God? Until the twentieth century the Christian consensus has been that *believing rightly matters*. Some Christian groups have emphasized that more than others, but nearly all across the spectrum of Eastern Orthodox, Roman Catholic and Protestant Christians have considered *right belief and confession about Jesus Christ and God as Trinity* absolutely crucial to vital, mature, God-honoring Christian existence. Those who have claimed to be Christian while at the same time rejecting the true humanity and deity of Jesus Christ and the triunity of God as Father, Son and Holy Spirit have rightly encountered serious opposition from Christian leaders and thinkers. In terms of belief, at least, this is what defines Christianity and sets it apart from mere religion, spirituality and philosophy. Jesus Christ as God and human and God as eternal community drawing humanity into fellowship with himself are shorthand for salvation. To be sure, salvation itself does not depend on what one believes. It depends on God's grace in Jesus Christ and one's response of repentance and faith, but wrong thinking about God and Jesus Christ and salvation can lead away from grace and proper response into false gospels of self-salvation.

## Diverse Christian Approaches to the Trinity

Earlier in this chapter we saw that a rough and basic consensus exists among Christians with regard to the Trinity and that the fundamental contours of that consensus may be found in the Nicene Creed and a few affirmations that have come to attach to it. For example, nowhere does the Nicene Creed say of God "three persons" *(hypostaseis),* but every historical theologian knows that the Cappadocian fathers, Basil and the two Gregorys, helped bring about the final form of the Nicene Creed in 381 at the Council of Constantinople by suggesting the distinction between *ousia* (substance) which is one in God and *hypostasis* (subsistence, person) which is three in God. Thus, the Nicene faith is often summed up as belief that *God is one substance and three persons.* Or, expressed more informally, it might be said that *God is one "what" and three "whos."*

Is there room within this orthodox belief for diverse interpretations and opinions? Indeed there is and equally orthodox Christian theologians have developed very different models of the Trinity based on Nicene trinitarian belief. The diversity about the Trinity within the Great Tradition of Christianity may be helpfully studied using the two main analogies of the Trinity: the *psychological analogy* and the *social analogy.* Some theologians have compared the Trinity with a single human person who always has distinct dimensions of personality. Others have preferred to compare the Trinity with a human community that always has some unifying force. The former is the psychological analogy and the latter is the social analogy—even where these terms are not explicitly used.

Augustine is no doubt the true father of the psychological analogy. In his book *De Trinitate (On the Trinity),* the great North African church father offered up several analogies in creation for God's three-in-oneness. But among his favorite analogies was the one now known as the psychological analogy in which he pointed out the compatibility of unity and diversity in human personality or mind. According to Augustine, the fact that humans are made in the image and likeness of God indicates that there should be traces of the Trinity in human nature itself. He finds the likeness in the structure of the human mind which, though one, is at the same time three: memory, understanding and will.[13] Together these three aspects or powers of mind are one mind and yet they are distinct powers of mind. Augustine and later Western trinitarian thinkers tended to find this psychological analogy the most helpful in explicating the meaning of God's triunity.

In varying ways post-Augustinian trinitarian thinkers in the Catholic and

---

[13]Augustine *On the Trinity* 10, *NPNF,* 1st ser., 3:134-43.

Protestant traditions developed it further. A twentieth-century Protestant theologian compared the Trinity with President Theodore Roosevelt who, although one integrated person, had three distinct roles that together made him who he was. He was father and family man, president and statesman, and rough rider and outdoorsman. Similarly, so the theologian argued, all persons have distinct dimensions and roles that make them the persons they are—public and private. This is just a dim analogy to the triunity of God. It is nothing more or other than a way of illustrating how it is possible for a single personal phenomenon to be both truly one and three.

Although neither Karl Barth nor his Catholic counterpart Karl Rahner (d. 1983) used the psychological analogy, their accounts of the Trinity borrowed heavily on Augustine's and the entire Western tradition's emphasis on the unity of God. Barth derived the Trinity from the reality of divine revelation itself. For him, the Trinity is an immediate implication of the structure of revelation as self-disclosure. If God truly reveals himself in revelation, then as revelation is threefold, revealer, revealedness and revelation itself, so God must be threefold—Father, Son and Holy Spirit: three distinct modes of being of the one being God who *is* his event of self-revelation.[14] Barth preferred the term "modes of being" to "persons" to express the threeness of God both in his self-revelation and in himself. For him, "person" too strongly connoted individuality while "mode of being" *(Seinsweisen)* connoted distinction without difference. Many commentators have regarded Barth's doctrine of the Trinity heavily influenced by Augustine and thus the link with the psychological analogy. However, Barth did not actually compare the Trinity with the human personality or mind; he merely treated the "persons" of the Godhead as conditions within God for self-revelation. It would be preferable to refer to Barth's view as a "revelational analogy," and yet it is true that in the end his view tends toward a similarity with the psychological analogies due to the overwhelming focus on God's unity. Karl Rahner also eschewed the term *persons* for the distinctions in God and, in his little book *The Trinity,* expressed preference for "distinct manner of subsisting."[15] Like Barth, Rahner preferred to emphasize the unity of God over the

---

[14]Karl Barth, *Church Dogmatics* 1/1: *The Doctrine of the Word of God,* part 1, ed. G. W. Bromiley and T. F. Torrance, trans. G. W. Bromiley (Edinburgh: T & T Clark, 1975), pp. 295ff. The entire chapter 11 deals with the threefold structure of divine revelation and its connection with the Trinity.

[15]Karl Rahner, *The Trinity,* trans. Joseph Donceel (New York: Seabury Press, 1974), pp. 109-15.

threeness of God, and *person* simply sounded too individualistic. Both great modern European theologians feared tritheism more than modalism.

The other main historical analogy for the Trinity is the social analogy, which tends to begin with the threeness of God and move toward the unity of divine being by comparing the Trinity with a human society or community. This approach is more typical of the Eastern Orthodox tradition, although some Western theologians have embraced forms of it as well. The term "social analogy" is of recent origin and used most often to describe the proposal for trinitarian theology set forth by twentieth-century British theologian Leonard Hodgson. However, like the psychological analogy, the social analogy has ancient roots and medieval echoes.

The Cappadocian fathers wrote much about the Trinity in the fourth century and often used analogies for God's three-in-oneness that drew on human social life. Gregory of Nyssa used the analogy of Jesus' three disciples Peter, James and John and argued that just as they are three identities and yet one as to their human nature so the Godhead is three identities and yet one divine nature or being. In his essay *On "Not Three Gods": To Ablabius,* the Cappadocian father emphasized the unity of Father, Son and Holy Spirit that transcends the unity of any three humans. For example, he stated there that the persons of the Trinity act in unison in all things, whereas any three human beings act apart at least some of the time. According to Gregory, then, there is an analogy, however dim and imperfect, between human groups at their best and the divine community of three persons who together make up one eternal Godhead. In the Middle Ages mystical theologian Richard of St. Victor (d. 1173) revived the social analogy in a treatise entitled *De Trinitate (On the Trinity).* He argued from the nature of love itself that God must be three distinct persons for otherwise, if God is by nature love, his love would be self-love which is a lesser form of love than other-love. Richard swam against the stream of Western trinitarian thought, and he and his followers—the so-called Victorines—were much criticized for allegedly coming too close to tritheism.

Twentieth-century Protestant thinker Leonard Hodgson became famous primarily for his revival of the social analogy in his Croall Lectures (Edinburgh) of 1943 published as *The Doctrine of the Trinity* (New York: Charles Scribner's Sons, 1944). There the Oxford professor argued that unity is not inconsistent with certain kinds of multiplicity and that, in fact, organic unity always incorporates multiplicity. The term he coined for the divine unity as well as for organic unity in creation is "internally constitutive unity." He saw this kind of unity as just as truly unitive as bare, mathematical oneness and perhaps even more so. According to Hodgson, revelation requires that we recognize three persons, each equally personal in the full sense of the word, as equally God, and reason and science tell us that there can be and is genuine unity among distinct parts.

Although they do not call their concepts of the Trinity "social analogy," twentieth-century German Protestant theologians Jürgen Moltmann and Wolfhart Pannenberg have developed trinitarian models in some ways similar to Hodgson's. Both emphasize the threeness of the divine persons and strive to show that their unity as one Godhead lies not in some underlying substance or subjectivity but in love—that is, community. In *The Trinity and the Kingdom,* Moltmann set forth a communitarian model of the Trinity in which the unity of Father, Son and Holy Spirit is a pattern for human social life. It is a "perichoretic unity"—a unity of interdependence and mutuality—rather than a substantial unity in which the persons are mere manifestations or dimensions of a single nature or underlying mind. According to the German theologian the Trinity is no "self-enclosed circle in heaven" but a dynamic community of fellowship open to creatures: "To throw open the circulatory movement of the divine light and the divine relationships, and to take men and women, with the whole of creation, into the life-stream of the triune God: that is the meaning of creation, reconciliation and glorification."[16]

Moltmann, who once studied with Barth, came to disagree strongly with the overwhelming favor of Western Christian thinking toward the psychological analogy and its starting point in divine unity. Some of Barth's disciples criticized Moltmann and his social analogy (or "kingdom analogy") for verging on tritheism. Advocates of the psychological analogy and advocates of the social analogy still share a common commitment to the orthodox vision of Nicene trinitarianism, though. All would say that God is both one (monotheism) and three (dynamic monotheism): *one being manifested eternally as three persons.* But they diverge over how best to picture and explain that fundamentally mysterious reality.

Other points of disagreement over the Trinity exist among Christian thinkers who are equally committed to the Christian consensual tradition

---

[16]Jürgen Moltmann, *The Trinity and the Kingdom,* trans. Margaret Kohl (San Francisco: Harper & Row, 1981), p. 178.

going back to the Nicene settlement of the fourth century and before that to the early church fathers. In 1054 when the Greek-speaking bishops of the East and the Latin-speaking bishops of the West excommunicated each other and their churches (so that the church became divided between Eastern Orthodoxy and Roman Catholicism) one of the issues dividing the two halves of Christendom was the Trinity and, most particularly, the insertion into the Latin form of the Nicene Creed of the phrase "and from the Son" (*filioque*). The Eastern bishops and theologians considered this not only illegitimate tampering with the unifying creed of Christianity but also reflection of the West's heterodox (less than fully orthodox) thinking about the Godhead. If the Holy Spirit proceeds from the Father *and the Son*—not only in time but also from all eternity—then the Spirit is subordinated to the Son and the unity of the Trinity is mangled. The West argued that the East could not distinguish the Son and the Holy Spirit due to its refusal to confess—following Augustine—that the Spirit proceeds from the Father and the Son.

Most Protestants who confess the Nicene Creed use the Western form with the *filioque* clause. However, from time to time and especially in the twentieth century, some Protestant theologians such as Moltmann have dropped the matter and urged all Christians to regard the three persons of the Trinity as proceeding from one another. That is, because they are eternally interdependent, there is no need to regard their relationships in the immanent Trinity as hierarchical. The "procession" of the Holy Spirit is "from the Father through the Son." Increasingly many Protestants are offering this formula as the alternative to the offensive (to the East) *filioque* clause. Free church Protestants such as Baptists, who generally do not recite the Nicene Creed, have tended to sit out this controversy.

### A Unitive Christian Vision of God's Triunity

Surely if God is God and not a creature, his inner life and its workings must be incomprehensible to finite minds. On the other hand, we must avoid using God's incomprehensibility as an excuse for refusing to trace the clues of divine revelation as far as they will take us in understanding God. God is not honored or glorified by lazy thinking about him. He revealed himself so that his human creatures might know him and be transformed by knowing him.

On the other hand, we must know where to draw the line of peering into God's mysterious, inner being. Too often theologians have transgressed that

line and speculated about the trinitarian relations within the eternal, immanent Trinity beyond anything warranted by God's self-revelation. The *filioque* controversy that split the medieval church in half is surely an example
of that. Revelation in Scripture indicates that the Holy Spirit is a divine person distinct from the Father and the Son and sent into the world by the
Father through the Son. But nowhere does it indicate an eternal procession
of the Spirit within the Godhead—either from the Father alone or from the
Father and the Son together. Many of the controversies about the Trinity—
as about many other theological subjects—arise from unwarranted and even
harmful speculation. How many angels can dance on the head of a pin?
Some medieval scholastic theologians debated the question because they
sought answers to every conceivable question and this was a way of asking,
what are angels? While there may be some profit in discussing whether
angels occupy space or not, it is difficult to see how the question of how
many can occupy a small space is relevant to anything. The same may be the
case with regard to certain debates about the Trinity.

Twentieth-century theologians such as Karl Barth, Karl Rahner, Jürgen
Moltmann and Catherine LaCugna have attempted to show that the Trinity
is not about a self-enclosed group of divine persons in heaven or the different manifestation of a single divine subjectivity. Rather, the Trinity is the
"mystery of salvation." Whatever cannot be related in some way to salvation
is irrelevant speculation. That means a new focus on the economic Trinity
without discarding all sense of immanent Trinity. It also now means a new
focus on the practical, spiritual and ecclesiastical (church-related) implications of the Trinity.

It seems that adherents to the psychological analogy and adherents to the
social analogy need each other for a balanced view of the Trinity. If pressed
too far and too one-sidedly the psychological analogy—or merely the traditional Western, Augustinian model of thinking about the Trinity—falls into a
kind of implicit modalism. So long as those who use the psychological analogy also confess God as eternally three distinct entities—whether the English
word *persons* is used or not—they are within the Great Tradition. There is
good reason to be cautious about the word *person* in modern discourse
about the Trinity though. Modern and postmodern people—especially in
the culture of Western Europe and North America—tend to think of *person*
as "individual self over against others." That is not what *hypostasis* meant to
the church fathers who brought about the Nicene settlement in the fourth

century. And it is not what *person* means in many cultures of the world. To be a person is to be a part of the community. One does not necessarily become more personal by asserting oneself against the group; one may become more personal by enhancing the common bond of fellowship within a group. And yet that is not what most people in twentieth-century Europe and North America think.

For such reasons Barth and Rahner both rejected *person* as the best term for the trinitarian distinctions. However, they, like Augustine and most Western Christian thinkers since Augustine, came very close to throwing the baby of multiplicity within God out with the bathwater of latent tritheism. The psychological analogy is always in danger of overemphasizing God's oneness to the detriment of God's threeness—the full personal reality of Father, Son and Holy Spirit. Augustine's "intellect, memory and will in one mind" is simply not sufficient by itself to depict the Trinity. Barth's "revealer, revelation and revealedness" as reiteration of a single divine subject—"God as Lord"—does not cut it either, and Barth himself seemed to realize this later in his career. The psychological analogy and the Western monistic model of the Trinity needs to be corrected, balanced and supplemented by the social analogy.

The social analogy needs to be corrected, balanced and supplemented by the psychological analogy as well. It is always in danger of falling into tritheism. Gregory of Nyssa's analogy of disciples Peter, James and John for the Father, Son and Holy Spirit inevitably implies three gods in spite of his arguments against that to his unknown correspondent Ablabius. Gregory also used the analogy of gold and individual coins: one substance and three instantiations of the one substance. Richard of St. Victor and his school of trinitarian thought in the Middle Ages risked reducing the Godhead to a ménage à trois in heaven, and certainly Joachim of Fiore, who was influenced by Richard, came very close to tritheism. Twentieth-century social analogy theologians have worked hard to avoid any hint of tritheism. Leonard Hodgson used the psychological analogy along with his social analogy while emphasizing the latter. His idea of "organic unity" for the unity of the Godhead is a great improvement over gold and coins or Peter, James and John. However, Hodgson and Moltmann and other social analogists struggle mightily to avoid falling into tritheism and barely succeed.

It should come as no surprise that because God is essentially incomprehensible we need more than one analogy drawn from creation to illustrate what his inner life is like. And analogies drawn from personal life are intrinsically better than analogies drawn from inanimate and nonhuman creaturely existence because only humans are created in the image of God and because God is personal—a *Thou* and not an *It*. It is crucial for the identity and integrity of Christianity that monotheism be preserved. But there is a difference between monotheism and *monarchianism*. The latter, unlike the former, implies a single, dominating subjectivity ruling over all. A case may be made that trinitarian theology is consistent monotheism while monarchianism is inconsistent with both trinitarianism and monotheism. If God is a single, dominating subjectivity—even with three manifestations—then who did he love before he created the world, and did he create the world to realize himself in and through it? (A person always needs another person or persons for self-realization.) The psychological analogy taken alone is in danger of falling into monarchianism. Monotheism that rejects inner multiplicity and organic unity of parts is in danger of falling into monarchianism as well. The social analogy must be supplemented by the psychological in order to avoid falling into tritheism, which is merely a form of polytheism (belief in more than one god). This is a classical case of both-and theology rather than either-or theology. We cannot have one model of the Trinity without the other one, even though they stand in tension with each other. How a single being can be faithfully and somewhat accurately described as *both* a single mind with multiple dimensions *and* a community of persons knitted together inseparably in a bond of love is beyond complete understanding. Nevertheless, divine revelation requires that God be described in both ways.

CHAPTER 7

# CREATION

## Good *and* Fallen

As soon as someone utters the word *creationism*, many listeners are conditioned to think of a particular theory of the origins of the universe, associated with fundamentalist Christianity. Unfortunately, creationism is thought to be the opposite of evolution and perhaps also opposed to science itself. However, the basic contours of the Christian idea of creation—which is not only about origins but also about nature—predate the so-called creation-evolution controversy by centuries. Long before Darwin proposed his theory of natural selection and long before certain fundamentalist opponents of evolution developed what has come to be known as "scientific creationism" or "young earth creationism," the Great Tradition of Christian belief and teaching had already settled the main issues of the doctrine of creation, and they had little to do with the age of the earth or the processes by which God may or may not have brought about life forms on it.

### Issues and Polarities of Christian Belief About Creation

Early Christians developed beliefs about creation—the universe—in response to religions, philosophies and worldviews that existed in their cultural environment. The Roman Empire was rife with myths and beliefs about the nature and origin of the universe. Most of them had nothing to do with what modern people think of as science; they were instead metaphysical and spiritual in nature and usually involved some ideas or stories about the gods or divine powers and forces. The early Christian apologists and church fathers drew heavily on Hebrew sources as they developed their own alternative belief about creation. They also sought out and used Hellenistic (Greek cultural) ideas about God and the world. Ultimately, however, the early Christians' inspiration for a distinctively Christian doctrine of creation came from reflection on divine revelation in Jesus Christ, through the prophets and apostles and in Scripture.

Throughout the centuries of Christian thought an implicit consensus emerged about certain fundamental beliefs regarding the universe. Some of the most important aspects of that consensus have little or nothing whatever to do with *when* God created the universe or life in it or *how* God created. Some church fathers and Reformers interpreted the Genesis account(s) of creation very literally; others interpreted them more allegorically. But they agreed on several important principles, to be explained in the next section, that have become the backbone, as it were, of the Christian worldview.

From time to time, however, tensions have arisen within Christianity over the nature of the universe and life in the universe. I have already alluded to a modern controversy over evolution and the age of the earth. But even more basic are tensions between Christian thinkers over the *metaphysical status* and *moral status* of the material, physical universe including bodies, natural processes, disasters, death, decay and evil. Some Christian thinkers have tended to emphasize the *goodness* of the world because God created it; other Christian thinkers have tended to emphasize the *fallenness* of the world because sin has invaded and corrupted it. This polarity in Christian thought is evidenced even in popular Christian songs. Some Christians love to sing "This World Is Not My Home (I'm Just a-Passin' Through)" while others prefer "This Is My Father's World." Some Christians view the world as little more than a series of trials—almost a purgatory—that one must go through in order to experience the bliss of heaven. Other Christians view the world as a gift of God—a home for humanity that God plans to redeem. The former focus on the curse on nature resulting from humanity's rebellion against God; the latter focus on the original blessing of God's presence with each particle and event of nature.

Most Christian theologians from the early church to the twentieth century have tried to maintain a balanced view of creation as *both* blessed *and* cursed, but such a balance is always kept only by conscious effort. Here our theme will be that Christian belief about creation has little to do with specific scientific theories about the age of the earth and the natural processes that led to the emergence of life. It has rather to do with embracing a certain *metaphysical* view of the status of the universe in relation to God and affirming a certain *moral* evaluation of the universe. Specifically, Christian belief about creation regards the universe as *good but not God* and *good but fallen under a curse.*

## The Christian Consensus About Creation

In his outstanding treatise on the Christian doctrine of creation titled *Maker of Heaven and Earth* (Garden City, N.Y.: Doubleday, 1959), twentieth-century Protestant theologian Langdon Gilkey summed up the Christian consensus about creation with three pregnant sentences: *God is the source of all that there is; creatures are dependent yet real and good;* and *God creates in freedom and with purpose.* While these statements well summarize most of basic Christian belief about creation, I think it necessary to add a fourth: *Creation is fallen under a curse and needs supernatural healing (i.e., redemption).* These four claims generally recapitulate in themselves all that revelation says about the natural world and all that the historic Christian consensus has taught about it. Of course, each one of these claims needs to be fleshed out in more detail. As they stand they are quite vague. In what sense is God the source of all that there is? Why did God create the universe? What does it mean that creatures are dependent? In what sense is creation fallen and what is the curse under which it exists? Here our aim will be to summarize very briefly the Christian consensus about these statements and about the questions surrounding them. Eventually we will also delve into the issues that tend to divide Christians who follow the Great Tradition of Christian thought about creation.

The most basic Christian confession about the universe—creation—is that God the Father Almighty is "maker of heaven and earth." This is the first sentence of the Apostles' Creed—a brief summation of the essence of the ecumenical Nicene Creed: "I believe in God the Father Almighty, maker of heaven and earth." Gilkey expresses this belief as "God is the source of all that there is." The biblical witness everywhere confirms this idea of the origin of the universe. Its first words declare that God created the heavens and the earth (Gen 1:1), and the first two chapters of the Bible express poetically how God's Spirit worked on the original creation to give it form and bring forth life. The Hebrew prophet Isaiah spoke for God about his creatorship of all things: "I am the LORD, who has made all things, who alone stretched out the heavens, who spread out the earth by myself" (Is 44:24). The apostle Paul affirmed God as the creative source of everything in his speech to the Athenian philosophers recounted in the New Testament Acts of the Apostles: "The God who made the world and everything in it is the Lord of heaven and earth and does not live in temples built by hands. And he is not served by human hands, as if he needed anything, because he himself gives all men life and breath and everything else" (Acts 17:24-25). Furthermore, according to Jewish tradition and earliest Christian proclamation, the Lord God Yahweh (God's name in Hebrew) is Lord, and if anything exists alongside him that he did not bring into existence and does not control then he is not Lord of that. God's lordship necessarily implies that he is the maker of everything outside his own being which alone is eternal.

The early church fathers faced a variety of religions and philosophies—some claiming to be Christian—that explained God's or the gods' creatorship as his craftsmanship of the universe out of eternal matter or (expressed mythically) out of the body of a slain monster. Many spiritually and philosophically-minded people of the Greek world and Roman empire could affirm a sense of divine creation of all things, but few besides Jews and Christians believed in one God who alone is eternal.

The Christian sects known as the Gnostics tried to combine pagan religion and Greek philosophy with Hebrew-Christian thought. They adapted a common belief about creation known as emanationism to their esoteric (mystical) form of Christianity. The idea was that God created the universe out of himself using his own divine substance. They also believed that some of this divine substance with which God created everything somehow fell into material form or was filched by fallen spirits and used to create matter. Thus, the Gnostics combined three ideas in their eclectic notion of creation: emanationism, dualism and biblical creationism. They taught that the real, underlying substance of all things is divine. For them, this is especially true of human souls or spirits. They also taught that some of that divine substance in creation fell into a material mode of existence which is the source of evil. This is dualism: belief in good and evil as two substances opposite one another. Finally, they drew on biblical teachings that God is the source of everything.

Against the Gnostics and certain other Greek-inspired philosophies and spiritualities, the Christian church fathers developed the doctrine of *creatio ex nihilo*—creation out of nothing. Nowhere is this stated explicitly in divine revelation, but like the Trinity it is a necessary implication of the clear revelation of God as the maker of all things in heaven and earth. If God fashioned the world out of "God stuff," then the universe would be worthy of worship. It would be fine, then, to worship "Mother Nature." But the prophets and apostles forbade worship of anything except God. To ward off false teachings and philosophies about the divinity of the universe (even of souls!) the church fathers and Reformers with one voice loudly proclaimed the doctrine of *creatio ex nihilo*. According to second-century church father, bishop and teacher Irenaeus:

> It is proper, then, that I should begin with the first and most important head, that is, God the Creator, who made the heaven and the earth, and all the things that are therein . . . and to demonstrate that there is nothing either above Him or after Him; nor that, influenced by anyone, but of His own free will He created all things, since He is the only God, the only Lord, the only Creator, the only Father, alone containing all things, and Himself commanding all things into existence.[1]

Church father and influential third-century theologian Tertullian also affirmed *creatio ex nihilo:*

> The fact of God being the One and only God asserts this rule, for He is the One-only God for the only reason that He is the sole God, and the sole God for the only reason that nothing existed with Him. Thus He must also be the First, since all things are posterior to Him; all things are posterior to Him for the reason that all things are by Him; all things are by Him for the reason that they are from nothing . . . for there was no power, no material, no nature of another substance which assisted Him.[2]

---

[1]Irenaeus *Against Heresies* 2.1.1, as quoted in Langdon Gilkey, *Maker of Heaven and Earth* (Garden City, N.Y.: Doubleday, 1959), p. 43.
[2]Tertullian *The Treatise Against Hermogenes,* chap. 17, as quoted in Gilkey, *Maker of Heaven,* p. 50.

The Protestant Reformers of the sixteenth century were no less firm about their confession of God's creation of everything out of nothing. For example, Calvin declared in his *Institutes,*

> For this, as I have elsewhere observed, though not the first principle, is yet, in the order of nature, the first lesson of faith, to remember that, whithersoever we turn our eyes, all the things which we behold are works of God. . . . Thence we shall learn that God, by the power of His Word and Spirit, created out of nothing the heaven and the earth; that from them He produced all things, animate and inanimate.[3]

Clearly, then, *creatio ex nihilo* is one of the most basic and universal Christian beliefs—even if many Christians have no idea what it means and have never been taught it. It is simply the clearest and most precise way of expressing the full import of "God is the source of all that there is," which is simply another way of saying "God alone is Lord of all!" It does *not* mean—as some have wrongly supposed—that God fashioned the universe out of a reality called *Nothing*. Ancient Greek philosophy had a concept of *Nothingness* as a reality. This is extremely abstract and scholars of Greek philosophy debate it endlessly, but suffice it to say that the church fathers and Reformers did not believe or teach that the universe is literally nothing or made out of a substance called *Nothingness (mē on)*. The latter idea would contradict the whole concept of *creatio ex nihilo,* which is meant to express and protect a mystery: that God spoke or commanded the universe into existence with everything in it—both material and spiritual. The whole heavens and earth that together comprise everything that exists outside of God came into being from God's command. That is not to say it came into being *as it now is* from God's sheer command, but it is to say that its original form which developed under the impulse and power of God's Spirit moving upon it began as the ultimate free lunch. It is sheer gift.

The idea that creation is somehow unreal because God brought it into existence "out of nothing" is surely not what the church fathers or Reformers intended either. Rather, as Gilkey helpfully affirms, the Christian concept of creation says that "creatures are dependent yet real and good." *Dependent* is implied necessarily by *creatio ex nihilo*. According to divine revelation as

---

[3]John Calvin *Institutes of the Christian Religion* 1.24.20, as quoted in Gilkey, *Maker of Heaven*, p. 43.

recorded in the biblical witness and according to the Great Tradition of Christian belief and teaching, the entire universe of "heaven and earth" exists "under God" and in complete dependence on him. The prophet Isaiah especially loved to emphasize this aspect of God's creatorship. In chapter 45, for example, he speaks for God: "I form the light and create darkness, I bring prosperity and create disaster; I, the LORD, do all these things" (Is 45:7). The same theme of God's total sovereignty over creation and creation's complete dependence upon God runs throughout biblical revelation. But even if Scripture nowhere explicitly spells it out, it is implied inexorably in the very idea of radical creation out of nothing. Some religions, philosophies and spiritualities assume that whatever is finite, dependent, must necessarily also be less than good. After all, only God is good. And yet, according to the creation accounts of Genesis, God created all things and saw that they were good (Gen 1:9, 12, 18, 21, 25, 31).

If God is good and even the very source of goodness, then how could he create anything intrinsically bad or flawed or evil? As one twentieth-century Christian philosopher has said very colloquially "God don't make no junk!" Even the world—a theater of great evil and suffering—came from the hand and word of God and is good in that God intended it to be the way it was. This is another truth about creation that many Christians miss or ignore. For some reason they assume that since the world contains evil, suffering and corruption it must be intrinsically evil or flawed. But how could God, who is both great and good, create something that is evil or flawed? As we will soon see, the Great Tradition of Christian belief about creation takes into account the flaws and even the evil and corruption that have come into creation, but that is not the same as affirming that creation itself is evil or flawed. Against many of the philosophies and religions of the Greek world and Roman empire, the early church fathers held fast to the confession that the universe God created was and is essentially good while also being *not God*. The great church father Augustine theorized the existence of "greater and lesser goods," and this has been taken up into Christian thought to help support and explain the reality of a creation that is both dependent—and therefore not God—and good, and therefore not to be disdained or even escaped. Augustine's idea was that only God is perfectly good—goodness itself. Any created thing would necessarily be a lesser good than God. And yet, a lesser good can still be good and not evil. But a lesser good than God is open to corruption. It can fall from its own level of goodness into some level of evil by turning away from its own source in God and its own good being.[4]

The third basic Christian concept about creation is that *God creates in freedom and with purpose*. The confession that God creates freely is the only confession consistent with God's transcendence (greatness), and the confession that God creates with purpose is the only confession consistent with God's personal presence (goodness). In fact, an argument could be made that these beliefs are little more than transcripts of the Christian doctrine of God in the context of the idea of creation. If God is truly great, then creation cannot be a limit on him. If creation was not created freely but out of any necessity it would form a limit on God's being. Furthermore, if the world were in any way necessary for God's being then creation and redemption would be as much for God as for the world itself and they would not be all of grace. If God is good then he created with a purpose. A randomly and capriciously wrought world would not be the work of a good God. In his great treatise on creation and history, church father and bishop Augustine expressed the sentiment of the whole Christian church: "And by the words, 'God saw that it was good,' it is sufficiently intimated that God made what was made not from any necessity, nor for the sake of supplying any want, but solely from its own goodness, i.e., because it was good."[5]

The fourth and final summary statement of Christian belief about creation is *creation is fallen under a curse and needs supernatural healing (redemption)*. Two passages of Scripture especially clearly confirm this: Genesis 3 and Romans 8. The Genesis passage quotes God the Lord informing Adam and Eve of a curse that has fallen upon the ground because of their disobedience. The Christian church has always interpreted that as referring to a distortion of the goodness of the created order evidenced in life depending upon death and in great suffering and tragedy built into the very fabric of the world as it exists after the fall outside the garden. The apostle Paul confirms this in Romans 8:18-24 where he writes of creation being subjected to "futility" (NASB, NRSV) and "bondage to decay"—a curse from which it will be freed in the future "glory" when Christ returns. This is a part of the

---

[4]See Augustine *Faith, Hope and Charity (Enchiridion)*, trans. Louis A. Arand (Westminster, Md.: Newman Press, 1955), chap. 4.
[5]Augustine *The City of God* 11.24, as quoted in Gilkey, *Maker of Heaven*, p. 78.

Christian answer to the so-called problem of evil. (It is "so-called" because in fact an argument could be made and has been made that disbelief in God has a greater problem with evil than does belief in God: what is *evil* if there is no ultimate standard of goodness?)

Although God is the Creator of everything, he is not the creator of evil. As the Cappadocian fathers and Augustine equally pointed out, evil is not a something, but the absence of the good. The fourth- and fifth-century church fathers explained and the Great Tradition of Christian belief has generally agreed that evil is not a substance. It has no ontological status. It is to good what darkness is to light: privation, absence. The curse that has fallen upon creation is not a thing, a substance, but a lack of something—just as a disease is not a substance but a lack of health. (Of course a disease may be caused by a substance, but the substance itself is not evil. Its location is wrong. The disease is a dis-order of the good system of a healthy organism.) God did not create evil even though he created everything, because evil is not a thing. God did create the possibility of evil. He created a universe in which evil could happen, but evil's appearance in a world that was wholly good was neither necessary nor inevitable.

## Alternatives to the Christian Consensus About Creation

Many people mistakenly believe that the main alternative to the Christian belief about creation is evolution. Ever since Charles Darwin published his controversial treatises on natural selection in the mid-nineteenth century much, if not most, controversy surrounding creation has involved the challenges of evolutionary theory as equated with Darwin's belief in natural selection as "survival of the fittest." Even in the late nineteenth century some conservative Christian theologians attempted to reconcile evolutionary theories of biological development of species with the Genesis account of creation. Others—for a century and a half—have focused on demonstrating their incommensurabilities. Every few years a new creation versus evolution controversy erupts. The most famous (or infamous) one was the so-called Scopes monkey trial in Dayton, Tennessee, in 1925, which became the basis for a play titled *Inherit the Wind*.

A careful study of historical Christian thought, however, reveals that the main alternatives to Christian belief in creation have not included evolution per se. Whether it should be added to the list is still a matter of disagreement and sometimes heated debate between Christian theologians, preachers and apologists. The main alternatives to the Christian concept of creation have been *dualism, monism* and *naturalism*. Some Christian critics of evolution argue that it is inescapably naturalistic. That is, they see evolutionary development of species from other species as inherently tied to a mechanistic if not materialistic view of the world. They argue that it should be rejected by all Christians simply because it reduces to naturalism—the belief that all of reality is governed by natural laws that are in principle scientifically discoverable in such a way that they can be expressed in mathematical equations. Whether all evolutionary explanations of biological development of species are naturalistic is a discussion that lies beyond the scope of this book. Here it must suffice to point out what these three main, general alternatives to Christian belief in creation are and why they have been and must continue to be viewed as incompatible with a Christian view of the world.

Once again, theologian Langdon Gilkey has summarized the three alternatives to Christian belief about creation most helpfully. In his modern classic *Maker of Heaven and Earth,* the University of Chicago Divinity School theologian classified these broad views of creation (all of which actually deny creation in any traditionally Christian sense!) as philosophies. They may also be religious worldviews and often are associated with religious and spiritual communities. Sometimes one or another stands at the center of a "Christian" community's belief system, in which case that community's Christian identification is placed in question. All three stand opposed to the Christian consensus about the cosmos and its origin and nature as summarized in the section here on the Christian consensus.

*Dualism* is any belief in two eternally existing, opposed realities. But how can that be a heresy? Some may ask, doesn't Christianity teach two opposed realities—God and Satan? The key operative word for distinguishing dualism from Christianity is *eternal.* The two opposed realities in dualism are both without beginning and without end and are both ultimate—equally powerful and real. In historic Christian belief God is the only eternal, ultimate being. Satan is a creature. Some critics of traditional Christian belief have suggested that its belief in Satan is a vestige of a Middle Eastern religious worldview that was dualistic. However, early Christian church fathers—especially Augustine—vigorously opposed any dualistic tendencies in Christian churches and their teachings. Satan was viewed by the early church fathers as well as the medieval theologians and

Reformers as a creature and not at all equal with God.[6]

Dualism appeared in early Christianity as a rival theology offered up by a religion named after its founder. They were the Manicheans and they flourished in North Africa when Augustine was bishop there (late fourth and early fifth centuries). They believed in a double dualism: two divine powers, one good and one sinister if not evil, and two ultimate ontological principles created by the two gods—spirit and matter. The Manicheans identified spirit as good and matter as the seat of all evil. Augustine and other early Christian leaders opposed this and all other forms of dualism because they implicitly deny the deity of God as the one maker of heaven and earth. Dualism introduces a god beside god and, while seeming to explain the origin of sin and evil in a sinister deity and its creation of matter, robs God of his ultimacy as Lord. It also detracts from the goodness of creation and makes hope for an ultimate triumph of the good over evil an illusion. All-in-all, the early church fathers and Christian thinkers throughout the ages have unanimously and firmly rejected dualism of both kinds. Any truly dualistic worldview is completely incompatible with the Christian life and worldview at nearly every point.

A second alternative to the Christian belief about creation is *monism*. Monism appears in many forms, and they all have the common feature of reducing all of reality to one substance—usually a spiritual substance identified with God or the divine. One form of monism is pantheism: the strict identification of creation with the divine being. A more common form of monism in the West that has plagued Christianity throughout most of its history is emanationism: its alternative to *creatio ex nihilo* is the belief that the one divine substance (God, Spirit, Mind) has send forth rays or emanations into the emptiness. All of reality, so emanationist monists say, is composed of some form or manifestation of the divine being, but some of these emanations from the "solar substance" or "ocean of light and love" (common terms for the one, central, eternal source of all emanations) have "hardened" and "forgotten" their true origin in God. That is how what we call matter came into existence and how sin and evil began.

Gnosticism is basically emanationist in its view of creation. Many Gnostic sects posed a serious threat and challenge to Christianity in the first through

---

[6]Jeffrey Burton Russell, *Satan: The Early Christian Tradition* (Ithaca, N.Y.: Cornell University Press, 1987).

the third centuries, especially in the Roman Empire. Emanationism has appeared and reappeared in Christian history as a kind of shadow of orthodox Christianity. Even after the many Gnostic teachers and sects were either stamped out or driven underground by the Constantinian church, the Gnostic worldview appeared in medieval European sects such as the Cathari and Albigenses. Various mystical teachers of Judaism and Christianity resurrected it during the Renaissance and Reformation eras, and in modern times it has been given new life by occultists and esoteric spiritual groups such as the Rosicrucians and Theosophists. Perhaps the most popular and influential form of emanationism in late-twentieth-century and early-twenty-first-century European and North American culture is the so-called New Age movement and its spiritual philosophy. Sir George Trevelyan, "father of the British New Age movement," delineated this contemporary version of ancient Gnosticism in two books: *A Vision of the Aquarian Age: The Emerging Spiritual World View* (Stillpoint, 1984) and *Operation Redemption: A Vision of Hope in an Age of Turmoil* (Stillpoint, 1985). According to Trevelyan, "everything is ultimately spirit, in different conditions of density" and the human person is a "droplet of divinity housed in the temple of the body."[7]

The church fathers rejected Gnosticism, and leading Christian thinkers have rejected it ever since because all forms of monism—emanationism included—detract from God's transcendence and commit the sin of idolatry with regard to creation, making it possible if not necessary to worship and serve created things rather than the Creator (Rom 1:25). The world—including humanity—is good because God created it with purpose and out of love, not because it is God or an extension of God. The Christian doctrine of *creatio ex nihilo,* creation out of nothing, was a theological product of early Christian reflection made necessary by dualism and monism. It is just as important in the contemporary Christian milieu as it was in the second and third centuries when it was developed. Without it the dualistic and monistic denials of the ultimacy of God over creation and tendencies either to demonize or idolize creation naturally arise even within Christian communities.

The third major alternative to Christian belief in creation is a modern one: *naturalism.* Dualism and monism have ancient roots; naturalism may

---

[7]George Trevelyan, *A Vision of the Aquarian Age: The Emerging Spiritual World View* (Walpole, N.H.: Stillpoint, 1984), pp. 1-2, 11.

have ancient precursors (e.g., certain Greek materialist philosophies) but it is by and large a product of the Enlightenment and scientific revolutions of modern, Western culture. Few, if any, religions are naturalistic. Some forms of modern liberal Protestant theology have attempted to construct a religious naturalism, but even that is an unstable middle ground unacceptable to both religious believers and most scientists. Perhaps the most influential naturalist of the contemporary Western world was the physicist and cosmologist Carl Sagan, whose book and documentary series *Cosmos* went far to impress upon school children's minds the idea that modern science left no room for belief in anything outside of or beyond the material universe ruled by scientifically discoverable and mathematically describable natural laws. Naturalism's idea of creation is rooted in chance. The universe is the ultimate accident. If it began with a "big bang," it was sheer happenstance and not at all the result of a divine intelligence or act of an omnipotent power. (Here it is important to note that belief in a "big bang" is not necessarily incompatible with Christian belief in creation, but naturalists—including many physicists who study the origins of the cosmos—tend to describe the "big bang" as an alternative to religious accounts of origins such as *creatio ex nihilo*. Why the two are so often pitted against one another by both naturalists and religious opponents of modern science remains a mystery.)

Naturalism is a foundational worldview that underlies many specific philosophies. For example, secular humanists are naturalists who interpret the human species as nature's highest product—matter becoming self-conscious and acquiring reasoning powers.[8] Many animal rights philosophers and "deep ecologists" share the same basic worldview with secular humanists (viz., nature is all there is), but reject the elevation of humanity to the pinnacle of nature as *speciesism*—a form of prejudice. Of course, naturalism and all philosophies inextricably based on it are incompatible with Christianity. While naturalism is not always touted as atheistic it is implicitly so. A peculiar form of illogical reasoning has led many people—including highly educated and intelligent people—to equate modern science with naturalism or to view the latter as the foundation of the former. This has resulted in gullible people on both sides of the science-religion debate assuming that they are necessarily locked in mortal combat. Once one sees that naturalism is a philosophy and that science does not depend on it to do its work, however, new vistas of

---

[8]Paul Kurtz, *In Defense of Secular Humanism* (Buffalo, N.Y.: Prometheus, 1983).

integration of Christian faith and scientific research and discovery open up. The problem with evolution, from a Christian point of view, is not that it is necessarily incompatible with Christian belief in God as the Creator. Rather the problem with evolution is that it is so often linked with naturalism in the minds of those who promote it, as well as in the minds (and writings) of those who reject it.

### Diverse Christian Beliefs About Creation

Almost all of the significant diversity and divisive debate about creation among Christians revolve around the thorny issues of the age of the earth and the origin of species. The production of books and articles, video tapes and lecture series by Christian apologists about this subject is way out of proportion to its importance in the overall scheme of Christian belief. Christian bookstores often carry more books about this than any other single topic. Few evangelical Christian young people can grow up in church or attend a Christian camp, school or conference without being faced with a barrage of propaganda about "the origins debate." This creates the impression in the minds of many Christians that the Christian doctrine of creation is about *how* and *when* the earth and life were created. By and large, however, the Christian consensus of belief about creation has included very little reference to *when* or *how* God created. What is so ironic in this particular locus of Christian belief and reflection is that many dyed-in-the-wool creationists who insist dogmatically on a young earth and sudden creation of species excluding any evolutionary processes fall unthinkingly into heresies such as equating finitude with evil or with the divine substance. They strain at gnats and swallow camels.

Among equally orthodox Christians one finds three main beliefs about the relatively unimportant issues of the when and how of creation: *theistic evolution, young earth creationism* and *progressive creationism*. Almost all Christian theologians and apologists who speculate about these issues fall into one of these three general approaches to relating modern science with biblical revelation.

In the seventeenth century, Irish Anglican Bishop James Ussher published a book in which he provided the year of creation itself. According to Ussher—whose work was based on his own study of the biblical chronologies and genealogies—God created the universe in 4004 B.C. Thus, many English-speaking Christians began to assume that the Bible teaches that creation is only about six thousand years old. This became the standard view of creation's antiquity for many Christians and they often confused the bishop's calculations and speculations with the Bible's own authority so that anyone who questioned that date for creation seemed to be questioning the Bible itself. Not very long after Bishop Ussher published his conclusion certain geologists began to contradict it based on their discoveries of fossils embedded in strata of rock formations in cliffs and river beds. Long before Charles Darwin published his controversial views about biological evolution, a conflict between biblical literalists and geologists was brewing. Geologists such as Charles Lyell argued that the earth must be millions of years old. Defenders of Bishop Ussher's young earth view appealed to the Noahic flood or to a supposed gap between a first creation and a second creation (or renovation of a creation ruined by a catastrophe) to explain the newly discovered fossil record and evidences of ancient upheavals in earth's crust and canyons created by aeons of erosion. Geologists and many who read their findings, however, were usually unimpressed by the argument from catastrophism. Eventually, Bishop Ussher's dating of creation was widely considered implausible.

In the nineteenth century, an English Christian who was also a geologist declared that he had the answer to this tension between modern cosmology based on the relatively new science of geology and the literally-interpreted biblical account of creation. The devout English Christian and scientist Philip Gosse proposed that God had created the universe *with the appearance of antiquity relatively recently.* In other words, according to this explanation, the world is really only about six thousand years old but "ideally" (in appearance) millions of years old. Few thoughtful people on either side of the growing divide between scientists and biblicists were convinced that this was a viable solution. To this day, and no doubt for a very long time to come, some conservative Christians—especially fundamentalist Protestants—argue that the universal, catastrophic flood of Noah's day adequately accounts for all of the evidence for an ancient earth and that the Bible must be interpreted as teaching that God created the world and all of life on it in a literal week of six twenty-four hour days. Organizations such as the Creation Research Institute publish books and documentary films attempting to demonstrate this point. Few university-trained scientists have been convinced. Fundamentalist Christians staked a great deal on a young earth and a denial of evolutionary development of species, especially of humanity. To most of them, it is a matter of dogma—absolute truth revealed directly by God's Word—and any accommodation of biblical interpretation to the theories of modern science regarding the age of the earth and the creation of a literal human couple (Adam and Eve) from which all humans are descended is anathema.

The scientific revolutions of the seventeenth through the nineteenth centuries—beginning with Copernicus and Galileo and continuing on especially with Darwin—created a crisis for traditional Christian belief about creation. Galileo argued persuasively that the Roman Catholic Church was wrong with regard to the solar system. Later he was proven correct. Isaac Newton—a devout Christian—provided a mathematically describable account of natural laws and seemed to demonstrate that the universe is a closed network of natural causes and effects. The great Enlightenment essayist and poet Alexander Pope honored Newton with a couplet: "Nature and nature's laws lay wrapped in night; God said 'Let Newton be!' and all was light"("Epitaph Intended for Sir Isaac Newton"). Darwin offered a plausible account of the natural development of species, including humanity. It appeared to many Christian thinkers that a paradigm shift was required in Christian belief about creation—including the creation of humanity.

As early as the late nineteenth century, certain Christian thinkers began to develop what has come to be known as theistic evolution—the idea that Darwin's theory of natural selection (including its wider background of belief in a world generally ruled by natural laws and created over aeons of time)—is true and not in conflict with essential Christianity. Theistic evolutionists believe that the biblical narratives of creation are to be taken seriously but not literally. In other words, they express theological truths, such as God is the Creator, through metaphor, poetry, myth and saga. Theistic evolution takes many forms, but all have in common a complete accommodation of Christian belief about the *how* and *when* of creation to the natural sciences and a tendency to view God as the intelligent designer behind and immanent power within the forces of nature that have given rise over millions of years to the universe and life on earth. Theistic evolutionists see no necessary conflict between Christianity—including a high view of Scripture as God's Word—and neo-Darwinism *so long as* the latter does not require naturalism and the former does not require a literal interpretation of the first few chapters of Genesis.

Throughout the twentieth century the tensions between Christians who hold firmly to *young earth creationism* (sometimes called "scientific creationism" by its proponents) and Christians who believe in *theistic evolution* have developed into all-out theological warfare that sometimes leads to political conflict. Some liberal Protestant theologians such as Langdon Gilkey have offered "expert testimony" on behalf of evolutionary science against fundamentalists who wish so-called scientific creationism to have equal time in public school science textbooks and classrooms. The media have made much of this situation of conflict and have generally ignored a broad middle ground view that includes many Christian theologians and scientists who teach at Christian colleges and universities. That little-known middle ground has come to be known by its proponents as *progressive creationism.* Progressive creationists—including leading evangelical theologian Bernard Ramm—believe that neither young earth creationism nor theistic evolutionism is a viable option for modern Christians. In his classic book *A Christian View of Science and Scripture,* Ramm pointed out the weaknesses of both views and argued for belief in a combination of ancient creation, evolutionary development of life and special acts of God at certain thresholds within the history of creation. According to Ramm, progressive creationism is the view that

> nature is permeated with the Divine activity but not in any pantheistic sense. The order is from blank and void to order and cosmos, from the seed to the full ear, from the cosmic to the organic, from the simple to the complex, from the sentient to the rational. The completed product is at the end of the process, not at the beginning.
>
> Putting together our picture we have something like this: Almighty God is Creator, World-Ground, and Omnipotent Sustainer. In His mind the entire plan of creation was formed with man as the climax. Over the millions of years of geological history the earth is prepared for man's dwelling, or as it has been put by others, the cosmos was pregnant with man. The vast forests grew and decayed for his coal, that coal might appear a natural product and not an artificial insertion in Nature. The millions of sea life were born and perished for his oil. The surface of the earth was weathered for his forests and valleys. From time to time the great creative acts, *do novo,* took place. The complexity of animal forms increased. Finally, when every river had cut its intended course, when every mountain was in its purposed place, when every animal was on the earth according to the blueprint, then he whom all creation anticipated is made, MAN, in whom alone is the breath of God.[9]

---

[9]Bernard Ramm, *The Christian View of Science and Scripture* (Grand Rapids, Mich.: Eerdmans, 1954), p. 155.

All three views of the *how* and *when* of creation are consistent with historic Christian belief insofar as they acknowledge that *God is the Creator ex nihilo of all reality outside himself* and that *creation is good but not God* and insofar as they avoid any hints of true naturalism, dualism or monism. Christian critics of young earth creationism (to say nothing of secular critics of the same!) tend to view it as obscurantist. To them it appears to be based on a refusal to accept the bare facts of modern scientific evidence and an unnecessarily literalistic and even wooden interpretation of the Genesis creation narratives. Even if that is true, and it probably is largely true, it does not make young earth creationism heresy. Being wrong is not always the same as falling into heresy.

Fundamentalists who insist on young earth creationism as part and parcel of authentic Christian belief in creation often argue that both theistic evolution and progressive creationism amount to denials of biblical authority and God's creatorship. Neither accusation is true. Both theistic evolution and progressive creationism take the Bible and science seriously and attempt to integrate the two creatively and faithfully. Progressive creationists tend to view both young earth creationism and theistic evolution as extremes. There is some truth to that perception. Young earth creationism ignores the fact that even the great early church father Augustine suggested a nonliteral reading of the "days" of creation as epochs of God's creative activity. It also elevates to dogmatic status—as part of the very essence of Christianity—a relatively eccentric interpretation of both the biblical genealogies (viz., Bishop Ussher's calculations which left no room for gaps) and of the scientific evidences for the great age of the earth and human life on it. On the other hand, theistic evolutionists are apt to jump too quickly and firmly to accept whatever theories of biological development of life on earth neo-Darwinian scientists offer, and they often fall into the trap of failing adequately to integrate the doctrine of creation with the best of modern science. Progressive creationism is an unfinished project, but it approaches the apparent conflicts between modern science and essential Christian truth better than the two main alternatives.

It is very unfortunate that questions of *how* and *when* God created have come to dominate Christian discussion of the doctrine of creation. In the meantime, while proponents of the three main views are arguing vehemently with each other and often hurling accusations at one another, the majority of Christians in the pews are untutored about the main contours of the historic

Christian belief in creation. Ask most of them about *creatio ex nihilo* (even in English translation) and they will be nonplused. There are other interesting questions and issues surrounding the doctrine of creation besides those that obsess so many Christians caught up in the arguments over the age of the earth and evolution. For example, Protestant thinkers have discussed for centuries the seemingly speculative question of *God's purpose for creating the universe.* All agree that God created *ex nihilo* and *freely with purpose,* but they do not always all agree about *why* God created the universe at all. Why creation? What was God's purpose? By and large, Reformed theologians—those in the tradition of the Swiss Protestant Reformers Ulrich Zwingli and John Calvin and their Scottish follower John Knox—view creation as "the theater of God's glory." Puritan preacher and theologian Jonathan Edwards—a brilliant and devoted Calvinist thinker—argued that God's purpose in creating the universe and human life and in everything God does is to glorify himself.

Twentieth-century Reformed theologian Karl Barth amended the traditional Reformed view by saying that creation is the "outer basis of the covenant" and that Jesus Christ is creation's "inner basis." By that he meant that God's entire and sole purpose in creating anything at all was redemption through Jesus Christ. Of course, for Barth, God is glorified in being in covenant relationship with humanity through Jesus Christ. The late twentieth-century German theologian Jürgen Moltmann has adjusted the Reformed concept of creation's purpose even more by suggesting that God created out of love—the overflowing love of the triune fellowship—and that God's glory and God's love are inextricably linked. One must not be elevated over the other. God glories in loving. Other Christian thinkers have suggested that God created in order to enjoy having a universe. For them the ultimate purpose of God in creation is an aesthetic one. God simply enjoys creating and the universe is like a work of art. In it God enjoys by expressing his artistic talents and powers.

All of these views of God's purpose in creation are viable products of reverent speculation. They only step outside of Christianity when and if they suggest that God *needed* to create the world *in order to actualize himself.* Such was and is the view of certain philosophers and theologians who follow them. The eighteenth-century German idealist philosopher G. W. F. Hegel argued in his speculative philosophy of religion that God created the universe in order to realize himself such that "without the world God would not be God." The world, then, is for Hegel God's counterpart and necessary to his very being. This is the essence of what is called *panentheism*—a philosophy of the God-world relationship found in the twentieth-century liberal theological movement known as process theology which, like Hegel, regards creation as necessary and coeternal with God. The result of any such view, of course, is a finitizing of God, a sacrifice of God's transcendent power and deity clearly contradicted by the apostle Paul's sermon to the Athenian philosophers in Acts 17 in which he declares that God needs nothing at all. Whatever God's exact purpose may have been in creation (and who can know the mind of God?) it must be one that was freely chosen and not imposed by any necessity.

## A Unitive Christian Vision of Creation

It is important that Christians look past the unnecessary and irrelevant debates that so often divide them from each other and focus on the core beliefs that have stood the test of time and are rooted firmly in original divine revelation in Jesus Christ and Scripture. Is there a contemporary vision of creation that is authentically Christian in those senses—rooted in revelation and consistent with the Great Tradition of Christian belief and teaching—that may unify Christians of various denominations and traditions? Why is this important? Besides the urgency of a unitive spirit among authentic Christian believers in an increasingly postmodern, pluralistic culture, there is also the urgency of the ecological crisis. Does Christianity have something to contribute to the unity of humankind and to the penultimate redemption of nature from destruction by pollution and exploitation? A rediscovery and reassertion of the essential Christian vision of creation as good because created by God with meaning and purpose would go far toward such unity and healing. If the world is God's good creation, as Christianity has always said when it is faithful to its own sources, then nature is worthy of being preserved and restored. Ultimately, of course, only God can renovate nature, and he promised to do it through the apostle Paul in Romans 8:19-23. In the meantime, however, Christians can anticipate God's restorative act and honor God's original creative act and declaration that its products were good by caring for the garden of nature. They are only likely to do it, however, if they have a strong belief in creation's essential goodness. Instead, so often, Christians assume from pious talk of "this world is not my home" and "the sweet by and by," that the physical world of creation—the earth—is not worthy of care.

Similarly, a unitive Christian belief about creation should hark back to the ancient and essential Christian belief that creation is not God but a reality under God's lordship. In an age when many who care for creation implicitly worship it as an extension of God (monism, emanationism), Christians need to hold fast together to the truth that the world of nature is entirely distinct from God—an order of reality under God and not of God's own substance.

Whether they prefer young earth creationism, theistic evolution, or progressive creationism and whether they are devoted to a view of the world as created for God's glory or for the covenant of redemption or out of divine aesthetic sensibilities, Christians can stand together in contrast to other worldviews, religions and philosophies that deify and worship nature or that reduce nature to an accident. Christians hold in common a heritage of a worldview that esteems the natural world highly while viewing it as less than God. The world is distinct from God and subordinate to God, but at the same time not separated from God and not alone or uncared for. Just as God raised the body of Jesus Christ from the tomb of death and glorified it to a new form of existence, so Christianity says God will raise creation from its bondage to decay—the curse under which it has fallen—and give it a new mode of glorified existence in new union of harmony with him (Rom 8:21). This vision of creation gives value to the world and hope for its eventual redemption; it motivates those who are grasped by it to work toward the healing of creation from all that corrupts it while at the same time acknowledging its ontological (not spatial) distance from deity.

# CHAPTER 8

# PROVIDENCE

## Limited *and* Detailed

Christians have always believed that the one true God, maker of heaven and earth, is also sovereign Lord of his creation. Both nature and history belong to him and he governs them and provides for them. As expressed by the popular Christian hymn "This Is My Father's World," "though the wrong seems oft so strong, God is the ruler yet." Another way of expressing Christian belief in God's providence is to affirm that God is *sovereign*. That is, God rules and reigns over all things such that no being and no event escapes his oversight and control. Scripture attests to God's providence or sovereignty repeatedly. In the Old Testament (as Christians traditionally call the Hebrew Bible) God says to the prophet Isaiah and through him to the people of Israel, "I form the light and create darkness, I bring prosperity and create disaster; I, the LORD, do all these things" (Is 45:7). The Psalms frequently testify to God's sovereign control of both nature and history. "Dominion belongs to the LORD and he rules over the nations" (Ps 22:28). In the New Testament Jesus emphasizes God's rulership: "Are not two sparrows sold for a penny? Yet not one of them will fall to the ground apart from the will of your Father. And even the very hairs of your head are all numbered" (Mt 10:29-30). The apostle Paul asserted God's authority and control in his speech to the Athenians. "And [God] is not served by human hands, as if he needed anything, because he himself gives all men life and breath and everything else. From one man he made every nation of men, . . . and he determined the times set for them and the exact places where they should live" (Acts 17:25-26).

These passages of Scripture, together with the beliefs already expounded in this book about God's greatness and creativity point undeniably toward what became and remains a powerful consensus of Christian belief about nature and history: *God is in charge and purposefully, powerfully guides nature and history such that his will always ultimately triumphs in and through (and sometimes in spite of) them.* As will be seen, Christian leaders and thinkers from the early church fathers through the medieval period and the reformations up into the modern and contemporary church have agreed together that nothing happens or can happen without God's permission and that God's ultimate will can never be thwarted; God always gets his way in the end. Whatever is happening in creation is within the purview of God's sovereign oversight, if not determinatively decreed, controlled and caused by God. Also, as we will see, many Christians qualify this consensus by distinguishing between two modes of God's will—God's *ideal* or *perfect will* and God's *permissive will.* For them, God's will always ultimately triumphs even if that includes allowing his perfect will to be thwarted by creaturely rebellion and refusal. Even they, however, affirm that in the end God wins and that whatever happens is at least allowed (permitted) by God; no creature can overcome God.

### Issues and Polarities of Christian Belief About Providence

Despite common affirmation of God's providence, the trouble is in the details of the doctrine. The Christian consensus must be identified and emphasized: *God is in charge of nature and history.* But what about evil and innocent suffering? Does God's providential sovereignty—his plan, power and control—extend to sin, immorality, inhumanity, cruelty, wars of aggression, genocide, abuse, torture, the pain of children, plagues and famine? Are these all "acts of God"? If so, in what sense is God good? If these are all "good" on some higher level such that God is justified in decreeing and causing them (even if only indirectly through secondary causes), then are they evil? And if they are not really evil why fight against them? The mind reels. What about free will? Are humans (let alone angels!) free moral agents such that we are truly responsible for our decisions and actions? Was Hitler God's instrument such that his genocidal cruelties were secretly willed and brought about by God? Or was Hitler (and other perpetrators of evil like him) a free and responsible moral agent whose war against everything good and godly temporarily thwarted God's perfect will?

While Christians have agreed that God is sovereign, that whatever happens in nature and history happens with God's permission, and that God's permission is always purposeful, Christians have not always believed alike about God's involvement with the manifest sin and evil in history and with the disasters of nature. Wide diversity and even acrimonious debate has existed among Christians over these issues. A well-known Christian layman and noted government official spoke to a college audience about his son's untimely death in a mountain-climbing accident and said, "God killed my son and that is what gives me the ability to accept my son's death." Another Christian spokesman of the same Protestant tradition said to a seminary audience, "when I lost my child I stopped telling grieving parents that God took their child; I no longer believe God makes bad things happen." And yet both men are noted, influential Christian spokesmen equally devoted to God and his church and equally believers in God's sovereignty and providential governing of nature and history.

It is important that Christians focus on their vast agreement about God's role in nature and history—God's sovereignty and providence—and allow for a certain amount of diversity of interpretation with regard to the details. Within the one great church of Jesus Christ over two thousand years both consensus and diversity have existed side by side. Occasionally, of course, a group of Christians decides to raise a particular interpretation of divine sovereignty and providence to the level of *status confessionis,* required doctrinal belief. Rarely does such a denomination or church believe other Christians who disagree are necessarily apostate. Some denominations and networks of churches insist only on the most basic belief in God's providence and allow tremendous diversity of interpretation within its ranks. Often, if not usually, however, tensions develop over time and divisions occur as people require more specific and dogmatic affirmations about God's control of nature and history. This has become one of the most divisive issues within Protestant Christian circles. Even within Roman Catholic theology some diversity of opinion about it coexists with the church's official, unifying teaching that God is sovereignly in control of all things.

## The Christian Consensus About God's Providence

The basis for Christian belief in God's sovereign, providential governance and control of all events both in nature and history has already been touched upon. Throughout Scripture the one God who is maker of heaven and earth and who is both perfectly great and perfectly good is also revealed as the one apart from whose power and permission absolutely nothing happens. Entire books of the canon of Scripture seem to have this truth as their primary theological witness. The book of Job, for example, narrates the mystery of God's involvement in the horrors of that righteous man's loss of health, property and family and ends with an affirmation of the importance of trust in God's goodness and mysterious ways. The New Testament book of Revelation points throughout to God's sovereign fulfillment of history in the completion of his plan through divine interventions and a new heaven and new earth.

There is a very real sense in which the entire Bible is one great "theodrama" of God's sovereign guidance of nature and history to a preordained end—the complete and perfect kingdom of God. And yet, that dramatic narrative plays out in a mysterious and complex manner through divine interaction with free agents. God always remains the superior partner in the relationship and is never thwarted, and yet humans play a significant role in how history unfolds. The Genesis story of Joseph indicates very directly that God orchestrated Joseph's life—including his brothers' conspiracy to sell him into Egyptian slavery—and yet, at the same time, it never detracts from the humans' roles in the plot and its stages. The same is true in the New Testament stories of Jesus' fate including his crucifixion. God planned for it to happen and somehow secretly and mysteriously orchestrated it, and yet there is no hint that those who betrayed, abandoned or executed him were less than fully free and responsible.

Scripture points to a paradox of divine-human synergism in history wherein God both proposes and disposes, and human agents also propose and dispose. And yet the outcome of everything is in God's hands and never finally or definitively in anyone else's hands. Human beings influence God but never thwart God. God controls human beings but never so as to rob them of freedom and responsibility. Nowhere is this paradox more clearly and yet subtly expressed than in Paul's great imperative, "work out your salvation with fear and trembling, for it is God who works in you to will and to act according to his good purpose" (Phil 2:12-13).

Based on these revelatory themes as well as on clear, logical deduction from the very nature of God as both great and good, the early church fathers, medieval thinkers, Protestant Reformers and post-Reformation Christian scholars and theologians all in chorus expressed the consensual Christian belief that *nature and history are sovereignly, providentially governed by God and nothing happens or can happen without God's permission.* Many people associate this high view of God's sovereignty over the courses of nature and history with the Protestant Reformer John Calvin. To be sure, Calvin highlighted it in a special way, and yet his own precursor, the Swiss Reformer Ulrich Zwingli, wrote an entire book on divine providence in which he stressed repeatedly God's providential control—even God's causation of sin and evil. Calvin's explication of the doctrine of providence was a bit more cautious and subtle than Zwingli's, even if in the end they amounted to the same view that has come to be called "meticulous providence," that is, belief in God's control of all details. It is wrong, however, to link Christian belief in God's sovereignty and providential governance of all things in creation exclusively or even especially with those Reformed Protestant theologians. The early church fathers also touted these beliefs as essential to Christianity.

They lived and wrote in a culture of confusion about the forces controlling human lives, natural events and history. The Greeks and Romans followed a bewildering array of teachings about why events occur, as did many within the early Christian churches. Dualism (as explained in the previous chapter) was a powerful and popular option that appealed to many people. It seemed to answer the question of evil by making it the work of an evil or demented god and a byproduct of matter. The Gnostics claimed that nature and history are not governed by God but are meaningless realms of fallen reality in which sparks of God's own substance have fallen; many Gnostics denied God's involvement in these realms. Followers of the pantheons of gods and goddesses attributed causation of events to those beings. Others, like the Stoics, believed that all is determined and as it should be; they tended to equate the divine with nature itself. For them providence was simply the blind outworking of divine nature.

Against all of these alternative beliefs the early church fathers asserted the Christian view that God is in charge and orders and arranges both nature and history for his own good purposes. In his five books *Against Heresies*, Irenaeus—with some justice considered Christianity's first real theologian—

affirmed both human free will and divine appointment and arrangement of all events. On the one hand he writes of "God thus determining all things beforehand," and on the other hand of "no coercion with God, . . . in man, as well as in angels, He has placed the power of choice."[1] Nowhere did Irenaeus or most other early Eastern church fathers attempt to iron out the seeming conflict between those two claims; they simply left them as truths in tension with each other but both undeniably true.

The first church father and theologian to attempt to develop a more rational, comprehensive and systematic account of God's sovereignty and providence was Augustine of North Africa. Before him the consensus was relatively simple and included equal weight placed on God's sovereignty and limited human freedom. The great North African church father Tertullian explicated Christian belief in divine sovereignty and providence more than any theologian up until Augustine almost two hundred years later. Tertullian followed the general trend of Eastern church fathers such as Irenaeus; he emphasized that absolutely nothing has ever happened or could happen without God's foresight and permission and that in many cases God directly intervenes to cause certain events to happen. At the same time, Tertullian taught that God's sovereignty never takes away the moral freedom and responsibility of human persons:

> It is not the part of good and solid faith to refer all things to the will of God in such a manner . . . that each individual should so flatter himself by saying that "nothing is done without His permission," as to make us fail to understand that there is a something in our own power.[2]

Tertullian stressed the unity-in-distinction of God's "absolute will" and "permissive will" and insisted that Christians believe that God perfectly and absolutely wills and renders certain some events and only passively permits other things such as sin and evil. According to the Christian attorney-turned-theologian, however, these are not two opposed wills of God but two sides of God's one sovereign will and power.

Two centuries later Augustine came closer to breaking the paradox in his own later writings on God's sovereignty and providence. To an extent greater than any Christian thinker before him the Bishop of Hippo inter-

---

[1] Irenaeus *Against Heresies* 1.520, 518, as quoted in Benjamin Wirt Farley, *The Providence of God* (Grand Rapids, Mich.: Baker, 1988), p. 82.
[2] Tertullian *On Exhortation to Chastity* 4.50-51, as quoted in Farley, p. 97.

preted God's providence as absolute, meticulous planning and controlling of all events. When Rome began to fall to invading tribes, many Christians wondered if God's will was being thwarted. They had come to identify Rome with the kingdom of God so that its fall to so-called barbarians raised serious questions about God's sovereignty. Augustine wrote a massive treatise on God's providence titled *The City of God,* in which he argued that no human society is identical with the kingdom of God and that God sovereignly and for his own reasons raises up and throws down human empires. According to Augustine, God's plan and purpose is never thwarted and never goes awry even if that seems to be the case to finite minds. God's foreordained plan is always being fulfilled in everything. Although he did not intend to deny free will and argued against fatalism, the great North African church father left little room for contingency in history. Christians are simply to trust that whatever is happening is somehow the outworking of God's sovereign plan. Even what seems to be evil is part of that great divine plan. While God does not cause evil, God plans for it and controls it. Even Satan is God's instrument. Augustine, then, is the real father of Christian belief in "meticulous providence."

Throughout the medieval era of Christianity, Catholic philosophers and theologians speculated endlessly about divine sovereignty and human free will. All agreed, however, that God is in charge of human affairs as well as of nature such that nothing happens or can happen without God's permission. Thomas Aquinas, almost certainly the most influential medieval theologian, argued that God is the cause of the entire network of events including all human decisions and actions, but he also argued that God's causality does not extend to direct causation of sin and evil. How can this be? In his massive, multivolume *Summa Theologiae,* the "Angelic Doctor" explained that God's causation of nature and history is complex such that while God is the cause of the whole and thereby the ultimate cause of each part (e.g., particular human decisions and actions), God's "final causation" (i.e., ultimate causation) of the whole works itself out in the details through "secondary causes" such as human wills. In this manner Thomas tried to reconcile Augustinian determinism with monastic belief in freedom and responsibility. Whether he was successful is still much debated. In any case, Thomas and all medieval Catholic theologians believed in and strongly promoted God's sovereign control over both nature and history such that nothing escapes God's plan, provision and governance.

The Protestant Reformers did not challenge the early and medieval Christian consensus about belief in God's sovereignty and providence. While Martin Luther and Ulrich Zwingli—the two earliest Protestant Reformers—may have disagreed about the nature of Christ's presence in the sacrament of the Lord's Supper, they agreed completely about divine providence. Zwingli wrote a treatise entitled *On Providence* in which he averred that "if anything exists, lives, and moves beyond the jurisdiction of the Deity, man can with equal right be said to be beyond God's jurisdiction. . . . Thus there will simply be no Deity."[3] In other words, Zwingli argued that if there is any real randomness, contingency or uncertainty in nature or history God is not God. The only alternative to meticulous providence, then, is atheism. Is God, then, the author of sin and evil? Zwingli did not shy away from that conclusion. Unlike many of his later followers Zwingli drew out and affirmed the logical conclusion of his strong view of divine omnicausality: "Upon God, as upon the head of the family, no law has been imposed. Therefore He sinneth not when He does in man that which is sin to man but not to Himself."[4]

John Calvin, who was influenced by both Luther and Zwingli but wished to present a somewhat more subtle doctrine of God's sovereign providence, explained in his *Institutes of the Christian Religion* that God foreordains everything that happens in nature and in human history but that God is not the cause of evil itself for sin and evil lie in the intentions of persons. God foreordains and controls all actions and all events, but does not cause the evil intentions of people's hearts and minds. While "no wind ever arises or increases except by God's express command"[5] (and Calvin makes clear that he includes in this sweeping affirmation of divine control all human decisions and actions), God is not stained by any guilt for the sin and evil that human beings conceive in their hearts. In the end, however, Calvin cannot escape the charge that he does make God the author of sin and evil in his strong account of meticulous providence:

> To sum up, since God's will is said to be the cause of all things, I have made his providence the determinative principle for all human plans and works, not only

---

[3]Ulrich Zwingli, *On Providence and Other Essays,* edited for Samuel Macauley Jackson by William John Hinke (Durham, N.C.: Labyrinth, 1983), p. 158.
[4]Ibid., p. 177.
[5]John Calvin *Institutes of the Christian Religion* 1.16.7, p. 206.

in order to display its force in the elect, who are ruled by the Holy Spirit, but also to compel the reprobate to obedience.[6]

The context makes clear that for Calvin God's compelling the reprobate to "obedience" means God's control over their decisions and actions such that they could not do otherwise than disobey. Reformed theology generally—following Augustine, Zwingli and Calvin—has affirmed this high, detailed view of God's sovereign control of nature and history and has often settled for appeal to mystery and paradox when asked how God is not, then, the author of sin and evil.

Many Protestant Christian theologians after the early stages of the sixteenth-century Protestant Reformation sought to soften the Augustinian-Reformed interpretation of God's sovereignty by affirming a Tertullian-like distinction between God's foreordination and God's permission. The seventeenth-century Dutch Protestant theologian Jacob Arminius strongly affirmed God's providence—to the extent of insisting that absolutely nothing whatever can happen in either nature or history without "divine concurrence"—but at the same time argued for divine self-limitation to allow for genuine human free will and to explain how God is sovereign and yet not responsible for sin and evil. Gradually a gap opened up and widened between Protestants who affirmed absolute divine sovereignty and meticulous providence and those who, like Arminius and his followers, affirmed a limited divine control over events such that God merely permits and does not foreordain or cause sinful, evil acts or innocent suffering.

A careful examination of the Great Tradition of Christian thought about God's role in nature and history reveals that the vast majority of Eastern Orthodox, Roman Catholic and Protestant thinkers of all major traditions have affirmed and do affirm God's sovereign control of the whole of both nature and history such that in spite of sin and evil God's ultimate will and purpose (as distinct from his perfect or ideal will for how he would like things to be) cannot be thwarted. The Christian consensus may be summarized in three broad affirmations: (1) God is the good and just governor of nature and history in that he not only created but also sustains, guides, provides for and judges everything; (2) Nothing at all can happen in either nature or history that God does not at least allow; (3) God's sovereign gov-

---

[6]Ibid., 1.18.2, p. 232.

ernance of nature and history is both "general" (i.e., through natural laws built into the processes) and "special" (i.e., extending to details of people's lives). Within that broad consensus there is plenty of room for real diversity and even disagreement about the details of God's involvement in natural events and human affairs.

## Alternatives to Christian Belief in God's Providence

The broad Christian consensus comes into focus when seen in the context of alternative views of God's involvement in nature and history. Occasionally even Christian thinkers have proposed beliefs about God's governance that implicitly if not explicitly deny not only the consensus but also the revelatory witness to God's greatness and goodness. It is only with great fear and trepidation and even tears that any of us should ever exclude fellow Christian believers from the sphere of authentic Christianity, but unfortunately that must happen occasionally. Three main alternatives to Christian belief in God's providence present such stark challenges to God's revealed nature and character and to the Christian consensus about God's relationship with nature and history that they must be condemned as contrary to Christianity, even if they are held and promoted by people who sincerely believe they are Christians. These three alternatives are *fatalism, Deism* and *process panentheism*. They are not denominations or organizations; they are views of God's involvement with the natural and social worlds that have become popular in pews and pulpits. Usually they are not labeled by these terms by the persons who hold them, but these labels do fairly describe three main alternative viewpoints that appear and exercise detrimental influence within Christian circles.

*Fatalism* is not identical with divine determinism. Augustine developed and affirmed a kind of divine determinism of all things in *The City of God*. In at least some of his writings Luther was a divine determinist as were Zwingli and Calvin. Many Christians believe in divine determinism as meticulous providence. The difference between true fatalism and divine determinism lies in the issue of *personal, purposive planning*. That is, true fatalism denies intelligent design (planning, purpose, involvement) within and behind history. To fatalists, nature and history (conceived as separate or as united) are ruled by blind forces that exclude not only contingency but also meaning and purpose. A famous 1980s bumper sticker cliché exclaimed, "Stuff happens!" (Well, it actually used a more earthy noun.) A popular coffee mug carried the expression "Life's a bitch and then you die!" These are vulgar expressions of a popular belief of many people around the world and which even occasionally appears in Christian churches and organizations. They express in vulgar ways the worldview that natural events and social-political events merely happen without any overarching plan or purpose and are therefore devoid of ultimate meaning. Nature is ruled by a blind watchmaker; history is simply a meaningless course of events without goal or direction. Fatalism adds into that nihilistic worldview, "whatever will be, will be," and so we humans need to find ways to adjust to, if not enjoy, inevitabilities.

How can fatalism—as described above—be held by Christians? To the extent that a person or group is actually committed to fatalism, authentic Christianity is lacking. However, there can be no doubt that many people who are members of Christian churches embrace fatalism instead of belief in divine providence. This writer has heard Christians exclaim fatalistically that "history is meaningless" and "this world is not my home [because it is ruled by fate and therefore meaningless], I'm just a-passin' through." Fatalism often appears in the guise of super-spirituality in which people who hold it combine it with an other-worldly focus. Nature and history are ruled by blind forces and no meaning exist in them, but a purely spiritual heaven exists where meaning is to be found. Some existentialist theologians have seemed to embrace such a Gnostic-like dualism. The German existentialist New Testament scholar and theologian Rudolf Bultmann strongly distinguished between *Historie* (events happening in ordinary world history) and *Geschichte* (the realm of personal history, self-understanding, psycho-spiritual history) and located meaning and purpose only in the latter. Fatalism comes in many guises and some of them appear to be very spiritual. On closer examination, however, all fatalism is antithetical to the biblical witness and the historic Christian consensus. If God is in charge (whether all-controlling or not), then nature and history cannot be meaninglessly ruled by blind forces of chance or mechanistic causes.

A second popular alternative to Christian belief in providence is *Deism*. Deism is a very broad category. Here it refers to that worldview that developed and rose to prominence in eighteenth-century Europe and North America together with the Enlightenment and scientific revolutions that tended to relegate providence to a general realm. That is, Deism views "divine providence" (often a term Deists use in place of *God*) as the divinely-established network of natural laws that govern both nature and history. For most Deists, both nature and history are full of meaning and purpose, but God is neither immanent (personally present and directly involved) nor intervening. In a popular image often associated with Deism God is pictured as a cosmic clock-maker who created the universe, built it to run according to natural laws immanent within its machinery, and then departed from it except, perhaps, as an observer. Whether such an image is true to the intentions of all the Deists of the eighteenth century (such as John Toland and Matthew Tyndal) is debatable, but popular Deism tends to view the realms of nature and history in such a manner. They are not ruled by blind chance or fate, but by divinely-instilled natural laws. Why is that inconsistent with Christian belief? Simply because it gives far too much current autonomy to creation and tends to rele-gate God to the status of a benign, absentee landlord of the universe. The popular song "From a Distance" (released in 1990) portrayed such a God-world relationship. In Deism, then, God exists and was involved at the begin-ning of the world, but God is now and into the indefinite future (and perhaps forever) uninvolved.

The only real value such a God can have is as an explanation for the beginning of the world (which naturalism, even with appeal to a big bang, cannot provide) and as a moral standard-giver. The great German enlighten-ment philosopher Immanuel Kant (d. 1804) was some kind of a Deist. For him, the main function of the idea of God was to guarantee moral objectiv-ity. Without God right and wrong would have little objective meaning. Such a "God," however, is at best a shadow of the intimately involved, transcen-dent-immanent God of the Bible whose creative and governing activity is continuing and who intervenes graciously, compassionately and powerfully in both nature and history. Prayer of supplication is meaningless within a deistic worldview. Do Deists exist today? Without doubt. In an article profil-ing the personal faiths of community leaders, a local newspaper featured a science professor of a large Christian university. The professor admitted to being a Deist as well as a member of a Methodist church.

The third main alternative to Christian belief in divine providence is *proc-ess panentheism*. Many forms of panentheism exist and all have in common belief that God and the creation are coeternal, reciprocally related, interde-pendent realities. Process theology is a twentieth-century form of philosoph-ical theology that has infiltrated and corrupted much of so-called mainstream Protestantism. It follows the metaphysical speculations of philos-ophers Alfred North Whitehead and Charles Hartshorne and attempts to

integrate them with biblical faith. In the end, however, process theology sac-
rifices the latter to the former. According to process panentheists evil and
innocent suffering—such as the holocausts of the twentieth century—are
neither caused nor even allowed by God. Process panentheists completely
reject any classical account of divine sovereignty and providence in order to
rescue God from responsibility for genocide. If God could have prevented
Auschwitz, they claim, he should have. If he didn't (but could have), then he
is not perfectly good. If he foreordained it (meticulous providence), then he
is positively evil.

Process panentheists such as Methodist theologian John Cobb, who
wrote *God and the World* (Philadelphia: Westminster Press, 1969), argue that
God's only recourse in the face of a recalcitrant world is *divine persuasion
toward the good*. God is neither all-powerful nor able to intervene to prevent
or interrupt evil. The world is not God's project and God is neither in charge
nor in control of it. And yet, Cobb and other process theologians claim to
believe in divine providence. How so? According to Cobb, "It no longer
means that God exercises a monopoly of power and compels everything to
be just as it is. It means instead that he exercises the optimum persuasive
power in relation to whatever is."[7] Thus, God is not responsible for the
world except to the extent he is able to lure it toward his vision of the greatest good. Never, however, will God's perfect will be achieved or accomplished. God's kingdom, according to process theology, is always coming
but never arriving. This vision of the God-world relationship may succeed in
getting God off the hook for sin and evil, but it does so only by sacrificing all
hope for any ultimate divine victory over the corruption of nature and history that has resulted from the fall of humanity into sin. Furthermore, it
undermines the efficacy of petitionary prayer and inevitably portrays God as
pathetic and powerless. Process theology turns the old proverb "man proposes but God disposes" on its head. Instead, it tells us, "God proposes but
man disposes." This is not Christianity.

### Diverse Christian Visions of God's Providence

In spite of considerable agreement about God's providential provision for
and governance of both nature and history (as described earlier in this chapter), Christians have developed different models or visions of divine sover-

---

[7]John B. Cobb Jr., *God and the World* (Philadelphia: Westminster Press, 1969), p. 90.

eignty—especially with regard to human freedom and the problem of evil. All Christians agree that God is sovereign (in spite of the claim of some Christians—especially of the strongly Reformed heritage—that sovereignty necessarily means meticulous providence by means of omnicausality). But what does sovereignty mean? Does belief in God's sovereignty and providence necessarily include belief that God foreordained, for example, the fall of humanity and all of its evil consequences? Does belief in divine providence necessarily include belief that God foreordains and somehow mysteriously wills the agonies of sick and abused children? Must a Christian believe that God willed and rendered certain (even if only through secondary causes) the Holocaust? These problems and questions have given rise over the centuries to different Christian perspectives on the details of providence. At the very least, as we have seen, Christian belief affirms that God is in charge of both nature and history and nothing can happen without his permission and everything that does happen has meaning and purpose. God fits it into a plan. But does God take risks? Or is everything that happens secretly willed and orchestrated by God?

Three main interpretations of divine providence have developed among Christian thinkers, and all three can be justified by appeal to divine revelation, Christian history, Christian experience and reason. In other words, while not all three can be equally true, all three are possibly valid views or models of divine providence and should be allowed to coexist within the community of Christians—even if some specific denominations choose to embrace one of them to the exclusion of the others. They are *meticulous providence, limited providence* and *open theism*. Among Protestants the first one is especially associated with the Reformed tradition that stems from Zwingli and Calvin, but it actually goes back to at least Augustine in the early fifth century. The second view is especially associated with Jacob Arminius and those who call themselves Arminians, although many who have never heard that label or used it for themselves hold a similar view. The third is a relatively recent development and may be seen as an adjustment of the second view. Here I will describe and examine each one briefly and show why each one is compatible with orthodox, consensual Christian belief.

*Meticulous providence* is that view of divine sovereignty in relation to nature and history already described as Augustine's, Zwingli's and Calvin's belief. Each added his own spin, but the essence of the model is absolute, meticulous planning, willing and controlling by God such that there is in nature no "maverick molecule" (contingency, chaos) and in history no "divine risk." Whatever happens in nature and history is completely, exhaustively willed by God and not merely permitted by God.

The very distinction between divine foreordination and permission is problematic in this view.[8] Some advocates of meticulous providence use the language of "permission" when speaking of God's relationship with sin and evil, but they make clear that such "permission" by God is never passive; it is active in that God wills it to happen while not actually, directly causing it. Some use the terminology of "rendering certain" when referring to the details of nature and history. Thus, they would say, God "renders certain" even sin and evil but in such a manner as to be untainted by guilt. God's sovereignty over nature and history, in this view, includes omnicausality, but some modes of God's causation are direct and unmediated and some are indirect—through secondary and even tertiary causes. According to Christian philosopher and theologian Paul Helm, the key to this view of providence—which he considers more than merely one option—is the belief that God never takes risks. The world contains no surprises for God; everything in it is exactly as God wants it to be. And yet, even then, proponents of meticulous providence have to introduce further subtle distinctions. God does not "want" or "will" everything in the same way. God may *wish* that his ultimate good (e.g., his glory) could be achieved without evils such as the Holocaust, and yet he *wills* the Holocaust because it is somehow necessary for the greatest good.

Belief in meticulous providence is pervasive within especially scholarly and pastoral circles in conservative Protestantism—especially those that are rooted in the Reformed tradition. It finds support in biblical references to God's sovereignty over nature and history and especially in Romans 9—11, where the apostle Paul attributes all kinds of things to God's mysterious, sovereign will and ways and forbids objection to God's deity on the basis of the phenomena of the world. Meticulous providence gives great hope and comfort to many people who seek nothing in tragedy except meaning. To trust that every tragic event somehow serves a greater purpose and is controlled by God is tremendously comforting to many Christians.

In addition, reason seems to support meticulous providence. If God is

---

[8]For a book-length and very astute exposition and recommendation of this view of divine providence, see Paul Helm, *The Providence of God* (Downers Grove, Ill.: InterVarsity Press, 1994).

God, so the argument goes, then how can anything—down to the least puff of existence—escape his control? Would such a God—who takes risks and has to cope with unwilled consequences—really be God? Would such a being be "the being greater than which none can be conceived?" Influential Reformed theologian and apologist R. C. Sproul implies in his writings and radio addresses that the only genuine alternative to meticulous providence is atheism. That is not to say that everyone who rejects meticulous providence is actually an atheist. Rather, Sproul and others like him simply believe that any authentic Christian who rejects meticulous providence is not thinking clearly.[9]

On the other hand, Christian critics of meticulous providence reject it because they see no way in which it can avoid making God the author of sin and evil—something even most Christian proponents of that view wish to avoid. One Reformed theologian who has turned against meticulous providence presents this critique quite forcefully in the context of the horrors of South African apartheid:

> There are distressingly many things that happen on earth that are not the will of God (Luke 7:30 and every other sin mentioned in the Bible), that are against his will, and that stem from the incomprehensible and senseless sin in which we are born, in which the greater part of mankind lives, and in which Israel persisted, and against which even the "holiest men" . . . struggled all their days (David, Peter). God has only one course of action for this and that is to provide for its atonement by having it all crucified and buried with Christ. To try to interpret all these things by means of the concept of a plan of God, creates intolerable difficulties and gives rise to more exceptions than regularities. But the most important objection is that the idea of a plan is against the message of the Bible since God himself becomes incredible if that against which he has fought with power, and for which he sacrificed his only Son, was nevertheless somehow part and parcel of his eternal counsel.[10]

The second Christian interpretation is the main alternative to the first: *limited providence*. Here *limited* means really *self-limiting* in the sense that this view believes that God *could* control nature and history meticulously but

---

[9]See R. C. Sproul, *Not a Chance: The Myth of Chance in Modern Science and Cosmology* (Grand Rapids, Mich.: Baker, 1999), and *Almighty Over All: Understanding the Sovereignty of God* (Grand Rapids, Mich.: Baker, 1999).

[10]Adrio König, *Here Am I: A Believer's Reflection on God* (Grand Rapids, Mich.: Eerdmans, 1982), pp. 198-99.

chooses not to. Instead, in this view, God restrains himself for the sake of a certain, limited degree of autonomy of both nature and human agency. Limited providence regards God as presently sovereign in both nature and history *de jure* (by right) but not yet sovereign *de facto* (in actuality); only in the future, when his kingdom fully arrives, will God be sovereign *de facto* as well as *de jure*. This view necessarily includes belief in divine risk in the sense that even if God foreknew all that would happen in creation (nature and history) down to the details (including sin and evil), he took a risk in deciding to create such a world and actually creating it, because it contains much that God does not perfectly, ideally will to happen—including his own suffering and death through Jesus Christ on the cross. This view affirms God's omnipotent ability to control and his permission of whatever is happening. But it portrays God's causality in providence as more general and less particular or detailed. The same South African revisionist Reformed theologian quoted above expresses this view well:

> It is better to proceed from the idea that God had a certain goal in mind (the covenant, or the kingdom of God, or the new earth—which are all the same thing viewed from different angles) that he will achieve with us, without us, or even against us. To use a few examples: together with us he brings the world to faith in himself; without us he gives us the new earth; and against us he will make his church one in the truth.[11]

The great Christian speaker and writer A. W. Tozer expressed a version of limited providence in his chapter on "The Sovereignty of God" in his classic *The Knowledge of the Holy: The Attributes of God: Their Meaning in the Christian Life.* There he presented a homely illustration of the God-world relationship in providence. God is like an ocean-liner captain taking his ship across the Atlantic from New York to Liverpool, England. On the journey many things happen on the ship that are against the captain's will, but he allows them to take place. Yet nothing that happens on the ship will stop it from arriving at its destination toward which the captain competently and inexorably steers it. So it is with God and nature/history, according to limited providence. God does not will the fall of humanity and all of its consequences, and he certainly does not will the Holocaust or the agonies of a dying child. He permits them. Why? In *Evil and the Christian God,* Christian

---

[11]Ibid., p. 199.

philosopher Michael W. Peterson argues that God permits some gratuitous evils (evils that are not necessary for the achievement of a greater good) in order to preserve the freedom and moral responsibility of the world. If God stepped in to halt every instance of gratuitous evil, the world would be a completely different place—one without the significant risk that is necessary for significant moral freedom.[12]

Critics of limited providence—such as R. C. Sproul and other strong believers in the Augustinian/Reformed model of meticulous providence—regard it as inconsistent with both reason and divine revelation. Many of its strongest critics argue that limited providence—which is a view widely held especially by non-Reformed Christians—gives too much credit to human freedom and agency, too little credit to divine power and sovereignty, and requires belief in uncaused effects. That is, if God is not the ultimate cause of even human acts of sin, what is their cause? The will, critics argue, cannot be the cause, because the will itself depends on desire for motivation. Where do the controlling desires of human beings come from? The debate between proponents of meticulous providence and limited providence will no doubt continue as long as Christians "see through a glass darkly" and not yet "face to face." And yet, they should embrace one another as fellow Christian believers within the one, invisible and universal church of God and know when and where to stop the polemical arguments against each other and work and worship together in spite of significant differences over details.

The third view is the most controversial one within orthodox Christianity, and some traditional Christian thinkers—especially those committed to meticulous providence—would place this one in the category of "alternatives to the Christian consensus," that is, in the category of heresies. It is variously known as *open theism* and *openness of God theology*. It was introduced to the Christian church for consideration by five authors in a volume titled *The Openness of God: A Biblical Challenge to the Traditional Understanding of God* (Downers Grove, Ill.: InterVarsity Press, 1994). The view of divine providence especially associated with open theism was also expounded in John Sanders's *The God Who Risks: A Theology of Providence* (Downers Grove, Ill.: InterVarsity Press, 1998). Nearly all open theists were previously believers in limited providence. They began to examine certain problems in that view such as how God can take risks if he knows with abso-

---

[12]Michael Peterson, *Evil and the Christian God* (Grand Rapids, Mich.: Baker, 1982).

lute, definite foreknowledge exactly what is going to happen and how humans can have genuine, libertarian free will (i.e., free will that is not compatible with determinism and in which the person can do otherwise) if God knows infallibly and exhaustively what they are going to do (because then they could not do otherwise). Open theists explored Scripture with fresh eyes and found numerous narratives about God changing his mind in response to prayers of supplication and concluded that both traditional beliefs about divine providence are mistaken. They reinterpreted providence as God's resourceful and powerful response to humanity within the frameworks of nature and history. According to open theism, God does not know with absolute certainty all that the future holds, but he is able to predict events and respond in such a way that his ultimate and final will for the future is never thwarted.

Open theism is a relatively new view of providence and may be only an adjustment to limited providence. If so, it is a significant adjustment and yet one that retains the essentials of a Christian view of divine sovereignty. In open theism God is omnipotent and interactive and assures that his will for history will be accomplished. Open theism has no hint of process theology's denial of divine sovereignty and power. Neither is there any hint of fatalism. Open theists tend to view meticulous providence as too close to fatalism, limited providence as an inconsistent and unstable middle ground, and process theology as hopelessly liberal in accommodation to Whitehead's organic philosophy. They are attempting to develop a new view that returns to the biblical narrative of a God fully and personally interactive with humanity who remains always the one in charge even if not in control. John Sanders expresses the open theist or risk-taking view of divine providence best:

> The survey of the biblical materials showed that God enters into genuine give-and-take relations with humans; what God wants does not always come about. The description of the divine nature as loving, wise, faithful and almighty promotes thinking of divine sovereignty in terms of general sovereignty, in which God chooses to macromanage most things while leaving open the option of micromanaging some things. This was God's sovereign choice. In grace God grants humans a role in collaborating with him on the course that human history takes. God provides "space" for us to operate and in so doing makes it possible that some of the specific goals he would like to see fulfilled may not come about. Nonetheless, God graciously works with us, being creatively resourceful, to achieve his overall project of establishing loving relationships

with significant others. God is yet working with us to open up new possibilities for the future. God faithfully works toward his overarching goals while remaining flexible as to how he brings these about.[13]

Open theism's critics have often treated it as a straw man rather than portraying it fairly and then revealing its true weaknesses. Many of its harshest condemnations have come from Reformed theologians whose arguments against open theism are familiar arguments against all limited providence (e.g., Arminianism in general). Some critics have attempted to lump it together with process panentheism, which is clearly a mistake in that open theists affirm *creatio ex nihilo,* divine omnipotence and God's supernatural intervention to bring about his ultimate closure to history in his kingdom. More cautious and fair critics have argued that open theism is suspect because it is in tension with the Great Tradition of Christian belief about God's absolute omniscience including foreknowledge, and that it has great difficulty explaining how God can prophesy future events that depend on human decisions and actions that seem to be morally free and responsible. To be sure, there are weaknesses in open theism, and whether it will be defeated by its critics and either disappear or move outside the circle of authentic Christianity is yet to be seen. But so far there is no good reason to condemn it as heterodox; open theism deserves to be treated as one legitimate option for interpreting and envisioning divine sovereignty and providence.

### A Unitive Christian View of Providence

Christians need to rediscover and rally together around a distinctively Christian view of God's sovereignty over nature and history in spite of deep differences about the details. Whether one prefers the strong Augustinian-Reformed model of meticulous providence or the Eastern Orthodox-Arminian model of limited providence or the contemporary open theism model, one can affirm with the Great Tradition and all true Christians everywhere that "though the wrong seems oft so strong, God is the ruler yet." A unifying vision of divine sovereignty and providence will seek to be faithful to the revelation of God in Jesus Christ and the biblical witness as well as to the main contours of the Great Tradition of Christian thought. It will avoid those worldviews such as fatalism, Deism and process panentheism that deny

---

[13]John Sanders, *The God Who Risks: A Theology of Providence* (Downers Grove, Ill.: InterVarsity Press, 1998), pp. 235-36.

God's gifts of purpose and closure to history. It will seek to avoid extremes that make God the author of sin and evil, thereby reducing their sinfulness and evilness and calling God's character into question, or that remove God from intimate and powerful involvement in the world.

It seems to this writer, and to many other evangelical Christians, that the best common ground for a unifying vision of divine sovereignty and providence lies somewhere in or around the view here labeled limited providence. Call it what you will, it is the view held by most Christians around the world and the one affirmed by all early Christian fathers up until Augustine in the early fifth century. It holds together, in some tension, essential Christian beliefs such as God's personal care and powerful involvement in both nature and history and human moral freedom and responsibility. It views God as most definitely in charge of the world without portraying him as the puppet-master who manipulates everyone and everything. It accounts for the polarities of revelation in which, for example, Jesus taught his disciples to pray, "thy kingdom come on earth as it is in heaven" (what is the point of praying that if God's will is always already being done—as meticulous providence claims?) and taught that God's "eye is on the sparrow."

# CHAPTER 9

# HUMANITY

## Essentially Good *and* Existentially Estranged

Ever since the Enlightenment of the seventeenth and eighteenth centuries Western thinkers—both secular and religious—have focused great attention on the nature of humanity. British essayist Alexander Pope expressed one aspect of the spirit of the Age of Reason in his couplet "Know then thyself; seek not God to scan; the proper study of mankind is man" *(Essay on Man)*. Before the cultural revolution known as the Enlightenment, most people thought they knew what humanity was. At least there was general agreement that humanity is a special creature of God's made in his image and likeness, composed of body and soul, fallen but redeemable.

**Issues and Polarities of Christian Belief About Humanity**
The Enlightenment and its aftermath raised serious questions about this consensus on the nature of humanity. The rise of naturalism throughout the nineteenth century and into the twentieth century seemed to pit modern science against belief in humanity's transcendent status over nature. Idealist philosophies and various forms of mysticism attempted to rescue humanity's special nature in the face of the new discoveries and theories of evolutionary

science by pointing to humanity's powers of consciousness and self-transcendence. All in all, the question of humanity's nature came to the forefront of philosophy, science and theology in new ways and with special urgency in the twentieth century.

And yet early Christian thinkers and church fathers wrestled with questions about humanity's nature and condition in their own pluralistic Greek and Roman culture. Many different views of humanity swirled around them, and they had to develop a rough consensus of Christian belief over against some of those views, especially when they infiltrated the churches. Are human beings pawns of the gods or godlets themselves? The Gnostics posed the most serious challenge to apostolic Christianity by promoting belief in humanity's (or some humans') inner divinity. In the face of such ancient and modern challenges Christians have developed out of the materials of divine revelation a rough consensus about human nature and existence. That consensus has seldom, if ever, taken on the status of dogma—essential belief—in the same way as the Christian consensus about Jesus Christ and the Trinity. Few creeds or formal confessional statements of Christian churches include detailed expressions of what must be believed about this subject. And yet, a careful reading of the church fathers, medieval Christian thinkers, Protestant Reformers and modern Christians reveals an amazing common ground of belief that distinguishes Christianity from all secular and pagan philosophies.

Unfortunately, many contemporary Christians are almost completely unfamiliar with this consensual Christian tradition of belief about humanity beyond its bare bones. They may know that Christianity includes belief in both physical and spiritual aspects of humanity (body, soul/spirit) and they may know that Christianity teaches that humans are created in God's image and likeness and that in spite of that they are fallen into sin, but they are often unaware of what those concepts of humanity mean and what they exclude. Many Christians, for example, confuse belief in a spiritual aspect of humanity with a Gnostic-like belief in inner divinity. They often tend also to interpret the "image of God" *(imago Dei)* that way or think of it as pointing to a physical likeness between humans and God. Finally, the whole concept of original sin—fallenness—is confusing to most contemporary Christians and is quickly being forgotten. It is important that Christians rediscover authentic Christian belief about human nature and existence in a time when many non-Christian ideas about humanity are infiltrating the churches.

What are the main issues surrounding Christian belief about humanity?

Three stand out as especially important: first, the dual nature of the human being as both natural-physical and transcendent-spiritual; second, the status of humans as created in God's image and likeness; third, the condition of humans as fallen, sinful, estranged from God and their own true being. These issues can be expressed in questions that pose false alternatives; the answer to all of them is a qualified *yes*. Are human beings part of nature or above nature? (Another way of presenting that same question asks, are human beings mortal or immortal?) Are humans essentially good or essentially evil? Are humans sinners because they sin or do they sin because they are sinners? These are not trick questions. They point to polarities in human nature and existence that Christian belief seeks to preserve.

According to Christianity, and in contrast with most other views of humanity, human beings are *both* animals (natural, biological beings who are mortal) *and* transcendent to nature (spiritual, possessing a supranatural quality, immortal). According to Christianity, humans are *both* essentially good *and* existentially estranged. According to Christianity, humans are *both* sinners because they sin *and* always already sinners. And yet these dual beliefs of Christianity have given rise to much confusion, conflict and controversy. In this chapter we will explore the basics of Christian belief about these matters and then examine alternatives to that Christian anthropology (view of human nature and existence). We will then continue to a description and critical evaluation of a few variations of belief about humanity within Christianity and conclude with a few remarks about a unifying Christian belief about humanity that is both faithful and relevant to the contemporary cultural situation.

## The Christian Consensus About Humanity

There are three essential Christian perspectives on human nature and existence that stand in stark contrast with most other anthropological viewpoints. First, *humans are both animal* (physical beings that are part of nature) and *spiritual* (beings that transcend nature and physical existence). Second, *humans are God's special creatures who possess the gift of God's own image and likeness.* Third, *humans are born "damaged goods" in the sense of inheriting a spiritual corruption that pervades every aspect of their being and leads inevitably to personal acts of disobedience to God* (that is, they are all sinners even before they commit "sins"). This third belief is known in Christian theology as "original sin" and "inherited depravity."

In each case, as in many other cases of Christian beliefs discussed in this book, there exists a tendency on the part of both Christians and non-Christians to identify the belief with one particular interpretation of it. That is something we want to avoid here. For example, Christians have always believed that humans are composed of both body and soul—nature (they are of the earth) and supernature (they possess an added gift above nature that makes them immortal and inescapably related to God). But some confuse this universal Christian belief about humans with some more specific interpretation of it such as "trichotomy," that humans are composed of three distinct and even separable aspects or entities: body, soul, spirit. Not all Christians have believed that. Disbelieving it does not mean one denies the Christian belief that humans are more than animals. We need to distinguish between the *basics* that bond Christians together over centuries in terms of their beliefs and perspectives and the *details* that arise as certain Christians speculate about the meanings and implications of the basics. Christians have always believed that humans are possessed of special dignity and value above all other creatures because they are created in God's image and likeness. Some Christians have identified that belief with some particular interpretation of what the *imago Dei* (image of God) means. This is something to avoid.

Christians have always believed that humans are sinful and in need of redemption by God's grace in Christ and through the Holy Spirit. Some Christians, unfortunately, have identified that basic, essential belief in original sin and total, inherited depravity with a particular theological interpretation of it. For example, some Christians simply assume that "original sin" means that humans are born guilty of Adam's and Eve's sin; some of those Christians assume that if a person does not believe in inherited or federal guilt (unified together with Adam) that person denies original sin. That is simply not the case.

Here our project and purpose will be to set forth as simply and briefly as possible the broad Christian consensus about these matters. In doing this we are faced with a difficulty in that these Christian views of human nature and existence have seldom been spelled out in authoritative books or confessional statements. They have remained primarily on the level of underlying assumptions. The church as a whole has seldom elevated them to the status of absolute essentials of Christian faith in the same way as it has elevated belief in the deity of Christ or the Trinity. And yet, as one reads Scripture, the church fathers and Reformers and other writings of influential Christians throughout the ages one sees that these basic beliefs have always been accepted even if they have not often been argued dogmatically.

Christianity views humans as *animals and more*. That is, human beings are animals. We are creatures made of the "dust of the ground" (Gen 2:7); we are finite, limited and physical beings whose destiny it is to die physical deaths. Everywhere biblical revelation assumes that human beings are animals (biological beings with genetic inheritance) and reflects that assumption in its stark realism about limitations, sickness, disease, physical frailty and bodily death. The Old Testament especially contains many references to human beings as "dust"—referring to the fact of finitude, material existence, bodily frailty and eventual demise. Some Christians have been tempted to view "dust" and "flesh" as evil containers or mere vessels of true humanity that is, they believe, essentially immaterial, spiritual and perhaps even divine. This is closer to the ancient Greek view of humanity than to Hebrew, biblical anthropology. To the Hebrews and early Christians the physical aspect of humanity is a good creation of God—a gift—even if one that has fallen into corruption due to sin. After all, as one Christian writer has vigorously asserted, "God don't make no junk." Genesis proclaims and Scripture everywhere supports the truth that even our bodies, though made of dust (finite, frail, now fallen) are creations of God proclaimed *good!* like everything else God creates.

The other side of this first Christian affirmation about human nature and existence is that although we are dust we are also spirit. Again, a misunderstanding lurks around this basic Christian perspective about humanity. Many people automatically assume that *spirit* is "divine substance" or a "spark of God." "God is Spirit; spirit is God" is a false equation. Scripture and Christian tradition strongly distinguish between the spirit of a person and God's Spirit. Human beings are souls (*soul* is often used in Scripture and in Christian thought as a synonym for the person before God); souls are composed of both body and spirit in union. This is, of course, a very brief summation of the general use of these terms in Scripture. Sometimes *soul* is used to designate the spiritual aspect of a person and the immaterial aspect that survives bodily death until the resurrection. However, for systematic purposes of expression it is best to speak of *soul* as the personal identity of the individual human being and *body* and *spirit* as the two sides or aspects of the soul.[1] Thus, in biblical revelation and, for the most part in Christian anthropology, human beings are "living souls" (persons inevitably and inescapably related to God) composed of both body (natural existence) and spirit (supernatural existence). Contrary to some folk theology, these are not equated with lower and higher natures of human beings. Instead, Christian anthropology values *both* body *and* spirit as two sides of the good creation of a human soul.

The great church father and defender of belief in the Trinity Athanasius, in his classic work *On the Incarnation,* affirmed the dual nature of humanity as both essentially mortal and transcending nature and mortality. Nothing found there is novel; Athanasius simply summed up the Christian consensus before him in a controversial context and his great prestige and authority helped seal whatever he wrote as of special value. In this book the fourth-century Egyptian bishop and theologian averred that humans—including Jesus Christ—are by nature mortal and "essentially impermanent" but also possess superadded gifts from God such as immortality and incorruption.[2] The great Western church fathers Tertullian and Augustine also taught the dual nature of humanity, as have all leading Christian thinkers since then. The main disagreement in this first area of Christian anthropology—which only reveals the more basic, underlying agreement—has been between those theologians of the church who taught *trichotomy* (three distinct aspects or components of every human person—body, soul and spirit as three separable substances) and those who taught *dichotomy* (two distinct aspects). Seldom has this debate led to anathemas or condemnations; it has remained for the most part a matter of heated opinionating. The influential books of twentieth-century Chinese Christian writer Watchman Nee have promoted trichotomy and led many lay Christians and pastors to assume that it is *the* biblical view, but the vast majority of Christians throughout history—including most of the church fathers and Reformers as well as most modern evangelical scholars—have been dichotomists.[3]

The second essential tenet of Christian anthropology is that humans are *essentially good.* Perhaps a better, less misleading way of expressing this Chris-

---

[1]For scholarly support for this usage of terms, see Dale Moody, *The Word of Truth: A Summary of Christian Doctrine Based on Biblical Revelation* (Grand Rapids, Mich.: Eerdmans, 1981), pp. 170-87.

[2]See H. D. McDonald, *The Christian View of Man* (Westchester, Ill.: Crossway, 1981), p. 54.

[3]For a helpful survey of this controversy, see ibid., part 2, pp. 47-100.

tian humanism is that humanity or human nature is essentially good *because it is the image and likeness of God.* Ask most Christians whether human nature is essentially good or essentially evil and the answer will often affirm humanity's essential evilness. However, the revelation of God in Jesus Christ and the biblical witness as well as the Christian consensual tradition affirms the essential goodness of human nature. What is *nature* in this sense? Humanity as God created it and still envisions it as his original special creation. According to the biblical witness God pronounced all that he created "good" (Gen 1:31). There was, according to all the early church fathers, no flaw in God's original creation.

Augustine, who is often mistakenly interpreted as viewing creation—including human nature—as evil, especially promoted the goodness of all substances and of creation itself. According to him, evil is only a perversion of goodness, and everything created is essentially good because God created it. Whence evil, then? "The only evil thing is an evil will." Evil, Augustine argued, enters the picture only when the good gift of free will is misused by humans. It is not a seed or germ already lying within human nature that caused sin and evil to appear. This view of humanity as essentially good but existentially estranged due to a misuse of freedom became the standard Christian view even through the period of the Protestant Reformation. When a Lutheran theologian named Matthias Flacius taught that human nature is Satanic, his view was condemned by the Lutheran churches of the sixteenth century. Contrary to the misconception of many Christians in the pews and, unfortunately, even in the pulpits, the Christian consensus has always been that human nature is good and not evil.

The goodness of human nature is clearly revealed in Jesus Christ who, Christians believe, was truly human and yet without sin. Sin cannot be an essential part of human nature if the Son of God through the incarnation became human and yet remained without sin. Luke tells us that Jesus "grew in wisdom and stature, and in favor with God and men" (Lk 2:52), and the second epistle of John condemns everyone (probably referring especially to those who call themselves Christians) who denies that Jesus Christ came in the flesh (2 Jn 7). Yet the epistle to the Hebrews makes clear that Jesus Christ was tempted "yet was without sin" (Heb 4:15). All in all, the revelation of Jesus Christ in the New Testament points to his true, authentic humanity and his perfect life morally and spiritually.

The goodness of human nature is also attested in the Psalms (among other portions of the Old Testament). Psalm 8 is a paean of praise to God for humanity's goodness as a gift from God: "You made him a little lower than the heavenly beings and crowned him with glory and honor" (Ps 8:5). Scripture also refers several times to humanity's creation in God's own image and likeness and never suggests that it is a completely lost dimension of human nature. Rather, the epistle of James forbids slander against fellow humans because they are "made in God's likeness" (Jas 3:9). The creation accounts of Genesis mention that humans were created in God's image and likeness (both male and female alike!). Church fathers such as Irenaeus of Lyons exploited this belief about humanity against the Gnostics who all demeaned human nature as opposed to the alleged divine spark within it. Irenaeus was the first Christian thinker to work out a relatively detailed explanation of the *imago Dei* in humanity, and all Christian writers after him who wrote about human nature added their own touches of interpretation to what he began.

Irenaeus made much of the use of two terms in Genesis 1:26—*image* and *likeness.* Many modern Hebrew scholars believe that this is merely an example of Hebrew parallelism and does not point to two distinct dimensions of the *imago Dei,* but Irenaeus and other early church fathers often assumed that "image of God" refers to that essential aspect of humanity that may be damaged by sin but cannot be lost and that "likeness to God" refers to that destiny of humanity which, when fulfilled, would complete our relationship with God but may be interrupted and temporarily lost without humans being less than truly and fully human.[4] This distinction may be more speculative than rooted in revelation itself, but the main point is that Irenaeus and other church fathers, as well as medieval theologians, Protestant Reformers and modern Christian thinkers, *all* have viewed humanity as special in creation because we bear a unique stamp of God; we reflect in our very being an icon of God. What that is, exactly, has been the subject of much disagreement and debate and the source of diversity within the Christian consensus, but the unanimous voice of Christianity has always been that humanity itself is good because it has—even if only as a relic—God's own image.

Even John Calvin, so often regarded as one of the greatest pessimists of human nature in the history of Christianity (because of his emphasis on total depravity), sang the praises of human nature or rather of God for creating

---

[4]For a good discussion of Irenaeus's and other church fathers' views of the image and likeness of God, see David Cairns, *The Image of God in Man* (London: Collins, 1973), pp. 79-107.

humanity good. In this regard Calvin—in concert with the entire church before him and afterwards—was a "Christian humanist" perhaps in spite of himself. In *Institutes of the Christian Religion* the Genevan Reformer affirmed that humanity is essentially good but existentially estranged, and he linked the essential goodness of human nature inextricably with the original creation of humans in God's own image and likeness (which he did not distinguish) and their restoration in heaven. According to Calvin:

> God's image is the perfect excellence of human nature which shone in Adam before his defection, but was subsequently so vitiated and almost blotted out that nothing remains after the ruin except what is confused, mutilated, and disease-ridden. Therefore in some part it now is manifest in the elect, in so far as they have been reborn in the spirit; but it will attain its full splendor in heaven.[5]

The extent to which the image of God is affected by the fall into sin is a subject of great debate within Christianity and among Christian theologians as well, but all agree—including Calvin—that original humanity, true humanity, essential humanity is good because humanity is created in God's own image and likeness.

The third main point of Christian anthropology is the counterpoint to the second: Christianity teaches and Christians believe that *human existence is estranged, fallen, corrupted*. In other words, even though humanity itself is something good, all humans besides Jesus Christ are living concrete lives estranged, alienated from God and from their own being in God's image. This is the doctrine of original sin or inherited depravity. Unfortunately, many people think that it is a denial of the essential goodness of humanity. This mistaken interpretation has even been promoted in popular Christian literature by certain Christian theologians who seem not to understand the traditional Christian viewpoint on human nature and existence. The greatest liberal Protestant theologian of the twentieth century, Paul Tillich, understood quite well and coined the phrase "essentially good but existentially estranged" to clear up this misunderstanding and express the paradox embedded in both revelation and the Christian heritage of reflection. Of course, some interpretations of existential estrangement—of original sin and inherited, total depravity—may indeed imply that human nature is *now*, since the fall of humanity, essentially corrupt and evil. But

---

[5]John Calvin *Institutes of the Christian Religion* 1.15.4, p. 190.

that is not at all necessary to the basic concept of original sin.

The Christian consensus about the human condition, as contrasted with essential humanity, is that our actual day-to-day lives are from birth on thoroughly pervaded by sin as tendency toward pride (self-idolatry), selfishness, disobedience to God. Our condition is that we are always already broken spiritually, psychologically, emotionally and physically. That is, according to classic Christianity, we are all always already sinners even before we commit conscious, willful transgressions for which we are culpable. We are born depraved or deprived, but that is not our real humanity. It is our diseased humanity. It is not our true nature even if it has become our second nature. But it is there at the beginning of our lives, even if only as an inherited time bomb ticking away within our spiritual lives inevitably leading us—insofar as we mature to conscious, moral awakening to right and wrong—toward becoming rebels against God in need of personal forgiveness and reconciliation with God.

Christian belief in original, inherited sinfulness is rooted firmly in divine revelation. Did Jesus Christ die for all people—the whole world? Are all people sinners without exception? The answers to these questions in the New Testament and in the writings of the church fathers are *yes* and *yes*. The medieval theologians and Protestant Reformers agreed. That is not to say that the teaching about original sin in the New Testament or belief about it in the writings of the Great Tradition of the church are simple; there is much ambiguity and disagreement about the details. Nevertheless, one cannot read the New Testament honestly and miss its realistic emphasis on universal human depravity. The epistle to the Romans especially emphasizes this truth and chapters one and five highlight it. Paul wrote in Romans 5:18, "just as the result of one trespass was condemnation for all men," and in the next verse, "just as through the disobedience of the one man the many were made sinners" (Rom 5:19). A careful study of any book of the New Testament will find the same assumption underlying it, even if expressed only between the lines. That is why Christ came: all humans are fallen and in need of redemption. We are all "born sinners."

This belief—at least in its general outlines—was assumed by all of the early church fathers, and they felt no need to spell it out dogmatically or in detail until someone with influence denied it. That first happened among Christians in Rome in the early fifth century. A monk from Britain named Pelagius arrived in Rome and began teaching that all people are born pure,

pristine, uncorrupted and fully able *if they will* to live lives in perfect obedience to God's revealed will without ever needing a special grace for forgiveness and restoration. Pelagius did not deny that many and perhaps most
people do fall into sin; he simply averred that it is not inevitable and that all
people are capable of not sinning just as Adam and Eve were capable of
either sinning or not sinning before they fell. Pelagius kept shifting his view
around to stay out of trouble with councils of bishops, but under great pres-
sure from Augustine he eventually fled Rome to Jerusalem and other parts of
the Eastern Roman Empire where he was better received by some Eastern
Orthodox bishops and theologians. When his heresy became clearer, however, his views were condemned by a universal council of Christian leaders in
431 at Ephesus.

In opposition to Pelagius, Augustine wrote several treatises on original sin
and inherited, total depravity. He argued that before the Fall the human
condition was *posse non peccare* (possible not to sin) but that after the Fall
our universal human condition is *non posse non peccare* (not possible not to
sin). He even went so far as to say that all babies are conceived in sin such
that they are born guilty of Adam's and Eve's sin. Scripture nowhere affirms
that clearly or unequivocally, and the entire Eastern Orthodox branch of
Christianity and many Protestants deny it. Fortunately, that detail, though
widely believed in Roman Catholic and some Protestant circles, is not a necessary aspect of the Christian consensus about the human condition.

From the Council of Ephesus (431) on, the Christian consensus has been
that all humans are born with and in the condition we call *sinfulness* such
that sin as corruption if not guilt is universally inherited and all people are in
need of repentance and faith and reconciliation through the work of Jesus
Christ on the cross. In other words, grace is a universal human need. God's
grace cannot be something for only a few or even merely for many; it is a
basic need of humanity due to the Fall at the beginning of history. It would
be possible to quote on this subject from almost any major Christian thinker
throughout church history; all affirmed some version of original sin as
human inability with regard to righteousness apart from Jesus Christ and
special grace from God. But because at least some people believe that John
Wesley, eighteenth-century founder of the Methodist tradition and himself a
priest of the Church of England, denied original sin, it might be useful to
refer to and quote from him. If Wesley affirmed belief in original sin, then
that points toward its universality in Christianity. Wesley considered himself

an evangelical catholic—a person who was interested in reforming Christianity while remaining true to the universal teachings of the early Christian fathers and sixteenth-century Reformers. In 1756 and 1757 Wesley wrote a treatise titled *The Doctrine of Original Sin.*[6] In it he claimed as essential Christian belief that

> Original sin . . . is no play of imagination, but plain, clear fact. We see it with our eyes and hear it with our ears daily. Heathens, Turks, Jews, Christians, of every nation, as such men as are there described. Such are the tempers, such the manners, of lords, gentlemen, clergymen, in England, as well as of tradesmen and the low vulgar. No man in his sense can deny it; and none can account for it but upon the supposition of original sin.[7]

In this essay and in his homilies (sermons) based on it, the great revivalist and reformer of Protestant Christianity affirmed unequivocally what the church has always taught: that every human person is corrupt because of what happened at the beginning of human history and all are in need of special grace for salvation. Wesley even went so far as to affirm universal guilt, although he mitigated that by equally affirming the universal application of Christ's atoning death and its benefits for setting aside the guilt of sin. In other words, Wesley and many other Protestants have come to believe that children are both guilty and innocent. They are guilty "in Adam" but innocent (or redeemed) "in Christ" until they mature to the point of conscious, willful rejection of God and his Son through embrace of sinful desires (what would today be called acting out). For the sake of Christ, on the basis of his atoning death for humanity, God mercifully does not impute the guilt of original sin to infants.

Is belief in original sin and inherited depravity an outmoded relic of Christianity's past? Not at all. The twentieth century has witnessed an astonishing revival of belief in the classic Christian doctrine of original sin even among liberal Protestants. One of the greatest twentieth-century Christian thinkers was Reinhold Niebuhr, whose portrait graced the twenty-fifth anniversary issue of *Time* magazine. In his numerous books Niebuhr—generally considered a moderately liberal, mainline Protestant theologian—promoted a renaissance of the doctrine of original sin stripped of belief in a literal, histor-

---

[6]For a nice summary of this essay including quotations from it, see Thomas Oden, *John Wesley's Scriptural Christianity* (Grand Rapids, Mich.: Zondervan, 1994), pp. 155-76.
[7]Ibid., p. 175.

ical Fall of an original couple in a paradise at the beginning of human history. Niebuhr embraced and promoted a paradox that came to be the essence of his "Christian realism." It is the paradox of human goodness and radical, universal evil as pride that inevitably gives rise to war, injustice, selfishness and all manner of atrocities both large and small. His Gifford Lectures, published as *The Nature and Destiny of Man* (New York: Charles Scribner's Sons, 1941-1949), may have been greeted by some liberal thinkers with scorn and dismay, but their overall effect was to confirm and convince most even moderately liberal Christians that the old Christian doctrine of original sin as built-in depravity (even if not inherited) is still relevant to the church and society in the modern world.

These three general Christian beliefs—humans as composed of a dual nature, humanity as essentially good because created in God's image, humans as universally fallen into sin—together form the inner core of what might be called Christian humanism. It is a realistic humanism that combines truths about humanity partially grasped and emphasized in one-sided ways by other religions and philosophies. It is humanism that regards humanity as having infinite value and dignity above and beyond any other creature and yet as corrupt and helpless apart from special grace from God. It is therefore a humanism that promotes hope and distrust: hope for the rise of humanity with God's help and distrust of human motives including our own. This humanism stands uncompromisingly opposed to three main alternative visions of human nature and existence. Examining them will help sharpen our focus on Christian belief and demonstrate how distinct it is among the anthropologies that battle for the minds and hearts of people in modern and postmodern society.

## Alternative Visions of Humanity

Three main general views of human nature and existence stand in stark contrast to Christianity and challenge it sometimes even within Christian circles. These are views that cannot be reconciled or made compatible with Christianity; they are non-Christian if not anti-Christian and should be exposed and rejected whenever they appear within the thinking of the church. The first is a peculiarly modern, Western view of humanity that is rooted in and based on naturalism. It is commonly known as *secular humanism* even though most of its manifestations do not publicly wear that label. The second is an ancient foe of Christianity that has formed a shadow attached to Christianity for two thousand years. It is based on an emanationist worldview of monism and can fairly be called *Gnosticism* even though that term is seldom used when it appears and exercises influence. The third alternative is the one taught by the British monk in Rome and other parts of the Roman Empire in the time of Augustine; it has reappeared from time to time within Christianity. It is seldom called by its technical name—*Pelagianism*—but it is a powerful and persuasive view of human nature that is probably more popular in folk piety, theology and spirituality than is classical Christian anthropology.

*Secular humanism* is a much overused category and label—especially in some fundamentalist quarters. In the 1970s and 1980s a few outspoken fundamentalist preachers and writers launched a campaign against "the religion of secular humanism" that they perceived being taught in most public schools. Many reacted to this religious assault on public education (as it was perceived and received by many educators) with indignation and scorn. Even many well-meaning Christians were tempted to toss the baby out with the bathwater by denying the very existence of secular humanism as a philosophy because certain extremists were overusing the term and the category for their own religious-political purposes. There can be no doubt of the existence of a modern philosophy, at the heart of which stands a naturalistic anthropology, and that this philosophy exercises a powerful and pervasive influence, and that "secular humanism" is as good a label for it as any. Even its leading proponents accept and use that label for their philosophy.[8]

What is secular humanism? Paul Kurtz explains it in terms of four "minimal principles": (1) antisupernaturalism [thus, a naturalistic foundation]; (2) ethics as human-centered [not God-centered]; (3) commitment to use of critical reason [as opposed to faith in divine revelation], and (4) humanitarian concerns [as opposed to interest in divine or spiritual concerns].[9] Expressed negatively, secular humanism takes man, Kurtz says, as

> a part of nature, even though man has his own unique dimensions, such as freedom. There is no break between the human mind or consciousness on the one hand and the body on the other, no special status to personality or "soul," and especially no privileged or special place for human existence in the universe

---

[8]Paul Kurtz, retired professor of philosophy at State University of New York, vigorously defends secular humanism and has launched his own campaign to defend it as that philosophy with the most cogency and usefulness in the modern, scientific world. Prometheus Press is the publishing company he founded and that publishes many books expressing a secular humanist viewpoint.

[9]Paul Kurtz, *In Defense of Secular Humanism* (Buffalo, N.Y.: Prometheus, 1983), p. 64.

at large. Thus, all claims to human immortality or eschatological theories of history are held to be an expression of wish-fulfillment, a vain reading into nature of human hope and fancy.[10]

Yet, according to Kurtz and other leading secular humanists, it is not a merely negative philosophy (viz., denying something traditionally believed) but more importantly a positive philosophy of human-centered ethics. Thus:

> Humanists have confidence in human beings, and they believe that the only bases for morality are human experience and human needs. Humanists are opposed to all forms of supernaturalistic and authoritarian religion. Many humanists believe that scientific intelligence and critical reason can assist in reconstructing our moral values.[11]

For secular humanists, values are all relative to humanity; humanity is the measure of good and bad, right and wrong. What promotes the common good promotes the happiness and fulfillment of each individual, and therefore the human happiness and self-fulfillment in harmony with the common good of humanity is the *summum bonum,* the greatest good. Of course, this begs many questions such as who gets to decide what is humanity's greatest happiness. What if the "greatest good for the greatest number" happens to require the elimination of a minority? Secular humanists are optimistic about the general benevolence of human society unshackled by superstition and ignorance, which they tend to associate with the influence of religion. The point here is about secular humanism's view of humanity. It regards humanity as essentially good, but not created in God's image or existentially estranged; as physical but not spiritual; as beset by problems such as biological self-centeredness, but not depraved. Secular humanists are not necessarily atheists, although the vast majority probably are agnostic with regard to knowledge of God or anything divine or supernatural. It has been recognized by many philosophers and even by the United State Supreme Court as a quasi-religion insofar as it provides for many of its adherents an alternative worldview and even a community of commitment for activism if not worship.

Most Christians readily recognize secular humanism as radically different from Christianity. It is quite easy to reject it when it appears in open,

---

[10]Ibid., p. 65.
[11]Ibid., p. 33.

organized, public forms such as humanist associations and organizations. But might some influence of secular humanist perspectives on humanity invade Christian minds and communities? One church newsletter warned of the influence of Christian humanism and portrayed that as a blending of secular humanism and Christianity in which people stay home from church to watch television evangelists! That is not exactly the sort of thing we are asking about here. Almost certainly the most significant threat to Christianity posed by secular humanism is the temptation to bifurcate life into separate, almost water-tight compartments and live according to a Christian worldview and anthropology in certain settings (home, church, religious organizations) and according to a secular worldview and anthropology in others (public settings, corporations, classrooms).

Another possible influence of secular humanism in Christian circles, however, is the adoption of totally utilitarian (productivity-centered or happiness-centered) ethics within them. The ironic situation is that many fundamentalist, anti-secular-humanist-crusading Christians link secular humanism with theistic evolution and even progressive creationism while organizing their Christian institutions along secular-humanist, utilitarian lines. Secular humanism has entered so pervasively and permanently into so many areas of culture and society that Christians cannot help being influenced by it; only a renaissance of God-centered and person-centered perspectives on human nature and existence that take seriously human fallenness can help guard Christian minds and communities against it.

The second main alternative to the Christian consensus of belief about humanity is *neognosticism*. By *neo* we mean "new form of something old." Gnosticism has already been described as an emanationist, ultimately monistic worldview that evolved in early Christianity and included a dualism between matter (evil) and spirit (good). Modern and contemporary forms of Gnosticism appear in various manifestations associated directly or loosely with the so-called New Age movement—a very diverse collection of esoteric, occult, mind-over-matter spiritual teachings and practices. Unfortunately, many New Age devotees also consider themselves Christians and attempt to combine their neognostic beliefs and practices with their Christianity.

Neognosticism/New Age philosophy tends to deny every major tenet of historic, classical Christianity by radically reinterpreting it in such a way that it is no longer recognizable. For example, most New Age followers affirm belief in humanity created in God's image and tout the essential goodness of human nature, but they interpret that in terms of a "spark of God" that forms the "higher self" in each person. They often then blend some kind of belief in reincarnation with that.[12] New Age anthropology reduces sin to spiritual ignorance of one's own "inner divinity" or "connection to God" and interprets the *soul* or *spirit* as an emanation of the divine substance. All in all, what makes neognosticism and New Age philosophy and spirituality so insidious is that many Christians and others cannot distinguish between Christian belief in the image of God and the inner man as a spiritual dimension of the human person from belief in "one's own God-self within." Similarly, many cannot distinguish between prayer and magic. Overall, the New Age worldview is radically alternative to Christianity even though there is some common ground between them in spiritual openness and affirmation of humanity's spirituality.

The third alternative to Christian anthropology is *Pelagianism,* which has already been described in relation to Augustine's debates with the British monk Pelagius. Pelagianism is still very much alive and well—even within Christian communities. It appears wherever people believe that human beings are born without flaw or fault and deny that sin is a condition into which all people are born. It appears wherever people imply that a simple act of will apart from special, supernatural grace from God can accomplish something truly spiritually good. It appears wherever the message is even subtly promoted that humans can by themselves initiate a right relationship with God (e.g., "God helps those who help themselves"). Even such a seemingly innocent and positive movement as wearing wristbands with the letters W.W.J.D. (What Would Jesus Do?) can manifest a Pelagian attitude toward Christianity—as if people are capable of doing what Jesus would do merely by choosing to act in Christlike ways without first being transformed by God's grace. Christian moralism comes in many disguises—some conservative and some liberal—but they all hide a basically Pelagian perspective on human action that attributes far too much power to humanity and too little dependence of the human being on God's supernatural grace.

## Diverse Christian Interpretations of Human Nature and Existence
Within the Christian consensus of belief about human nature and existence

---

[12]For an excellent survey and critical examination of New Age philosophy, see John P. Newport, *The New Age Movement and the Biblical Worldview* (Grand Rapids, Mich.: Eerdmans, 1998).

there is plenty of room for differing interpretations about details. However, for the most part, Christian denominations have avoided sharp controversy and division over these matters. Most of the different interpretations arise from the speculations of individual Christian scholars and theologians. A few matters of interpretation, however, have become tests of fellowship within certain Christian tradition-communities. Here space allows only the briefest and most inadequate treatment of these diverse viewpoints within the Christian consensus. Only some of them will be touched on; many will be neglected. They will be explained and examined in the order of the three main Christian beliefs about humanity described earlier in this chapter.

While all Christians agree that human beings are composed of natural-physical and supernatural-spiritual dimensions, sharp disagreement has arisen among Christian scholars about the number and relationship of these parts of human personhood. The great medieval scholastic theologian Thomas Aquinas argued from Scripture and philosophy for two distinct and even separate substances that together make up a whole human being: body and soul. (To Thomas and many other Christian theologians *soul* is simply a term for the spiritual aspect of a person that survives bodily death; it could be called *spirit* just as well.) Thomas was a *dichotomist* and a *dualist* with regard to human composition. The Roman Catholic Church has generally followed his viewpoints. Thus, the immaterial substance of human nature is immortal and exists in a conscious state after bodily death awaiting reunification with the body in the resurrection. Many Protestants agree with this dichotomy and equate *soul* and *spirit*—two terms that are sometimes used interchangeably in the New Testament for the immaterial but conscious aspect of the human person that is especially related to God and survives physical death.

The alternatives to dichotomous dualism (or dualistic dichotomy) are *trichotomy* and *holism*. Some early church fathers, such as Irenaeus and the Alexandrian theologians, who were especially influenced by Platonic philosophy believed in three distinct substances or dimensions of human nature—body, soul and spirit. Plato and his school of Greek philosophy taught a tripartite psychology very similar to Christian trichotomy, and some scholars argue that trichotomy derives more from Greek philosophy than from divine revelation. According to trichotomy, the soul is a mediating organ of the human being; it is the animating life force that surpasses the merely physical body but does not survive bodily death. Some trichotomists equate the soul with consciousness as well as with life force. According to this view, spirit is the higher substance or dimension of a human person that radically transcends physical and animating life-force substances and is capable of communing with God both while in the body and when out of it after death.

Holism is the relatively recent view that human beings are unified entities that cannot be sliced up into separable substances; soul and spirit are merely terms for the whole person who is also physical but not merely material.[13] Persons, holists argue, are ensouled bodies and embodied souls; they cannot be divided. Most holists must deny any conscious intermediate existence of the dead and affirm in its place an immediate postmortem transition into the resurrection or else "soul sleep" in which the dead are truly dead—unaware if not nonexistent—until the resurrection.

The view that seems to take into account most adequately all of the biblical materials as well as receive the support of the majority of Christian thinkers down through the centuries is dichotomy, but traditional dichotomy can benefit from some influence of holism. Christian theologian John W. Cooper calls such a view "holistic dualism," in which any separation of the immaterial soul-spirit from the physical body is always only at best temporary and not ideal; until the resurrection the dead may be conscious but not in an ideal state. The body is part of human personal identity, but persons may be and are conscious and "held by God" in the intermediate, non-bodily state after death until the resurrection.

The specific meaning of the *imago Dei* has been much debated among Christian theologians. Irenaeus assumed that the image of God refers to the reasoning capacity of human beings as well as to their souls or spirits, while the likeness of God refers to their destinies of being Christlike in redemption. Over the centuries of Christian thought, many patterns and viewpoints have developed including some that identify the image of God with powers of reason, immortality, conscience, ability to respond to God's Word, freedom, and having dominion over the earth. No major Christian thinker has identified the *imago Dei* with a bodily likeness or likeness of countenance with God. The problem in these various definitions is that most of them are too narrow and limited. Why identify the image of God in humanity with one aspect or function? Why not simply regard it as *personhood*—that psycho-

---

[13]An excellent survey of these and other Christian and philosophical views of the composition of human beings is John W. Cooper, *Body, Soul & Life Everlasting: Biblical Anthropology and the Monism-Dualism Debate* (Grand Rapids, Mich.: Eerdmans, 1989).

spiritual ability and function that transcends mere nature and physicality through reasoning ability, need and capacity for community and cultural creativity, development of language and communication, worship and self-transcendence, freedom and responsibility?

Few denominations of Christianity have ever pronounced what their members (let alone all Christians) must believe about the precise identity of the *imago Dei*. It is theologians who have frequently developed and promoted such theories, and there are far too many of these even to touch on them all here. Our view is that most of them do contain an element of truth and the problem with each one is its attempt to monopolize the whole significance of humanity in the *image of God* for one facet of human nature and existence. It is best, we believe, to draw the truth from many, if not all of them together and regard the *imago Dei* as a multifaceted, diverse collection of Godlike qualities in humanity that together may, with proper qualifications, be called personhood.

Finally, tremendous diversity exists among Christians about the details of original sin and inherited, total depravity. While all Christians believe that humanity is fallen and in need of redemption, some Christians believe and teach that each infant is born guilty of Adam's sin, and some expressly deny that, arguing instead for acquired guilt at the age of accountability. Inherited guilt and total depravity (e.g., as bondage of the will to sin) is the strongest and most common view of original sin in the Augustinian-Lutheran-Reformed tradition of Christian anthropology. In reaction against Pelagianism and Semi-Pelagianism, Augustine and his followers asserted that all of humanity together is fallen in Adam. "In Adam's fall we sinned all" was the saying taught to Puritan school children in the seventeenth and eighteenth centuries. Humanity, this view says, is a "mass of perdition," and no human being can escape condemnation without special grace from God through baptism or conversion to Christ. That relegates even infants to hell unless they are among the elect (predestined to salvation) as in much traditional Lutheran and Reformed theology, baptized as in classical Catholic thought or covered by the atonement of Jesus Christ until they reach the age of accountability as in Wesley's theology. Many free church Protestants such as most Baptists and Pentecostals believe that God regards infants and children as innocent in spite of original sin until they mature to the age of accountability ("awakening of conscience") and commit their own sins willfully.

During the Protestant Reformation, Zwingli and those of his followers who broke away from the magisterial Reformed churches—the so-called Anabaptists—denied inherited guilt and believed only in inherited depravity as corruption of nature leading inevitably to personal acts of transgression at the age of accountability. Anabaptists such as Balthasar Hubmaier and Menno Simons and all of their followers—including most Baptists later—embraced the view that Zwingli (not Calvin) taught: infants are innocent (because of Christ's provision of grace by his death), and original sin is a propensity to sin in which all people are born without guilt, but all free, morally responsible and mature persons do eventually sin guiltily and need repentance and forgiveness.[14] Menno Simons, one of the leading Anabaptist writers of the Reformation, argued against belief in inherited guilt (or at least the guilt of infants) and thus rejected infant baptism as unnecessary and unbiblical. But he did not deny original sin as inherited corruption. According to Simons:

> We [Anabaptists] also believe and confess that we are all born of unclean seed, that we through the first and earthly Adam became wholly depraved and children of death and of hell: with this understanding, however, that even as we fell and became sinners in Adam, so we also believe and confess that through Christ, the second and heavenly Adam, we are graciously helped to our feet again and justified. . . . To innocent and minor children sin is for Jesus' sake not imputed. Life is promised, not through any ceremony, but of pure grace, through the blood of the Lord, as He Himself says: Suffer the little children to come unto me and forbid them not; for of such is the kingdom of heaven.[15]

Simons's view is the one held by most Baptist and many other evangelical Protestant theologians. It is, of course, believed by all Anabaptists including Mennonites as well as by all Pentecostals and many in the Pietist traditions. The various Methodist groups tend to hold this view in spite of John Wesley's own tendency to embrace belief in baptismal regeneration of infants. On the other hand, many staunchly traditional and conservative Roman Catholics, Lutherans, Episcopalians/Anglicans and Reformed theologians still accept the Augustinian view that all of humanity is guilty and condemned—including infants—because of Adam's first sin. Their only hope for salvation, then, should they die before maturity and conscious repentance

---

[14]Ulrich Zwingli, "Declaration of Huldreich Zwingli Regarding Original Sin, Addressed to Urbanus Rhegius," in *On Providence and Other Essays,* edited for Samuel Macauley Jackson by William John Hinke (Durham, N.C.: Labyrinth, 1983), pp. 32.

[15]Menno Simons, "Foundation of Christian Doctrine," in *The Complete Writings of Menno Simons,* ed. J. C. Wenger, trans. Leonard Verduin (Scottsdale, Penn.: Herald, 1984), pp. 130-31.

and faith, lies in being among the elect predestined by God to be among his covenant people or, as in Catholic theology, in the sacrament of baptism. Virtually no Christian denomination teaches that all unbaptized people—especially unbaptized infants—are automatically damned. Even the Catholic Church recognizes a "baptism of desire." The debate revolves around whether all infants are saved, in spite of original sin and through the grace of Christ, or whether only some infants are saved by the grace of Christ through special election by God or the sacrament of water baptism.[16]

## A Unifying Christian Perspective on Human Nature and Existence

One of the hottest flash points of controversy between people of differing worldviews and belief systems lies in the age-old question, what is man? (Today, of course, inclusive language rephrases the question: what is humanity? The problem is that *humanity* is collective and so the question asked that way implies an aggregate and tends to leave the individual person out of view; *man* had the advantage of referring to both the individual and the collective of all humans even though, of course, it is now widely viewed as favoring the male of the specifies.) Philosophers and theologians of all religions and no religion explore that question and attempt to answer it. The physical universe is increasingly being understood and explained by the various sciences, but the mystery of human nature and existence remains just that—largely a mystery. The contemporary battle for the mind going on in pluralistic cultures centers around that mystery. Are humans merely "naked apes"? Or are humans godlets? One secular scientist and philosopher has suggested that human beings are nothing more than "digestive systems that know they will die." Some New Age spiritualists proclaim human beings divine and possessed of all the power, intelligence and wisdom of the universal Spirit or God. Does Christianity have a distinctive message about humanity or is it compatible with all of these views?

At its best, in the whole and in the main, Christianity has always viewed humanity as having infinite dignity and value above the rest of nature because humans are created in God's image, loved by God and redeemed in Christ. At the same time, Christianity has always viewed humanity as

---

[16]Many Christian theologians and church leaders simply relegate the fate of unbaptized infants and children to mystery and appeal to God's mercy and justice. This does little to satisfy inquiring minds, however.

degraded, worse than animals, corrupt and condemned. The Christian message about humanity is *paradoxical* and yet *not contradictory*. The seventeenth-century French Christian philosopher, scientist, inventor and lay theologian Blaise Pascal wrote an outline for a book of Christian apologetics entitled *Pensées* (Thoughts) based on this paradox: man as a king sitting on a crumbling throne, possessed of both great glory and at the same time degraded by sin. Other Christian writers such as twentieth-century theologian Reinhold Niebuhr have also portrayed humanity as a paradox and argued that this dual account of human nature that refuses to reduce humans to animals or elevate them to divine beings is the only one that adequately explains the true human situation.

In a postmodern culture in which humanity is precariously situated in philosophy, psychology and science, every denomination of Christianity needs to hold forth a unified vision of humanity that undergirds the values of respect for human life and basic human rights while at the same time acknowledging human limitations and evil tendencies. Such a unified vision can best be forged through a creative retrieval of the Great Tradition of Christian belief about humanity created in God's image, possessed of both body and soul/spirit, and fallen into sin. Such a creative retrieval of traditional Christian belief involves two steps or stages. First, the essence of the belief has to be discovered and recovered from the layers of speculation and interpretation with which it has become entangled. In other words, the belief needs to be rediscovered in all its simplicity. Second, the simple core of the belief has to be re-expressed with relevance to the contemporary situation. In other words, the essential Christian concept must be translated into a contemporary idiom that speaks to the peculiar needs and problems of the contemporary social context. The basic, unifying Christian perspective on humanity, for example, includes the relatively simple (not simplistic) idea that all human beings are *both* unique and possessed of special dignity and value because they are created in the image of God *and* corrupted from birth by a spiritual disease that prevents them from being fulfilled apart from God's saving grace.

This dual truth, virtually unique to Christianity, can speak powerfully to the needs of modern and postmodern people who are perplexed by a myriad of questions arising out of technology, politics, economics and spiritualities. It can speak powerfully to the ethical dilemmas of this pluralistic culture where technology is racing ahead of all construals of human nature and existence. On the basis of our belief in humanity's special dignity and value Christians can applaud and support those advances in science and technology that truly enhance human life; on the basis of our belief in humanity's fallenness and proclivity to evil Christians can and must raise warning flags about the tendency of those advances to outrun reflection about their benefits for the common good as well as the good of individuals and minorities.

# CHAPTER 10

# JESUS CHRIST

## God *and* Man

Belief in and about Jesus Christ lies at the heart of Christianity; most of the discussion and controversy over right belief (orthodoxy) in the first few centuries of Christianity revolved around questions of the nature of Jesus Christ. Over the intervening centuries such questions have arisen in new ways and given rise to new rounds of debate in spite of certain doctrinal settlements achieved by the undivided Christian church of the first four to five centuries. A saying often repeated in Christian churches and movements states "Christianity *is* Christ." That is simply another way of saying that the person of Jesus Christ is the most important reality for Christianity and therefore believing rightly about him is absolutely crucial to preserving authentic Christianity. When the World Council of Churches formed as an umbrella organization for cooperation between over one hundred denominations of Christians worldwide, the question of a criterion for membership was raised and seriously considered. What makes a group of people such as a church or a denomination Christian? Are all that say they are Christian and have that word in their charters or names really Christian? Are there groups that do not necessarily highlight the word *Christian* for some good reason but really are Christian? Which denominations would be admitted? On what grounds? The final agreement was and remains that the one belief that must be affirmed by any denomination that wishes to join the WCC is "Jesus Christ is God and Savior." Some modern theologians scoffed and argued that even the New Testament nowhere explicitly or directly calls Jesus *God*. But the WCC held to its decision and to this day belief in Jesus Christ as both God and Savior (and one may safely assume this includes his being human) is the sole, necessary affirmation for authentic Christianity.

## Issues and Polarities of Christian Belief About Jesus Christ

Despite general agreement on this affirmation of Jesus Christ as God and Savior, problems remain for theological reflection and explanation. What does it mean to say that one person is both God and human? What is the nature of Jesus Christ's savior status? How did he and does he save? Can a person believe that Jesus Christ is a mixture of humanity and deity (or divinity) or must one agree with the early Christian councils that proclaimed his two natures? Numerous questions and problems surrounding the person of Jesus Christ have arisen and still arise among Christians. In the 1980s a major Protestant denomination in the United States struggled with the necessity of belief in and affirmation of Jesus Christ's deity by its ordained clergy. In Canada a controversy arose over an official of the largest Protestant body who seemed to deny that core, historic Christian belief. Among more conservative Christians questions still arise from time to time about Jesus' humanity. Could he have become ill? Could he have sinned? Such questions seem speculative and do sometimes waste time. However, they relate to the larger issue of who Jesus Christ was and is.

Massive volumes and sets of volumes have been published by Christian theologians dealing with the history of theological reflection and dogmatic pronouncements by churches about the person of Jesus Christ. Any good theological library contains shelves of such tomes. Here only the briefest account of Christian belief about the person of Christ can be given. Much that is truly important will have to be left aside. Readers are urged to pick up a volume about Christology (the area of theological reflection that deals with the person of Christ) and become acquainted with some of the finer points.[1]

---

[1]An excellent midlevel introduction to Christology for nontheologians with some background in Christian belief (such as may be provided by this chapter and ones like it in other books) is

This chapter continues in the usual pattern and thus will follow this brief introduction to the issues and questions surrounding Christology with an exposition of the historic Christian consensus, a discussion of some major alternatives to that orthodox consensual tradition, an examination of some diverse interpretations of orthodox Christians, and close with a brief statement of a unifying vision of belief about the person of Christ for today.

Christianity is Christ. Who is Christ? What is Christ? The earliest Christian explainers of Christian belief—the fathers of the first few centuries—faced doubts about Christ's true humanity and then about his true deity. Gnostics especially questioned whether the Savior from heaven could be truly human. Adoptionists questioned whether the model of perfect humanity could be truly divine. Nestorians (followers of a Christian bishop named Nestorius) questioned whether a person could be both truly human and truly divine and really be one person. Eutychians and Monophysites (followers of a Christian monk named Eutyches) questioned whether a divine-human person could have dual natures or whether such a one must be a third something—a hybrid of divinity and humanity. In modern times, the main issues surrounding the person of Christ have to do with his deity. Hardly anyone questions Jesus' true humanity; many liberal theologians question his ontological (having to do with substance and being) deity. Perhaps his deity is nothing more than his function on behalf of God as God's human representative? The Christian church has historically allowed greater diversity in other areas of belief than this one. There is no dogma of human nature and existence that unifies all Christians (even if there is an implicit unifying belief as shown in the previous chapter). Christian belief about the sacraments and the end times, the second coming of Christ and so-called millennium are about as diverse as one can imagine. When it comes to doctrine about the person of Christ—Christology—however, we have a much clearer and more detailed necessary belief, even if some modern theologians challenge it. That is because all the bishops of the Christian church met in three universal councils during the fourth and fifth centuries to hammer out a unifying belief about Jesus Christ to counter the swelling tides of heresies within the church. And nearly all the great Protestant Reformers of the six-

---

Donald G. Bloesch, *Jesus Christ: Savior & Lord* (Downers Grove, Ill.: InterVarsity Press, 1997). This is one of seven volumes comprising evangelical theologian Bloesch's magnum opus Christian Foundations. Each volume and the set as a whole provide excellent introductions to major Christian beliefs for those who already have a basic understanding of them.

teenth century embraced and affirmed that consensus of the first four ecumenical councils.

## The Christian Consensus About Jesus Christ

Stating the Christian consensus of belief about the person of Jesus Christ is simpler and more straightforward than almost any other locus of Christian belief. The fourth ecumenical (universal) council of Christian bishops gathered—after great turmoil and controversy—in 451 at the city of Chalcedon near the capital city of the Roman Empire known as Constantinople (modern Istanbul). The council developed a definition of correct, unifying Christian belief that culminated a long controversy among Christians and became the orthodox statement on Christology for all Christians (Eastern Orthodox, Roman Catholic, most Protestants) for more than fifteen hundred years. In the nineteenth and twentieth centuries liberal-leaning Protestant thinkers raised questions about the language and conceptuality of the Chalcedonian Definition (which is often mistakenly called the Chalcedonian Creed), but it has survived into the twenty-first century as a unifying statement of most Christians. Even those church bodies that eschew formal creeds and doctrinal statements are indebted to it and rely on it whenever they say that Jesus Christ is both God and man or both divine and human and yet one Savior and Lord. Chalcedon is considered an official statement of belief by the Orthodox and Catholic churches as well as by nearly all Lutherans, Reformed Christians (e.g., Presbyterians), Episcopalians/Anglicans (Church of England) and some smaller branches of Protestantism. The numerous noncreedal and nonconfessional Protestant churches such as most Baptists, Pentecostals and other independent evangelical bodies of Christian believers may not recite the Chalcedonian Definition or print it in their worship books or statements of faith, but by and large they do affirm its content.

The Chalcedonian Definition is this crucial Christological affirmation:

> Following, then, the holy fathers [of the Nicene Council and Council of Constantinople], we unite in teaching all men to confess the one and only Son, our Lord Jesus Christ. This selfsame one is perfect both in deity and also in humanness; this selfsame one is also actually God and actually man, with a rational soul and a body. He is of the same reality as God as far as his deity is concerned and of the same reality as we are ourselves as far as his humanness is concerned; thus like us in all respects, sin only excepted. Before time began he was begotten of the Father, in respect of his deity, and now in these "last

days," for us and on behalf of our salvation, this selfsame one was born of Mary the virgin, who is God-bearer in respect of his humanness. [We also teach] that we apprehend this one and only Christ—Son, Lord, only-begotten—in two natures; [and we do this] without confusing the two natures, without transmuting one nature into the other, without dividing them into two separate categories, without contrasting them according to area or function. The distinctiveness of each nature is not nullified by the union. Instead, the "properties" of each nature are conserved and both natures concur in one "person" and in one *hypostasis* [subsistence, entity]. They are not divided or cut into two *prosōpa* (individual persons), but are together the one and only and only-begotten Logos of God, the Lord Jesus Christ. Thus have the prophets of old testified; thus the Lord Jesus Christ himself taught us; thus the Symbol of the Fathers [Nicene Creed] has handed down to us.[2]

This model of the person of Jesus Christ, carved out at the Council of Chalcedon, drawing on writings of several influential church fathers and leaders and completely consistent with Scripture is known in Christian theology as the doctrine of the *hypostatic union*. *Union* refers to the union of two natures; *hypostatic* refers to the one person of the Son of God, the Logos who became human in the incarnation through the Holy Spirit and Mary. Thus, *hypostatic union* is the belief in a perfect union of two distinct but never separate natures—one human and one divine—in one integral, eternal divine person. What the fathers and bishops gathered at Chalcedon seemed to be saying was that whereas the doctrine of the Trinity says God is *one what and three whos*—one divine substance shared equally by three distinct persons—so Jesus Christ on earth and now in heaven because of the incarnation is *two whats and one who*—two distinct but never separate natures (divine and human) and one integrated person, the eternal Son of God, the second person of the Trinity. They never intended this model to be an explanation of the mystery of the incarnation; rather they intended it to be a paradoxical protection of the mystery against rationalizing explanations that effectively destroy the mystery.

Does belief in the hypostatic union find support in divine revelation and the earliest traditions of faithful Christian believers? It does, even if nowhere was it spelled out either in Scripture or in the first generations of post-apostolic church fathers. The Gospel of John begins with a strong affirmation of

---

[2]John H. Leith, ed., *Creeds of the Churches: A Reader in Christian Doctrine from the Bible to the Present,* rev. ed. (Richmond, Va.: John Knox Press, 1973), pp. 35-36.

the incarnation: one who was "with God and was God" became human (Jn 1). Yet Luke's gospel refers to the same person on earth as increasing in wisdom and stature and favor with God and man (normal human development) (Lk 2:52). Jesus Christ acted as God by forgiving people's sins and was condemned at his trial for making himself equal with God. While he never stood on a hilltop, stretching out his arms, proclaiming "I am God; come worship me!" he did go around implicitly acting as if he thought he was God. He repeatedly said that people's decisions about God and his rule (kingdom of God) were made in the form of decisions about him—Jesus Christ. Apostles like Paul may not have declared Jesus Christ to be God, but they more than implied it. Philippians 2 contains an early Christian hymn ("Carmen Christi," Phil 2:6-11) that refers to the Son of God's *kenosis* (self-emptying) by laying aside his privileges as God in order to take on the form of a servant.

The fact that early Christians worshiped Jesus Christ as God is well-attested by non-Christian writers of the second century. The anti-Christian Roman philosopher of the mid-second century Celsus ridiculed Christians for worshiping a man as God:

> Now, if the Christians worshiped only one God they might have reason on their side. But as a matter of fact they worship a man who appeared only recently. They do not consider what they are doing a breach of monotheism; rather, they think it perfectly consistent to worship the great God and to worship his servant as God. And their worship of this Jesus is the more outrageous because they refuse to listen to any talk about God, the father of all, unless it includes some reference to Jesus: Tell them that Jesus, the author of Christian insurrection, was not his son, and they will not listen to you. And when they call him Son of God, they are not really paying homage to God, rather, they are attempting to exalt Jesus to the heights.[3]

Thus a pagan Roman opponent of Christianity provides strong evidence that the same basic idea later expressed at the Council of Chalcedon was already well-known as a basic Christian belief by Christianity's critics only about one hundred years after the apostles.

The early church fathers vigorously asserted and defended the true humanity and true deity of Jesus Christ long before the ecumenical councils established official church doctrine about the person of Jesus Christ. Limita-

---

[3]Celsus *On the True Doctrine: A Discourse Against the Christians,* trans. R. Joseph Hoffmann (New York: Oxford University Press, 1987), p. 116.

tions of space prevent a thorough treatment of these early Christian affirmations of what later came to be formalized as the doctrine of the hypostatic union. But a few notable examples can be provided. The influential late-second-century and early-third-century Latin church father and theologian Tertullian wrote about the incarnation of the Word (Logos, Son of God) as Jesus Christ:

> The Word, therefore, is incarnate; and this must be the point of our inquiry: How the Word became flesh,—whether it was by having been transfigured, as it were, in the flesh, or by having really clothed Himself in flesh. Certainly it was by a real clothing of Himself in flesh. For the rest, we must needs believe God to be unchangeable, and incapable of form, as being eternal. But transfiguration is the destruction of that which previously existed. For whatsoever is transfigured into some other thing ceases to be that which it had been, and begins to be that which it previously was not. God, however, neither ceases to be what He was, nor can He be any other thing than what He is. The Word is God.[4]

Tertullian continues by arguing that the incarnation must not mean that the Word (second person of the Trinity) transformed himself into a human being because then he would no longer be what he was—God. Rather Jesus Christ must have been of "two substances"—the divine substance of the Word (eternal) and the human substance of man (mortal). These two substances, according to the North African father, cannot mix or mingle. Rather:

> We see plainly [in Jesus Christ] the twofold state, which is not confounded, but conjoined in One Person—Jesus, God and Man. Concerning Christ, indeed, I defer what I have to say. (I remark here), that the property of each nature is so wholly preserved, that the Spirit on the one hand did all things in Jesus suitable to Itself, such as miracles, and mighty deeds, and wonders; and the Flesh, on the other hand, exhibited the affections which belong to it.[5]

At about the same time Tertullian wrote about Christian beliefs in the Latin-speaking, Western portion of North Africa (Carthage and its environment), Origen was writing as a Christian philosopher in the Greek-speaking, Eastern portion of that region of the Roman Empire. In his great exposition of Christian philosophy titled *On First Principles,* the Alexandrian thinker

---

[4]Tertullian *Against Praxeas* 27, *ANF* 3:623.
[5]Ibid., p. 624.

explained the incarnation of Christ as a union of two natures in the one person of the eternal Word, the Son of God (chapter 6). Like Tertullian, Origen went to great pains to distinguish the two natures—human and divine—in Jesus Christ while preserving his unified person. He used the analogy of an iron in a fire in which two entirely distinct substances unite—as can be seen in the iron poker becoming red with heat—while remaining distinct. Yet another great North African Christian, Augustine of Hippo, expressed a pre-Chalcedonian view of Jesus Christ that foreshadowed the hypostatic union doctrine. In his handbook of doctrine titled *Faith, Hope and Charity* the great bishop wrote:

> Wherefore, Christ Jesus, the Son of God, is both God and man. He is God before all ages; man in our own time. He is God because He is the Word of God, for *the Word was God*. But He is man because in His own Person there were joined to the Word a rational soul and a body. Therefore, so far as He is God, He and the Father are one; but so far as He is a man, the Father is greater than He. Since He was the only Son of God, not by grace but by nature, in order that He should also be full of grace He became likewise the son of man; and the one selfsame Christ results from the union of both. . . . Being God and man did not make Him two sons of God, but one Son of God: God without beginning, man with a definite beginning—our Lord Jesus Christ.[6]

The litany of great Christian thinkers, theologians, bishops and Reformers who affirmed the hypostatic union of two natures in Christ could continue. Suffice it to say that this unifying doctrine of Christianity found agreement in Thomas Aquinas, the leading Catholic thinker of the medieval period, as well as in the writings of the great medieval Eastern Orthodox theologians. The Protestant Reformers all accepted it as true Christian belief, and some of them included the Chalcedonian Definition in their books of creeds and confessions of faith. The Church of England included it among its list of authoritative Christian statements; the Puritan divines (preacher-theologians) all gave the basic idea of Chalcedon great weight and authority. The Presbyterian Westminster Confession of Faith uses the concepts of Chalcedon to express the doctrine "Of Christ the Mediator" (chapter 8). The radical reformers such as Servetus of Spain and Socinus of Poland were roundly condemned by the main Protestant Reformers for casting aside the incarna-

---

[6]Augustine *Faith, Hope and Charity (Enchiridion)*, trans. Louis A. Arand (Westminster, Md.: Newman, 1963), p. 43.

tion and rejecting the Chalcedonian Definition. The leading Anabaptist leaders such as Menno Simons affirmed the basic idea of the hypostatic union without acknowledging the special authority of the Definition of Chalcedon. Some of Menno's critics claimed that he departed from orthodoxy by teaching a strange doctrine of the "celestial flesh of Jesus Christ"—that the humanity of Christ actually began in heaven before the virginal conception and birth on earth—but there is no evidence that the great founder of the Mennonite tradition who also influenced the English Quaker (Friends) movement and other radical Reformation movements ever questioned the two natures of Jesus Christ or the incarnation. Nor did the early Methodist revivalists such as John Wesley and George Whitefield.

Not until the rise of liberal Protestantism in the nineteenth century did the hypostatic union and Chalcedonian Definition come under attack and find rejection in the mainline churches of the Reformation. It became a flash point of controversy between conservative and liberal Protestants throughout much of the twentieth century. Conservative theologians as diverse as Karl Barth of Switzerland and Carl F. H. Henry of the United States defended the basic Chalcedonian model of the person of Jesus Christ as essential to authentic Christian belief.[7]

One can say without much fear of contradiction that through two thousand years of Christianity belief in something like the "one person, two natures" idea of Jesus Christ has reigned supreme among most Christians. Christianity claims that this one man of Nazareth who died in Palestine on a Roman cross and rose from the dead nearly two thousand years ago is both truly God and truly human and yet not a mixture of those two kinds of being—divine and human—but a union of them in one fully integrated person, the person of the Son of God, the second person of the Trinity.

---

[7]This is easier to document in Carl F. H. Henry's case than in the case of Karl Barth. See Henry's book *The Identity of Jesus of Nazareth* (Nashville: Broadman, 1992). Some scholars may object that Karl Barth did not affirm the Chalcedonian hypostatic union model of the person of Jesus Christ preferring instead his own "two states" or "two conditions" model to the classical "two natures" model of the person of Christ. However, in *Church Dogmatics* 4/2: *The Doctrine of Reconciliation*, chap. 64, para. 2, "The Homecoming of the Son of Man," the Swiss theologian rejects abandonment of the "two natures" Christology. His account of the two states of Jesus Christ—humiliation and exaltation—is his own interpretation of it. His only concern with the hypostatic union concept is the danger of presupposing that we already know apart from Jesus Christ what "human nature" and "divine nature" are and must be.

## Alternative Views of Jesus Christ

Alternatives to orthodox Christology are too numerous to mention let alone describe. Here we will focus on those views of the person of Jesus Christ that have arisen within the church among Christians and challenged the Christological consensus in some significant way. Six main Christological heresies arose during the first few centuries of Christian history and all have reappeared from time to time within Christian circles. Seldom are they promoted using the names that have been given them by Christian theologians. However, it is helpful to know those names and so they will be used here even though they may sound technical and very unfamiliar to most readers. Each one first arose during the first four centuries of Christian history and each one contributed to the need for a unified response by Christian thinkers and leaders. The Chalcedonian Definition responded to them in its hypostatic union model of the incarnation. By 451, then, the Christian consensus was considered official in the Roman Empire and had the force of law behind it. Dissenters—of which there were many—had to be quiet about their views of Jesus Christ or else move to areas of the empire where orthodox, catholic leaders had little power. In a few geographical areas alternative Christologies became semi-official and the churches in those areas broke away from the rest of the bishops of the empire. This was the case, for example, with the Coptic Church of Egypt, which disagreed with Chalcedon for many years and developed its own style of liturgy and leadership.

The first alternative Christology was *docetism,* promoted by Gnostics within the Christian churches. The Gnostics believed that matter is either evil or so corrupt that the heavenly redeemer could not combine with matter. Thus, they denied the true humanity of the Savior. This came to be known as *docetism* after the Greek word for *appear.* To the Gnostics Christ only appeared to be human and fleshly; in fact, he was only spiritual. Those who held a docetist Christology suggested that perhaps Christ only pretended to have human frailties and be tempted. Perhaps he only faked his suffering and death. More sophisticated docetists held a dualistic Christology that strongly distinguished between "Christ," a heavenly, spiritual redeemer, and "Jesus," the human taken over by the Christ and used as his instrument for a time on earth. Some of the docetists believed that Christ entered into the man Jesus at the latter's baptism by John the Baptist. Most believed that the redeemer left the body of the man Jesus before he died on the cross. In any case, all docetists denied the full and true incarnation of the

Son of God in humanity. In one way or another they spiritualized the incarnation so that it was not a true incarnation at all.

The apostles and early church fathers firmly and even vehemently rejected docetism. Citing passages from the New Testament that pointed to Jesus' humanity did not help very much because of the dualistic model of docetism that could answer those passages by referring the limitations and frailties to the man Jesus and arguing that the spiritual Christ in him was not in view. The second-century church father Irenaeus, bishop of the Christians in Lyons in Gaul (France) worked hard to refute docetism by arguing that if Christ did not take on true humanity like our own then we are not saved. His argument in *Five Books Against Heresies* was that in order to save us Christ had to reverse the sin of Adam in the "very same formation" as Adam. Christ's saving work, Irenaeus asserted, was "recapitulation"—a process of going through all the stages of human life in a human nature (not merely pretending to be human) and obeying where the first man, Adam, disobeyed. The overall thrust of Irenaeus's and later church fathers' polemics against the Gnostic docetists was that if they were right humanity was not saved. The incarnation as union of divine and human natures in the person of the Son of God came to be viewed as itself a saving reality. The cross was just one part of it.

Docetism still exists within Christian circles, especially in folk religion and folk theology. Many Christians mistakenly believe that if Jesus Christ was truly God he could not really suffer or be tempted and that he must have experienced omniscience and omnipotence at all points throughout his life. This definitely weakens the message of the incarnation—that God became human, taking on humanity for our sakes so that our humanity might be healed and restored.

The second main challenge to orthodox Christology was the opposite of docetism. *Adoptionism* was promoted by Paul of Samosata, a bishop of Christians in Syria. He and his followers believed that Jesus Christ was only human but a very special human—one "adopted" by God as his special prophet and "son." According to most adoptionists this happened at the baptism of Jesus, but other adoptionists have attempted to root it in God's own eternal intention to raise up a special man to reveal him in a unique way. Adoptionism, then, does not necessarily imply that Jesus Christ was nothing but a "divine pick up," to use theologian John A. T. Robinson's inelegant phrase. For most adoptionists, such as many liberal Protestant theologians of the nineteenth and twentieth centuries, Jesus Christ fulfilled among humans within history an eternal divine plan: he was a human being perfectly fulfilling the image of God and God's ideal for humanity. The key characteristic of all adoptionist Christologies is an affirmation of Jesus Christ's uniqueness in relation to God combined with a denial of his ontological deity (equality with God's own eternal being). Most adoptionists describe Jesus as "the human face of God"[8] or "God's deputy and representative among men." They pay great homage to the man Jesus Christ while rejecting his equality with God and the classical doctrine of two natures.

The early Christian leaders firmly rejected adoptionism. In fact, the first synod or gathering of bishops that excommunicated one of their own excluded bishop Paul of Samosata from Christianity in the middle of the third century. The Christians felt that adoptionism robbed Christianity and the gospel itself of power. The gospel is God incarnate for us; adoptionism reduces the gospel to a message of following God as the man Jesus did. It ultimately ties in with a "gospel" of self-salvation because it reduces Christ to an example.

Adoptionism has reappeared throughout the centuries of Christianity. In the Reformation decade Servetus and Socinus, two radical reformers, taught their own forms of adoptionism. The Unitarian denomination began in England in the late nineteenth century with an adoptionist Christology that led to a denial of the Trinity. Friedrich Schleiermacher, the father of modern Protestant theology in the nineteenth century, incorporated a sophisticated form of adoptionism into his system of Christian belief that he entitled *The Christian Faith.*[9] In it he interpreted Jesus Christ as the "perfectly God-conscious man" and tried to defend his Christology by saying that the "potency" of God-consciousness in Christ constituted a veritable existence of God in him. The other great liberal Protestant theologian of that century, Albrecht Ritschl, reduced the preexistence of Christ to an eternal intention in God's mind. Unfortunately, adoptionism has become the norm for modern liberal Protestant Christianity. Conservative and evangelical theologians oppose it vigorously as a fatal denial of a core belief of Christianity.

The third major heretical Christology is *Arianism*. Because this was already

---

[8]John A. T. Robinson, *The Human Face of God* (Philadelphia: Westminster Press, 1973).
[9]Friedrich Schleiermacher, *The Christian Faith,* ed. H. R. Mackintosh and J. S. Stewart (Philadelphia: Fortress, 1976).

discussed in the earlier chapter on the Trinity, I will not describe it at length here. Suffice it to say that Arianism is little or nothing more than a sophisticated form of adoptionism that pushes the origin of Christ back before his birth as a baby in Bethlehem and claims that he was God's first and greatest creature but not God or equal with God. Modern Jehovah's Witnesses (The Watchtower Bible and Tract Society) confess this Christology without calling it Arianism. They believe that Jesus Christ was the incarnation of the archangel Michael. This Christology suffers all the same defects as adoptionism; it reduces Jesus Christ to a creature and robs him of his exalted status as worship-worthy deity. How a mere creature—whether human or angelic—can redeem lost and sinful humanity is an unanswerable question. Redemption has to be redefined as pulling oneself up by one's moral and spiritual bootstraps following the good example set by Jesus Christ. That is not the gospel of the New Testament or of the Christian church over two millennia.

In order to understand the other three christological heresies it is important to know about a controversy that erupted among Christians in the Roman Empire in the late fourth and early fifth centuries. The details of the controversy are too numerous and complex to recount here, but before continuing the controversy itself must be described briefly: Two major cities of the Greek-speaking, Eastern Roman Empire vied for power and influence over the new, relatively small capital of Constantinople. They were Alexandria in Egypt and Antioch in Syria. The Christians in each city held somewhat different views on a variety of theological subjects and wanted their perspectives to dominate the church of Constantinople where the emperor worshiped. Alexandrian Christians and those under their theological influence emphasized the deity of Jesus Christ and were very suspicious of any talk of his "two natures" because they felt that took something away from his being fully and truly divine. They were more than willing to say that Jesus Christ was and is both God and man, truly divine and truly human. They affirmed and confessed the Nicene Faith in the triunity of God including the Son of God's oneness of substance with the Father and the Holy Spirit. But they did not like "two natures" talk of Jesus Christ. They preferred to think and speak of Jesus Christ as the one-natured God-man. Antiochian Christians were appalled by the Alexandrian resistance to the two-natures formula about Jesus Christ. They emphasized his two natures so much that to the Alexandrians they seemed to be dividing Jesus Christ into two distinct persons. To the Antiochians the Christians of Alexandria seemed to be denying the full reality of true humanity and true divinity in Christ and suggesting that he was a hybrid of God and man—a third something that is neither fully and truly human nor fully and truly divine.

The fourth christological heresy arose out of that controversy between the two patterns of thinking about Jesus Christ. It is known in the annals of Christian history as *Apollinarianism* after Apollinarius, a Christian bishop of the Eastern Roman Empire who lived at Laodicea in the fourth century. Apollinarius taught that Jesus Christ did not have a human rational soul or spirit. That is, according to his tripartite or trichotomous view of humans Apollinarius believed that the incarnation of God in Jesus Christ could easily be explained by saying that he was a human body and soul (animating life force) without a human rational soul (mind, spirit); in Jesus Christ, so Apollinarius argued, the place of a human rational soul or spirit was filled by the divine Logos/Word, the eternal Son of God, the second person of the Trinity. Thus, in Apollinarianism Jesus Christ was literally "God in a bod." Of course, Apollinarius did not put it quite that way, but his concept of Christ's deity and humanity can fairly be expressed by that phrase.

Something like this model of Jesus Christ seems to be the popular default Christology of many untutored Christians. The problem is, of course, that if Jesus Christ was merely "God in a bod" and did not have a human rational soul—which in Apollinarianism is the "higher nature" and seat of reason, will and worship—then he was not truly human. The church fathers recognized this as a very serious mistake that could eventually undermine salvation itself for, as Gregory of Nazianzus declared, "What God has not assumed [taken to himself in incarnation] is not saved."[10] That is, if Jesus Christ is the mediator between God and humanity and if the incarnation is itself necessary for salvation, then the incarnate Savior Jesus Christ must have had full and complete humanity and full and complete deity—two unmutilated, complete and perfect natures. Besides, how could Jesus Christ have grown in stature and wisdom and favor with God and man as testified in Luke 2:52 if he did not have a human rational soul or mind?

The fifth christological error appeared on the heels of Apollinarianism. It arose out of Antioch and was first proclaimed in Constantinople by the Antiochian patriarch (super-bishop) of the imperial city. His name was Nestorius, and in the early fourth century he affirmed the two complete and unmuti-

---

[10]Gregory of Nazianzus *Epistulae* 101.7, NPNF VII, p. 440.

lated natures of Christ in a way that seemed to divide the person of Jesus Christ into two persons working in harmony. According to Nestorius, the "person" of Christ was actually a "moral union" of two persons like a perfect marriage. The eternal Son of God entered into a unique relationship with the human Jesus Christ from the latter's very beginning in the virgin Mary. What was born of Mary, however, was only the human one—the Son of David. Throughout his life on earth the human one and the divine one worked entirely in concert with each other although only the human one was born, experienced limited knowledge, grew in wisdom, suffered and died. The divine one, the Word of God/Logos/Son of God, performed the miracles and remained untouched by any weaknesses, frailties, suffering, increase in knowledge and wisdom or death.

Of course, the other church leaders recognized this model as problematic (to say the least!). It is not a true incarnation. Again, it is merely a sophisticated new form of adoptionism. The older adoptionism—which also arose out of the Antiochian region—was non-trinitarian. It viewed Jesus Christ as only a man who held a special relationship with God the Father. There was, in that view, no eternal Son of God or Holy Spirit. Nestorius was fully trinitarian, but he seemed to be repeating the error of adoptionism with regard to Jesus Christ who he reduced to a man in a special kind of relationship with God—only now it is the eternal Son of God who is in view. The leaders of Christianity met at Ephesus in 431 and condemned Nestorianism as heresy because it amounted to a denial of Jesus Christ's true divinity and the Son of God's true humanity. As appealing as it may be, Nestorianism completely undermines the crucial Christian idea of incarnation. A modern form of Nestorianism has arisen among certain liberal Protestant theologians. British process theologian W. Norman Pittenger tried to breathe new life into the old Antiochian heresy in his 1959 book *The Word Incarnate* (Digswell Place, U.K.: James Nisbet).

The sixth and last Christological heresy was developed in direct response to Nestorianism by an elderly monk of Constantinople who was devoted to the Alexandrian viewpoint. His name was Eutyches, and his error has been called both *Eutychianism* and *Monophysitism* (meaning "belief in one nature"). He and his followers in Constantinople and around the empire were so appalled at the Nestorian denial of the unity of the person of Christ that they emphasized it in a one-sided way by denying that Jesus Christ could have two full and complete natures. According to Eutyches and all monophysites, Jesus Christ's humanity was "like a drop of wine in the ocean of his divinity." In other words, while he *had* a human nature *in theory* it was actually swallowed up by his divinity so that he was really a hybrid of humanity and divinity. The Christian leaders gathered at the Council of Chalcedon in 451 condemned that view as well as its main rival, Nestorianism, and all other heresies regarding the person of Christ. The wording of the Chalcedonian Definition reflects its rejection of all these alternative Christologies. Monophysitism survived among Christians in certain regions of the Middle East. So did Nestorianism. These smaller, regional, nonorthodox, noncatholic denominations have existed mostly under Muslim rule for centuries.

### Diversity Within Christian Belief About Jesus Christ

The immediately preceding description of the six major alternatives to Christian belief about Jesus Christ might mislead someone to think there is no diversity in Christianity with regard to belief about the person of Jesus Christ. It is true that Christian leaders of all major traditions and denominations have been more protective of Christology than any other area of Christian belief. Any significant departure or deviation from belief in the incarnation as hypostatic union is viewed as heresy if not apostasy by all relatively conservative Christian theologians and leaders. Nevertheless, the Chalcedonian Definition did not answer all questions about the person of Christ and left much room for further exploration and speculation about the subject within its "four fences" (the description of Christ's two natures as without division, separation, confusion, mingling).

So long as one does not deny the full and true deity and humanity of Christ and so long as one does not divide him into two persons or describe his being as a hybrid of two natures one is permitted to speculate far and wide about his being and person. For example, during the Protestant Reformation there was much debate and disagreement between Luther and his followers and Zwingli, Calvin and their Reformed disciples over whether Jesus Christ could be present bodily in the sacrament of the Lord's Supper. Luther and the Lutherans insisted that because of the incarnation the very humanity of Jesus Christ—including his glorified body—is "ubiquitous." That is, the man Jesus Christ is not limited to heaven; he can be everywhere at the same time because he is God as well as human. To the Reformed theologians this seemed to undermine the humanity of Christ so they rejected Luther's view and argued that even now, after his resurrection and ascension, the man Jesus is bodily located in heaven and is not omnnipresent except through the Holy Spirit who is the Spirit of Christ making him present with all of his people everywhere.

In the nineteenth century, Protestant theologians began to discuss the true humanity of Jesus Christ during his earthly life in new ways. A debate arose that continued into the twentieth century and will almost certainly continue until Christ returns. Some theologians argued that for the purpose of the incarnation, in order to live a truly human life, the divine Son of God "emptied himself of all but love" (to borrow a phrase from Charles Wesley's hymn "And Can It Be"); he laid aside his attributes of glory and went through a normal human development of growth, temptation, limitation and then suffering and death. In this view, which has come to be known as "kenotic Christology,"[11] Jesus Christ had two natures and was one person but was also limited in knowledge and power because of a voluntary decision of self-restriction or self-limitation made by the Son of God who became Jesus Christ. Kenoticists appeal especially to the famous *kenosis* (emptying) passage in Philippians 2:5-11.

According to the leading kenotic thinkers such as Anglican bishop Charles Gore, Congregational evangelical theologian P. T. Forsyth and Canadian Baptist thinker Russell F. Aldwinckle, the divine Son (Word, Logos) did not set aside his attributes of deity, but he did restrict their use so that he was not even conscious of them in his human life on earth. He chose to receive everything from God his Father and from the Holy Spirit. Thus, he could and he did live a truly human life. He was not merely possessed of an impersonal nature, as some would have it, but he was a real man just like others (without sin) who was also God without being aware of it all of the time. This leaves open many questions about when and how Jesus became aware of his deity and to what extent he used his divine powers, but kenotic Christology includes any model of the person of Christ that begins with a basically Chalcedonian framework of "one person, two natures" and then explains the coexistence of two natures in Christ by referring to a self-limitation of the Son of God's divine nature.

The main competing model to kenotic Christology is the "two minds" or "two consciousnesses" model which denies any limitations of knowledge or power in Jesus Christ and attaches two wills and two consciousnesses to his

---

[11]For an excellent survey of this christological model. see Donald G. Dawe, *The Form of a Servant: A Historical Analysis of the Kenotic Motif* (Philadelphia: Westminster Press, 1968).

single personhood. This view is explained (rather awkwardly) in the twentieth-century classic *God Was in Christ* by Scottish theologian Donald M.
Baillie (1948), which some critics have viewed as almost Nestorian in its
emphasis on the distinction between the humanity and deity of Christ. An
arguably more conservative and traditional explanation of this model of
hypostatic union is given by the Christian philosophical theologian Thomas
V. Morris in *The Logic of God Incarnate*,[12] in which the author argues that
one person can possess two distinct minds or consciousnesses. An analogy
might be a computer that uses two programs simultaneously or an ordinary,
healthy person who knows more than she knows that she knows and occasionally recalls subconscious or repressed memories and data knowledge.

Kenotic Christology is perfectly consistent with Christian consensus
Christology so long as it does not go so far as to say that the heavenly
Logos/Son of God gave up his attributes of deity in order to become
human. Some kenotic Christian thinkers may have leaned that far in trying
to affirm Jesus' true humanity. Most, however, do not, and it is not at all
necessary to kenotic Christology to go that far. The vast majority of kenotic
Christian thinkers merely aver that the Son of God voluntarily laid aside the
*conscious awareness and use of* attributes of glory.[13] He was still always—even
as Jesus Christ the baby lying in a manger in Bethlehem—both truly God
and truly human.

Two-minds or two-consciousnesses Christology is likewise perfectly consistent with Christian consensus Christology so long as it does not suggest
that Jesus Christ was really two persons—one human and one divine—working in harmony. That would be Nestorianism and a denial of the incarnation
itself. Kenotic thinkers tend to view two-minds Christology as too close to
Nestorianism for comfort. How can two consciousnesses really exist in one
person if that person is healthy and not mentally ill? And if one of the two
consciousnesses is said to be latent, subconscious, repressed in some way—is
that not a major concession to kenotic Christology? Why not go all the way
with true kenoticism? Two-minds or two-consciousness thinkers tend to
view kenotic Christology as implicitly Eutychian or Monophysite in that it
seems to favor the unity of the person of Jesus Christ over his possession of

---

[12]Thomas V. Morris, *The Logic of God Incarnate* (Ithaca, N.Y.: Cornell University Press, 1986).
[13]See for example P. T. Forsyth, *The Person and Place of Jesus Christ* (London: Independent
   Press, 1946).

two distinct natures.

Both groups of thinkers need to acknowledge that the mystery of the incarnation is too deep of a mystery for human speculation to explain and that their models are only that—models of a mystery. They should accept each other as fellow Christian believers so long as they both affirm the single, unified personhood of Jesus Christ and his two distinct but inseparable natures.

There are, of course, many other contemporary models of the person of Jesus Christ such as liberation Christology (Christ as liberator of the poor and oppressed) and revelation Christology (Christ as full revealer of the heart and mind of God). These are not really so much attempts to elucidate consensus Christology as they are attempts to relate Jesus Christ to contemporary social and spiritual questions and needs. They can be fully in harmony with consensus Christology or they may be substitutes for it. Each one must be carefully examined in the light of the biblical revelation of Jesus Christ and the Chalcedonian Definition.

## A Unitive Christian View of the Person of Jesus Christ

Christians have always used a variety of models and metaphors for expressing the unique significance of Jesus Christ as God and Savior: friend, liberator, reconciler, king, healer, judge, mediator, sacrificial lamb, rock, mother, counselor, teacher, example, messiah. All can be legitimate ways of expressing Jesus Christ's significance for the world and for Christians. New models and metaphors arise as the gospel is taken to and grasped by new groups of people in different cultures. In some universes of thought Christ is embraced and revered as hero or ancestor or victorious conqueror. Is there a basic, universal Christian belief about Jesus Christ that all these diverse metaphors must build on and return to? Is there a criterion by which newly-developed metaphors and models should be judged so that there are not many Christs? There is. It is the one finally agreed on by the leaders of early, undivided Christendom that was simply an outworking in formal language of the apostolic witness itself: *Jesus Christ as God incarnate; one unified person—the eternal Son of God equal with the father; of two distinct but never separate natures, human and divine.* This unified and unifying Christology is admittedly a mystery. It does not say everything about Christ that needs to be said in particular cultures and contexts. It merely rules out those models of Christology that would reduce Jesus Christ to something less or other than "truly human and truly divine"—the God-man who alone can be Savior of the world.

Merely functional Christologies that attempt to describe Jesus Christ solely in terms of his human accomplishment as a prophet, revealer, model of love and so forth cannot suffice; if Jesus Christ was not God there is no particular reason to suppose he cannot be surpassed. People who settle for a merely functional Christology will inevitably begin looking for another Christ or at least allowing for the possibility of many Christs. Christianity is Christ, and that means that at its very center it necessarily includes belief in and affirmation of Christ's full deity. He does not merely "have the value of God for us" as one liberal Protestant theologian expressed Jesus' deity; he is God for us, as Karl Barth never tired of saying. At the same time, we must remember that he was and is not only truly human, but also the true human. From Jesus Christ we learn not only the will and character of God but also our own humanity.

# CHAPTER 11

# SALVATION

## Objective *and* Subjective

Christianity is a religion of salvation. Just as "Christianity is Christ," so also "Christianity is the gospel of Christ as Savior." When the early church fathers debated the doctrine of the person of Christ and sought to construct a unifying belief about his deity and humanity (incarnation) they were primarily concerned to protect the reality of salvation through Christ. The apostle Paul wrote in his second epistle to the Corinthians that "God was reconciling the world to himself in Christ" (2 Cor 5:19), and the same basic message echoes throughout the New Testament writings and those of the early Christian church fathers. Christians have always believed that Jesus Christ is both *Lord* and *Savior,* and they have sought to keep the two titles inextricably tied together. Any Christology that undermines salvation through Christ was rejected; any view of salvation that does not do justice to Christ's sole and unsurpassable mediatorship and leaves room for other saviors and lords or for salvation by some other means was rejected. *Salvation* has been interpreted in relation to the fallen human condition of alienation from God as well as inward corruption of nature. Christianity says that Jesus Christ reversed this condition or provided for its reversal by his life, death and resurrection from the dead.

## Issues and Polarities of Christian Belief About Salvation

As usual, simple and straightforward appeal to divine revelation in Scripture does not seem to suffice to render verdicts in controversies. Problems and questions have arisen throughout the history of Christian thought. While all Christians have always agreed that Jesus Christ is the Savior of the world (how could anyone consider himself or herself a Christian or be considered a Christian by anyone else and deny that?) they have not always agreed on the details of *how* Christ saves humans. Was his very life as the incarnate one—his union of deity with humanity—somehow saving? If so, how is that to be understood and explained? Was his life as the God-man on earth perhaps only or primarily a journey to the crucifixion where, by his death, he accomplished salvation for humanity? If so, how is his death saving? Why did he (or anyone!) have to die in order for humanity to be reconciled to God? Did Christ's saving work on behalf of humanity actually accomplish salvation? That is, was it an objectively "done deal"? Or is there something for humans to do? Is a certain response to Jesus Christ's life and death required for anyone to benefit from his work? These and other questions have been asked by inquiring minds over the centuries. They are fair and reasonable questions, which Christian theologians have attempted to answer.

Like most other areas of Christian belief this one—the "work of Christ," as it is called in theology—is extremely complex and space constraints prevent exhaustive treatment of all its aspects. Therefore, the focus here will be on the heart of the matter: the Christian belief in Christ's atonement. *Atonement* is an English word that means reconciliation. That is, atonement refers to the work of Christ by which he brought humanity and God together in spite of humanity's sinfulness and God's holiness. Christians have always believed in atonement by Christ, but they have not always agreed on how he accomplished it for us. It has been left to theologians, scholars and church leaders to work that out. Here our procedure will be the usual one. We will begin with a brief description of the Christian consensus about Christ's atonement. Then we will proceed to an examination of some alternatives to Christian belief and follow that with a delineation of several major Christian models of atonement that provide most of the diversity about this subject in Christianity. Finally, we will wrap it up with a few brief remarks about how Christians might unify around this area of belief.

## The Christian Consensus About Christ's Atonement

In the previous chapter we saw that the World Council of Churches—accused by many conservatives in all major branches of Christianity of being too liberal—at least sets one major belief-criterion for membership: "Jesus Christ is God and Savior." (It assumes that everyone believes Jesus Christ was human, so that goes without saying.) The last chapter examined the Christian consensus about the first part of that confession—Jesus as God incarnate. Here we examine the Christian consensus about the second part—Jesus as Savior of the world. Unfortunately, here we cannot turn to a unifying creed setting forth as detailed a statement as that contained in the Chalcedonian Definition about Jesus' humanity and divinity. No major unifying council of the undivided church (i.e., before the division between Eastern Orthodoxy and Western Catholicism) ever promulgated an official Christian belief about the atonement. All the major Christological creeds—from Nicea through Chalcedon through the so-called Athanasian Creed—say that Jesus Christ is Savior, but none sets forth what Christians must believe about *how* he saves. The consensus of Christian belief about Christ's atonement on behalf of fallen, sinful human beings must be discerned from the writings of the great church fathers, medieval theologians, Reformers and modern Christian thinkers.

What appears more prominently than consensus in those writings is diversity. Some of the church fathers described Christ's accomplishment of salvation primarily in terms of his uniting deity (divine nature) with humanity (human nature). Others described it more in terms of his ransom of captive human beings from Satan. Later, in the medieval era, certain theologians of the church developed latent themes such as sacrifice into elaborate theories of satisfaction and penal substitution. Luther preferred the imagery of battle—Christ invading the territory of the evil powers and principalities and conquering them, thus freeing humans from their domination. Some medieval and modern Christians have preferred to think of Christ's atonement as his moral influence on humanity. In a later section of this chapter we will examine these diverse theological models of Christ's atonement, but here our concern is with discovering and describing the unity of belief underlying them.

That basic unity of Christian belief about Christ's atonement finds first expression in the New Testament itself. Almost every book of the New Testament from Matthew to Revelation at least touches on Christ's life and death as the sole basis for the salvation of humanity through the grace and mercy of God. As usual, the apostle Paul summarizes this earliest Christian perspective best:

> You see, at just the right time, when we were still powerless, Christ died for the ungodly. Very rarely will anyone die for a righteous man, though for a good man someone might possibly dare to die. But God demonstrates his own love for us in this: While we were still sinners, Christ died for us.
>
> Since we have now been justified by his blood, how much more shall we be saved from God's wrath through him! For if, when we were God's enemies, we were reconciled to him through the death of his Son, how much more, having been reconciled, shall we be saved through his life! Not only is this so, but we also rejoice in God through our Lord Jesus Christ, through whom we have now received reconciliation. (Rom 5:6-11)

Paul continues in the same epistle by emphasizing that Christ's death was not only an objective reconciliation but also a transforming event in which we participate. By faith in Jesus Christ and his cross we die with him to our own fallen, sinful natures. The first epistle of Peter offers the same basic perspective as Paul and other New Testament writers:

> To this you were called, because Christ suffered for you, leaving you an example, that you should follow in his steps.
>     "He committed no sin,
>         and no deceit was found in his mouth."
> When they hurled their insults at him, he did not retaliate; when he suffered, he made no threats. Instead, he entrusted himself to him who judges justly. He himself bore our sins in his body on the tree, so that we might die to sins and live for righteousness; by his wounds you have been healed. For you were like sheep going astray, but now you have returned to the Shepherd and Overseer of your souls. (1 Pet 2:21-25)

Any impartial reading of the New Testament documents cannot help but reach the conclusion that, although the writers describe the details of Christ's atonement in their own ways, an underlying unity of belief exists throughout: *Jesus Christ's life and death objectively provide for reconciliation between God and humanity and make possible forgiveness and transformation of those who believe and trust in him.*

The apostolic consensus reflected in the New Testament writings is also found across the writings of the church fathers. The second-century bishop and theologian Irenaeus, who was an important link between the late second-century Christians and the apostles because he had been taught by Polycarp, one of John's disciples, emphasized the Christian consensus in his five books *Against Heresies.* In the first book the bishop of Lyons writes about the unifying tradition of Christian belief handed down by the apostles and includes in it the one faith (belief) in salvation through Christ Jesus, the Son of God, who became incarnate "for our salvation." He specifically mentions the major events of Jesus' life, death ("passion") and resurrection as part and parcel of his saving work. Throughout his five books Irenaeus expounds the salvation wrought by Christ in great detail focusing especially on his own pet theory that Christ "recapitulated" the life of Adam and by each act reversed Adam's disobedience so that humanity itself could have a new beginning. Christ, according to Irenaeus, was our "second Adam," the new head of a new human race. Included in his redeeming work was his sacrificial death which Irenaeus compares with Adam's disobedience: Just as Adam disobeyed and fell from fellowship with God at a tree (the tree of the knowledge of good and evil), so Christ faced a "tree" (the cross) and obeyed God even unto death. There is no question that for Irenaeus the incarnation of the Son of God as Jesus Christ brought about salvation and that all who embrace him by faith and participation in his church are forgiven and renewed. His obedience overcomes Adam's and our disobedience; his "passion" (suffering and death) becomes the basis for our eternal life.

Approximately one hundred and fifty years after Irenaeus developed his great concept of Christ's saving work for humanity as recapitulation, the influential church father Athanasius wrote his classic defense of Christ's deity titled *On the Incarnation of the Word (De Incarnatione).* There the bishop of Alexandria and defender of the doctrine of the Trinity also wrote about Jesus Christ's saving work and staked it on his being God incarnate—both truly human and truly divine. Throughout *De Incarnatione,* Athanasius emphasized the necessity of the incarnation for salvation and worked out further the idea of saving incarnation—that the unity of humanity and divinity in Christ actually transforms human existence by overcoming death. He also wrote about the cross of Christ as a ransom, a sacrifice for sins, a conquest and a reconciliation of God and humanity. According to the Egyptian Christian leader:

> And so it was that two marvels came to pass at once, that the death of all was accomplished in the Lord's body, and that death and corruption were wholly done away by reason of the Word that was united with it. For there was need

of death, and death must needs be suffered on behalf of all, that the debt owing from all might be paid. Whence, as I said before, the Word, since it was not possible for Him to die, as He was immortal, took to Himself a body such as could die, that He might offer it as His own in the stead of all, and as suffering, through His union with it, on behalf of all, "Bring to nought Him that had the power of death, that is the devil; and might deliver them who through fear of death were all their lifetime subject to bondage."[1]

Later in the same work Athanasius avers that Christ's death has universal significance and is the one basis of salvation for all people:

> He [Christ] it is that was crucified before the sun and all creation as witnesses, and before those who put Him to death: and by His death has salvation come to all, and all creation been ransomed. He is the Life of all, and he it is that as a sheep yielded His body to death as a substitute, for the salvation of all, even though the Jews believe it not.[2]

Athanasius's view of Christ's atonement is not unique among the early church fathers; rather, it is representative of their consensus.

The great Augustine of North Africa taught the saving significance of Christ's life and death and pinned any and all hope of salvation—both objective (reconciliation) and subjective (transformation) on Christ and his atoning work for humanity. One of his major objections to Pelagius and his denial of original sin was that if Pelagius was correct Christ's atonement and especially his death on the cross would not be necessary for everyone—as it clearly is. In his doctrinal handbook *Faith, Hope and Charity.* Augustine asserts the vicarious sacrifice of Christ for human sins and for humanity's salvation:

> Christ was . . . begotten and conceived of no lust of carnal concupiscence. For this reason He brought with Him no original sin. Again, by the grace of God He was most intimately united in a wonderful and ineffable way in one Person of the Word. . . . Yet, because of the likeness of sinful flesh in which He came, He was Himself called sin, destined as He was to be sacrificed in order to wash away sin. In fact, under the Old Law sacrifices for sins were called sins. And He, of whom those sacrifices were but shadows, was Himself truly made sin . . . that is, a sacrifice for sin by which we might be reconciled to God.[3]

---

[1]Athanasius *On the Incarnation of the Word* 20, *ANF,* 2nd ser., 4:47.
[2]Ibid., 37, p. 56.
[3]Augustine *Faith, Hope and Charity (Enchiridion),* trans. Louis A. Arand (Westminster, Md.: Newman, 1963), p. 49.

Like Athanasius before him, then, the Latin North-African father Augustine viewed the life and death of Christ as humanity's reconciliation with God. Scattered throughout his numerous writings are many images and metaphors of Christ's atonement, including victorious conquest and ransom, but in and through all he held forth the unifying vision found in all the church fathers—that Christ's life and death are the basis for the salvation of humanity.

The same unified theme of the gospel of salvation through Christ's life and death is found highlighted in the medieval theologians and the Protestant Reformers. Medieval monk and theologian Anselm wrote a classic book about the atoning work of Christ titled *Cur Deus Homo (Why God Became Man)* in which he attempted to explain rationally the necessity of Christ's death as the God-man for the salvation of humanity. Before explaining his rational theory of Christ's atonement and how it reconciles people with God and God with people, the great abbot and archbishop of Canterbury echoed Irenaeus and other early church fathers by extolling the mercy of God in sending Christ to save humanity:

> It was fitting, surely, that just as death had entered into the human race because of the disobedience of man, so by the obedience of man [Jesus], life should be restored. Further, just as the sin that was the cause of our condemnation had its origin in a woman, it was equally fitting that the author of our justification and salvation should be born of a woman. It was also fitting that the devil, who conquered man by tempting him to taste of the fruit of a tree, should be conquered by a man through suffering he endured on the wood of a tree. There are also many other things which, carefully considered, show a certain indescribable beauty in this manner of accomplishing our redemption.[4]

Anselm continued in the rest of *Cur Deus Homo* to unfold a theory of *how* Christ's death on the cross accomplished our redemption, but he placed before it his affirmation of the universal faith of the church going back to the apostles that only through Christ has God saved humanity or provided for humanity's salvation. Approximately two centuries later another great medieval theologian, Thomas Aquinas, echoed the same basic gospel, and in his *Summa Theologiae* argued that only through Christ's merits, earned by his obedient life and sacrificial death, are humans saved.

---

[4]Anselm "Why God Became Man," chap. 3 in *Why God Became Man and The Virgin Conception and Original Sin*, trans. Joseph M. Colleran (Albany, N.Y.: Magi, 1969), p. 68.

The Protestant Reformers loved to extol the cross of Christ above all else; for them the death of Christ became the focal point of the gospel, taking precedence even over his obedient life, victory over temptation and resurrection (none of which they denied). Martin Luther developed a "theology of the cross" to counter what he viewed as a late medieval tendency in the Catholic church to revel in a "theology of glory" that elevated human powers of reason and moral achievement over the sheer gift of God's grace through the scandalous death of the Son of God at the hands of sinners. Luther viewed the suffering of Jesus Christ as both the suffering of God (the Son) and the suffering of a man (Jesus) and did not emphasize, as some before him tended to, the impassibility of the divine nature even in the cross event. For Luther, the divine-human suffering was the outworking for all of humanity of the great wrath and love of God so that God might be reconciled with sinners and sinners might be both reconciled and transformed. The German Reformer used many images and metaphors for the atoning work of Christ. One of his favorites was the image of a great battle in which the Son of God invades the territory of Satan and conquers sin, death and Satan by his death and resurrection (the *Christus Victor* theme). But overall and in general, Luther agreed with the Christian consensus before him that the work of Christ on behalf of humanity was an absolutely necessary saving sacrifice through vicarious suffering of the penalty of sin.[5]

John Calvin also agreed entirely with the Christian consensus about the centrality and necessity of Christ's redeeming life and atoning death. He wrote of them in terms of Christ's three "offices" of prophet, priest and king, but he described the center of Christ's saving work as his substitutionary death for the sins of humanity: "This is our acquittal: the guilt that held us liable for punishment has been transferred to the head of the Son of God."[6] Calvin holds out no hope and explicitly denies any hope for salvation apart from Christ's death to assuage the wrath of God and win our acquittal; he also interprets the inclusive work of Christ beginning from his earthly life and continuing to his intercession in heaven after his resurrection as necessary for human transformation into restoration of God's image. All Protestant Reformers—including the Anabaptists—viewed Christ's death on the

---

[5]See Paul Althaus, *The Theology of Martin Luther*, trans. Robert C. Schultz (Philadelphia: Fortress, 1966), pp. 201-18.

[6]John Calvin *Institutes of the Christian Religion* 2.16.5, pp. 509-10.

cross as the salvation of humanity, and used many different images and models to describe how that atonement works to bring about reconciliation and peace between God and fallen humans.

What then is the Christian consensus about the atoning work of Christ? Is there any universal agreement of belief about Christ's saving achievement on humanity's behalf that defines authentic Christianity? In spite of tremendous diversity of language, imagery, theoretical explanations, theological constructs and even denominational distinctives about the subject, the unified voice of Christianity about this subject is clear: *Jesus Christ provides salvation for the world (humanity) by his life, death and resurrection.* I might add that this consensus includes belief that *God acted in Christ's death on the cross to reconcile the world (humanity) with himself and to make possible the forgiveness and transformation of sinners.* These exact words are not found in any creed or confessional statement, but they summarize well the belief of all Christians across two thousand years of church history. Anyone who denies them (as opposed to interprets them in a certain way) is in danger of forfeiting his or her right to be considered an authentic Christian. Christianity is the saving work of Christ in his life, death and resurrection.

### Alternatives to Christian Belief About Salvation Through Christ

Just as there is no unifying creed or confession of faith that formally states what all Christians must believe about Christ's saving work, so there is no formal list of heresies about the atonement that the church as a whole rejects. Nevertheless, from time to time Christian theologians and leaders have found it necessary to identify and condemn certain views about Christ and salvation that seem to deny the gospel itself. There are, in other words, beliefs and teachings about the life and death of Jesus Christ that lie outside the pale, as it were, of authentic Christianity. Persons who firmly believe in and promote such views may call themselves and their churches Christian, but they cannot be accepted as truly Christian insofar as they deny the Christian consensus from the New Testament through the modern churches of all major denominations. It seems that two main alternative visions of the atonement of Christ have appeared to challenge the Christian consensus that Christ accomplished salvation for humanity and that he is the only hope of an individual's reconciliation with God which leads to transformation, restoration of the image of God and eternal life with God in heaven. They do not have precise, technical names in historical theology and they are not tied exclusively with one person or group in church history. Thus, I will simply describe them and explain why each one deviates so far from the Christian consensus of belief—rooted as it is in divine revelation—that they are not options for authentic Christian life and faith.

The first main alternative to orthodox Christian belief in Christ's atonement is *the idea that Christ's saving work is not necessary for everyone.* Some so-called Christians have attempted to develop a view of salvation that leaves Christ's death, for example, as a necessary rescue mission by God for only some people; other people are able to save themselves or be saved by some other means than through Christ. This heresy was taught by Pelagius in the early church, resurrected by Socinus and his followers (the Socinians) in the sixteenth century, promoted by certain Unitarian and liberal Protestant theologians in the nineteenth and twentieth centuries (such as Hastings Rashdall in *The Idea of Atonement in Christian Theology* [1919]), and openly articulated by pluralists in the late twentieth and early twenty-first century.

This belief is, of course, closely connected with denial of original sin and affirmation of a basically uncorrupted human nature. Many who hold this view—not a few liberal Protestant Christians among them—believe that Christ's main work on behalf of humanity was entirely subjective—provision of a moral example of God's love and will. In this view, what humanity needs is not so much atonement in the form of reconciliation with God or conquest of evil powers that hold them hostage and in slavery to sin; what humanity needs is an object lesson of God's love and acceptance and self-sacrificing service. Jesus Christ's life and death provided that and only that. Modern pluralists such as John Hick, liberal Protestant theologian and philosopher of England, argue that Christ's life and death provide that only for Christians and people in the Western, primarily European and North American contexts dominated by Christianity. For him, people in other contexts find redemption through other saviors such as Muhammad, Krishna and Buddha. All the prophets and mediators of all the great world religions, pluralists say, provide equal access to "the Real"—whatever God may be behind the many masks and faces of the gods.[7]

Of course, proponents of religious pluralism (in the sense described

---

[7]For John Hick's pluralistic account of Christ as one savior and lord among many, see his contribution to Dennis L. Okholm and Timothy R. Phillips, eds., *Four Views on Salvation in a Pluralistic World* (Grand Rapids, Mich.: Zondervan, 1996).

above) and of Christ's atonement as merely a moral example for humanity to follow do not explicitly deny the reality of Christ's saving work on behalf of humanity. They limit and qualify it in such a way as to reduce it to something quite different from what it always has been in Christian belief. These views of Christ's saving work may appeal to modern and postmodern people who find religious claims of exclusivity troubling, but they sacrifice the intrinsic Christian "scandal of particularity" (Christ's uniqueness and unsurpassable-ness as Savior and Lord) in favor of accommodation to cultural worship of human goodness and tolerance. The limb of Christ's universal lordship and atonement for the sins of humanity cannot be amputated without killing the patient—authentic Christianity. Similarly, the surgery of reinterpreting the atoning work of Christ as mere moral example through voluntary martyr-dom effectively destroys the patient whose very life depends on the gospel of Christ's work as the objective mercy and grace of God for the justification and renewal of all humanity. It leaves the door open to the possibility that some, perhaps many, can save themselves by moral effort alone; it opens the possibility that Christ might be surpassed by a more recent moral example through martyrdom.

Pluralism and moral example theology of the atonement go together; they have found each other in the late twentieth century and early twenty-first century. They are preferred by many Christians and non-Christians because they appear to fit well with the tolerant, humanistic spirit of the age and they avoid the offense of Christ and his cross by reducing them to one path to self-salvation. In the end, however, this approach is fundamentally non-Christian. It capitulates to romantic philosophies and spiritualities that take seriously neither the human predicament nor the grace of the cross. They are far from the center of Christianity as expressed in the consensus of belief about Christ's atonement from the New Testament through two thou-sand years of Christian history.

The second major alternative to Christian belief about Christ's saving atonement is a fairly recent one. It is the view promoted by at least some members of the Korean-based religion known as the Unification Church or simply Unificationism. The church is relatively small in North America, but in some parts of Asia it is large and fast-growing, and it has branches all over the world. Unificationists look to the Korean-born prophet Sun Myung Moon as a latter-day messiah to unify world religions and cultures by means of a philosophy known as "the divine principle." Some followers regard him

as "the Lord of the Second Advent," although Moon has not openly
declared himself in that role. Unificationism claims to be Christian. The
church's official name is The Holy Spirit Association for the Unification of
World Christianity. It possesses great wealth and power and its members
tend to be passionate in their commitment to changing the world into God's
kingdom along the lines laid down by Moon and his associates in books such
as *The Divine Principle*. Unificationism teaches that Jesus Christ was supposed to be the savior of the world and he actually did accomplish a major
aspect of salvation—the spiritual salvation of setting aside the guilt of the
first ancestors' sins and providing indemnity for the sins of all who repent
and believe in him.[8] However, according to unification theology, Christ died
before he was able to finish his mission, which included establishing a new
humanity by marrying and having children purified of the Satanic nature
implanted in humanity by the fall of Adam and Eve in the primeval garden.
Thus, another savior is to appear—the Lord of the Second Advent—who will
complete the work of Christ and establish the kingdom of God on earth.

While pluralism and moral-example thinking about Christ's saving work
are associated with secularization processes in culture and Christianity, teaching about and belief in the unfinished work of Christ yet to be completed by
a new messiah (such as many believe Sun Myung Moon to be) is associated
with extreme sectarianism. Some view the latter belief as cultic; it is certainly
far out of step with the consensus of Christian belief about the finished work
of Christ down through the centuries of church history. John's gospel in the
New Testament recounts Jesus' last words, "It is finished" (Jn 19:30), and
Christians have always believed and taught that Christ accomplished all that
was necessary for salvation. All that remains for salvation to be fully realized
is repentance and faith in Christ and his finished work in his life, death and
resurrection. The message of an incomplete atonement by Christ yet to be
finished by another messiah is a gospel different from the Christian gospel. It
is demeaning to Jesus Christ and it opens a Pandora's box of frightening
possibilities with regard to new christs, saviors, lords and messiahs.

No doubt some knowledgeable readers will be dissatisfied with our reduc-
tion of heresies about Christ's saving work to these two. What about the
numerous partial theories of Christ's atonement that have appeared

---

[8]For an account of unificationist theology by a unificationist theologian, see Young Oon Kim,
*Unification Theology and Christian Thought* (New York: Golden Gate, 1975).

throughout Christian history? Is there not one model of atonement that stands out as normative for Christian belief? Are not all the others (described in the next section here) false? Some Christian theologians do elevate one particular theory or model of Christ's atoning work to the status of dogma and require belief in it of all who call themselves Christians. Some denominations of Christianity have made belief in one particular atonement theory a matter of *status confessionis*, required confession of belief. But only a few hard-core fundamentalists have insisted that all who affirm other theories of atonement cannot be Christians. (Many fundamentalist Protestants of the twentieth century included John Calvin's and the Puritans' "penal substitution theory" among the few "fundamentals of the faith." Many conservative Protestant denominations require affirmation of that theory by candidates for ordination to ministry.) The big picture of Christian belief, however, includes as absolutely normative only belief that Christ's life, death and resurrection are God's unique, special, unsurpassable provision of salvation as reconciliation and transformation for humanity. Exactly *how* God reconciled the world to himself by means of Christ's death on the cross is the subject of much speculation and theological reflection and is a reason for great diversity among Christians.

### Diverse Christian Beliefs About Christ's Atoning Work

Why did Christ (or anyone, for that matter!) *have to die* in order for humanity to be saved from the effects of sin such as alienation from God, condemnation by God and conscience, corruption of nature and eternal death? Why couldn't God simply declare that humans are forgiven? These are questions that arise quite naturally once the absolute centrality and necessity of Christ's atoning death on the cross is recognized as at the heart of Christian belief and proclamation. Over the centuries Christian thinkers have attempted to answer such questions by developing theories or models of the atonement—explanations of why it was necessary for salvation and how it achieved salvation. Occasionally, as noted earlier, one such model is promoted by a theologian or church or denomination as the one crucial model such that its denial or neglect is tantamount to denial of the atonement itself. More often, however, these views have been proposed by individual Christian scholars to help inquiring Christian minds understand the heart of the matter and answer their questions; they have not usually been presented to the exclusion of all other viewpoints.

Christian theories of atonement have been divided into at least two categories by scholars who study historical theology: *objective* and *subjective*. In fact, however, that is a somewhat artificial and misleading dualism. All of the Christian theories of atonement developed by constructive theologians attempt to be both objective and subjective. *Objective* here means that in the cross event something is actually achieved on behalf of humanity by God in Christ; atonement itself happens outside of the individual human subject even if it remains to be realized and appropriated by him or her. Any view that regards Christ's death on the cross as a payment of a required penalty by Jesus Christ to God on behalf of humanity is objective. *Subjective* here means that the cross makes possible or enables a necessary response within the human person needing salvation and that the actual benefit of Christ's death is in that response. Any view that regards Christ's death on the cross as an example or a transforming influence on humanity is subjective. Most, if not all, Christian models of the atonement contain both objective and subjective elements. The moral example heresy of the atonement discussed in the previous section of this chapter is exclusively subjective, which is why it has been rejected by all orthodox Christians.

Here my approach will not be to categorize and divide legitimate Christian theories of Christ's atoning work; I will simply set forth several of the major views developed in Christian history and briefly analyze and evaluate them. Each one has some insight into the cross of Jesus Christ and its saving benefit; each one by itself leaves something of Christ's work for humanity out of view. All together provide a well-rounded, holistic theological account of the atonement. I will conclude by arguing that one theory in particular seems to express the heart of the gospel even if it is insufficient by itself to encompass all that the gospel of Christ's death on the cross says about how we are saved.

The earliest theory or model of atonement in Christian history was the so-called *ransom theory*. It is first found in somewhat definite form in the second-century speculative Christian theologian and church father Origen of Alexandria. It appeared repeatedly in many early Christian writings and gradually became the most popular explanation of how Christ's death on the cross saved humanity. It draws on New Testament imagery and language about Christ ransoming people and being paid as a ransom for them (e.g., Mk 10:45). The ransom theory (as opposed to the New Testament imagery and language of Christ as a ransom) proposed that Christ's death on the cross was necessary because Satan had captured humanity due to Adam's sin and the original sin that spread to all of his posterity and held them in bondage. Because Satan's hold on humanity was legal, God had to deal justly even with Satan, so he paid his Son Jesus Christ to Satan on the cross in order to win back his beloved human creatures. The great Cappadocian church father Gregory of Nyssa—who was influenced by Origen—expressed the ransom theory in chapters 22—26 of his *Great Catechism* in terms of God fishing for humanity using Christ's humanity on the cross as bait. Pope Gregory I (Gregory the Great) took up this theme in the sixth century and made it the virtually unanimous version of atonement. It has very few proponents in the modern church because it portrays God as having to deal fairly with Satan, thus implying a dualism, and at the same time depicts God as tricking Satan because, so all agreed, Satan could not keep Christ because of his holiness and deity. This theory contains a certain hint of antiquated superstition.

In the Middle Ages Anselm of Canterbury was eager to replace the ransom theory with a more rationally intelligible model of the atonement that would also be biblically faithful and true to the impulses of Christian piety and worship. In his *Cur Deus Homo* the archbishop explained how Christ's death was a "satisfaction" paid by the sinless man Jesus to the honor of God. For him, the atonement was not so much a conquest as a transaction, and he explained it in terms of the feudal contract that held his own society together in the eleventh century. In feudal societies a code of honor bound together various groups of people within a hierarchy of power and influence. A vassal served a lord and received from him a piece of land, a manor house, protection or some other payment. The vassal was required to give his lord honor—obedience and service. If a vassal dishonored his lord by betraying him in some way he owed him a "satisfaction"—a debt of some kind. The ultimate debt a vassal might owe his lord would be his life. According to Anselm this system provides the basis for understanding why Christ had to die:

> The restoration of human nature ought not to be neglected, and . . . it could not be accomplished unless man paid to God what he owed for sin. But this debt was so great that, although man alone owed the debt, still God alone was able to pay it, so that the same person would have to be both man and God. Hence it was necessary that God assume human nature into the unity of His person, so that the one who in his nature owed the debt and could not pay it, should be, in His Person, able to pay it.[9]

---

[9]Anselm *Why God Became Man*, p. 155.

According to Anselm and those who followed his thought about the
atonement (which came to include most medieval Catholics), Christ's death
was the substitutionary payment of a debt owed by humanity to the honor of
God, which was robbed or wounded by sin. In order to uphold cosmic justice and order, God absolutely must receive a payment of such satisfaction.
While some have accused Anselm of portraying God as bloodthirsty and like
Shakespeare's Shylock having to have his pound of flesh, in reality Anselm
attributed Christ's redeeming work of paying the penalty for humanity's sins
to God's own love, mercy and compassion. Anselm's theory is highly objective; it depicts the atonement of the cross as a transaction between God and
Jesus Christ. When Christ dies, *it* is truly *finished*. God's honor is satisfied,
his wrath is assuaged, humanity's penalty of eternal death is set aside. All that
remains is for humans to accept the benefit of Christ's death for themselves
through faith, sacraments and works of love. Although Anselm's *satisfaction
theory* echoes New Testament themes of a debt paid by Christ and is echoed
later by Calvin and other Protestant theologians in their theory of Christ taking our deserved punishment, it is so connected with the medieval feudal
system of European society that few in the modern world can understand or
accept it.

Another medieval theologian of Europe named Peter Abelard attempted
to provide an alternative theory of atonement to ransom and satisfaction.
Abelard was a maverick theologian and philosopher in Paris during the late
eleventh and early twelfth centuries. He was strongly dissatisfied with
Anselm's model of Christ's atoning work on behalf of humanity and
attempted to develop an explanation that would do greater justice to God's
love and include humanity in reconciliation. The unfortunate Abelard (who
was castrated by thugs paid by his wife's uncle and who was constantly
hounded by a church inquisition) is often accused of reducing the cross of
Christ to a moral example. That is simply not true. Rather, the young Pari-
sian Christian thinker suggested that Christ's main work of redemption on
the cross was provision of a *moral influence* that changes the perspective of
humanity and causes them to trust God and repent of their sins. For
Abelard, God does not so much need payment of a penalty and certainly
does not need to deal with the devil; God needs sinful people to repent and
throw themselves on his mercy. They don't because they fear and hate God.
Christ enters the picture as the divine-human mediator who demonstrates
God's great love and who, by laying down his life for humanity, causes a

change in sinners' hearts so that they are drawn to God. It is not merely an example; it is a transforming influence. An analogy might be Mahatma Gandhi's idea of *Satyagraha*—causing change in the hearts of enemies by self-sacrificing love. Most Christian theologians consider Abelard's model of the atonement too subjective, although it is sung by even conservative evangelical Protestants all over the English-speaking world. The great hymn "When I Survey the Wondrous Cross" lyrically expresses Abelard's atonement model.

The fourth main Christian theory of atonement is not so much a rational explanation as a dramatic expression of conquest. During the Reformation Luther drew on New Testament themes of battle and early Christian concepts of Christ as victor over Satan and death and developed what has come to be called the *Christus Victor* (Christ the victor) model. It has been championed in the twentieth century especially by Swedish Lutheran theologian Gustaf Aulén in his book *Christus Victor: An Historical Study of the Three Main Types of the Idea of the Atonement.* According to Luther and Aulén, the heart of Christ's atoning work for humanity is his victorious invasion and conquest of Satan's territory where humans have been held captive. It is not so much a ransom paid—and certainly not to Satan!—as a spiritual battle. Regarding this motif of Christ's redemption, Aulén says, "its central theme is the idea of the Atonement as a Divine conflict and victory; Christ—Christus Victor—fights against and triumphs over the evil powers of the world, the 'tyrants' under which mankind is in bondage and suffering, and in Him God reconciles the world to Himself."[10]

The only problems with this view are that it falls short of being a rationally intelligible model that answers the question, why did Christ have to die? and it does not include an account of human guilt and response. It is too objective to suffice as a comprehensive account of atonement by Christ, and it is too dramatic, too poetic to provide a rational answer to the question. That is not to dismiss the Christus Victor concept as unimportant. It is great sermonic material! However, alone it cannot satisfy inquiring minds who want theologically meaningful constructive models that answer the *why?* question.

The fifth theological theory of the atonement rose to prominence during the Protestant Reformation as an adjustment to Anselm's medieval satisfaction

---

[10]Gustaf Aulén, *Christus Victor*, trans. A. G. Hebert (New York: Macmillan, 1969), p. 4.

theory. It is Calvin's and the Reformed theologians' *penal substitution* model of the atonement. Some version of it is most familiar to orthodox, conservative Protestants and especially those in the numerous denominations under the influence of Calvin, the Puritans and great evangelical preachers such as Jonathan Edwards, Charles Spurgeon and Billy Graham (to choose one from each of the last three centuries). Calvin began his explanation of the atonement by describing the problem: "in some ineffable way, God loved us and yet was angry toward us at the same time, until he became reconciled to us in Christ."[11]

Christ reconciled God to us and us to God because "the burden of condemnation, from which we were freed, was laid upon Christ."[12] In other words, Jesus Christ suffered the punishment humanity deserved and thus God's righteous anger and tender love were reconciled; his wrath was assuaged and his compassion expressed. Because of his death on the cross Christ's righteousness can be imputed to us by God just as our sinfulness was imputed to him. Calvin concludes, "Not only was salvation given to us through Christ, but, by his grace the Father is now favorable to us."[13]

The basic structure of Calvin's and the Reformed theologians' model is similar to Anselm's. Calvin even referred to Christ's payment of a debt owed by humanity to God. And yet, a subtle shift appears here. In Calvin's and the Reformed model of "penal substitution" (i.e., substitute punishment) the focus and emphasis are on *punishment*. The penalty born by Christ for us is not a satisfaction paid to the wounded honor of God, but capital punishment as retribution deserved for disobeying God's law. Like Anselm's medieval model this one is strongly objective, but it includes a subjective note insofar as human beings must respond appropriately (repentance and faith) in order to benefit from what Christ accomplished for them. Many critics have argued that this model, like Anselm's, portrays God too negatively and introduces a disjunction between God the Father and the Son of God in which the former is angry, wrathful and punitive and the latter is loving, kind and forgiving. Be that as it may, there can be little doubt that Calvin's Reformed theory of the atonement has biblical underpinnings in the sacrificial system of the Old Testament and in especially the apostle Paul's strong emphasis on Christ turning aside the wrath of God for us.

---

[11]Calvin *Institutes* 2.17.2.
[12]Ibid., 2.17.4.
[13]Ibid., 2.17.5.

These five models of the atoning work of Christ are not the only ones that have appeared in church history; they are just the most influential ones. Others includes a *governmental theory* developed by the seventeenth-century Dutch Arminian theologian and statesman Hugo Grotius and a *perfect vicarious penitent* theory spun out by nineteenth-century Scottish Presbyterian theologian John McLeod Campbell and incorporated by C. S. Lewis in *Mere Christianity*. Most "new theories" are versions of older ones; the five described here and the heretical "moral example" theory pretty well cover all the possibilities. Of course, it is very possible for new models or new versions of these models to appear in cultures being newly touched by the gospel and where indigenous, contextualized theological reflection is young.[14]

For the most part, Christian denominations have avoided identifying any one theory with orthodox belief in the atonement, but in some cases one model or theory has been favored by groups of Christians. Certainly the Eastern Orthodox family of churches tends to favor something like the ransom theory without payment of the ransom to Satan. Overall, however, Eastern Orthodox Christians tend to shy away from rational explanations in favor of embracing mystery. They view the incarnation itself as saving and do not search for theories or models of the cross that set it apart as the single primary focus of Christ's saving work. The Roman Catholic Church enshrines Anselm's basic insight into the objective, finished work of Christ while leaving the door open to additions from other views. The Lutheran churches lean heavily toward Luther's dramatic Christus Victor theme, and the Reformed churches stick close to Calvin's model unless they have been liberalized, in which case they portray Christ's saving work as providing a subjective moral example for basically good people to follow. The Episcopalians and Methodists maintain a broad outlook that holds up the Christian consensus without requiring any particular model. Most Baptists and Pentecostals fall back on Calvin's penal substitution theory without necessarily making it a matter of required doctrine.

### A Unified Christian View of Atonement

Christians need to rediscover and revalue the underlying, essential Christian

---

[14]For examples of possibly new models of Christian thinking about the atonement in non-Western cultures, see Joel B. Green and Mark D. Baker, *Recovering the Scandal of the Cross: Atonement in New Testament & Contemporary Cultures* (Downers Grove, Ill.: InterVarsity Press, 2000).

belief about Christ and his atoning work for the salvation of humanity. In this modern-postmodern era of Western civilization and culture many voices are being raised both against any traditional belief about atonement by Christ's death on the cross and in favor of elevating one particular model of atonement over all others, even to the exclusion of others. Certain outspoken and fairly radical liberation theologians—especially so-called womanist theologians—argue that any traditional theory of the atonement condones violence and sanctions child abuse. Such radical revisionists would like to substitute for salvation-by-death (i.e., Christ's atoning death on the cross) a view of Christ's crucifixion as a martyrdom and a symbol of what powerful religious and political leaders within hierarchical systems of domination always do to prophets. At the other end of the spectrum of theological reflection stand certain outspoken conservative theologians who argue that only the Reformed penal substitution theory developed by Calvin and promoted by theologians such as nineteenth-century Princeton professor Charles Hodge is biblically and theologically correct. Many of these ultra-conservative theologians insist that Christ's death on the cross be viewed by all true Christians as propitiation (appeasement) of God's wrath by means of a vicarious infliction of punishment on God's Son for the sins of the world (or for only the elect).

In the midst of this conflictual situation it is important to discover a unifying Christian view of Christ's saving work on behalf of the human race. The best way to do that is to go back to the sources of Christian reflection and retrieve the simple faith in Christ's saving life, death and resurrection that united the early Christians and the Protestant Reformers in spite of their uses of various models for communicating it and making it intelligible within their own cultural contexts. The early church of the first century believed that "God was in Christ reconciling the world to himself" and that in some mysterious way beyond full human comprehension Christ's death on the cross was a sacrifice for sins, a conquest of evil powers that enslave and an example of perfect love for disciples of Jesus Christ to follow. No one explanation does justice to all that happened on the cross. It was clearly *both* an objective transaction in which something happened in the cosmic, divine order of universal history (as symbolized by the veil of the Jerusalem temple being torn in half [Mt 27:51]) *and* a subjective example and influence that demonstrates God's love and justice and draws people to God in repentance and faith (as expressed in Jesus' statement that when he was "lifted up" he would draw all people to himself [Jn 12:32]). Theological reflection can fall into unwarranted speculation at times, which seems to have happened in the history of Christian reflection on the work of Christ. While there is nothing wrong with reverent speculation and construction of modest models to explain and communicate transcendent mysteries, Christian thinkers must be careful not to baptize any theologically speculative construction (theory, model) as the one and only true Christian belief to the exclusion of all other possible perspectives.

Having said that, it is now also important to say that belief in the objectivity of Christ's atonement is absolutely necessary to the gospel itself. The good news of revelation and Christian proclamation is that God acted in a decisive, objective way in Jesus Christ and his death, graciously and powerfully changing the situation of alienation and spiritual corruption that disrupted the world with the fall of humanity. The gospel cannot be reduced to a merely subjective atonement in which Christ offers an object lesson of God's great love; such a subjective view of the meaning of Christ's death can only be a facet and not the centerpiece of Christian belief and proclamation. Unfortunately many contemporary Christians—even many who consider themselves biblically serious and evangelically-committed—tend to reduce belief in Christ's atonement to a subjective model and neglect or ignore the objective accomplishment of God in Christ. One does not necessarily need to embrace a full-fledged satisfaction theory or penal substitution theory of Christ's work in order to affirm that what Christ accomplished by his death was a unique transaction that effectively reconciled God's justice and love in the face of human disobedience and rebellion and made it possible for God to forgive all who come to him through Christ by faith.

# CHAPTER 12

# SALVATION

## Gift *and* Task

The previous chapter dealt with one major aspect of salvation that is part of Christian belief: Christ's accomplished work for humanity, especially on the cross (atonement). We saw that Christ accomplished an objective reconciliation between God and humanity as well as a subjective example and influence that draws sinners to God in repentance and trust. There is a very real sense, then, in which salvation must be seen by Christians as something that has already happened within history. Salvation is something Christ achieved for humanity. "It is finished" (Jn 19:30).

**Issues and Polarities of Christian Belief About Personal Salvation**
While Christ accomplished salvation in the past, Christianity also says that salvation has another aspect—its application to persons and its appropriation by them. In this chapter we will examine Christian belief and beliefs about that second aspect: *If a person becomes saved (reconciled with God through forgiveness of sins as well as inwardly renewed so that the inherited corruption of sin is being healed) why and how does that happen?* This is the issue of the so-called *ordo salutis,* order of salvation, including the question of God's agency

(initiative, will, action) and the human person's agency and how they work together. What does God have to do with this personal salvation? What does the person who is saved have to do with it? Is it all of God? Is it a cooperation between God and the human person? What is involved in this aspect of salvation?

Two problems present themselves immediately when examining this area of Christian belief. First, while there is some basic agreement, a rough consensus, among Christians of all major traditions, what stands out as most obvious is the disagreement and diversity. This area of belief was largely the cause of the great division that took place within Christendom during the Protestant Reformation of the sixteenth century. Luther believed that the Catholic church of his day was implicitly denying the gospel of salvation by God's grace alone. Once Protestantism developed as a permanent branch of Christianity separate from Eastern Orthodoxy and Roman Catholicism, Protestants themselves began to disagree about issues related to salvation. Many of the most profound divisions within Protestantism have to do with differing beliefs about salvation. Second, this area of Christian belief is extremely complex, with numerous questions, issues, problems and perspectives. It is impossible to deal with even all the important ones in one chapter. Our approach here will be the usual one and will necessarily have to leave aside many important questions and specific beliefs of theologians and denominations. Readers already quite knowledgeable will have to forgive this inevitable and inescapable oversimplification.

In what follows we will deal first with the rough Christian consensus about personal salvation. (I am trying to avoid the phrase "individual salvation," as that may imply that salvation is totally individualistic; it is not. We want to avoid any neglect of the community aspect of salvation in which God works with and through groups of people.) In spite of very strong disagreements among Christians about the ins and outs of personal salvation, a minimal but important consensus defines authentic Christian belief in this area known to theologians as *soteriology* (doctrine of salvation). After explaining the Christian consensus about salvation we will turn to its alternatives—heresies about salvation. Again, there are many views of salvation that lie completely outside of Christianity in world religions and even philosophies. We will examine only those that have arisen within Christianity that pose a very serious threat to the gospel and to the unison voice of historical Christianity. After that we will look into several of the major diverse viewpoints held by Christians and Christian communities about personal salvation. Finally, as always, we will close with a few brief remarks about a unified Christian perspective on salvation.

## The Christian Consensus About Personal Salvation

According to all major Christian traditions over two thousand years of reflection and proclamation, personal salvation is both *gift* and *task*. As we will see later, some Christians have emphasized the gift aspect of personal salvation more than the task side, while others have highlighted the task side more than the gift side. And yet, no major Christian denomination or influential Christian leader or thinker has ever denied that in some senses salvation includes both. Much of the diversity of Christian thought arises from differing estimations of the weight that should be given to salvation as sheer gift of God's grace and how much to salvation as human acceptance by faith and perhaps faithfulness. Nevertheless, underlying that diversity there is agreement: salvation is primarily a gift in which the initiative is God's and yet there is something for the human person to do even if only to accept the gift.

The basis for Christian belief that salvation is both gift and task lies in divine revelation itself. In the Old Testament God reminds his people Israel repeatedly that they are chosen by him and that his choice is not based on their goodness but on his grace alone (Deut 7:7-9; 9:6). The New Testament communicates the same message regarding the church and personalizes it by applying it to individuals as well. In his epistle to the Ephesians the apostle Paul reminds his readers that "it is by grace you have been saved, through faith—and this not from yourselves, it is the gift of God—not by works, so that no one can boast" (Eph 2:8-9). The epistle of James provides the counterpoint: "You see that a person is justified [reconciled with God] by what he does and not by faith alone" (Jas 2:24). Gift and task. This paradox of personal salvation is expressed succinctly by the apostle Paul in his epistle to the Philippians: "continue to work out your salvation with fear and trembling, for it is God who works in you to will and to act according to his good purpose" (Phil 2:12-13). Gift and task. The entire biblical witness presents this paradox even if in certain isolated passages it seems to promote one side more than the other. The only way to reconcile these seemingly conflicting motifs of revelation is to regard salvation as both sheer divine gift (provided, offered) and necessary human response (accepted, maintained). This is indeed the paradox embraced by Christian belief over the centuries.

One of the first Christian writings outside of the New Testament canon is *The First Epistle of Clement,* written by the bishop of the church at Rome to Christians at Corinth around 95 or 100. The author, who almost certainly knew some of the apostles, urges his readers to remember that they are saved not by works but by faith and also that they must not give up on good works and love:

> being called by His will in Christ Jesus, [we] are not justified by ourselves, nor
> by our own wisdom, or understanding, or godliness, or works which we have
> wrought in holiness of heart; but by that faith through which, from the begin-
> ning, Almighty God has justified all men; to whom be glory for ever and ever.
> . . . What shall we do, then, brethren? Shall we become slothful in well-doing,
> and cease from the practice of love? God forbid that any such course should be
> followed by us! But rather let us hasten with all energy and readiness of mind
> to perform every good work.[1]

Later in the same epistle the early church father and bishop writes, "How blessed and wonderful, beloved, are the gifts of God! Life in immortality, splendour in righteousness, truth in perfect confidence, faith in assurance, self-control in holiness!"[2] About one hundred years later Irenaeus extolled the gift of salvation through Jesus Christ received by faith: "Inasmuch, then, as in this world some persons betake themselves to the light, and by faith unite themselves with God, but others shun the light, and separate them-selves from God, the Word of God comes preparing a fit habitation for both."[3] The entire context of Irenaeus's writings against the Gnostic heretics makes clear that salvation is made possible wholly and entirely by God's mercy and grace through Jesus Christ.

The North African church father and theologian Tertullian wrote a trea-tise titled *On Repentance* that expresses the paradox of salvation as both gift and task. According to Tertullian, the very possibility of repentance leading to salvation is a work of God's grace. He refers to salvation as the "fruit of repentance" sown by God. The blessing of salvation he attributes wholly and entirely to God's mercy, and good deeds, including repentance, he attributes both to God's work as well as to the human person's. There is simply no other way to understand this subtle essay on repentance by the great Chris-

---

[1]Clement of Rome *The First Epistle of Clement* 32 and 33, *ANF* 1:13.
[2]Ibid., 35, p. 14.
[3]Irenaeus *Against Heresies* 5:28, *ANF* 1:556.

tian attorney-theologian of Carthage than as an expression of the paradox of salvation as a mysterious combination of God's grace and human "work" in the sense of repentance and amendment of life, which are themselves ultimately God's work in the human person. Sensing the danger that some people may rely so heavily on God's grace—if all is of God—that they may become morally and spiritually careless, Tertullian emphasizes the necessity of striving toward sinlessness and harshly warns against presumptuousness with regard to salvation. But the entire treatise, which appears quite harsh and even legalistic, must be read in the light of the first two chapters where the author clearly attributes all goodness to God's mercy and final causation.[4] The same basic pattern may be discerned in all of the writings of the church fathers insofar as they deal extensively with salvation; all goodness—including every blessing, from desire for God to repentance and faith to forgiveness and inward renewal through partial participation in the divine nature ("divinization")—is attributed to divine mercy and grace, while human persons are urged and even sternly commanded to repent and be faithful.

This paradox of salvation is affirmed by the third-century church father and bishop of Carthage Cyprian, who is often perceived, especially by Protestants, as a legalist who contributed to a moralistic approach to salvation in Catholic Christianity. While it is true that Cyprian helped develop a penitential system for restoring lapsed Christians (who had denied Christ under persecution) and argued that there could be no salvation for those who abandon the catholic church, it is clear that he believed salvation to be a mysterious combination of God's agency and human reception. For Cyprian, salvation is wholly a gift of God and at the same time wholly a matter of human repentance and faith. In his *Epistle to Donatus,* also known in church history as Cyprian's first epistle *(Epistle I),* the North African bishop recounted his own dramatic conversion experience which, he wrote, took place "by the agency of the Spirit breathed from heaven" at baptism.[5] He rejected any boasting by those who have experienced this "new birth":

> Anything like boasting in one's own praise is hateful, although we cannot in reality boast but only be grateful for whatever we do not ascribe to man's virtue but declare to be the gift of God; so that now we sin not is the beginning

---

[4]Tertullian *On Repentance, ANF* 3:657-66.
[5]Cyprian *Epistle I,* para. 4, *ANF* 5:276.

of the work of faith, whereas that we sinned before was the result of human error. All our power is of God; I say, of God. From Him we have life, from Him we have strength, by power derived and conceived from Him we do, while yet in this world, foreknow the indications of things to come. Only let fear be the keeper of innocence, that the Lord, who of His mercy has flowed into our hearts in the access of celestial grace, may be kept by righteous submissiveness in the hostelry of a grateful mind, that the assurance we have gained may not beget carelessness, and so the old enemy creep upon us again.[6]

Clearly, in spite of his reputation for legalism and moralism, Cyprian believed that every good that Christians possess, from new birth through faithfulness to death, is the gift of God and work of God's agency; at the same time he clearly believed that people must work to maintain the gift of God through keeping a grateful heart. Later, in his treatise *On the Unity of the Church*, Cyprian wrote, "but how can we possess immortality, unless we keep those commandments of Christ whereby death is driven out and overcome, when He Himself warns us?"[7] If we read this in the light of his earlier testimony and affirmation of God's grace and agency (power) in salvation, however, we may safely assume that Cyprian believed that Christians' very desire and ability to keep God's commandments comes from God himself—that is, from the Spirit of God poured into their hearts.

Augustine also affirmed the paradox of salvation as both gift and task. Much to the dismay of his critic and opponent Pelagius the North African bishop and church father penned the prayer, "O God, command whatever thou wilt, but give what thou dost command." Pelagius, who denied original sin and taught that humans have a natural ability to live sinless lives apart from any supernatural assistance of divine grace, considered Augustine's prayer permission to sin and keep on sinning until the desire for sin ceases and power to live sinlessly arrives. Augustine explained later what he meant: "Even if men do good things which pertain to God's service, it is He Himself that brings it about that they do what He commanded." In his handbook of doctrine, *Faith, Hope and Charity*, Augustine explicitly affirmed this paradox of salvation:

> if the action [salvation] is from both, that is, from the will of man and from the mercy of God, then we accept that saying "it is not of him that willeth, nor of

---

[6]Ibid.
[7]Cyprian *On the Unity of the Church (Treatise I)*, para. 2, *ANF* 5:421.

him that runneth, but of God that showeth mercy," as if it meant: "the will of man alone does not suffice if the mercy of God be not also present." But then neither does the mercy of God alone suffice if the will of man is not also active. . . . the entire work is to be credited to God, who both readies the will to accept assistance, and assists the will once it has been made ready.[8]

Just as Cyprian, one hundred and fifty years earlier, had gone on to emphasize the works side of salvation lest people rely so much on God's grace and power that they "depart from innocence" (i.e., sin more that grace may abound), so Augustine goes on in his later writings to emphasize the grace side of salvation lest people follow Pelagius into thinking they can save themselves apart from the supernatural work of God's grace within them. In one of his final treatises, titled *On the Predestination of the Saints,* the Bishop of Hippo affirmed unconditional election (absolute predestination) and denied free will that could limit or resist the work of God's sovereign grace in those whom God has chosen to save out of the "mass of perdition." During the Protestant Reformation Luther and Calvin hark back to this later writing of Augustine's. None of them, however, entirely denied the human role in salvation; they simply gave priority to divine grace and attributed even human choices and actions—insofar as they are meritorious—to God.

The paradox of salvation as both gift and task—with the priority of grace over works—was officially affirmed and elevated to the status of doctrine (if not dogma) at a synod of Western bishops in 529 (Second Synod or Council of Orange). Certain monks and theologians had been disputing Augustine's theology for over a century, and finally the church's leaders took steps to settle the matter. The so-called Semi-Pelagians had been arguing that not only was Augustine wrong to teach unconditional predestination and irresistible grace, but that he was also wrong about the *initium fidei*—initiative of faith in people being saved. John Cassian, for example, wrote that at least in some cases the good will of a human being precedes divine mercy and grace.[9] The synod of 529 decided that all faithful Christians should believe otherwise. The bishops gathered there affirmed that even the beginning of a good will toward God is a work of God's grace. They also, however, condemned any

---

[8]Augustine *Faith, Hope and Charity (Enchiridion),* trans. Louis A. Arand (Westminster, Md.: Newman, 1963), pp. 39-40.

[9]For a scholarly account of Semi-Pelagianism, see Rebecca Harden Weaver, *Divine Grace and Human Agency: A Study of the Semi-Pelagian Controversy* (Macon, Ga.: Mercer University Press, 1996).

belief in divine predestination to evil or sin and allowed faithful Christians to believe in free will cooperating with divine grace. During the later Middle Ages and Renaissance some Catholic thinkers and leaders seemed to undermine the priority of divine grace by focusing too much on human acts of penitence. It was against this unofficial theology of the Catholics of Europe more than against the older, official theology of the church that the Protestant Reformers reacted.

Throughout the Protestant Reformation and post-Reformation eras Christian leaders, Reformers, and theologians have always attempted to hold together in paradoxical tension the grace of God and the agency of human persons in salvation. Without doubt, the magisterial Reformers (Lutherans, Reformed and Church of England) tended to emphasize the role of divine grace so much that human agency seemed to take a back seat. In reaction to that emphasis on the absolute sovereignty of grace and perceived implicit rejection of genuine free will (except to sin), the Anabaptists and Arminian Remonstrants of Holland emphasized human agency in salvation while affirming the "prevenience of grace"—that God's assisting grace goes before and is absolutely necessary for even the repentance and faith of sinners who accept Christ and become saved.

During the Great Awakening of the eighteenth century, the great evangelical revivalists and theologians such as John Wesley and George Whitefield disagreed about predestination and free will while agreeing that salvation is wholly a work of God's grace received by human persons. They interpreted grace and free will differently, as we will see in our section on diversity of Christian belief about salvation. In any case, there should be no real doubt that *all major Protestant Reformers and their post-Reformation disciples as well as modern Christian theologians* affirmed and proclaimed *both* divine grace *and* human agency in salvation.[10] Of course they have described that paradox in different ways, and sometimes those differences have caused controversy and division between Protestants—just as they caused the division within Christendom itself during the Protestant Reformation of the sixteenth century. But that is a matter for consideration in the section on diversity of Christian belief about salvation later in this chapter. Suffice it to say here that *Christians all together believe that salvation as reconciliation with*

---

[10]See Alan P. F. Sell, *The Great Debate: Calvinism, Arminianism and Salvation* (Grand Rapids, Mich.: Baker, 1983).

*God and inward renewal from the corruption of inherited depravity and toward the restoration of the image of God is wholly and completely a work of God's grace while at the same time also an event and process involving human agency.* That is, for Christians, salvation is both gift and task.[11]

## Alternatives to the Christian Consensus About Salvation

Two major challenges to the Christian consensus about personal salvation as a paradoxical combination of both gift and task, grace and response, have arisen in church history. They are *Pelagianism/Semi-Pelagianism* and *apokatastasis/ universalism*. These are broad categories with many variations within them, but each one has an essential element that creates its category. Pelagianism and Semi-Pelagianism have already been briefly described. They share the common feature of placing the initiative of salvation in the autonomous human will apart from any special, assisting and calling grace of God. In other words, they at least (sheer Pelagianism may go further) deny the necessity of *prevenient grace*—the calling, convicting, enabling and assisting grace of God that overcomes the bondage of the will to sin and allows a person to respond freely to Christ and the Holy Spirit. Denial of prevenient grace is tantamount to denying original sin and the gratuity (giftness) of salvation (Eph 2:8).

Semi-Pelagianism is associated in church history with a group of monks of Southern Gaul—especially around the city of Marseilles (which is why they are sometimes known as the Massillians)—who campaigned against Augustine's strong belief in original sin and predestination and in the process fell into denial of the absolute necessity of grace for the beginning of the process of salvation. They broke apart the paradox of grace by placing priority on human initiative and free will over God's assisting grace. Semi-Pelagianism has appeared many times throughout the history of Christianity without that label. The Protestant Reformers believed that many of the Roman Catholic leaders and theologians of their day had fallen into Semi-Pelagianism. Many of the radical reformers—especially the rationalists such as Socinus of Poland—taught a Semi-Pelagian doctrine of salvation. The Deists and early Unitarians and liberal Protestant theologians of the eighteenth and nine-

---

[11]For two twentieth-century theologians of different Protestant traditions (Reformed and Arminian-Wesleyan respectively) who equally affirm the paradox of salvation as both gift and task in harmony with the Great Tradition of Christian thought, see D. M. Baillie, *God Was in Christ: An Essay on Incarnation and Atonement* (London: Faber & Faber, 1948); and Thomas Oden, *The Transforming Power of Grace* (Nashville: Abingdon, 1993).

teenth centuries appeared more Semi-Pelagian than Christian in their views on human goodness and moral achievement apart from any special, supernatural assisting grace of God.

No Semi-Pelagian ever set out to contradict hundreds and thousands of years of Christian tradition, let alone divine revelation itself. Semi-Pelagians have never considered themselves heretics or deniers of Christian belief. Few, if any, Christian theological volumes blatantly deny the sovereignty and necessity of grace. Semi-Pelagianism appears more in what Christians do not say about salvation than in what they actually do say. Or in some cases it appears in folk religion and folk theology among Christians. It is perhaps the common default theology of many people in pews and more than a few in pulpits. It is expressed in clichés such as "God helps those who help themselves" and "if you take one step toward God, he will come the rest of the way to you." Popular religious and even Christian jargon is filled with this attitude expressed in many different ways; most people who express it are totally unaware that it is antithetical to the Christian message.

Perhaps the single most influential Semi-Pelagian in modern church history is the great nineteenth-century American revivalist Charles Finney, who left an indelible stamp on not only North American but also world evangelical Christianity. Finney wrote numerous books on theology and revival, organized and led hundreds of mass evangelism campaigns, served as president of Oberlin College in Ohio, and was a tireless and effective social reformer. In spite of his many great achievements, Finney's expressed views on salvation were more consistent with Semi-Pelagianism than with orthodox Christianity. He more than implied that gracious works of God, in and for individuals and groups of people, wait upon human initiative and that all people are capable by will power alone of repenting, exercising faith in Christ, and living virtually sinless, holy lives.[12] Critics of Finney's theology and revival methods are quite right to suggest that he became a major conduit of enlightenment rationalism, individualism and humanism into conservative evangelical Christianity.[13] No doubt his motives were pure, but his theology was pernicious.

---

[12]See Charles Finney, *Systematic Theology* (Minneapolis: Bethany House, 1976), chaps. 31-33: "The Notion of Inability," "Natural Ability" and "Gracious Ability," in which Finney denies inherited depravity (natural inability) and the necessity of prevenient, enabling grace (gracious ability) for the first exercise of the will toward God and the good.

[13]See Michael S. Horton, "The Legacy of Charles Finney," in *Premise* 2, no. 3 (1995) <www.capo.org/premise/95/march/horton-f.html>.

From at least the time of Finney, North American Christianity included a strongly Semi-Pelagian flavor—especially in the social gospel endeavors of liberal Protestants and in the revivalist Evangelicalism of more conservative churches and organizations. The emphasis on individual freedom, will power, decision and moral accomplishment often pushes aside any serious emphasis on God's grace as the source of all true goodness, including every first impulse toward what is good. This Semi-Pelagian or even Pelagian emphasis on the human ability and initiative in salvation found acceptance and expression in several fringe movements of North American Christianity that arose around the same time as Finney's ministry. Mormons and Seventh-day Adventists have tended to promote Semi-Pelagian views of salvation, although the latter have been moving more toward orthodox Protestant Christianity in the second half of the twentieth century.

The second challenge to the Christian consensus about the paradox of salvation as both gift and task, grace and response, is *apokatastasis/universalism*. These two terms are virtually synonymous; they refer to belief in the ultimate, unconditional reconciliation of all humans (if not all creatures including angelic and demonic spirits) with God. The early church fathers Origen and Gregory of Nyssa both apparently affirmed this belief, which was condemned as a heresy by the Second Council of Constantinople in 553. It was revived by the founders of the Unitarian and Universalist movements in the late eighteenth and early nineteenth centuries and became almost a defining feature of liberal Protestant theology in the later nineteenth and entire twentieth centuries. In spite of his rejection of liberal Protestant theology, the great Swiss twentieth-century dialectical theologian Karl Barth seemed to affirm something like a doctrine of *apokatastasis* in which all people are saved in Christ quite apart from their responses to him. However, Barth was notoriously oblique about this matter; on the one hand he affirmed that all are elect and forgiven in Jesus Christ and on the other hand he wrote that the church should not preach an *apokatastasis*.[14] Other twentieth-century theologians have not been as subtle in affirming unconditional, ultimate reconciliation or universalism. "Theologian of hope" Jürgen Moltmann has averred that "through his sufferings Christ has destroyed hell. Since his resurrection from his hellish death on the cross

---

[14]Karl Barth, *Church Dogmatics 2/2: The Doctrine of God*, ed. G. W. Bromiley and T. F. Torrance, trans. G. W. Bromiley et al. (Edinburgh: T & T Clark, 1957), p. 477.

there is no longer any such thing as 'being damned for all eternity'."[15]

Just as Semi-Pelagianism breaks the Christian paradox of salvation as both gift and task by elevating task and human responsibility and ability to initiate salvation over grace, so *apokatastasis*/universalism breaks it by elevating gift and divine grace toward everyone over task so that human beings really play no crucial role whatever in their salvation. The one heresy nullifies "for God is at work in you" and the other one negates "work out your own salvation." Divine revelation and the Great Tradition of Christian belief affirm both. It may not be a heresy to *hope for* universal salvation and it is certainly not a heresy to *call for* human exercise of the will toward God and the good. Semi-Pelagianism and universalism are heresies because they move beyond calling and hoping to believing and teaching that human willing takes priority over divine grace *or* that God's sovereign grace sets aside the necessity of human decision.

### Diversity Within Christian Belief About Salvation

True Christian belief about salvation affirms the gospel—the unconditional good news that fallen, alienated, corrupted and guilty human beings may receive forgiveness, reconciliation and inward renewal toward restoration of the image of God as a free gift through the simple appropriation process of receiving it by repentance and faith. Jesus Christ has accomplished all that is necessary for our salvation on our behalf (gift); all that is required is appropriate response by human persons (task). When people respond appropriately they receive the full benefit of Christ's atonement (gift). There is no question of having to earn the gift of salvation. That would be a sheer contradiction. The paradox of Christian belief about salvation—a paradox embedded in revelation itself and not at all contrary to reason—is that the gift must be received and that even the reception is, in some sense, a gift. At least the desire and the ability to receive it are gifts of grace. This consensus about personal salvation leaves many questions unanswered, and attempts to articulate those questions and answer them have led to tremendous diversity and sometimes rancorous division among Christians.

All of this Christian diversity revolves around the enormously complex issue of the *ordo salutis*—order of salvation. What does God do and what do

---

[15]Jürgen Moltmann, *The Coming of God: Christian Eschatology*, trans. Margaret Kohl (Minneapolis: Fortress, 1996), p. 254.

human persons do in the process of whole salvation? In what order do these aspects or dimensions of salvation happen? Unfortunately, the New Testament does not lay out a clear, unambiguous plan of salvation in the sense of a logical or chronological ordering of how personal salvation begins and unfolds and comes to completion. Different Christian theologians and communities have proposed such and have often committed themselves to a specific plan or map of salvation.

The New Testament uses terms for various events and processes such as election, predestination, conversion, repentance, faith, justification, regeneration and sanctification. It describes gifts such as forgiveness of sins, reconciliation, union with Christ, peace with God, inner renewal, being filled with the Holy Spirit, enduement with power and glorification. Nowhere does it provide a neat, precise, orderly description of all these facets of whole salvation and how they take place or in what order they happen.

In order to understand the diversity of Christian perspectives on the *ordo salutis* it is necessary to study four main Christian interpretations of salvation. These are not completely mutually exclusive perspectives; they sometimes overlap each other within particular Christian theologians' and Christian communities' accounts of how salvation happens. I will divide them into two pairs for ease of examination and comprehension. The first pair of perspectives is *monergism* and *synergism*. Monergism is any belief that God is the sole sovereign agent in salvation and that even the task side of salvation is secretly and entirely the work of God in the person being saved. Monergism is often associated in people's minds with Calvinism, but in fact it existed long before Calvin developed his theology in sixteenth-century Switzerland. It originated at least with Augustine in the fourth and fifth centuries and may have more ancient roots. (Strong believers in monergism argue, of course, that it was the view held and taught by the apostle Paul.)

Synergism is any belief that salvation is a cooperative project and process in which God is the superior partner and the human person being saved is the inferior but nevertheless crucial partner. Synergism is often associated in people's minds with Arminianism, but in fact it existed well before Jacob Arminius developed his Protestant version of synergism in Holland in the seventeenth century. It may be found in the Greek church fathers, medieval Eastern Orthodox and Roman Catholic thinkers, and in the great Renaissance Catholic reformer Erasmus of Rotterdam. (Of course, strong believers in synergism argue that *it* was the view held and taught by the apostle Paul.)

The second pair of Christian perspectives on the *ordo salutis* are *Roman Catholic* and *Protestant*. The Eastern Orthodox view is not very different from the Catholic order of salvation. During the Protestant Reformation Luther, Zwingli, Calvin and the other Reformers sought to revive the true New Testament gospel of salvation by grace through faith alone. They and their Protestant followers emphasized justification—God's declaration of a person as righteous on account of his or her faith in Jesus Christ—as the centerpiece of salvation. The Catholic Church responded by formalizing its own view of salvation as a process involving both faith and "works of love," and identified justification with sanctification—God's renewing work of making persons who participate faithfully in the sacraments actually inwardly righteous. The decisive difference between the classical Protestant view and the orthodox Catholic view lies in the nature of justification within the order of salvation as well as in the role of faith. Protestantism elevates faith (viewed as personal trust in Christ and his completed work of atonement on the cross) and inflates justification (viewed as a forensic or declaratory work of God in which God imputes Christ's righteousness to persons being saved). Catholic theology promotes the necessity of works of love (viewed as participation in the sacramental system plus giving to the poor and striving for personal purity) together with faith and inflates sanctification (viewed as a process of being inwardly cleansed from sinful attitudes and actions by indwelling grace through the sacraments).

The *monergist Christian view of salvation,* most commonly associated with the theology of John Calvin, came to special systematic theological expression in the Canons of Dort, which were promulgated by the Reformed divines (ministers and theologians) of the Protestant Synod of Dort that met in the Netherlands in 1618-1619. Dort did not intend to create any new beliefs but only to clarify what the theologians and church leaders gathered there considered classical Reformed Protestant belief about salvation. They were responding to a group of synergists known as the Remonstrants, who were followers of the Dutch Protestant theologian Jacob Arminius (d. 1609). Dort's canons of Reformed doctrine were later summed up by the acronym TULIP, the letters of which stand for *total depravity, unconditional election, limited atonement, irresistible grace, perseverence of the saints.* Not all Christian monergists affirm all five of these points, and even those who do (so-called five-point Calvinists) debate their meaning among themselves. Here I simply wish to point out a pattern especially in Protestant Christian monergism (there are some Catholic Christian monergists) by illustrating it with these five points.

The pattern or inner logic begins with the universal human condition of total depravity, which simply means complete helplessness even to seek God or will the good. Total depravity does not mean that all people are equally bad or even that fallen people cannot achieve some modicum of "civil goodness" (e.g., just societies). It only means that there is no spiritual health left in humanity after the Fall; people are born totally dependent on God's grace for any spiritual accomplishment. Unconditional election is God's solution to this situation of complete human spiritual depravity, and it is also, monergists argue, the only view of the beginning of salvation that protects the giftness of salvation. God sovereignly predestines some fallen people to be saved. Limited atonement, also known as definite atonement and particular atonement, is the peculiar view of some Calvinists that Christ's atoning death on the cross was only intended by God for those he unconditionally elects or predestines to salvation. Monergists believe that God applies the grace of regeneration (new birth by God's Spirit) to the elect so that they respond to God's effectual call with repentance and faith. The elect cannot resist God's grace. Finally, of course, those unconditionally elected by God to be saved will persevere in grace and not fall from it.[16]

Monergists support their belief in God's absolute control over salvation and their denial of libertarian human free will (i.e., not determined but able to do otherwise) to accept or reject God's saving grace by appealing to certain passages and themes in Scripture as well to the more basic belief in salvation as gift. They argue that if salvation is truly gift, then it cannot be chosen by human persons. Such a free choice would make God dependent on humanity and give the human person who chooses salvation a reason to boast; he or she would be earning salvation by choosing it. Scripture passages used to support monergism include John 14—17, where Jesus refers several times to his disciples and those who come after them (the church) being chosen and given to him by the Father; Romans 9—11, where the apostle Paul promotes God's sovereignty in choosing people to bless; and Ephesians 1, where Paul extols God's election and choice of the church for

---

[16]For an excellent modern account and defense of the Reformed Protestant Christian monergist belief about salvation, see Anthony A. Hoekema, *Saved by Grace* (Grand Rapids, Mich.: Eerdmans, 1989).

special blessing. Most monergists do not rely solely on a few proof passages, however, but appeal to a synoptic vision of the whole of revelation and Scripture as well as to God's greatness and human depravity.

The *synergist view of salvation* is not the opposite of the monergist view, as one might mistakenly suppose. The opposite of Christian monergism would be Pelagianism—a heresy rejected by all Christian churches. Synergism is not the belief that humans save themselves; it is the belief that salvation is by grace alone but requires free reception and not resistance by human persons. Two examples of Christian synergism are the Catholic reformer Erasmus, who was roughly contemporary with Luther, and the seventeenth-century Dutch theologian Arminius. John Wesley, founder of the Methodist tradition, was also a synergist with regard to salvation. Erasmus was provoked into a public and published debate with Luther over free will. In his treatise titled *On Free Will,* he criticized Luther for embracing and promoting monergism. (Luther's followers—Lutherans—have not all been monergists.) Luther responded harshly with his own essay titled *On the Bondage of the Will.*[17] Erasmus argued that in spite of a few Scripture passages that, taken in isolation and out of context, seem to teach monergism, Scripture as a whole assumes and teaches human free will. In order to avoid Pelagianism and Semi-Pelagianism, Erasmus affirmed that a resistible, prevenient (going before) and assisting grace of God liberates the human will from bondage to sin and enables it to accept salvation or reject it. The Catholic reformer insisted that salvation is all of God's grace but that humans must accept grace freely; he also insisted that even free acceptance of God's grace is made possible by grace. The initiative, then, is God's; the decision is the human person's.[18]

About a century later the Dutch Reformed theologian Arminius taught a Protestant version of the same synergistic view of salvation earlier expounded by Erasmus. Reformed theologians are fond of treating Arminius's theology—Arminianism—as Semi-Pelagian or even Pelagian. That is simply dis-

---

[17]These treatises have been published together in several formats. They may be found together in E. Gordon Rupp and Philip S. Watson, eds., *Luther and Erasmus: Free Will and Salvation* (Philadelphia: Westminster Press, 1969).

[18]For readers who have only heard that Erasmus was a Semi-Pelagian or have only read Luther's response to Erasmus, which is sometimes published by itself and which clearly misrepresents Erasmus's synergistic view of salvation as Semi-Pelagian if not purely Pelagian, see Erasmus, *On the Freedom of the Will,* chap. 3, in ibid., pp. 79-85.

tortion and misrepresentation. Arminius opposed the monergistic teaching of his Dutch colleague Franciscus Gomarus at the University of Leiden and argued that election is not unconditional; predestination refers to God's foreknowledge of who will freely accept his offer of salvation through Christ. He based human ability freely to believe in Christ, repent and be saved on the "prevening" (prevenient) grace of God.[19]

About one hundred and twenty-five years later, the English revivalist and Methodist founder Wesley taught the same basic synergistic view of salvation based on belief in God's prevenient grace enabling fallen sinners to respond freely to God's offer of saving grace. Contrary to the misleading polemics of monergistic critics, Christian synergism—as taught by Erasmus, Arminius and Wesley—is not Semi-Pelagian because it places the initiative in salvation entirely on God's side—in prevenient (calling, convicting, enabling, assisting) grace. Christians synergists believe that repentance and faith are not gifts of God effectually imparted to elect individuals; they are genuinely free responses of persons whose depraved wills have been liberated by the prevenient grace of God through the proclamation of the Word of God. Two arguments in favor of synergism are that Scripture everywhere presupposes such human freedom and responsibility and that a God who orchestrates sin and salvation, saving only some persons when he could sovereignly save all, may be great but cannot be truly good.

Eastern Orthodox and Roman Catholic beliefs about salvation tend to be strongly synergistic although some Catholic theologians have affirmed a kind of monergism. The latter can point back to the great church father Augustine, highly revered within Catholic theology, who clearly ended his life and career a monergist. However, Catholic theology forbids any extreme monergism that would go so far as to attribute sin and evil or eternal damnation to God's agency. The Protestant house is divided by monergism and synergism. A few Protestant denominations have attempted to allow both perspectives within their ranks, but division over this issue of predestination versus free will seems inevitable insofar as Christians care about interpreting Scripture and developing sound doctrines. Some will come to monergistic conclusions; others will arrive at synergistic ones. The former will attribute salva-

---

[19]For Arminius's view of synergism, including his account of predestination as foreknowledge and prevenient grace, see his "A Declaration of the Sentiments of Arminius," in *The Works of James Arminius,* trans. James Nichols and William Nichols (Grand Rapids, Mich.: Baker, 1996), 1:581-732 (especially pp. 653-57).

tion entirely and exclusively to the sovereign predestination and irresistible power of God; the latter will attribute salvation to a combination of divine grace and free human response. With a few notable exceptions evangelical Christian leaders have come to accept each other in spite of these differences. The National Association of Evangelicals—an umbrella organization of approximately fifty theologically conservative Protestant denominations— includes both committed monergists and ardent synergists.

Whether they are monergists or synergists, all Protestants agree that *salvation is an entirely free gift of God's grace received by faith alone,* whereas Catholics believe that *salvation is a gift received by faith and works of love.* The Catholic *ordo salutis* begins with water baptism, which is normally administered by a priest to an infant of faithful Christian parents. Catholics believe that baptism, rightly administered and not received deceptively (e.g., by an adult who does not truly have faith in Jesus Christ) automatically imparts the grace of justification into the life of the person being baptized. The "grace of justification" is also the "grace of sanctification;" they are one and the same grace— the inwardly purifying and transforming grace of God that washes away the guilt of sin and makes one a child of God. Salvation, then, is the process of being made inwardly righteous that begins with baptism, continues with a life of faithfulness to God through his church (e.g., regular participation in the sacraments such as Eucharist—the Lord's Supper—and penance—confession of sins to a priest) and ends sometime after death when a person has been totally purified in purgatory. In Catholic belief, faith that saves is interpreted as faithfulness. There is no whole salvation "by faith alone" without faithful involvement and participation in the divinely established means of grace.[20] Catholic theologians do not consider this "salvation by good works," however, because every "merit" received in the process is a gift of God and therefore not truly earned. All merit belongs to Christ; the individual being saved is simply accepting Christ's merits through participation in the sacraments.

Conversion, according to Catholic thought, is a lifelong process beginning with baptism, continuing through confirmation and penance and other sacraments, involving lifelong transformation by God's grace inextricably bound up with acts of contrition for sin and love for God and others, and ending with the discipline of purgatory that prepares a person for the face-to-face

---

[20]For a lucid explanation of the Catholic view of salvation, see *The Church's Confession of Faith: A Catholic Catechism for Adults* (San Francisco: Ignatius Press, 1987).

encounter with God in heaven. Catholic theology views the classical Protestant belief in justification by grace through faith alone at a moment in time (either at the baptism of an infant or conversion of an adult) as presumptuous and possibly even antinomian (rejecting law). That is, according to traditional Catholic theology—going back to at least the Council of Trent where the Roman Catholic hierarchy responded definitively to the Protestant Reformers in the mid sixteenth century—the Protestant belief neglects the task side of the paradox of salvation in favor of an overemphasis on the gift side.

The Protestant Reformers and their followers viewed the Catholic belief about salvation as a thinly disguised form of works-righteousness; to them it emphasized far too much the task side of salvation and implicitly undermined the gospel of salvation as wholly and entirely a gift of God's grace that cannot be earned. Luther never tired of reiterating that no works of any kind—however good they may seem—can earn any portion of righteousness and that righteousness can only be imputed, not imparted, to sinners. In his 1518 *Heidelberg Disputation* the Reformer wrote:

> works contribute nothing to justification. Therefore man knows that works which he does by such faith are not his but God's. For this reason he does not seek to become justified or glorified through them, but seeks God. His justification by faith in Christ is sufficient to him. Christ is his wisdom, righteousness, etc., as I Cor 1 [:30] has it, that he himself may be Christ's action and instrument.[21]

All faithful Protestants follow Luther in utterly rejecting any dependence of God's grace in salvation on human works; justification is viewed by Protestants—both monergists and synergists alike—as a declaration by God that a person is righteous with Christ's own righteousness even though that person is still a sinner in thought, word and deed. How does justification happen? Although Protestants disagree among themselves about predestination and baptism (infant versus adult believers only) and many other details, they all agree that justification is a once-for-all, momentary event of being declared righteous by God that takes place when a person repents and trusts in Christ alone. Whereas Catholic doctrine views justification as capable of increasing, Protestant doctrine views it as complete at the moment of conversion to Christ.

---

[21]Martin Luther, *Heidelberg Disputation*, para. 25, in *Martin Luther's Basic Theological Writings*, ed. Timothy F. Lull (Minneapolis: Fortress, 1989), pp. 46-47.

Sanctification is distinct from justification; the former is a process of growth in repentance and righteousness; the latter is its beginning. Justification has to do with one's position vis-à-vis God—reconciliation and forgiveness. Sanctification has to do with one's inward, spiritual condition. It is the process of being conformed inwardly to that righteousness received as a gift by faith alone at conversion. Luther and Protestants in general—of all denominations—appeal to Paul's epistles to the Romans and the Galatians for special support for their belief in salvation as justification by grace through faith alone. In both epistles, so Protestants believe, the apostle rejects any dependence of salvation on human works and bases it entirely and exclusively on faith as trust in Christ.

Protestants disagree among themselves about the precise structure of the *ordo salutis*. Lutherans tend to begin the order of salvation with God's sovereign decision regarding who will be saved and locate justification and the new birth (regeneration by the indwelling of the Holy Spirit) at the moment of water baptism received by faith in Christ. (In the case of infants Luther appealed to an "incipient faith" in the child and to the parents' faith and affirmed that the baptized child will need to express his or her own faith at confirmation.) Sanctification grows out of justification at baptism and ends with glorification at the moment of death or in the future resurrection. Many Anglicans agree completely with the Lutheran teaching about the order of salvation. Other Anglicans and Episcopalians adopt the Reformed perspective that begins the order of salvation with God's eternal decree of election (predestination) and views justification and regeneration (forgiveness and inward renewing by the Holy Spirit) as works of God's grace that begin with baptism (as inclusion in the covenant people of God) but only come to full fruition when embraced by the elect person by faith later in life.

Conversionist Christians, including most traditional Methodists, Baptists, Pentecostals and many other evangelical Protestant groups, tend to view the order of salvation differently. There are many specific orderings of the elements or aspects of salvation among conversionists, but all place justification-regeneration at conversion, which is interpreted as a personal decision to repent of sin and accept Christ as Savior and Lord. Most Methodists baptize infants, but they view infant baptism as a sacrament of prevenient grace or infant dedication. Baptists, Pentecostals and many other evangelicals reject infant baptism and acknowledge water baptism only of those who have already made a conscious decision to repent and trust in Christ alone for salvation. Pentecostals add to the Protestant order of salvation a "second definite work of grace" called "Baptism of the Holy Spirit" (more correctly "infilling of the Holy Spirit") interpreted as an enduement with power from God such as the disciples received on the Day of Pentecost (Acts 2). Holiness Protestants such as Nazarenes and Wesleyans believe it is possible for Christians to become "perfected in love" at some point in the process of sanctification.

There are numerous variations on the Protestant *ordo salutis*. What they all have in common is justification as a momentary and complete event—a gift solely by the grace of God that cannot be earned—and sanctification as a process of growth in righteousness after justification. Protestants disagree among themselves about the roles human decision and baptism play in the order of salvation as well as about how to practice baptism. Because they emphasize the sovereignty of God in salvation, most traditional Lutherans and Reformed (e.g., traditional Presbyterians and members of the Christian Reformed Church as well as some Anglicans and Episcopalians) tend to play down the role of human decision in salvation and play up God's electing decree and irresistible calling through the Word of God and the sacraments. Because they emphasize the relational aspect of salvation, many free church Protestants (e.g., many Baptists and all Pentecostals) tend to play down the role of God's sovereign, irresistible power in salvation and play up the human person's free decision either to accept or reject God's saving grace. Of course, at their best, these Christians also emphasize the necessity of prevenient grace that enables sinners to make such free choices regarding salvation.

## A Unifying Christian Perspective on Salvation

Can Christians find significant common ground among themselves with regard to personal salvation? It may seem unlikely. Not only are the differences profound; hard feelings often exist between members of various Christian traditions. The Protestant Reformation may have happened centuries ago, but many Catholics and Protestants still regard each other as barely Christian if Christian at all. Suspicion and even hostility exist between some adherents of different Protestant denominations as well. Aggressive, dogmatic Reformed Protestants often go out of their way to insult Arminian Protestants who believe in libertarian free will and who emphasize decision by calling them Semi-Pelagians and arguing that their synergistic belief in salvation as involving cooperation of the human will with divine grace is

covertly Roman Catholic.[22] Some of them simply declare it heresy.[23] Some
Arminian Protestants return the favor by treating Reformed theology (Calvinism) as near-heresy if not outright heresy.

Nevertheless, all of these Christian traditions have much in common in
contrast to the various philosophies and theologies of self-salvation
embraced and promoted by numerous sects, cults and New Age spiritualities. Since the Second Vatican Council (Vatican II) of the 1960s Roman
Catholic and Protestant theologians have engaged in vigorous and produc-
tive dialogues and have often discovered that in spite of continuing differences of belief they share a common faith in salvation as both gift and task.
Adherents of different Protestant traditions are accepting each other as
equally evangelical in spite of occasional renewed tensions caused by aggressive and divisive voices on the extreme fringes of monergism and synergism.

There is a common element to Christian belief about salvation and it goes
back to the consensus rooted in the New Testament and early church fathers
that reconciliation with God and transformation into the image of God and
Christlikeness are gifts that also involve human participation—even if that
participation is interpreted as a gift also. No authentically Christian theologian or group denies that salvation is ultimately a gift of divine grace and
mercy wholly won by Christ and acquired by individual persons through
faith. Disagreements erupt only when theologians and groups of Christians
attempt to pin down more precisely the exact nature of salvation as gift and
task by, for example, overdefining faith in an exclusionary way that makes
any other possible interpretation a denial of the gospel itself.

By no means am I arguing here for a minimalist account of Christian
belief such that everyone ought to embrace a lowest-common-denominator,
generic Christianity stripped of all but its most common traits. Rather, I urge
Christians of various traditions to keep matters of difference in perspective.
What defines Christian belief in this area is not every minute detail of an *ordo
salutis* or monergism or synergism. What defines it is belief that salvation is
wholly a gift of grace—not at all deserved or earned—and at the same time
received by persons through grateful reception by repentance and faith.

---

[22]Michael S. Horton, "Evangelical Arminians: Option or Oxymoron?" in *Modern Reformation*,
    May-June 1992.
[23]One anonymous evangelical reviewer of this book's manuscript declared synergism heresy and
    implied an incompatibility between Arminian theology and faithfulness to the Bible.

# CHAPTER 13

# THE CHURCH

## Visible *and* Invisible

**M**any readers may be surprised to find a whole chapter on the subject of Christian belief about the church. Is there a Christian doctrine of the church? Why is church a subject of Christian belief? The fact that such questions are inevitable and, in late modern and postmodern culture, understandable reveals the need for a consideration of Christian belief about the church.

### Issues and Polarities of Christian Belief About the Church

For much of Christian history, the Great Tradition of Christian thought held the church, the "body of Christ," in high regard, and even after the undivided visible church split and then fragmented, most Christian leaders and theologians considered the church an important aspect of Christian belief and witness. The very idea of authentic, vital Christianity apart from the church was virtually unheard-of before the twentieth century. And yet, we find ourselves now in a situation where in many places Christians seem to believe that the church is nothing more than an optional support group for Christians who need it or a tool of evangelism to win people to Christ. Many

Christians regard their own "personal relationship with God" their "church." Many others consider their transient small Bible study or prayer group their "church." Many seem to believe that there is no church for them; they look upon the church as too formal, institutional, filled with hypocrites, money-grubbing or old-fashioned. And yet they commune with God through Bible reading, prayer, meditation and perhaps even watching favorite Christian television programs on a regular basis.

What is wrong with the situation just described? It is certainly out of step with the Great Tradition of Christian belief about the church. In early Christianity it was said, "the church is the ark [as in Noah's ship] of salvation," and "outside the church there is no salvation." The second-century North African bishop Cyprian went so far as to warn those who would divide or abandon the church, "he can no longer have God for his Father, who has not the Church for his mother."[1] As we will see, the Great Tradition of Christianity, at least up until recently, has included belief in the unity of the church and even the necessity of the church for authentic Christian living if not for salvation itself.

The questions that surround Christian belief about the church may seem strange to people who shop for church as they shop for anything else. These questions have to do with the true nature of church: What makes a group of people *church*? Is any group of Christians that gathers for worship, Bible study or prayer automatically church? Or are there certain necessary marks or characteristics of church that must be present in some degree for a group of Christians to be a manifestation of the church of Jesus Christ? Can the church be divided? Can there be more than one true church? Is there an invisible church or is the church by nature always visible? What unifies the church? What should be the church's structure? How should it be governed? What are the church's sacraments or ordinances? What do they have to do with salvation and vital Christianity and how should they be practiced? The different answers to these and similar questions provide much of the diversity of Christianity. Denominations that believe nearly identically about everything else often remain separate from one another because of differences over church government and sacraments.

Because of the tremendous complexity of Christian perspectives about the church we will necessarily treat this area of Christian belief in a somewhat

---

[1]Cyprian *On the Unity of the Church (Treatise I)*, para. 6, *ANF* 5:423.

cursory manner that will seem wholly inadequate to the already initiated. We will have to simplify and even oversimplify the subject in order to treat it in one chapter. The approach will follow the usual pattern, although the size of sections will differ somewhat from earlier chapters. The Christian consensus about the church will be explained very briefly; there is not much of a consensus. The alternatives to that consensus—"heresies about the church"—will be quite brief as well because our view is that most of the diversity of Christian belief about the church is legitimate; we might think otherwise if we were Roman Catholic, though. The largest section here will be the one on diversity of Christian belief about the church and sacraments. At last we will conclude with a brief statement of a unifying vision of the church.

### The Christian Consensus About the Church

Is there some essential Christian belief about the church that can be drawn from both divine revelation and the Great Tradition of two millennia of Christian thought? The Nicene Creed, formulated finally at the First Council of Constantinople in 381 and widely accepted as the unifying creed of Christendom, says that the church is *one, holy, catholic* and *apostolic*. It also confesses belief in *one baptism for the remission of sins*. If we back up into the New Testament itself we find a strong emphasis on the unity of the church in the apostolic writings.

The apostle Paul especially stresses that the church, though made up of many individuals, is essentially united (1 Cor 12), and he bases that unity on the foundation of the "apostles and prophets" as well as on the cornerstone which is Christ (Eph 2:20). So strongly does Paul promote the unity of the church that he identifies it with Christ (1 Cor 12:27); just as Christ cannot be divided so the church must not be divided even though it is composed of many members. Paul's identification of the church with Christ—which should not be taken to mean that the church is literally Jesus Christ but should be taken to mean that it is mystically one with him and represents him in a special way—is very revealing. For him and for the early church after the apostles, the corporate community of God's people, united by "one Lord," "one Spirit," "one faith," "one baptism," is the locus of union with Christ. There is no hint of Lone Ranger Christianity in the New Testament; there is no suggestion that a person can be vitally united with Christ and growing spiritually apart from the church. The assumption throughout is that the church is the indispensable vehicle of Christian spiritual life, the locus of Christ's special presence and the Spirit's power.

The early Christian church after the apostles valued the church very highly, and the writings of the second-century church fathers are filled with references to the church, its leaders and the sacraments. Notable examples are the epistles of the early second-century Christian leader Ignatius who ordered his Christian readers to obey their bishops (overseers), remain united and observe the Lord's Supper or Eucharist as the "medicine of immortality." The late second-century bishop of Lyons Irenaeus appealed to the unity of the faith of the church to contradict the various Gnostic groups that were dividing Christians in his time. For him, as for other early church fathers who succeeded the apostles as leaders of Christians in the Roman Empire, the church, though spread throughout the world and speaking many languages, is united by one apostolic faith and therefore it is "catholic" (universal) and not divided into levels of spiritual prowess and enlightenment as the Gnostics claimed.[2] The most notable example of an early church father emphasizing the unity of the church and the importance of its sacraments is third-century Bishop Cyprian of Carthage. His *Treatise on the Unity of the Church* is a classic of early Christian reflection on the universality of the one true church that cannot be divided or abandoned. Cyprian goes so far as to say that "he cannot possess the garment of Christ who parts and divides the Church of Christ."[3]

A little more than one century after Cyprian the second ecumenical (universal) council of Christian leaders met at Constantinople and put the final touches on the Nicene Creed; they described the church as *one, holy, catholic* and *apostolic*. By *one* they meant that the church is united; there cannot be two or more churches. They clearly did not mean congregations. What they were trying to avoid was the situation that later developed—denominationalism. By *holy* they did not mean morally perfect, but "set apart by God" for service and worship. By *catholic* they did not mean what that term later came to signify; they meant "universal across time and space." By *apostolic* they meant carrying on the ministry and teaching of Jesus' own apostles. The early church fathers strove to avoid the kind of division that later came to be a seemingly permanent feature of Christianity.

Even Luther, who is often blamed for dividing the church, valued the

---

[2] See Irenaeus *Against Heresies* 1.10.1, *ANF* 1:330-31.
[3] Cyprian, para. 7, p. 423.

unity of the true Christian church and defended his new "evangelical" (Protestant) church movement as a restoration of the church rather than as a split
from or division within the church. Insofar as the church became divided,
Luther believed, it was not living up to its true essence and needed to be
united once again. But for him, as for the other Protestant Reformers, peace
and unity were less important than truth. While they highly esteemed the
marks of the true Christian church as one, holy, catholic and apostolic, they
also came to believe that the true church does not exist where the people of
God are not truly gathered (that is, where only priests and monks are considered the church) and where the Word of God is not rightly proclaimed (that
is, where the gospel of salvation by grace through faith alone is denied or
neglected) and where the sacraments are not rightly administered. The
Reformers believed that the Roman Catholic Church of their day had
become heretical if not apostate and was therefore not truly apostolic. They
did not intend to create denominationalism, although that became the unin-
tended consequence of their movement and of the pope's refusal to heed
their calls to reform the church.[4]

The Christian consensus regarding the church, then, is relatively simple
and straightforward: *the church is a divinely-instituted community where
Christ is present by his Spirit and is essentially one, holy, catholic and apostolic.*
Protestants tend to interpret the church's oneness and catholicity as invisible
rather than institutional, whereas Catholics view them as intrinsically bound
to the institution of the bishops in apostolic succession and especially the
bishop of Rome as pope. Protestants, for the most part, understand the
church's apostolicity as its continuing in the traditions of the apostles in its
teaching and preaching, whereas Catholics interpret it as the existence of a
hierarchy of bishops in apostolic succession. Protestants add the essential
marks of "Word of God rightly proclaimed" and "sacraments rightly administered" to the four Nicene marks of the church. There are other differences,
not only between Protestants and Catholics but also, of course, between various Protestant groups. All share in common, however, a strong belief in the
church as a sacred means of grace.[5] The church is the normal context within
which grace happens, as it were, and where faith that appropriates grace is

---

[4]See John Calvin's section on the church in *Institutes of the Christian Religion* 4.1, especially
paragraph 9, "The marks of the church," pp. 1023-26.
[5]Again, John Calvin may be cited as a source. In his *Institutes,* the Swiss Reformer refers to the
church as a means of grace. Ibid.

strengthened. Nowhere in the Great Tradition of Christianity before the twentieth century can one find the uniquely modern phenomenon of "churchless Christians."

## Alternatives to the Christian Consensus About the Church

Some Christian traditions and communities have declared certain beliefs about the church heretical, but our concern here is to examine perspectives about the church that are radically inconsistent with the Christian consensus outlined in the first section of this chapter. That is, just because one branch of Christianity considers a belief profoundly mistaken does not mean that it is such. For members of that denomination or tradition it may be, but for us what constitutes a heresy or radical alternative to Christian belief is not determined by one denomination or theologian or Christian community. The Roman Catholic Church, for example, officially considers belief in the existence of a true, invisible, universal church that is not institutionally under the authority of the magisterium (bishops, cardinals, pope) a heresy. For Roman Catholics, the one true church is constituted by the bishops in fellowship with each other and all together with and under the pope. Many Protestants consider that belief a heresy. That is not my perspective here. Within our own denominations we may consider it so, but in this book I wish to take a larger view and consider the essence of Christianity above, behind and beneath all the particular denominations. We should acknowledge, of course, that some of those do consider themselves the one true church and view all or most of the others as defective at best.

There are several beliefs about the church and the sacraments (ordinances) that have arisen throughout church history and still exist in some form that contradict the Great Tradition of Christian belief. To the extent that people consciously affirm these beliefs they are falling short of authentic Christianity. Two of these will be the focus of our attention here: *sectarianism* and *rejection of the two ordinances of baptism and the Lord's Supper*. *Sectarianism* has several meanings, but here it refers to the belief or attitude that the unity of the church is unimportant and that the true essence of the church may exist without unity. It is manifest in the "baptizing" of denominationalism as normative and especially in the identification of a particular denomination with the church universal itself. Negatively, it is manifest in utter rejection of all ecumenical cooperation, dialogue and fellowship among true Christians. It often involves belief in the purity of the church so that persons who belong to Christian communities other than the one considered pure are rejected as not truly Christian for that reason alone.

Sectarianism has many faces and comes in many degrees. One of the first manifestations of sectarianism within Christianity was the second-century movement known as Montanism. The Montanists were followers of a Christian prophet named Montanus and they established their own churches known as "The New Prophecy," perhaps the first Christian sect. They rejected the catholic church because it did not accept the claims of Montanus to be inspired by the Holy Spirit. The bishops of the catholic church near Pepuza in Asia Minor, where Montanus maintained a headquarters, met and excommunicated him and his movement from the universal church. Montanus and his followers apparently believed that they were the true church of Christ to the exclusion of all others.

Such sectarianism has appeared repeatedly throughout Christian history and especially in the modern world. Many new religious movements founded by latter-day prophets and self-proclaimed messiahs stand over against the universal church and condemn or ignore it. To them all other denominations are not merely defective or lacking the fullness of truth or spiritual life; they are apostate or at least so distorted or lifeless that they are imposter churches that God has totally abandoned. Sectarianism cuts itself off from the church universal, the Great Tradition of Christianity. It tends to view God as its own possession. It elevates the holiness of the church—which it falsely identifies with its own perceived passion and purity—over the unity and apostolicity of the church. The antidote to sectarianism is trust that God has always been present in his church across space and time, preserving it in spite of human resistance. It is also spiritual humility that recognizes that all particular forms of the church are flawed.

The second major alternative to the Christian consensus of belief about the church has to do with the sacraments or ordinances. From the New Testament through modern Christianity two ceremonies or rituals have been practiced in various ways by all faithful Christians and churches: water baptism and the Lord's Supper. Others have been added by certain traditions of Christianity, but these two are and have always been observed and celebrated throughout the body of Christ. Christ instituted both of them and commanded his disciples to continue observing them; the apostles practiced them and wrote about them in their inspired epistles; the earliest Christian writings after the apostles—the apostolic fathers of the second century—are replete with references to them and sometimes with detailed instructions about how to observe them.[6]

During the Protestant Reformation some mystical, radical sects spawned by the Reformation began to argue that all outward rites and ceremonies, including water baptism and the Lord's Supper, are unnecessary and perhaps worse. George Fox, the seventeenth-century English founder of the Quaker movement (Society of Friends) rejected all sacraments and ceremonies, including baptism (except an inner, mystical "baptism of the Spirit") and the Lord's Supper. Certain reforming social Christian groups of the nineteenth century neglected these two ceremonies, and to this day the Salvation Army does not observe them. The Jesus movement of the early 1970s that spread from California throughout North America and into Europe tended to dismiss everything formal associated with Christianity, often including the institutional, organized church and sacraments or ordinances. (This was not true of all so-called Jesus People, but the Jesus movement had a lasting influence that diminished the importance of allegedly formalistic ceremonies for many young Christians.) In the last quarter of the twentieth century some evangelical Protestant churches and denominations dropped requirements of water baptism and observance of the Lord's Supper. They became optional and died out in many independent churches.

For the most part, the second alternative to the Great Tradition is a heresy of neglect. Very few Christians would make a point of rejecting all sacraments and ordinances, but many care little about them and, unfortunately, their pastors and leaders accommodate to that disinterest. This is a heresy, especially insofar as neglect of the sacraments becomes institutionalized. While Christians may legitimately disagree among themselves about the significance of the sacraments, they must not drop them altogether. That is not permitted by the New Testament or by the Christian consensual tradition.

## Diversity Within Christian Belief About the Church

Christians agree that the church of Jesus Christ is one, holy, catholic (universal) and apostolic. They also agree that the church should observe two special ceremonies instituted by Christ—baptism and the Lord's Supper.

---

[6]See for example the *Didache*, also known as the *Teaching of the Twelve Apostles*, which many consider the earliest Christian writing outside the New Testament, in *The Apostolic Fathers*, trans. J. B. Lightfoot and J. R. Harmer, ed. and rev. by Michael W. Holmes, 2nd ed. (Grand Rapids, Mich.: Baker, 1989), pp. 145-58.

However, Christians do not agree about the specific interpretations of these or about whether there may be more marks of the true church and more sacraments/ordinances. The diversity of Christian belief about these matters is extensive and the disagreements very profound. Dialogue between representatives of different Christian denominations and traditions has led to some agreement, but strong differences of belief remain and often keep Christians of various denominations from worshiping with each other. The main areas of disagreement have to do with the nature of the church's *unity* and with the *sacraments/ordinances.* There are also significant differences about the proper form of *church government (polity).*

The Roman Catholic Church insists that the unity of the church—its oneness—is *visible and institutional.* It also believes and teaches that the only proper form of church government is *hierarchical and episcopal*—centered around the bishops under the authority of the pope who is considered the Apostle Peter's successor as the bishop of Rome. Finally, the Roman Catholic Church believes in and observes *seven sacraments:* baptism, confirmation, penance, Eucharist (the Lord's Supper or the Mass), extreme unction, ordination and marriage. According to Roman Catholic belief, there is no authentic manifestation of the church of Jesus Christ outside of its own history and hierarchical order. The church *is* the body of believers in fellowship with the priests governed by the bishops appointed by the pope. This is the one, true, visible and institutional body of Christ on earth; there is no invisible church. The First Vatican Council (Vatican I) declared this doctrine of the church (which the bishops gathered there believed to be the historic consensus of the church) in 1870:

> No one should ever believe that the members of the Church are united with merely internal, hidden bonds and that, therefore, they constitute a hidden and completely invisible society. For the eternal wisdom and power of the Godhead willed that, to these spiritual and invisible bonds by which the faithful through the Holy Spirit adhere to the supreme and invisible head of the Church, there should be corresponding external, visible bonds also in order that this spiritual and supernatural society might appear in external form and be conspicuously evident. Consequently, there is a visible teaching authority which publicly proposes dogma that must be interiorly believed and openly professed. There is a visible priestly office which publicly supervises and takes care of the visible mysteries of God [sacraments] by which interior sanctification is conferred on men and due worship is paid to God. There is a visible

governing body which orders the union of the members among themselves and which guides and directs the whole external and public life of the faithful in the Church. Finally, the whole body of the Church is visible; and not only the just or the predestined belong to it, but also those who are in sin, but who are linked with it by their common profession of faith. Thus the Church of Christ on earth is neither invisible nor hidden; but it is placed in clear view like a city set upon a mountain, high and brilliant, impossible to hide, and like a lamp on a lampstand that is illuminated by the sun of justice and shines on the whole world with the light of its truth.[7]

The Second Vatican Council (Vatican II) softened the perspective of the Catholic church somewhat with regard to Christians who are not members of the Roman Catholic Church, but it did not change the historic Catholic belief in the visibility and institutional hierarchy of the church. Even in the post-Vatican II era, in which the Catholic Church has reached out to "separated brethren" (Protestants) as fellow true believers in Jesus Christ, the Roman Catholic belief in the church's visible and institutional unity under the pope around the bishops has remained intact. The Church of Rome throughout the world is the only true Christian church; all other groups of Christians are "ecclesial communities," religious clubs or parachurch organizations.

Most Protestant denominations and traditions believe in the *invisible unity of the church;* the church universal is spiritually united rather than institutionally united. The Lutheran *Augsburg Confession* states that the unity of the church resides in the gathering of believers among whom the gospel is preached in its purity and the sacraments (baptism and the Lord's Supper) are administered according to the gospel. While many Lutherans consider the visible and institutional unity of the church an ideal—something to hope and strive for—Lutheran doctrine does not confine the true church to any institution or organization.

The Church of England and many of its sister churches in the worldwide Anglican communion agree with the Lutheran doctrine of the church while preserving their own version of visible unity under the British monarch (supreme governor of the Church of England) and the bishops in apostolic succession. It rejects the papacy of Rome.

---

[7]*The Church Teaches: Documents of the Church in English Translation* (St. Louis: B. Herder, 1955), pp. 89-90.

The Reformed branch of Protestantism (e.g., Presbyterians) explicitly embraces and affirms the invisible nature of the church's unity and universality. The *Westminster Confession* (1648) says that "the catholic or universal Church, which is invisible, consists of the whole number of the elect, that have been, are, or shall be gathered into one, under Christ the head thereof," and "the visible Church, which is also catholic or universal under the gospel (not confined to one nation as before under the law) consists of all those, throughout the world, that profess the true religion, and of their children; and is the kingdom of the Lord Jesus Christ, the house and family of God, out of which there is no ordinary possibility of salvation."[8] In other words, Reformed Protestants believe, the church universal is not identical with any one denomination or national church, but is invisible and spread throughout the world in many visible churches, denominations and sects. It consists of all the elect of God and is neither disconnected from visible congregations and denominations nor identical with any one of them. The invisible body of Christ is also visible in that it is manifested in many different gatherings of Christians, but the latter do not exhaust or confine the true church.

While all Protestants believe that the true church is one and that its unity transcends particular denominations such that the one, true body of Christ is in some sense invisible in its universality, and while all Protestants tend to locate the presence of the true church in the right proclamation of the gospel (Word of God) and practice of the sacraments/ordinances, Protestants disagree among themselves about the proper structure and government of the visible church as well as about the nature of the sacraments/ordinances of baptism and the Lord's Supper.

The three main forms of church government or polity found among Protestants are *episcopal, presbyterian* and *congregational.* Episcopal polity is centered around the office of bishop. The worldwide Anglican communion of churches—the Church of England and its many national sister churches—is one of the more hierarchical Protestant denominations. The spiritual leader of the Anglican Communion worldwide is the archbishop of Canterbury who is appointed by the British Parliament. The archbishop has nothing like the authority of the Roman Catholic Pope. Outside of England, bishops of the

---

[8]See John H. Leith, ed., *Creeds of the Churches: A Reader in Christian Doctrine from the Bible to the Present,* rev. ed. (Richmond, Va.: John Knox, 1973), p. 222.

Anglican churches (manifested in the United States primarily in the Episcopal Church) are generally elected by clergy and lay representatives from their dioceses with confirmation from a majority of other bishops from within their national churches. Bishops are the spiritual leaders of their dioceses and have authority to confirm laity and to ordain priests and deacons. Individual congregations have considerable control over their own affairs, but all worship according to a Book of Common Prayer. The bishops of the Anglican communion are all ordained in apostolic succession. That is, they can trace their pedigree of ordination back to one of the apostles of the first-century Christian church. Generally speaking, traditional Anglicans/Episcopalians regard churches that are not in fellowship with bishops in apostolic succession as defective at best and sectarian at worst. Some Methodist denominations are also episcopal in polity, but they do not look to the monarch of England or the archbishop of Canterbury and they do not ordain their bishops in apostolic succession. In the United States Methodist bishops are elected by ministers and lay leaders of congregations and confirmed in their office by fellow bishops. They are primarily administrators as well as spiritual cheerleaders.

The Lutheran branch of Protestantism is not as unified organizationally or hierarchically as the Anglican communion. While Lutheran churches look to bishops as administrative leaders, the role of Lutheran bishop differs from one synod and national group of churches to another. Some Lutheran denominations are more episcopal-hierarchical and some are more presbyterian and even congregational. In most Lutheran fellowships of churches, each congregation exists in fellowship with a bishop who may or may not be ordained in apostolic succession, and such apostolic succession is often interpreted as a spiritual and doctrinal continuity rather than a traceable pedigree of organizational ordination throughout history. Many Lutheran bishops are elected by the pastors and lay delegates to synods and conventions. Individual Lutheran congregations and their pastors are accountable to their bishops and to each other even though they have a great deal of autonomy with regard to their own internal affairs.

Reformed denominations follow much the same pattern as most Lutheran groups but without the office of bishop. All Reformed churches exist in a pattern of *presbyterian accountability* in which each congregation is governed by its own elected elders or presbyters who, in turn, join together with other Reformed teaching and ruling elders in conclaves that together make important decisions for the denomination. The presbyterian polity is nonhierarchical and representative; it revolves around congregationally-elected leaders who send delegates to assemblies that make important decisions on behalf of the region or national group of churches.

Many Protestant churches—especially those in the free church tradition (i.e., that came into existence apart from any government sponsorship)—follow the *congregational* polity. Each congregation is completely autonomous and there are no bishops or authoritative representative bodies over them. Congregations elect their own internal leaders—often deacons as well as ministers—own their own property, decide what their form of worship will be, determine their own relationships (or lack of them) with other congregations and write their own constitutions and by-laws (if any). Their "denominations" are really nothing more than conventions of voluntarily cooperating independent congregations. The purpose of such conventions is to pool congregations' voluntarily contributed resources for missions and evangelism, education, charitable work and publication. Congregationalists, Baptists, Churches of Christ, most Pentecostals and all Anabaptists such as Mennonites are organized according to this congregational polity.

Forms of church structure and government provide much of the diversity within Christianity, but equally contributing to that diversity are different views of the sacraments or ordinances. Only the Roman Catholic Church believes in and practices seven distinct sacraments. It views them as "means of grace," visible ceremonies performed by duly ordained priests representing bishops, that truly communicate sanctifying and justifying grace to the faithful people of God. In Catholic doctrine baptism performed correctly by a qualified priest of the church automatically washes away the guilt of original sin as well as of all actual, willful sins that may have been committed before baptism (if any) so long as the grace of baptism is not being resisted by the recipient. There is no need for personal faith for baptism to be effective. This is known as "baptismal regeneration," being born again of God's Spirit through baptism. Of course, the Catholic Church does not baptize unrepentant or faithless adults. Only children of believing parents in communion with the church are considered automatically saved by baptismal grace alone apart from personal repentance and faith.

The other sacraments (all mentioned above) are also considered true means of grace and normally may only be administered by a priest. The most important sacrament after baptism is the Eucharist or mass (called the Lord's Supper or Communion by most Protestants). The Catholic tradition believes in "transubstantiation," the transformation of the substance of bread and wine into the body and blood of Jesus Christ. The "accidents" (taste, smell, appearance) remain bread and wine, but when the priest pronounces the words of consecration, "this is my body; this is my blood; do this in remembrance of me," the elements become "in substance" actually the body and blood of Christ such that Christ's humanity is present, resacrificed and eaten by the recipients whose faith is thereby strengthened. Supernatural union with Christ is enhanced by frequent, faithful participation in this sacrament. For Roman Catholics, the sacraments are just as important as the proclamation of the Word of God. The two are inseparable for the health of the church and individual Christians.[9]

Protestants reject the sacramental theology and practice of the Roman Catholic tradition. But they disagree profoundly among themselves about the nature of the ceremonies of baptism and the Lord's Supper.[10] Almost all Protestants believe in and practice only those two ceremonies as the ones instituted by Christ and handed down by the apostles and view them as sacraments or ordinances. A few Protestants, mostly of the Anabaptist tradition, add foot washing as a third ordinance. Some Protestants, most notably Lutherans and traditional Anglicans/Episcopalians, believe that baptism and the Lord's Supper or Eucharist are true means of grace in the sense that they strengthen faith and the believer's relationship with God. Many of them view infant baptism as regenerative in that it inserts the child into the covenant people of God and brings him or her the benefits of Christ's atoning work on the cross. Of course, as Protestants, they believe that the sacraments, including infant baptism, convey grace only in connection with faith. In the case of infants the faith of the parents and of the congregation may stand in for the faith of the child until he or she is old enough to confirm by faith what was done in baptism. Sacramentalist Protestants—especially traditional Lutherans—believe that the humanity of Jesus Christ is truly present "in, with and under" the elements of bread and wine in the Eucharist or

---

[9]For a contemporary, authoritative and relatively simple account of the Roman Catholic sacramental theology, see *The Church's Confession of Faith: A Catholic Catechism for Adults* (San Francisco: Ignatius Press, 1987), pp. 271-325.

[10]For lucid accounts of Protestant differences about the sacraments/ordinances, see Alasdair I. C. Heron, *Table and Tradition: Toward an Ecumenical Understanding of the Eucharist* (Philadelphia: Westminster Press, 1983); and Donald Bridge and David Phypers, *The Water That Divides: The Baptism Debate* (Downers Grove, Ill.: InterVarsity Press, 1977).

Lord's Supper. This has come to be known as "consubstantiation," even though that is not a term favored by Lutherans. It differs from the Roman Catholic interpretation of the Eucharist in that the bread and wine remain wholly bread and wine, but they are more than symbols. They become vehicles of the risen, glorified body and blood of Christ and strengthen faith.

During the first decade of the Protestant Reformation in Europe, the Swiss Reformer Zwingli strongly disagreed with Luther's view of the sacraments of baptism and the Lord's Supper. At first he favored believer baptism over infant baptism, but when he could not get the city council of Zurich to go along with that he defended infant baptism as a ritual parallel in the new covenant with circumcision in the old covenant. In other words, he viewed it as a rite of inclusion in the elect people of God and not as regenerative. Zwingli criticized Luther for sticking too close to the Catholic dogmas and practices regarding the sacraments, especially the mass or Eucharist. For Zwingli, the Lord's Supper was just a memorial meal commemorating Christ's death. He denied any "real presence" of Christ's body in, with or under the elements of bread and wine. Luther denounced Zwingli for this departure from tradition and fervently defended his own sacramental view of both baptism and the Lord's Supper—including consubstantiation. Underlying their differences about the Lord's Supper were disagreements about Christology; Luther believed in the principle of *communicatio idiomatum*— the communication of divine attributes to the humanity of Christ such that in his risen and exalted condition he could be present everywhere (ubiquity). Zwingli denied this principle and argued that if the incarnation means anything, it means that Jesus Christ, as a man, is located in heaven and is not ubiquitous. The argument over the Lord's Supper deeply divided early Protestantism.

John Calvin and his followers developed a view of the sacraments that was somewhere between Luther's and Zwingli's interpretations. For the majority of Reformed Protestants, baptism and the Lord's Supper are true sacraments in that they convey faith-strengthening grace when received with faith. But baptism is not automatically salvific, and the Lord's Supper, though more than a symbolic ceremony, has no real, bodily presence of Christ. For Calvin and his followers, baptism—including infant baptism—is the "sign and seal" of God's acceptance of the person into the church, which is Christ's body and the covenant community of God's people. They reject any interpretation of baptism as magical; it does not automatically save anyone. However, in Reformed theology, even infants receive spiritual benefits and blessings from being baptized even though they must grow up to embrace and not reject their place in the covenant between God and his elect people if they are to make their election and calling sure (i.e., be assured of their eternal salvation by God's electing grace). For Calvin and his followers, the Lord's Supper has a mystical, spiritual power without magic. The Holy Spirit uses it to promote and strengthen union with Christ whenever Christians participate in it with faith.

In 1525 a group of Zwingli's followers broke from his early Reformation in Zurich, Switzerland, over baptism. They came to be called Anabaptists because they "re-baptized" persons who had been baptized as infants. (Of course, they did not consider it rebaptism at all; they rejected infant baptism as anything more than moisture on the head.) Conrad Grebel and Felix Mantz were the first two Swiss Brethren—as the first Anabaptists were called—and their belief that baptism is symbolic of conversion to Christ and therefore should follow conscious repentance and faith was taken up later by Mennonites and Baptists. In the modern world a significant portion of Protestants practice "believer baptism" either by effusion (pouring) or immersion (dunking in water) and view it as a public act of commitment to Christ and his church rather than as a means of grace. Most of these Christians follow Zwingli's view of the Lord's Supper; it is for them a memorial meal rather than a sacrament. These Christians, whether they are Mennonites, Baptists or Pentecostals, prefer to call baptism and the Lord's Supper ordinances rather than sacraments because they do not believe that any outward ceremony actually conveys grace. Ordinances are observed because Christ commanded them and because they symbolize vividly the work of Christ for and within believers. For these Christians, the ordinances of baptism and the Lord's Supper are "visible words"—powerful object lessons that both teach and proclaim salvation and strengthen memory and hope.

Underlying these differences between Christian groups are certain historic commitments of tradition-communities. All of them can marshal Scripture passages to support their views. The Roman Catholic beliefs about the church and sacraments are rooted in tradition as much as or more than in Scripture. A major Catholic commitment is to the visible unity of the church, a principle that trumps many others. Protestants may value the unity of the church, but much more important for them is the purity of the gospel. In their view the existence of the church depends more on its faithfulness to the truth of the gospel of salvation by grace through Christ alone by faith alone than on its visible, institutional unity. Protestants in the free church tradition such as Anabaptists, Baptists and Pentecostals value the "priesthood of every believer," and that Protestant principle often takes precedence over ecumenical vision and continuity with the Great Tradition of historical Christianity. Yet, in spite of very significant differences of belief about the church and sacraments, Christians do agree that the church is established and maintained by God as the body of Christ and temple of the Holy Spirit and that on some level, in spite of appearances, it is unified, holy, universal and apostolic. All authentic Christians highly value at least the two sacraments or ordinances of baptism and the Lord's Supper even if they disagree about their meaning and observance.[11]

## A Unifying Christian Vision of the Church and Sacraments

Underlying the numerous Christian visions of the true nature of the church and its visible, organizational structure and the sacraments is a basic, bedrock unity of belief: the church is the people of God, founded by Christ himself to be the community of the Holy Spirit and the anticipation of his future kingdom. Furthermore, the church is one, holy, universal (catholic) and apostolic. Baptism and the Lord's Supper or Eucharist are permanent means of grace—however that is understood—until Christ returns. Almost without doubt significant differences of understanding of these realities will remain among Christians until history ends. But Christians can return to their basic, underlying agreement about the church and use it as common ground for mutual understanding, respect and cooperation for mission and service.

Christian common ground about the church is summed up in the four universal marks of the church stated in the Nicene Creed. The church of Jesus Christ is *one*. There is only one true church and it is the mystical body of Christ, the fellowship of all true believers in him throughout the world. Catholics and some Protestants may identify it in a special way with some specific organization, but almost all modern Christians realize that it transcends visible hierarchies, flow charts, buildings and budgets. It even transcends bishops and denominations. It exists wherever two or three people gather in the name

---

[11]Christian groups that do not observe baptism and the Lord's Supper are defectively Christian—as are most Christian denominations and churches at some point. It does not have to be a completely black and white, either-or situation. Some groups that call themselves Christian could be more authentically Christian by observing the sacraments/ordinances of baptism and the Lord's Supper, but that is not to say their members are not Christians at all.

of Jesus Christ to worship and serve, but it also takes concrete form in organized congregations and their connections with each other. As the great twentieth-century Swiss Protestant theologian Emil Brunner reminds us, its essence is fellowship, and yet fellowship always has an outer form.[12] The church is united in its fellowship—between believers and Christ, and between believers and other believers in the Holy Spirit. Even if this visible unity may never be institutional, it can still be a real unity. There is only one church of Jesus Christ, but there are and always will be (before Christ's return) many organizations in which it comes to expression.

The church is *holy*. That is, the one true church of Jesus Christ spread throughout time and space is set apart to God by the Holy Spirit. In spite of the manifest flaws and faults of its leaders and its members, the church is God's dwelling place on earth and has a unique call and destiny. Its purpose is to glorify God among all people and to anticipate the perfect community of the future when God will be with his people in the kingdom of God. It is a supernatural community of faith, hope and love. It is also a community of discipline in which people are held accountable and called to live in repentance before God. Some Christians will always view the church as a mixed assembly of true believers and false professors of faith in Christ, while others will always view it as a community composed only of true believers. But all may agree that the church is called to holiness, not only in ethical conduct but also in its spiritual focus on God and God alone. Worship, in other words, is not for entertainment or any other human-centered purpose; it is for God's glory and enjoyment.

The church is *catholic* or *universal*. It exists across barriers of language, ethnicity, culture and nationality. It extends down through time since the Day of Pentecost and until Christ returns and, perhaps in some form, throughout eternity. Denominations, individual congregations, conventions and parachurch organizations are manifestations of the church universal; they are never the church itself. That is not to dismiss them as without value. Their value exists, however, in their service to Christ as portions of his extended body of all true believers. Denominations and congregations, conventions and parachurch organizations come and go, but the church has always existed and will exist forever. It is spiritual, mystical and invisible yet

---

[12]Emil Brunner, *The Misunderstanding of the Church*, trans. Harold Knight (London: Lutterworth, 1952).

not at all ethereal or illusory. We hope and pray for the day when all true believers in Jesus Christ will realize this in such a way that sectarianism will fade away. As that happens, Christians of many different denominations will retain their specific, historical identities while joyfully worshiping with each other and eagerly cooperating with each other in mission and service.

Finally, the church is *apostolic*. The unity, holiness and universality of the church cannot be separated from its apostolic nature. The apostolicity of the church is its continuation in the faith and experience of the apostles of Jesus Christ who received the Holy Spirit on the Day of Pentecost. It is the church's continuing reform by the Word of God and the Holy Spirit; it is the church's faithfulness to the gospel of Jesus Christ as incarnation of God as well as sole Lord and Savior of the world. Wherever the gospel proclaimed by the apostles is faithfully preserved and proclaimed, even if in contemporary translation and contextualization, the church is present. Of course, many Christians will consider the apostolicity of the church a visible succession of ordained bishops who can trace their pedigrees, as it were, back to the apostles. Others will consider it a spiritual reality distinct from any visible, organizational hierarchy. Underlying both views is belief in the continuity of the church from the apostles down to the contemporary world and until Christ returns and afterwards.

A unifying Christian vision of the church may seem to be a pipe dream, but in reality it need not be that. In spite of continuing debates between theologians and church officers, the laity (ordinary church members) are already forging ahead with visible, if not institutional, unity of the church. While bishops and theologians, denominational executives and seminary professors anxiously discuss how to achieve "visible and institutional unity of the churches," ordinary lay Christians in movements such as the charismatic movement, lay renewal weekends, men's and women's Christian movements, base communities, Bible study groups and ecumenical worship services are already practicing visible unity across denominational lines. While there are certain dangers in this post-denominational Christian grassroots practice, it is also full of promise and hope for Christian unity that has not been achieved by all the efforts of ecumenical meetings and organizations. Perhaps the time has come for denominational Christian leaders to catch up with the practice of their laypeople and drop the barriers to full fellowship that have stood so long in the way of the church's unity.

# CHAPTER 14

# LIFE BEYOND DEATH

## Continuity *and* Discontinuity

The final two chapters of our book will deal with Christian beliefs about the future. In classical theology the term for this very large and complex subject is *eschatology*. Some readers may find it odd that I devote two entire chapters to this topic after devoting only one to what many Christians would consider much more crucial beliefs of the Christian faith. The only defense is that there are so many questions and issues and proposed answers related to eschatology that they require two chapters. Traditionally eschatology is divided into two distinct, interrelated areas of study and belief: *individual destiny* (life after death) and *the destiny of the world* (the end of the world as we know it). These areas of belief concern many people very intensely.

**Issues and Polarities of Christian Belief About Life Beyond Death**

Some of the bestselling novels in both Christian and secular bookstores deal with visions of the future that purport to be based on divine revelation. Some of them seem to be based more on speculation. Religious and secular movies portray life after death and the end times; many hymns, choruses and

gospel songs sung in church and recorded by Christian artists have eschatological themes. It is somewhat ironic that so much attention is paid to these
issues by religiously-committed and secular people while most Bible scholars
and theologians either ignore them entirely or make very modest claims
about knowledge in eschatology. One leading twentieth-century Protestant
theologian quipped, "We should not want to know too much about the furniture of heaven or the temperature of hell!" His caution seems to have
fallen on deaf ears. That is quite understandable because everyone faces
death sooner or later, and inquiring minds want to know what Christianity
says about the future of the individual person and of the world as a whole.

In this penultimate chapter of the book we will deal only with Christian
beliefs about the future of individual human persons. There is a general
Christian consensus about life beyond bodily death even though its details
are minimal. Everyone has heard of heaven and hell, but what about the
intermediate state? The New Testament refers to a place or condition after
bodily death and before the resurrection of the body called paradise. What is
the resurrection and when will it occur? What about judgments and everlasting life or consignment to eternal flames? Are these important Christian
beliefs? Polls show that about one quarter of adult North Americans say they
believe in reincarnation. Is that compatible with Christianity? What about
purgatory? Do all Christians believe in that or is it a doctrine only of the
Roman Catholic Church? These are some of the questions that arise in this
locus of Christian belief. They all revolve around the future fate of individual
human persons; the next chapter will deal with the distinct but related locus
of Christian belief about the future fate of the entire world, including
Christ's return to earth (parousia) and the kingdom of God in its completion and fulfillment.

As usual, we will first explore the Christian consensus about the future of
individuals beyond bodily death. We will see that there are a very few, basic
ideas about the future destiny of individuals agreed on by almost all Christians down through the ages. Then we will critically examine some of the
main alternatives to the Christian consensus—including belief in reincarnation. The unity of classical Christian belief will seem more significant once
the alternatives that lie outside the consensual tradition become apparent as
alternatives or heresies. After examining the alternative beliefs we will turn to
a study of the diversity of Christian beliefs about individual life beyond
bodily death. Purgatory is a distinctive belief of one major branch of Chris-

tianity; Protestants generally reject it. We will see that there is diversity among Protestants as well. Finally, I will make a few remarks about a unitive Christian vision of individual life beyond death. My hope is that this chapter and the next one will give readers some perspective for understanding classical, historic Christian belief in relationship to the plethora of popular books, movies, songs and folk beliefs about the future.

## The Christian Consensus About Life Beyond Death

Christianity has always been a religion of hope; Christians have always agreed that for those who trust in God's promise through Jesus Christ and who repent of their sins death is not the end of life but the doorway into eternal life—a transformed, personal existence with God in heaven. Christianity has always been a material religion as well; Christians have always believed (except when they forget their common faith) that the body participates in redemption and future eternal life. Finally, Christianity has always had a dark side that warns of judgment for those who live against God's mercy, grace and compassion and who refuse to repent and accept the salvation offered through Jesus Christ. Christians have always believed in hell as well as in heaven. Christianity necessarily and essentially holds out a promise given through Jesus Christ that death is not the end but, in the words of twentieth-century Protestant martyr Dietrich Bonhoeffer, "the beginning of life." By no means does this focus on the future make Christianity other-worldly. If that is its result it is due to distortion based on misunderstanding. Rather, the focus on the future fills this life and this world with meaning and purpose. Many evangelical Protestant Christians have sung, "This world is not my home; I'm just a-passin' through." But that song and the message it conveys are not meant to belittle or demean the world God created and in which we Christians are to be stewards. Rather, it reflects the reality of a future world beyond this present age under the domination of sin and its consequences. Christians also sing, "This is my father's world." This is God the Father's world, but our home is in its future. Here we are pilgrims and stewards who look forward to bodily redemption in a transformed world without sorrow, sickness, sin or death.

Four concepts sum up the Christian consensus about personal life beyond bodily death: *resurrection, judgment, heaven* and *hell.* Unfortunately, many Christians have focused their attention on folk religious notions about life after death. The main one is that when people die their souls go either to heaven to be "forever with the Lord" or else to hell and "everlasting fire." The common picture of life after death formed by many Christians is an amalgam of notions drawn from eclectic sources such as Greek mythology and philosophy, spiritualism (the "silver cord that breaks" and "summerland"), accounts of near-death experiences, Scripture and popular poetry and literature. This common picture—which has little to do with revelation or the classical Christian tradition—leaves bodily resurrection in the future completely aside and focuses intensely on the non-bodily but fully conscious and recognizable existence of individuals in an afterlife realm that is described using biblical images such as "pearly gates," "streets of gold" and "mansions." Many people even take seriously the accretions of legend such as Saint Peter at the pearly gates. In place of all these notions, Scripture and Christian tradition emphasize bodily resurrection of all the saints (all people who died in a state of grace through faith) together when Christ returns at the end of history as we know it. Very little is said in either Scripture or Christian tradition about the so-called intermediate state of souls between bodily death and bodily resurrection. The focus of almost all hope is on that which is yet future for everyone—the glorious resurrection and heaven when Christ returns.

The classical locus of biblical revelation with regard to resurrection is Paul's first epistle to the Corinthians, chapter fifteen. There are certainly many other references to resurrection in the New Testament and possibly a few in the Old Testament, but in 1 Corinthians 15 we have a sustained discussion of the Christian belief in bodily resurrection that leaves little or no room for doubt that, insofar as the New Testament is believed to be God's inspired Word, God has revealed through his apostles that the life to come in heaven with God is bodily and not ghostly or ethereal. Heaven will be populated by persons with bodies and not by disembodied spirits. In 1 Corinthians 15 Paul corrects those Christians at Corinth who questioned the redemption of bodies and viewed life after death as immortality of souls without bodies:

> how can some of you say that there is no resurrection of the dead? If there is no resurrection of the dead, then not even Christ has been raised. And if Christ has not been raised, our preaching is useless and so is your faith. More than that, we are then found to be false witnesses about God, for we have testified about God that he raised Christ from the dead. But he did not raise him if in fact the dead are not raised. For if the dead are not raised, then Christ has not

been raised either. And if Christ has not been raised, your faith is futile; you are still in your sins. (1 Cor 15:12-17)

Paul closely links Christ's bodily resurrection with the general resurrection of all the dead in the future and uses the former as the paradigm for understanding the latter. Shortly after, in 1 Corinthians 15:35-49, he argues that our future resurrections will be like Jesus Christ's, and he seems to suggest that Christ's was the beginning of the future resurrection happening ahead of time. He calls the resurrection body (both Christ's and ours in the future) a "spiritual body," while clearly intending that to be understood as more than some ethereal, ghostly soul substance. For Paul there is continuity and discontinuity between the body that dies and the body that God raises in the future, just as there was continuity and discontinuity between Christ's buried body and his glorious, raised body. The apostle returns to this subject in his epistle to the Philippians 3:20-21: "But our citizenship is in heaven. And we eagerly await a Savior from there, the Lord Jesus Christ, who, by the power that enables him to bring everything under his control, will transform our lowly bodies so that they will be like his glorious body."

The bodily resurrection of all people at some time after death has played a prominent role in Christian teaching throughout history. In spite of a pronounced tendency among untutored lay Christians to focus attention on immortality of souls and neglect bodily resurrection, the fathers of the church, medieval Christian thinkers, all the Protestant Reformers and faithful modern Christian biblical scholars and theologians have emphasized the bodily resurrection as the blessed hope of believers in Christ. One of the first Christian writers after the apostles was Clement of Rome, who was bishop of the Christians in the imperial capital in the last decade of the first century. In his epistle to the Corinthian Christians, *1 Clement,* he strongly affirms the bodily resurrection, even going so far as to illustrate it with the legend of the Phoenix—a mythical bird of Arabia that was said to rise out of its own ashes.[1] Irenaeus included the resurrection in his magisterial summary of the united faith of Christians dispersed throughout the world: "The Church, though dispersed throughout the whole world, even to the ends of the earth, has received from the apostles and their disciples this faith: . . . [Jesus

---

[1]"The Letter of the Romans to the Corinthians (I Clement)," chap. 25, in *The Apostolic Fathers,* trans. J. B. Lightfoot and J. R. Harmer, ed. and rev. by Michael W. Holmes, 2nd ed. (Grand Rapids, Mich.: Baker, 1989), pp. 42-43.

Christ's] manifestation from heaven in the glory of the Father 'to gather all things in one,' and to raise up anew all flesh of the whole human race."[2] The same influential second-century church father argued against the Gnostics that future redemption is bodily just as Christ's new life after death was bodily: "In the same manner, therefore, as Christ did rise in the substance of flesh, and pointed out to His disciples the mark of the nails and the opening in His side (now these are the tokens of that flesh which rose from the dead), so 'shall He also,' it is said, 'raise us up by His own power.'"[3]

Irenaeus, like almost all the church fathers, leaves no doubt that the resurrection will be corporeal and not merely "spiritual" and that the expectation of such holistic salvation—body, soul and spirit (Irenaeus embraced a trichotomous view of human persons)—is part and parcel of the blessed hope of Christians for their future redemption. The same emphatic teaching about the bodily resurrection of all people in the future can be found in Irenaeus's contemporaries Tertullian (*Apology* 48) and Origen (*On First Principles* 2.10). These three church fathers lived in different parts of the Roman Empire, wrote in different languages (Greek and Latin), and probably did not know of each other. They all believed that they were simply handing on what the apostles themselves had taught; they displayed no consciousness of innovating or speculating. Moreover, affirmation of bodily resurrection would have been entirely contrary to the cultures in which they lived and wrote.

The fourth- and fifth-century North African church father and bishop Augustine taught that the hope of believers for life everlasting through Jesus Christ is a hope for bodily resurrection. In his summary of Christian doctrine entitled *Faith, Hope and Charity,* the Bishop of Hippo devoted an entire chapter to it. He wrote that "no Christian may in any way doubt that the bodies of all men, those already born and those yet to be born, those who have died and those who will die, are to rise again,"[4] and he argued that resurrection bodies would be perfect bodies without deformities, each one being approximately thirty years of age and in perfect strength—no matter at what age or in what condition the person had died. While some of the details of Augustine's teaching about the resurrection seem speculative, there is no

---

[2]Irenaeus *Against Heresies* 1.10.1, *ANF* 1:330.
[3]Ibid., 5.7.1, p. 532.
[4]Augustine *Faith, Hope and Charity (Enchiridion)*, trans. Louis A. Arand (Westminster, Md.: Newman Press, 1963), chap. 23, p. 82.

doubt that in general he was simply communicating what was believed by the whole church (excluding Gnostics) about the future life.

The Roman Catholic tradition carried on this consensual tradition regarding resurrection of bodies and requires belief in it by all the faithful. This is clearly reflected in one of the most recent authoritative summaries of Catholic teaching, *The Church's Confession of Faith: A Catholic Catechism for Adults:* "God wills, calls, and loves the whole man, who is one in body and soul. The whole man includes his relation to the world and to his fellow men, which relation expresses itself in the body. The hope for bodily resurrection is not some later, foreign addition to faith in God. It too is an internal consequence of faith."[5] The catechism explains further that resurrection bodies are not to be conceived of as either grossly material or purely spiritual; they will be transformed and transfigured bodies. The only analogy to this, the official Catholic catechism states, is Christ's own resurrection body that prefigures our future redeemed bodies.

The Protestant Reformers of the sixteenth century and their later followers of all major Protestant traditions and denominations concurred completely with the early church and Catholic consensus regarding the future destiny of persons after bodily death. Three major Protestant doctrinal statements—the *Augsburg Confession* (Lutheran), the *Dordrecht Confession* (Anabaptist/Mennonite) and *The Westminster Confession of Faith* (Reformed/Presbyterian)—all equally confess the hope of bodily resurrection when Christ returns as a basic Christian belief. The Reformers and theologians behind these doctrinal statements taught the bodily resurrection in complete agreement with Augustine and the entire Christian tradition going back to the second-century church fathers and the apostle Paul himself.

John Calvin devoted several pages of his *Institutes of the Christian Religion* to the subject and left no doubt where he stood on the matter. chapter 25 of book 3 is titled "The Final Resurrection" and there the Geneva Reformer rejected belief in immortality of souls as understood by ancient Greek philosophy and some Renaissance philosophers in favor of a future resurrection of bodies understood as parallel with Christ's own bodily resurrection. That is, Calvin adamantly stated that the bodies with which we rise will be the very same bodies in which we died although they will be trans-

---

[5] *The Church's Confession of Faith: A Catholic Catechism for Adults* (San Francisco: Ignatius Press, 1987), 5.2.3, p. 336.

formed, just as Christ's was transformed to a new mode of existence fit for heaven. The Anabaptist Reformer Menno Simons wrote an essay "The Spiritual Resurrection," which is really about the new birth; for Menno every person must have what modern-day evangelical Christians call a "born again experience." He labeled this "spiritual resurrection" and in the process made clear that *future resurrection*—guaranteed by Christ's death and resurrection and our own spiritual resurrection by repentance and faith in the new birth—is bodily and not "spiritual."[6] John Wesley—the eighteenth-century Church of England reformer, revivalist and founder of the Methodist tradition—also taught bodily resurrection in his essay "On Eternity," where he affirmed that "death does not end the life of the soul or even finally of the body, since in the resurrection body and soul are reunited."[7]

It would be impossible to discover any single point of greater agreement in the history of Christian thought than this one: *the future bodily resurrection of the dead is the blessed hope of all who are in Christ Jesus by faith.* Over two millennia the church's leaders and faithful theologians have unanimously taught this above the immortality of souls and as more important than some ethereal intermediate state between bodily death and bodily resurrection when Christ returns. And yet, as we lamented earlier, it seems that the vast majority of Christians do not know this and neglect belief in bodily resurrection in favor of belief in immediate postmortem heavenly, spiritual existence as ghost-like beings (or even angels!) "forever with the Lord in heaven." One possible explanation for this sad situation of radical, if unintentional, departure from Christian tradition (to say nothing of from Scripture!) is the unacknowledged influence of *spiritualism* (belief in and practice of communication with the dead) on Western Christianity in the nineteenth century.

The other concepts of the consensual tradition of Christian belief—*judgment, heaven, hell*—need less explanation and defense from historical theology as they are rarely questioned or even seriously neglected among faithful, believing Christians. One can go through the same church fathers and confessional statements cited in favor of bodily resurrection as essential Christian belief about the future destinies of persons and find much material about Christ's return (to be dealt with in the next chapter of this book) and judg-

---

[6]See *The Complete Writings of Menno Simons c. 1496-1561,* trans. Leonard Verduin, ed. J. C. Wenger (Scottdale, Penn.: Herald, 1984), pp. 53-62.
[7]Thomas Oden, *John Wesley's Scriptural Christianity* (Grand Rapids, Mich.: Zondervan, 1994), p. 32.

ment of all people and their assignments to either heaven or hell. The revelational basis for belief in future heaven or hell after judgment may be found especially in Jesus' own teachings. Matthew 24 and 25 are sometimes called "the little apocalypse" because they contain Jesus' warnings about catastrophic future events surrounding the Son of Man's return and his judgment of the peoples of the earth and their consignments to heaven ("the kingdom" and "eternal life") or hell ("eternal punishment").

The terms *heaven* and *hell* are used throughout the New Testament and in church history for two distinct stages or aspects of personal eschatology. Generally speaking, however, Christian theologians have identified them with the ultimate future destinies of persons who have been judged by Christ when he returns. The so-called intermediate states of souls between bodily death and bodily resurrection receive very little attention in either Scripture or church tradition. Jesus refers in John 14 to a "place" he was going to prepare for his disciples so that when he returned they could be there with him forever. This place is generally understood in Christian thought to be heaven, whereas *paradise,* a restful oasis, is the term preferred for the state of souls that die in communion with Christ before he returns and opens heaven for them. John Calvin cautioned against too much attention to this intermediate state:

> Now it is neither lawful nor expedient to inquire too curiously concerning our souls' intermediate state. Many torment themselves overmuch with disputing as to what place the souls occupy and whether or not they already enjoy heavenly glory. Yet it is foolish and rash to inquire concerning unknown matters more deeply than God permits us to know. Scripture goes no farther than to say that Christ is present with them, and receives them into paradise that they may obtain consolation, while the souls of the reprobate suffer such torments as they deserve.[8]

While *paradise* is the usual English term for the intermediate abode of the righteous souls who restfully wait for their future gathering together with Christ to enjoy heaven in their glorified bodies after the resurrection, there is no specific term for the opposite intermediate abode of the "reprobate," as Calvin called those who die without being reconciled with God through Christ. Nevertheless, the virtually unanimous belief of Christian theologians

---

[8]John Calvin *Institutes* 3.25.6, p. 997.

down through the ages has been that such intermediate abodes do exist, though we know very little about them, and that they are not the focus of the blessed hope or of dire warnings in either Scripture or Christian proclamation and exhortation. Those are rather our yet future everlasting existences as resurrected bodies in either heaven or hell.

**Alternatives to the Christian Consensus About Life Beyond Death**
Many beliefs about life after and beyond bodily death exist in the world; many of them are associated with particular cultures and their dominant religions. Some are philosophical in nature and not tied to any specific culture, tribe or religion. Here we will critically examine only those beliefs about life after and beyond bodily death that have gained some influence among Christians. Thus, we will be dealing only with what may be called heresies about life after death that are embraced by some Christians and that seriously conflict with normative Christian belief as outlined above. One of these is *immortality of souls to the neglect or exclusion of bodily resurrections*. It is not as common among Christian scholars and theologians as among unsophisticated and biblically semiliterate laypeople. It is the common, default belief of folk Christianity—the informal, unreflective beliefs and practices of many Christians that are drawn more from comfortable slogans, legends and stories than from biblical materials or doctrinal, theological traditions. The pronounced influence of nineteenth-century *spiritualism*[9] in Europe and North America has much to do with this situation; many conservative Christians who would never darken the door of a spiritualist medium or attend a séance actually hold beliefs about the afterlife much more like spiritualists than like the church fathers or Reformers of Christianity.

Another heresy about life after death that is gaining greater acceptance among Christians is *reincarnation* or *transmigration of souls or spirits*. While this belief about personal destiny used to be associated with oriental religions and Western occultism, it is now widely accepted by members of Christian churches in Europe and North America and promoted by a few Christian theologians. The final heresy that we will examine here is *objective immortal-*

---

[9]Here *spiritualism* is being used as a general label for a variety of individuals and groups that arose on the margins of Christianity in Europe and North America and gained prominence and influence—even among many Christians—in the nineteenth century. Among its most noted "theologians" were the Swedish nobleman and mystic Emanuel Swedenborg and the American spiritualist thinker and medium Andrew Jackson Davis.

*ity*—belief that the only existence of persons after bodily death is their enduring influence on the world and presence in God's memory. Objective immortality denies any conscious, personal survival of bodily death including resurrection. The dead are extinct, but their impact lives on. That is their objective immortality as opposed to subjective immortality. This view is widely held by liberal Protestant theologians who follow what is known as process theology.

Many Christians (and others) will be surprised to see *immortality of souls* mentioned here as a heresy. And yet, if bodily resurrection is true Christian belief about the ultimate destiny of persons, immortality of souls cannot be consistent with authentic Christianity. "Immortality of souls"—as we are using the phrase here and as it is usually understood in the history of philosophy, religion and spirituality—is the belief held and promoted by the ancient Greek philosophers and schools of religion and by the nineteenth-century spiritualists who profoundly influenced North American Protestant church life. It is represented by the lyrics of numerous gospel songs such as "I'll Fly Away," which compares the soul at bodily death with a bird flying from prison bars (i.e., a cage). Far too many Christian ministers fall back on this idea in funeral sermons and graveside devotions where the "dear, departed loved one" is said to have left this mortal body to be forever with the Lord.

The ancient Greek philosophers and the numerous mystery religions and cults of the Greek and Roman empires all held some form of this same belief about life beyond bodily death. The body (*sōma* in Greek) was compared with a tomb (*sēma*), and the soul (*psychē*) pictured as yearning for escape into some everlasting realm of purely spiritual delight unlimited and unburdened by physical existence of any kind. Many Christians who consciously embrace immortality of souls to the exclusion of bodily resurrection have no idea of its ancient roots in Greek philosophy and Gnostic spirituality. They prefer to base it on a few passages in Scripture that, if taken out of context, seem to portray those in paradise as enjoying the fullness of God's presence and their own redemption. In fact, however, one simply cannot read the entire New Testament and miss its reservation of redemption for the future—when Christ returns visibly in judgment. The sad and simple fact seems to be that many Christians have unthinkingly accepted ancient Greek and modern spiritualist images of life after death as "Summerland" because it is comforting to think of their loved ones as already in heaven and not as awaiting a bodily resurrection which would mean a certain incompleteness until then.

No major Christian theologian has ever taught immortality of souls in this sense and no significant Christian denomination teaches it as an alternative to resurrection. However, the heresy of soul immortality is common in a variety of neognostic and spiritualist churches that may be found in virtually every city in North America. The Swedenborgian churches—many of which were established in America by the frontiersman Johnny "Appleseed" Chapman—teach immortality of souls and a kind of transmigration of souls in realms of spiritual travel after bodily death. These images and ideas have worked their ways into the hearts and minds of millions of members of mainline and evangelical Christian churches and have pushed aside interest and belief in bodily resurrection.

*Reincarnation* is a term that designates several different beliefs about personal life after death that all portray souls as departing from dying bodies and eventually entering new ones. It is sometimes known as "transmigration of souls" (especially when it includes belief that disembodied souls or spirits may enter nonhuman bodies) or "re-embodiment" (a term preferred by many adherents of the so-called New Age movement).[10] Polls have shown that as many as twenty-three percent of adult Americans say they believe in some kind of reincarnation.[11] Some Christians—including a few Christian theologians—have embraced the idea as compatible with divine revelation if not Christian tradition. One occasionally hears the claim that early Christians believed in and taught reincarnation, but that it was declared heretical by an early Christian Roman emperor and expunged from the canon of inspired Scripture and excluded from Christian teaching. This is patently false and nothing more than a kind of religious legend—similar to urban legends that are widely accepted as true in spite of the fact that not a shred of evidence supports them. The idea that reincarnation—in any sense—is compatible with Christian belief or was ever taught by any significant church father has been thoroughly debunked by evangelical theologian Mark Albrecht (Wheaton College) in *Reincarnation: A Christian Appraisal* (Downers Grove, Ill.: InterVarsity Press, 1982). And yet Protestant philosophical theo-

---

[10]For scholarly but accessible discussions of many ideas of life after death, including reincarnation, see Geddes MacGregor, *Images of Afterlife: Beliefs from Antiquity to Modern Times* (New York: Paragon House, 1992).

[11]George Gallup, *Adventures in Immortality* (New York: McGraw Hill, 1982), pp. 137-38.

logian Geddes MacGregor (University of Southern California) has argued that certain versions of reincarnation are compatible with the true essence of Christianity in *Reincarnation in Christianity* (Wheaton, Ill.: Quest Books, 1978).

If there is a prooftext that completely undermines any idea of reincarnation it is Hebrews 9:27: "Just as man is destined to die once, and after that to face judgment." Of course, those who insist on attempting to make reincarnation fit with Scripture and authentic Christian belief claim that in this passage judgment refers to karma—the law of retribution in which souls re-enter bodies based on their moral and spiritual performances in previous embodiments. However, that ignores the clear reference to one death per person. In the final analysis, however, the reason that reincarnation must be rejected as completely incompatible with authentic Christianity is not because one verse of the New Testament seems clearly to exclude it. The larger reason is that reincarnation inevitably devalues the body and denies bodily resurrection. Which body would be raised? Which body of the series possessed by the soul is the one true body of the person? Reincarnation cannot possibly do justice to the value of bodily existence as part of God's good creation. Belief in it reduces bodies to mere vehicles of spiritual evolution out of which souls or spirits—the true, higher self—wish to grow. Finally, of course, reincarnation is impossible for Christians for Christological reasons. It devalues the incarnation and raises unanswerable questions about Jesus Christ's embodiment both before and after the resurrection. For these and many reasons reincarnation in all its forms must be pronounced incompatible with Christianity.

The last major alternative to Christian belief about individual eschatology is *objective immortality*. The term was apparently coined by twentieth-century philosopher Alfred North Whitehead, who inspired the school of liberal theology known as process theology. Whitehead's definition of the term is disputed even among his followers, but it seems that he meant that individual entities such as persons survive biological death only in their continuing contributions to the whole networks of which they were parts and in God's memory, which preserves all values. Thus, objective immortality excludes personal, subjective, conscious existence after bodily death. Bodily resurrection is considered a symbolic expression of the new existence of the soul or self that died, a new existence in the environment and the mind of God. One of the most influential proponents of objective immortality does not call it that, but expresses and recommends the idea in her book *God and Gaia: An Ecofeminist Theology of Earth Healing*. The author's name is Rosemary Radford Ruether, and she is a Catholic professor of Christian theology and ethics at a Protestant seminary. She is also the leading feminist theologian of the late twentieth century and early twenty-first century. In *God and Gaia* Ruether writes of the traditional Christian theological view:

> This concept of the "immortal self," survivable apart from our particular transient organism, must be recognized, not only as untenable, but as the source of much destructive behavior toward the earth and other humans. . . . The cutting of the life center [by bodily death] also means that our bodies disintegrate into organic matter, to enter the cycle of decomposition and recomposition as other entities. . . . Is there also a consciousness that remembers and envisions and reconciles all things, as the Process theologians believe? Surely, if we are kin to all things and offspring of the universe, then what has flowered in us as consciousness must also be reflected in that universe as well, in the ongoing creative Matrix of the whole.[12]

This is, of course, little different from sheer extinction of persons by death—the naturalistic, atheistic denial of personal survival of death of any kind. Can Christianity or even religion survive the amputation of such an important limb of the body of belief as personal existence beyond bodily death? It does not seem so. And yet, some Christian theologians are arguing for just that amputation. Few, if any, lay Christian people follow them. While the heresy of immortality of souls is popular in folk religion and almost nonexistent among theologians, the heresy of objective immortality is popular in some academic theological circles and almost nonexistent among Christians in the pews. There is nothing to support objective immortality (to the exclusion of subjective personal life beyond death) in biblical revelation or the Great Tradition of Christianity. It flies in the face of the Christ-centered criterion of Christian thought. Christ rose from the dead and is alive! He lives and will return to raise all of the dead to new, transformed existence fit for heaven or hell. This is the consensus of the biblical witness and of the Christian heritage of belief. The only reason for believing in objective immortality is sheer accommodation (even capitulation) to modern naturalism.

Do these three fairly obvious alternatives to classical Christian belief about

---

[12]Rosemary Radford Ruether, *God and Gaia: An Ecofeminist Theology of Earth Healing* (San Francisco: HarperSanFrancisco, 1992), pp. 251-53.

personal destiny after and beyond death exhaust the possibilities? Are there no other significant, influential heresies in this locus of Christian belief? There may be, but these are the three main categories. They are not precise, clear-cut beliefs; they are rather broad ways of thinking about life beyond death with variations and some diversity within each one. Not all process theologians, for example, will agree wholly with Rosemary Radford Ruether's account of objective immortality, but most, if not all, share with it the denial of personal, subjective, conscious, individual existence of human beings after their bodily deaths. They reject not only bodily resurrection but also any ego-survival of death; they locate immortality in God's memory or nature's reservoir of values. The situation is the same with reincarnation and immortality of souls—each one allows for certain variations of interpretation within its general category.

Some Protestant readers may wonder why the Catholic doctrine of purgatory is not examined in this section on alternatives to Christian belief. Others may look for what is called "annihilationism" here. Finally, what about "soul sleep"? These are beliefs about personal life after death that are held by many Christians and that are doctrinal beliefs of some Christian denominations. The reason none of them is described and examined here is that while they may be considered aberrations and deviations from the majority view of Christians, they are not radically opposed to or inconsistent with the Christian consensus. They are at best opinions about life beyond bodily death and the ultimate destinies of individual persons; if they are heretical that appears when they are elevated to the status of required doctrine or even dogma. Of course, some specific Christian denominations, churches and organizations do exclude these beliefs as inconsistent with their own confessional traditions and doctrinal statements, but many do not. That is why they will be treated under the category heading of diversity in this area of Christian belief—not because I recommend them or believe they are valid but because it is possible for an authentically Christian person to hold them without (in our view) needing correction to become more fully and truly Christian in terms of beliefs.

## Diverse Christian Beliefs About Life Beyond Death

All Christians do or should believe in bodily resurrection as the ultimate destiny of all persons. All Christians do or should also believe in future judgment and heaven and hell, even if they do not claim to know very much about "the furniture of heaven or the temperature of hell." Christians who happen to believe in reincarnation or immortality of souls (to the exclusion of bodily redemption) or objective immortality are believing contrary to the Great Tradition of Christianity and the conflict is serious. They should change their beliefs in order to become more truly and authentically Christian. However, there are many different views about secondary matters of personal eschatology within orthodox Christianity. Some of them have to do with the nature of the so-called *intermediate state* between bodily death and bodily resurrection. Others have to do with the *nature of hell*. Finally, some relate to the *nature of heaven*.

Strangely, perhaps, the latter—the nature of heaven—gives rise to the fewest and least hostile differences of belief among Christians. One is hard pressed to find and describe such debates even though differences of opinion are well known. Some Christians believe that heaven will be a renewed earth—a transformed and transfigured creation and not another dimension of reality from this world. They base this on the apostle Paul's references in Romans 8 to a future liberation of creation—from bondage to decay. Others believe that heaven will be quite different from this world and that the differences are dimensional. That is, there is no continuity between heaven and earth. Some Christians believe that heaven will have levels. The apostle Paul referred to three levels or spheres of heaven in 2 Corinthians 12. It would seem, however, that he was speaking of a vision of paradise that he received. Many Christians believe in rewards in heaven; some resurrected people who are given entrance to heaven, they believe, will be awarded something for their lives or deaths (e.g., martyrdom) that others in heaven will not receive. John Calvin, for one, strongly affirmed this. Other Christians are repulsed by the thought of rewards or different levels of glory in heaven. These differences about heaven are just about on the level of different views of its "furniture"—that is, whether people will have their own living quarters and whether their pets will be there and so forth. One article in a weekly news magazine reported a popular baseball coach's belief that there will be baseball in heaven! These opinions all fall into a relatively low level of importance as neither Scripture nor Christian tradition point toward anything very clearly. Whatever one chooses to believe about these matters is relatively unimportant.

On the other hand, genuine debates and controversies have taken place among Christians about the *nature of the intermediate state*. A few Christians deny any conscious existence of human beings between bodily death and bodily resurrection. This view is known by its critics as "soul sleep." Most Christians throughout history have believed in some kind of conscious condition of persons, "souls," out of the body, while affirming the nonultimacy of this state; it is some kind of waiting for resurrection, judgment and either heaven or hell. Roman Catholics and a few Protestants believe in purgatory as one sphere of the intermediate state; most Protestants strongly deny it. Eastern Orthodox Christians also deny purgatory even as they pray for the souls of the dead. Here we will discuss these various options of belief beginning with the view involving the richest and most detailed intermediate state and ending with the vanishing intermediate state—soul sleep. Between them we will discuss the standard Protestant belief (not folk theology) in the intermediate state as anticipatory conditions of waiting for future judgment and fulfillment or punishment.

*Purgatory.* The word itself used to send shivers up and down the spines of most Protestants. Belief in it was a flash point of controversy during the Protestant Reformation and between Catholics and Protestants for many years. Only after the Second Vatican Council (Vatican II) in the 1960s did that controversy begin to die down largely because Catholic theologians began to redefine purgatory in ways not so offensive to Protestants. Purgatory is, according to Catholic theology, the place where souls of persons who died in a state of grace but with the stain and corruption of sin still clinging to them spend some period of time before being admitted to paradise. Purgatory is variously conceived by Catholic theologians as either purification by fiery punishment or as a kind of spiritual development toward perfect penance and preparation for the vision of God in paradise and in heaven after the resurrection. Medieval images of purgatory tended to portray it as hellish. The only significant difference between purgatory and hell in Dante's poetic descriptions of the various dimensions of the afterlife was that purgatory was temporary whereas hell or Hades was permanent. Those in purgatory were believed always eventually to be purified and admitted to paradise and then to heaven. Thomas Aquinas provided one of the most scholarly medieval Catholic descriptions of and justifications for purgatory:

> But by sin the soul is unclean in its disordered union to inferior things. To be sure, the soul is purified from this uncleanness in this life by penance and other sacraments . . . but it does at times happen that such purification is not entirely

perfected in this life; one remains a debtor for the punishment, whether by reason of some negligence, or business, or even because a man is overtaken by
death. Nevertheless, he is not entirely cut off from his reward, because such
things can happen without mortal sin, which alone takes away the charity [love]
to which the reward of eternal life is due. . . . They must, then, be purged after
this life before they achieve the final reward. This purgation, of course, is made
by punishments, just as in this life their purgation would have been completed
by punishments which satisfy this debt; otherwise, the negligent would be better off than the solicitous, if the punishment which they do not complete for
their sins here need not be undergone in the future. Therefore, if the souls of
the good have something capable of purgation in this world, they are held back
from the achievement of their reward while they undergo cleansing punishments. And this is the reason we hold that there is a purgatory.[13]

The theological basis for belief in purgatory, then, was (and sometimes is
still) belief that even good Christians often die without having received full
pardon for their sins; they must still suffer the "temporal consequences" for
those. One can understand, then, why Luther, Calvin and the other Protestant Reformers rejected belief in purgatory; it seems to them to undermine
the gospel of salvation as free gift. The Roman Catholic response was and
still is that while eternal life in heaven is a free gift that cannot be earned, one
must suffer the temporal punishments for his or her sins and enter heaven
truly righteous.

The Roman Catholic Church appeals to several passages of Scripture to
justify its doctrine of purgatory. One of the main texts is in what Protestants
call the Apocrypha—the noncanonical books between the two testaments.
In 2 Maccabees, one of the thirteen books considered canonical by Roman
Catholics but rejected by Protestants, reference is made to prayers for the
dead (12:48). Catholics also point to 1 Corinthians 3:15 and Matthew
12:32 and 5:26 as supporting passages. These are interpreted as teaching
fiery purgation and repentance and forgiveness after bodily death. Protestants interpret them in other ways. Ultimately, however, the reason Catholics
believe in purgatory—however it is understood—is that they believe one
must be essentially morally and spiritually perfect before entering into the
presence of God. However, the idea of purgatory has undergone a radical
transformation in modern Catholic thought. One Catholic priest explained

---

[13]Thomas Aquinas, quoted in Robert C. Doyle, *Eschatology and the Shape of Christian Belief*
(Carlisle, U.K.: Paternoster, 1999), pp. 121-22.

to me that purgatory is nothing more than a momentary cleansing that a Christian soul experiences "in a flash" after death. He averred that such souls go immediately into paradise after that. The semi-official Catholic adult catechism reinterprets purgatory:

> Popular talk about the "poor souls" [in purgatory] is justified so far as their "poverty" is understood to mean that they cannot be actively but only passively purified and sanctified. But they are not really "poor souls" so much as souls who experience the whole wealth of the mercy of God and who are a substantial step ahead of us in the realization of human hope and in nearness to God. Their pain before God's face is that they are not yet pure enough to be able to be wholly filled and beatified by his love. They suffer only the purifying pain of his love. In this love, all members of the one body of Christ are united in solidarity. . . . Of course, it is not as if Jesus Christ had not done enough for our redemption by his suffering and death. He did more than enough. But he lets us participate in the effects of his saving work.[14]

While the portrayal of purgatory in modern Catholic thought is less offensive to Protestants, the very idea of purgatory goes against the classical Protestant belief in complete salvation as full and free "by grace through faith in Christ alone." It implies a need for some kind of addition to Christ's suffering and death as a condition for whole salvation. On the other hand, Protestants should admit that the Catholic concept of purgatory is far from what it was when Luther so vehemently protested it and the Church of England (to name just one Protestant tradition out of all) condemned it in its statement of faith. Many Catholics at the beginning of the twenty-first century believe that purgatory is nothing more or less than a kind of spiritual formation after death that prepares souls for entrance into God's comforting presence in paradise. One question that remains unanswered, of course, is why the thief on the cross next to Jesus was able to enter paradise that very day—immediately upon death (Lk 23:42-43). All quibbling aside, however, the Catholic-Protestant disagreement over the afterlife will no doubt continue; it can only be hoped that devout Christians on both sides will also recognize and acknowledge their common ground of belief.

The traditional Protestant view of the afterlife—life beyond bodily death—includes belief in *two intermediate states* as opposed both to the Catholic belief in three (paradise, purgatory and the realm of the con-

---

[14]*The Church's Confession of Faith* 5.3.3.

demned who died in mortal sin) and to some Protestants' belief in so-called soul sleep. Although it has been criticized as inherently dualistic with regard to the physical and spiritual aspects of human persons, classical Protestant belief in conscious existence of disembodied souls between bodily death and resurrection finds much support in Scripture. Jesus declared Abraham, Isaac and Jacob alive and not dead in Mark 12:24-27. Of course, they had already died physically, so Jesus must have been referring to their continuing existence in an intermediate state. The gospel story of the transfiguration of Christ with Moses and Elijah appears to support traditional belief in an intermediate, conscious state of those who have died, as does Jesus' story of the rich man and Lazarus. The apostle Paul certainly seemed to believe in such an intermediate state when he wrote, "For to me, to live is Christ and to die is gain. If I am to go on living in the body, this will mean fruitful labor for me. Yet what shall I choose? I do not know! I am torn between the two: I desire to depart and be with Christ, which is better by far; but it is more necessary for you that I remain in the body" (Phil 1:21-24). It is also argued that Paul's enigmatic reference to visiting paradise, the "third heaven," points toward his belief in an intermediate existence (2 Cor 12:1-6).

There are fewer biblical references to the abode of the dead who died condemned. The images of hell as a "lake of fire," and "outer darkness" refer to the future destination of those who reject God's mercy and are judged harshly by God for their lack of faith and lives of evil. Bible readers have plumbed Scripture for information about the names and natures of the places or conditions of the souls who died, but Scripture remains relatively opaque about the intermediate states. Nevertheless, John Calvin speculated cautiously about the intermediate states while warning against too much curiosity about the dead:

> Now it is neither lawful nor expedient to inquire too curiously concerning our souls' intermediate state. Many torment themselves overmuch with disputing as to what place the souls occupy and whether or not they already enjoy heavenly glory. Yet it is foolish and rash to inquire concerning unknown matters more deeply than God permits us to know. Scripture goes no farther than to say that Christ is present with them, and receives them into paradise that they may obtain consolation, while the souls of the reprobate suffer such torments as they deserve.[15]

---

[15]Calvin *Institutes* 3.25.6.

Calvin's view is the classical Protestant interpretation of the afterlife before and until Christ's return to judge the living and the dead (i.e., those who have died and are bodily raised when he appears). Very little information is included in this classical Protestant vision of the intermediate state. Certainly, however, it does not require literal fire for the damned or literal pearly gates and streets of gold for the saved. These are images of existence after bodily resurrection and judgment in the ultimate eschaton—after the coming of Christ. Where are the dead now and what is life like for them? Any answers to those questions would be purely speculative and not at all normative for Christian belief. That is why the third option, commonly known by its opponents as "soul sleep," is not all that objectionable.

Some Protestants believe that the only intermediate state of souls is either nonexistence until bodily resurrection or else unconscious, sleep-like waiting for resurrection when Christ returns. The only term commonly used for these ideas is *soul sleep*. The main Protestant group that holds this idea as doctrine is the group of denominations of Adventists. (The Watchtower Bible and Tract Society, commonly known as Jehovah's Witnesses also believes in soul sleep because the sect is an offshoot of the older, larger Adventist movement.) Many non-Adventist individuals also deny conscious intermediate states of the dead, but all Adventists share this belief in soul sleep. The idea is that bodies and souls belong together and are, in fact, inseparable. Thus, when the body dies the soul dies too. Or as some prefer to say, the soul, which is the entire person before God, "sleeps" until resurrection. What will be raised is the whole person in a new, transformed existence—body and soul/spirit. In this view, then, the dead are completely unaware of anything including any passage of time. When they are raised they will not be aware of having "slept" or of having been nonexistent for some period of time. Adventists and others who embrace this belief about personal eschatology base it on the numerous biblical passages that refer to the dead as "asleep" or "sleeping."

Critics of soul sleep—in either of its versions—point out that such references are counterbalanced by references to the souls of the dead as being in some place. Jesus' promise to the dying thief on the cross next to him can hardly be squared with belief in soul sleep or any denial of conscious, intermediate existence of souls after bodily death: "I tell you the truth, today you will be with me in paradise" (Lk 23:43). Nevertheless, soul sleep is no longer considered a heresy by even most conservative Protestant theologians. Many have even embraced a version of it in which persons are said to skip over intervening time between bodily death and resurrection and enter immediately into the resurrection and heaven after death. In this view, paradise is heaven. The problem with that interpretation, of course, is that it requires believing that the second coming of Christ and the general resurrection of all the dead have already happened—even if only "for those who have died." This seems clearly contrary to the apostle Paul's own comforting message to the worried Thessalonian Christians who had been seduced into believing that the resurrection had already happened (2 Thess 2). It also seems clearly contrary to the same apostle's references to the state of being "away from the body and at home with the Lord" upon bodily death (2 Cor 5:8). Finally, belief that persons who die simply skip over the rest of time and enter immediately after death into resurrection, judgment and either heaven or hell seems to require belief that time itself is either an illusion or so able to operate according to different rules that history becomes unreal. The biblical narrative and worldview do not devalue time and history but assume their reality—even for the dead (Rev 7:9-17).[16]

A final area of significant diversity in Christian belief about personal eschatology—life beyond death—has to do with the *nature of hell*. While most Christians throughout history have believed that hell is everlasting torment of the wicked—whether literal flames or not—some Christians believe that hell is extinction. This controversial interpretation of hell is known as *annihilationism* and *conditional immortality*. (The two can be distinguished, but they are nearly identical in essence.) Belief that hell will be everlasting, conscious punishment of some kind (not necessarily fire and brimstone) is shared by the vast majority of Christians down through history—Eastern Orthodox, Roman Catholic and Protestant—and is based on several passages of Scripture including Jesus' own words about Gehenna—a fiery, smoke-filled dump near Jerusalem that Jesus used as an image of the destination of Satan and those who obey him (Mt 18:9; 25:41)—which Jesus called "eternal fire." Revelation 20 refers to a future "lake of fire" into which death and Hades are to be thrown together with all of God's enemies; these are described as a place where they will be "tormented day and night for ever and ever."

---

[16]Oscar Cullmann, *Christ and Time: The Primitive Christian Conception of Time and History*, trans. Floyd V. Filson (Philadelphia: Westminster Press, 1950), pp. 231-242.

Annihilationists—including all members of the various Adventist denominations, churches and organizations—believe that the everlastingness of hell is extinction. That is, persons who are consigned there are punished and shown mercy at the same time; God punishes them by burning them up completely and shows them mercy by allowing them to cease existing as rebellious persons under condemnation. It is God's form of mercy killing and capital punishment. Annihilationism has been embraced by a number of conservative, evangelical theologians outside of Adventist circles. Edward Fudge published a book-length study and defense of it in 1982; Clark Pinnock and John Stott, two notable evangelical scholars, have endorsed it (Stott "tentatively"), as has Anglican evangelical theologian Philip Edgcumbe Hughes.[17] The rise of interest in and affirmation of annihilationism has predictably given rise to a reaction; many conservative evangelical theologians have resurrected the old polemical labels of heresy and aberrational teaching to marginalize those evangelicals who would dare to embrace a belief that was once relegated to the sectarian margins of Protestantism. This hardly seems like a valuable expenditure of time and energy. Annihilationism does not strike at the heart of the gospel or even deny any major Christian belief; it is simply a reinterpretation of hell. More importantly, its harsh condemnation by a few fundamentalists should not deter Christians from accepting one another as equally believers in the gospel of Jesus Christ in spite of differences of opinion about the nature of hell. Contrary to what some fundamentalist critics have charged, annihilationism is not tantamount to universalism or *apokatastasis*. It is simply a minority view of the nature of hell, not a denial of hell.

## A Unitive Christian View of Life Beyond Death

In contrast to its main alternatives and in spite of some serious differences of opinion, the common ground shared by all believing Christians about personal life after or beyond death is truly significant. In a society and culture in which approximately twenty-three percent of adults—including many who consider themselves Christians—admit to believing in reincarnation and in which some Christian theologians and many secular thinkers deny any personal existence after death, Christians of differing opinions about the details

---

[17]See Edward W. Fudge, *The Fire That Consumes: A Biblical and Historical Study of Final Punishment* (Houston, Tex.: Providential, 1982); and David L. Edwards and John Stott, *Evangelical Essentials* (Downers Grove, Ill.: InterVarsity Press, 1988), pp. 312-29.

of personal eschatology should be able to work together and affirm their common faith in God's promises for the future. Honest, rigorous debate is not thereby excluded, but openness to each other's particular viewpoints and especially to each other in spite of relatively minor differences of opinion is necessary. Most Protestants will almost certainly never embrace purgatory, although they should acknowledge the significant changes in that idea in recent Catholic thought, and should cease misrepresenting it. Similarly, Catholics and most Protestants are not likely to endorse annihilationism or soul sleep, but they can and should recognize that many Christians who do hold those beliefs also share with the Great Tradition of Christian thought the main perspectives about personal life after death such as bodily resurrection, judgment, heaven and hell.

Rather than arguing with each other and especially against each other, Christian theologians and leaders of all major Christian traditions ought to focus attention on helping untutored lay Christians grasp essential Christian belief about life beyond death and separate that from the welter of folk beliefs that they tend to pick up from movies, television programs, popular literature and songs. Christian ministers of all denominations need to proclaim the blessed hope of future resurrection at funerals and strictly avoid pandering to what relatives of the deceased want to hear. Far too much emphasis has been placed on the "furniture of heaven and temperature of hell" in funeral sermons and at gravesides. Our Christian hope resides in the future of Jesus Christ and his raising of all the dead to stand before him in judgment and in his mercy and grace as well as his vindication of the righteous will of God against unrepentant evildoers. Our hope resides not in "mansions over the hilltop" but in a "new heaven and new earth" in which God will dwell with us and we with him. Christians of all traditions believe in these promises and their fulfillment more than in detailed scenarios of the intermediate states or of heaven and hell.

# CHAPTER 15

# THE KINGDOM OF GOD

## Already *and* Not Yet

Christians have always believed and confessed that "our God reigns" and "Jesus is Lord." On the other hand, Christians have also always admitted that God's reign is, in some sense, future. In what has come to be known as the Lord's Prayer, Jesus instructed his disciples to petition God for the kingdom: "your kingdom come, your will be done on earth as it is in heaven" (Mt 6:10). It seems, then, that Jesus believed in a heavenly rule and reign of God at all times as well as a future—eschatological—consummation and manifestation of God's rule and reign. The apostle Paul referred to this same paradox of the "already and not yet" character of God's kingdom in his first letter to the Corinthians where he wrote:

> Then the end will come, when he [Jesus] hands over the kingdom to God the Father after he has destroyed all dominion, authority and power. For he must reign until he has put all his enemies under his feet. The last enemy to be destroyed is death. . . . When he has done this, then the Son himself will be made subject to him who put everything under him, so that God may be all in all. (1 Cor 15:24-28)

According to Paul, then, Christ already reigns (and God's kingdom is inseparable from Christ's reign if Christ is God the Son) and yet must establish that reign by destroying all opposing "dominion, authority and power." We have already noticed this paradox of God's sovereignty in the chapter on divine providence. God is already and always sovereign *de jure* (by right and might) but only sovereign *de facto* (in fact by all things being according to his perfect will) in the future. God's kingdom, as the correspondence of the world of nature and history with God's will, is a hope and a promise; Christians pray for it and believe in its coming fervently. What is this world coming to? The Christian answer is "to the kingdom of God." At the same time, Christianity says and Christians believe that the kingdom of God is already real. It is not an exclusively future reality; it is also a present reality. God is in charge; nothing happens unless God allows it to happen. "And though the wrong seems oft so strong, God is the ruler yet." On the other hand, Christians confess, this "present evil age" (the systems of the world within history) resists and opposes God. So, Christians believe that the fullness of God's kingdom is eschatological. Even as the earliest Christians of the Roman Empire confessed "Jesus is Lord!" they also prayed "Maranatha!"— "come quickly, Lord Jesus."

### Issues and Polarities of Christian Belief About the Kingdom of God

The cover of *Time* magazine's June 25, 2001, issue asked, "How Will the Universe End?" It is a universal human question. Inquiring minds want to know what the future holds not only for me but also for all of us. How will the world end? What is the end of history and of humanity? Is there hope for this world of nature and history or is the future just more of the same or possibly obliteration? Christians believe that God has answered these questions in admittedly somewhat opaque language and imagery. As we will see, Christians do not all agree on the specific details about that answer or how to interpret the imagery and the language in which it is couched. There is tremendous diversity within Christianity about the end of the world as we know it—universal, world eschatology. Such diversity has always existed among Christians.

In the second century the church father and bishop Irenaeus presented a relatively detailed description of the end of the present world and the events surrounding Christ's return and the establishment of God's visible rule and reign. Some of what he wrote reads as if it were taken out of certain late-twentieth-century popular Christian books about the end times. Around the same time, the church father Origen presented his own speculative scenario of the future that bears little concrete resemblance to Irenaeus's more florid account. Origen's description of universal eschatology—the end of the world as we know it—emphasizes a gradual dawning of God's kingdom as people grow in their understanding of God through Christ. Apocalyptic elements (images of conflict and catastrophe) are not entirely absent from Origen's eschatology, but they are not as prominent in his writing as in Irenaeus's.

The same kind of diversity is noticeable in the age of the Protestant Reformation. Most of the so-called mainstream or magisterial Reformers such as Luther and Calvin played down the apocalyptic imagery of the New Testament in favor of Christ's present but hidden rule and reign and a kind of reverent agnosticism about the future. Many of the so-called radical Reformers such as the Anabaptists tended to emphasize the conflictual and future nature of the inauguration of God's kingdom. In the twentieth century Protestant Christians sometimes divided into separate denominations over issues of universal eschatology such as whether there would be or would not be a literal one-thousand-year reign of Jesus Christ—kingdom of God—on earth in the future after Christ returns. Millennialists affirm it; amillennialists deny it. Some conservative Protestant Christians elevate detailed belief about the events of the end times to the status of doctrine or even dogma. Other Christians tend to view the matter as less absolute and relegate it to the category of opinion.

As we will see, all Christians have always believed that the world as we know it will end with the return of Jesus Christ; they have always also believed that Christ is not absent now, but that his rule and reign (and God's through him) is hidden and visible primarily in and through the church, which anticipates his kingdom when he returns. Christians believe and have always believed that when Christ returns the kingdom of God will be established and revealed in a new way and that eventually God will create a new heaven and new earth that will last forever. But how should these revealed truths about the future be interpreted? How should the enigmatic New Testament book of Revelation and other biblical apocalyptic books and passages be understood? Do they refer to events that were already happening when they were written or to future events or to both? What will Christ's return be like? Is it imminent? Will it be visible and literal, surrounded by catastrophic events and figures such as the antichrist and the great beast? Will Christ personally and visibly rule and reign on the earth for a millennium? Will the new earth joined with heaven be somehow continuous with this world or an entirely new environment? These are just some of the questions that surround universal eschatology and sometimes obsess Christian futurists. Limitations of space will preclude any thorough, detailed examination of these issues and problems. We must settle for brushing with broad strokes and attempting only to portray the general contours of the Christian eschatological landscape.

We will follow the usual pattern in our treatment of this locus of Christian belief. First, I have already described some of its issues, questions and problems. Next, I will explain the basic Christian consensus about universal eschatology. Third, we will critically examine two alternatives to the Christian consensus that have plagued Christianity from within. After that, we will explore three main Christian approaches to universal eschatology that provide much of the diversity about this subject within Christianity. Finally, I will briefly propose a unitive Christian vision of the future of the world and humanity that affirms the historic Christian consensus. My hope is that this chapter will help readers to take very seriously the Christian hope—confident expectation—for the future that is rooted in God's revealed promises and thus become realistic optimists about the future of the world. It is also my hope that readers will be able to put into perspective the plethora of competing visions of the future that appear on the bookshelves of many Christian (and now also secular) bookstores and realize that they are often nothing more than one author's or one Christian tradition's interpretation of divine revelation and Christian hope.

## The Christian Consensus About Universal Eschatology and the Kingdom of God

Have Christians ever agreed about the nature of the future end of the world and the events surrounding it? A glance through church history and across denominations of Christians might convince one that no such agreement has ever really existed. There is and always has been tremendous diversity within Christianity about Christ's return and God's reign in the future. The creedal affirmations of the undivided early church and the confessional statements of the major branches of Christianity say very little about universal eschatology; no controversy about the subject ever arose within Christianity comparable with the controversies about the Trinity, deity and humanity of Christ and salvation by grace. The Protestant Reformation was not at all about eschatology, even though a few radical Protestant Reformers and movements embraced eschatological beliefs that most of the Reformers either rejected or neglected.

But is there anything in this area of belief among Christians that is recognizable as universally Christian? Are there any beliefs that one must hold in order to be authentically Christian? Or to put the same question negatively, are there any beliefs the denial of which make one less than authentically Christian? There are. Three major doctrines stand out as universally affirmed by all Christians—except those that must be reluctantly considered heretics—for two millennia. The first one is that *Jesus Christ will return to the earth.* This is sometimes known as belief in the *parousia* which means "appearing" or "coming." Christians of all traditions, tribes and denominations have looked forward to the second coming of Jesus Christ. The second universal Christian belief about the collective future is that *when Christ returns he will establish or completely manifest the rule and reign of God—the kingdom of God—that is already at work within history.* The third unifying Christian belief about universal eschatology is that *in the end God will create a new heaven and new earth that will endure forever.* Most Christians consider the new heaven and new earth continuous with the original creation—their redemption through renovation. A few consider that future reality an entirely new creation after destruction of this world. All agree that resurrected and redeemed humans will dwell with God and God will dwell with them in a utopia that will never end.

When Jesus ascended back to his Father in heaven angels appeared and told the disciples, "this same Jesus, who has been taken from you into heaven, will come back in the same way you have seen him go into heaven" (Acts 1:11). Christians have always lived by this promise in hopeful expectation that their Lord and Savior will return. This future event is known among Christians by a variety of terms: second advent, second coming, return of Christ, parousia. It is rooted not only in the angels' witness to the disciples but also in numerous biblical affirmations. Jesus spoke often of his own return after a departure. The disciples did not understand his enigmatic sayings until they reflected back on them after Christ's death, resurrection and ascension. One particularly revealing passage where Jesus instructs the disciples about his leaving and returning is John 14. There Jesus says:

> Do not let your hearts be troubled. Trust in God; trust also in me. In my Father's house are many rooms; if it were not so, I would have told you. I am

going there to prepare a place for you. And if I go and prepare a place for you, I will come back and take you to be with me that you also may be where I am. (Jn 14:1-3)

The context of this saying makes clear that Jesus was not referring to some planned seclusion from which he would return; Jesus spoke often and clearly of his departure by death and subsequent return. The apostles and other writers of the New Testament also emphasized Jesus' return. Paul's Thessalonian letters include significant portions that address the second coming of Christ and events surrounding it. One easily discerns between the lines of these two letters a context of controversy; someone was confusing the Christians in and around Thessalonika about the parousia and resurrection. Paul instructs them that Jesus Christ will return visibly to raise the dead and gather his people to him (1 Thess 4; 2 Thess 2). He comforts them by stressing the fact that Christ's return will be a very public event so they could not have already missed it and by telling them that God's own people will not be surprised because they will be able to discern the signs of Christ's imminent return in the world around them. Only for others will the parousia be like a "thief in the night" (1 Thess 5:2-5).

Second Peter 3 contains instruction and exhortation to early Christians about the public, catastrophic events of Christ's second coming. Much of the book of Revelation deals with the same subject in symbolic language and metaphor. Nevertheless, it is clear that the author of Revelation believed in a coming of Christ at the end of world history. Near the end of his Apocalypse the visionary writer quotes Jesus Christ: "Behold, I am coming soon! Blessed is he who keeps the words of the prophecy in this book" (Rev 22:7). The New Testament contains far too much material about the return of Christ to dismiss it or minimize its importance for Christian belief; for Christians, history's meaning is provided by its end: History ends with God intervening by sending Jesus Christ to judge the world and establish God's visible rule and reign among people.

The early church fathers agreed that Jesus Christ will return; they disagreed about the details of the parousia and all that would lead up to it and come afterwards. They also agreed that while God's kingdom is somehow within the church and hidden in the world, its fulfillment is future and will come when Christ returns. The earliest church fathers who wrote much about the subject of Christ's second coming were adventists and millennialists. That is, they believed in the imminence, visibility and catastrophic nature of the parousia and in an earthly, historical utopia after it. Later church fathers began to soften the harsh apocalypticism of the second- and third-century writers, and they tended to identify the kingdom of God more with the church before Christ's second coming than with a post-parousia earthly utopia. These two visions of the early church fathers were not necessarily in conflict, but they emphasized different themes. The difference is understandable in light of the persecutions of Christians before Constantine (the first self-identified Christian Roman emperor) and their favored status after the so-called conversion of the empire.

Late-second- and early-third-century Christian teachers Irenaeus and Tertullian were clearly apocalyptic millennialists with regard to Christ's return. Their contemporary Origen, who was much more philosophically minded, clearly believed in the second coming of Christ but tended to portray events leading up to it and following it less dramatically. That is, he allegorized much of the New Testament language about eschatology. Irenaeus and Tertullian interpreted the same language more literally. All three of them clearly affirmed a real parousia of Christ—unlike the Gnostics who tended to spiritualize it as an inward, mystical realization of the "Christ" within each person. Irenaeus's description of the return of Christ and events surrounding it is the most detailed and graphic of the three. In book five of *Against Heresies* the influential bishop and church father wrote several chapters about the end times in which he quoted heavily from the book of Revelation and summarized the end of the world as we know it this way:

> But he [the writer of the book of Revelation] indicates the number of the name [of the antichrist] now, that when this man comes we may avoid him, being aware who he is: the name, however, is suppressed, because it is not worthy of being proclaimed by the Holy Spirit. For if it had been declared by Him, he [antichrist] might perhaps continue for a long period. But now as "he was, and is not, and shall ascend out of the abyss, and goes into perdition," as one who has no existence; so neither has his name been declared, for the name of that which does not exist is not proclaimed. But when this Antichrist shall have devastated all things in this world, he will reign for three years and six months, and sit in the temple at Jerusalem; and then the Lord will come from heaven in the clouds, in the glory of the Father, sending this man and those who follow him into the lake of fire; but bringing in for the righteous the times of the kingdom, that is, the rest, the hallowed seventh day; and restoring to Abraham

the promised inheritance, in which kingdom the Lord declared that "many coming from the east and from the west should sit down with Abraham, Isaac, and Jacob."[1]

Clearly Irenaeus was both an adventist and millennialist with regard to his belief about the return of Christ and events at the end of world history. Similar themes are echoed in Tertullian's writings and especially in his *Five Books Against Marcion* 4.39. There the Christian lawyer and theologian of Carthage argues vehemently for Christian belief in a literal return of Jesus Christ and establishment of God's rule and reign on earth against the heretic Marcion and others who tended to spiritualize biblical apocalyptic literature.

The late-fourth- and early-fifth-century bishop and church father Augustine of Hippo may not have been either an adventist or millennialist with regard to the second coming of Christ and the kingdom of God in the future, but he did agree entirely with Irenaeus and Tertullian and all the other fathers of the church about Christ's literal, bodily return. In *Faith, Hope and Charity* he contradicted those who spiritualized and allegorized the second coming of Christ:

> But as to our belief concerning what Christ will do in the future, namely, that He will come from heaven to judge the living and the dead, this does not pertain to our life as we live it here; for neither is it a part of what He did on earth, but of what He will do at the end of the world. It is to this that the Apostle referred when he goes on to say: When Christ shall appear, who is your life, then you shall also appear with Him in glory.[2]

In his massive treatise on divine providence and God's sovereignty over world history entitled *The City of God,* Augustine often refers (especially in book 20) to the "coming of the Lord Jesus Christ to judge the quick [i.e., living] and the dead." Lest anyone attempt to spiritualize that event the bishop wrote, "and of this judgment He [Jesus] went on to say, 'And hath given Him authority to execute judgment also, because He is the Son of man.' Here He shows that He will come to judge in that flesh in which He had come to be judged."[3]

Unlike several earlier church fathers, Augustine treats the church as the

---

[1] Irenaeus *Against Heresies* 5.30.4, *ANF* 1:560.
[2] Augustine *Faith, Hope and Charity (Enchiridion),* trans. Louis A. Arand (Westminster, Md.: Newman, 1963), chap. 54, p. 57.
[3] Augustine *The City of God* 20.6, *NPNF,* 1st ser., 2:425.

kingdom of God and the present age—before Christ's return—as the "tribulation age" described in the New Testament. He also regards this present age as the millennium of Revelation 20—the one-thousand-year rule and reign of Christ during which Satan is bound, the antichrist appears, and Satan is loosed for a season to tempt the nations. Thus, Augustine was not an adventist or millennialist in the usual senses of those terms. He did, nevertheless, believe most fervently in the eventual bodily return of Jesus Christ and the consummation of God's plan to perfect the "City of God" (kingdom of God) which is until then a hidden and spiritual reality.

A quick perusal of the great creeds and confessional statements embraced and promulgated by the Protestant Reformers demonstrates their firm belief in the future return of Christ as a public event. The Augsburg Confession, which unites Lutherans, states in Article 17:

> It is also taught among us that our Lord Jesus Christ will return on the last day for judgment and will raise up all the dead, to give eternal life and everlasting joy to believers and the elect but to condemn ungodly men and the devil to hell and eternal punishment.[4]

Luther himself was somewhat obsessed with the parousia; he believed Christ would return during his own lifetime or soon afterwards, and he regarded the office of the papacy as the antichrist mentioned in the book of Revelation. On the other hand, the great German Reformer forbade his ministers from preaching from the book of Revelation since he did not believe anyone could know what it means and he considered attempts to interpret it divisive and dangerous. Calvin and Wesley, for all their differences, also equally believed in the literal, public, future return of Jesus Christ, although they were very uncomfortable with detailed speculations about the end times and especially with attempts to set dates for Christ's return. Like Augustine, Calvin tended to emphasize the church as the kingdom of God and viewed the millennium as the present church age and the time after the return of Christ as fulfillment of God's rule and reign through the church. His view of the kingdom of God, in other words, was more progressive and less apocalyptic and catastrophic than many Christians'. Wesley also tended to identify God's kingdom with the spiritual presence of Christ through the Holy Spirit

---

[4]John H. Leith, ed., *Creeds of the Churches: A Reader in Christian Doctrine from the Bible to the Present,* rev. ed. (Richmond, Va.: John Knox, 1973), p. 73.

both now and in the future; no more than Calvin did the founder of Methodism focus his attention or that of his followers on details of the end times. And yet, neither Calvin nor Wesley nor their faithful followers ever doubted or questioned the future return of Christ to the world.

Only in the nineteenth and twentieth centuries did certain liberal Christian theologians begin to cast doubt on and even deny the realistic parousia in the future. In reaction to liberal "demythologizing" of the return of Christ and its related events at the end of world history, many conservative Protestant theologians and lay biblical interpreters developed a new, aggressive form of adventism and millennialism that tended to elevate belief in Christ's imminent return and even an earthly, literal thousand-year reign of Christ on earth after the parousia to the status of essential Christian belief. Universal eschatology became a flash point of debate in the so-called liberal-fundamentalist controversy within Protestantism in the late nineteenth and early twentieth centuries. One side of that controversy tended to become obsessed with detailed speculation about the end times and an overly literalistic interpretation of biblical apocalyptic literature. The other side tended to dismiss universal eschatology as myth. Most Christians began to forget the great heritage of Christian belief in the basic theme of Christ's return to establish or fulfill God's kingdom, which became swamped in eschatological fever or else neglected in fear of unsophisticated supernaturalism and reveling in mythology.

In the midst of that situation appeared a new movement of theology that came to be known as "Theology of Hope," associated primarily with two German theologians, Wolfhart Pannenberg and Jürgen Moltmann. During the 1960s through the 1990s these two academic theologians reintroduced realistic eschatology—including public parousia and establishment of God's kingdom on earth—into so-called mainstream theology without including feverish apocalyptic speculation about the end times. Although Moltmann may be some kind of millennialist, neither theologian of hope is an apocalypticist. Neither encourages other-worldly waiting and watching for the parousia; both promote belief in a new appearing of Jesus Christ and God's kingdom on earth as the unity of humanity with each other and with God.[5]

---

[5]See Jürgen Moltmann, *The Coming of God: Christian Eschatology*, trans. Margaret Kohl (Minneapolis: Fortress, 1996); and Wolfhart Pannenberg, *Systematic Theology*, vol. 3, trans. Geoffrey W. Bromiley (Grand Rapids, Mich.: Eerdmans, 1998).

Christians have also always believed in two realities closely related to Christ's future return: *the consummation of God's kingdom* and *the new heaven and new earth*. Of course, they have interpreted these in different ways, but the Christian consensus is clear that when Christ returns, God's kingdom—already inaugurated by Christ's resurrection and the sending of the Holy Spirit to the church—will be completed, and eventually God will renew his creation in a new world that unites heaven and earth. Jesus spoke to his disciples about the futurity of the kingdom of God:

> "There will be signs in the sun, moon and stars. On the earth, nations will be in anguish and perplexity at the roaring and tossing of the sea. Men will faint from terror, apprehensive of what is coming on the world, for the heavenly bodies will be shaken. At that time they will see the Son of Man coming in a cloud with power and great glory. When these things begin to take place, stand up and lift up your heads, because your redemption is drawing near." He told them this parable: "Look at the fig tree and all the trees. When they sprout leaves, you can see for yourselves and know that summer is near. Even so, when you see these things happening, you know that the kingdom of God is near." (Lk 21:25-31)

At the same time, Jesus also instructed the disciples and others about the presence of the kingdom: "the kingdom of God is within you" (Lk 17:21). In Jesus' teaching about the kingdom, then, we can clearly see the paradox of "already but not yet." The same pattern can be observed throughout the New Testament. Few, if any, Christians question or doubt the presence of God's kingdom as a spiritual experience within believers' hearts and minds and within the community of God's people. Not all are aware, however, of the Christian belief about its future fulfillment. And yet that is also part of the revelatory witness of Jesus and the apostles. I have alluded earlier to Paul's reference to the futurity of the kingdom of God in 1 Corinthians 15; there are many others in the apostles' epistles in the New Testament. In 2 Timothy Paul mentions in close connection Christ's appearing, judgment and kingdom (2 Tim 4:1). The epistle to the Hebrews points readers forward to a future "city" that, unlike any earthly city, will endure (Heb 13:14). Second Peter promises a future "new heaven and a new earth, the home of righteousness" (2 Pet 3:13). The final three chapters of the book of Revelation seem to describe a future kingdom of God after Christ's return when Satan will be bound and there will be no temptation as well as a future new heaven and new earth where "there will be no more death or mourning or crying or pain, for the old order of things has passed away" (Rev 21:4). Perhaps the most intriguing canonical passage about the future new order belongs to Paul and appears in the middle of the eighth chapter of his epistle to the Romans: "I consider that our present sufferings are not worth comparing with the glory that will be revealed in us. The creation waits in eager expectation for the sons of God to be revealed. For the creation was subjected to frustration . . . in hope that the creation itself will be liberated from its bondage to decay and brought into the glorious freedom of the children of God" (Rom 8:18-25).

Christians have never reached consensus about whether the future kingdom of God in its fulfillment and the new heaven and new earth are one and the same. Some Christians have clearly distinguished them (millennialism), and others have identified them. This difference of opinion will become clearer when we discuss the diversity of Christian beliefs about universal eschatology. For now it must suffice to say that all Christians have always believed on the basis of the New Testament that Christ's parousia will usher in a consummated kingdom of God and a new heaven and new earth in the form of a new world order without sickness, sin or death.

We have already seen how early church fathers Irenaeus and Tertullian taught about the future end of the world as we know it. Both of them included with Christ's second coming the judgment of the nations and a perfected earthly social order ruled over by Christ. They viewed the new heaven and new earth as an everlasting reality after the millennial reign of Christ. Their contemporary North African church father and theologian Origen wrote more about the new world order after Christ's return than about the apocalyptic events surrounding that parousia. Two eccentric tendencies stand out in Origen's eschatology. First, he seems to have believed in ultimate, universal reconciliation of all things with each other and with God (*apokatastasis*) as an essential component of the future kingdom of God and consummation of God's plan in a new heaven and new earth. Second, he portrayed the dawning of the consummation as gradual and progressive rather than sudden and catastrophic. In spite of these eccentric elements, Origen's eschatology included the general features of the Christian consensus beginning with the New Testament itself. He was well aware of most, if not all, of the apostolic writings and was a great scholar of those and other canonical and noncanonical scriptures. While he tended to interpret apoca-

lyptic literature allegorically—which is how he could view the coming of
Christ and the inauguration of the future kingdom of God as progressive—
Origen definitely believed in and taught a future new order of things after
Christ returns. Typical of Origen's philosophical style is his contrast between
what the Stoics believed about the future and what Christians believe about
it in his *Against Celsus:*

> The Stoics, indeed, hold that, when the strongest of the elements prevails, all
> things shall be turned into fire. But our belief is, that the Word shall prevail
> over the entire rational creation, and change every soul into His own perfec-
> tion; in which state every one, by the mere exercise of his power, will choose
> what he desires, and obtain what he chooses. . . . The consummation of all
> things is the destruction of evil.[6]

Later, North African church father Augustine adamantly rejected Origen's ultimate, universal reconciliation belief, but agreed with Origen and
the entire orthodox-catholic church before him and of his time that after
Christ returns a new order of things devoid of sin and evil will appear.
Augustine called this new world order "the city of God" and contrasted it
with the future "city of the devil" which will be thoroughly evil.

> But after the resurrection [i.e., after Christ returns], when the general judg-
> ment has been held and concluded, there will remain two cities, each with its
> own boundaries—the one Christ's, the other the devil's; the one embracing
> the good, the other, the bad, with both consisting of angels and men. For the
> one group the will to sin will be impossible, for the other, the power to do so.
> Nor will any manner of death remain. The former will live truly and happily in
> eternal life, the latter will drag on, miserable in eternal death—unable to die;
> for both are now without end.[7]

These two very different early Christian fathers both equally reflect common Christian belief in the future fulfillment of God's rule and reign over
creation and in a complete renovation of creation in its union with heaven.

The Protestant Reformers all affirmed the same future hope for a world of
peace, harmony and justice as well as a perfected, renewed world united with
heaven as the early church fathers. Luther and Calvin and their followers,
including the English Protestant Reformers—the so-called magisterial

---

[6]Origen *Against Celsus* 8.72, *ANF* 1:667.
[7]Augustine *Faith, Hope and Love* 26.111.

Reformers—all viewed the true church of Jesus Christ as the kingdom of God on earth within world history, but they all also looked forward to a future time after Christ returns when the spiritual impulses of righteousness hidden within the church and mixed there with sin would prevail and permeate all of creation. They tended to stress continuity between the future kingdom of God in its consummation and perfection and the present kingdom of God hidden within the spiritual lives of believers and made manifest in the proclamation of the gospel within the church and its affects on individuals and society. Yet there can be no doubt that the Reformers and their faithful followers also realized and affirmed realistic hope for future renewal and unimaginable change in the physical creation and social order. Calvin wrote in his *Institutes*:

> But since the prophecy that death will be swallowed up in victory will only then [at the final resurrection of the dead] be fulfilled, let us always have in mind the eternal happiness, the goal of resurrection—a happiness of whose excellence the minutest part would scarce be told if all were said that the tongues of all men can say. For though we very truly hear that the Kingdom of God will be filled with splendor, joy, happiness, and glory, yet when these things are spoken of, they remain utterly remote from our perception, and, as it were, wrapped in obscurities, until that day comes when he will reveal to us his glory, that we may behold it face to face.[8]

The Genevan Reformer continued after that to caution against curious speculation about the details of heaven and encouraged Christians to be content with what has been clearly revealed and can be known from divine revelation without speculation. Many Christians have not heeded Calvin's warnings against eschatological speculation and have attempted to add to the basic Christian consensus about universal eschatology numerous details about the "furniture of heaven and temperature of hell"—that is, highly speculative guesses and hunches about the end times and the ultimate future of all things that seem more imaginative than solidly rooted in divine revelation, Christian tradition, reason or common Christian experiences of worship, prayer and transformation.

**Alternatives to the Christian Consensus About Universal Eschatology**
Very few heresies have appeared within Christianity that have to do with the

---

[8]John Calvin *Institutes of the Christian Religion* 3.10.

end times. So long as Christians affirm the three minimal beliefs of promise and hope described above they are usually considered well within Christian boundaries of belief. Of course, some denominations, churches and organizations have chosen to include more detailed beliefs in their official statements of faith and ministers of those groups and organizations must at least pay lip service to those. For example, in the twentieth century many fundamentalist Protestant denominations, churches and organizations have required belief in a literal one-thousand-year millennial reign of Christ on the earth after his parousia and some have gone so far as to require belief in a secret "rapture" of all true believers at the beginning of the "great tribulation" that is believed to precede the parousia. Premillennialism is one Christian interpretation of the events of the future, but it is hardly the only orthodox Christian view.

Belief in a so-called rapture (i.e., secret departure of true believers from the earth seven or three and a half years before the public appearing of Christ) is catching on among Christians and even non-Christians through popular novels and movies. It is not part of the great consensus of Christian belief. Nor is it heresy. It is the interpretation of a group of Christians; the vast majority of Christians had never heard of it until the twentieth century and even the 1960s when it was popularized by writers such as Hal Lindsay. The point is that Christian eschatology allows for great diversity and variety about details. There are two main alternative beliefs that have arisen and gained some popularity in the twentieth century. They have more ancient roots, but they are particularly sinister because of their wide acceptance in the modern Christian churches. The first one is *radically realized eschatology*, and the second one is *extreme adventism*. Neither of these is embraced officially by any major Christian denomination; they are rather theological perspectives of the future held by individual Christian scholars, ministers and a few laypeople. They are valid Christian perspectives taken to extremes, and that is what makes them alternatives to Christian belief.

*Radically realized eschatology* is any view of universal eschatology that claims the parousia, kingdom of God, and new heaven and new earth have already been realized. It is the belief that

> eschatological expectation . . . is not so much a looking forward to certain events which will happen in the future, but rather, apprehending Jesus Christ in repentance and faith in every moment when we confront him. It is in a real

sense a timeless eschatology. The eschatological moment is very much *now*, when eternity breaks into time in the Word of judgment and grace, and creates faith and a life centred in God.[9]

As we have already seen, the paradox of the kingdom of God in Scripture and in the tradition of Christian teaching about universal eschatology includes an element of realized eschatology. That is, there is a sense in which the kingdom of God already is actual. It is "within" or "among" the people of God and hidden within the church and the world. But classical Christian belief acknowledges a future fulfillment of the kingdom of God inaugurated by a realistic return of Christ to this world. Radically realized eschatology errs by denying that future aspect except as possibly a gradual increase in the kingdom's intensity. Radically realized eschatology reduces the coming of Jesus Christ and his kingdom and God's new heaven and new earth to a spiritual, existential reality within the hearts and lives of believers and within the church.

The Gnostics of early Christianity embraced a realized eschatology insofar as they believed that all the promises of God *could be* experienced in their fullness outside of world history and apart from the physical world. They considered time and matter evil or at least tending toward evil, and so they could not hope for redemption within time or of the world.[10] Church fathers such as Irenaeus, Tertullian and Augustine contradicted Gnosticism's overly realized eschatology and argued that Christ's return, the resurrection of everyone, the kingdom of God, the judgment and new heaven and earth will be real events and states of affairs within creation and not outside of it.

Certain forms of liberal and neo-orthodox Protestant theology in the modern world have paralleled ancient Gnosticism's overly realized eschatology. For some of them, the kingdom of God is "always coming but never arriving"—an impossible ideal hovering above history and achieved in moments of justice or transformed self-understanding in authentic existence through faith in the cross of Christ. The twentieth-century German New Testament scholar and theologian Rudolf Bultmann seems to have embraced a fully realized eschatology in which the return of Jesus Christ—the parou-

---

[9]Robert C. Doyle, *Eschatology and the Shape of Christian Belief* (Carlisle, U.K.: Paternoster, 1999), p. 261.

[10]For an excellent description and examination of ancient and modern Gnosticism and its realized eschatology, see Carl A. Raschke, *The Interruption of Eternity: Modern Gnosticism and the Origins of the New Religious Consciousness* (Chicago: Nelson-Hall, 1980).

sia—and the consummation of the kingdom of God take place in every moment where a person is confronted by Jesus Christ through the Word of the Cross (proclamation of the gospel) and responds in absolute faith. Bultmann demythologized the supernatural narratives and apocalyptic literature of Scripture and found their true meaning not in outer history but in inner history—the existential self-understanding of persons before God.[11]

Existentialist, consistently realized eschatology is not the only form of that heresy. There are more conservative forms as well. Bultmann and others like him seem to have been driven to radically realized eschatology by aversion to the supernatural. However, forms of radically realized eschatology that are heavily supernaturalistic exist as well. For example, some persons associated with certain manifestations of the charismatic movement affirm a realized eschatology known informally as "Kingdom Now" theology. Not all of them deny futuristic, realistic universal eschatology, but they have in common a nearly exclusive focus on the realization of God's kingdom in its fullness within this present world age. There is little or no need for future hope; real Christian hope is for the Holy Spirit's transformation of Spirit-filled men and women into "the manifest Sons of God" here and now.

Whereas classical Pentecostalism and most early charismatics—especially in the so-called mainline denominations—enthusiastically affirmed the imminent return of Jesus Christ and sometimes fell into a certain otherworldly asceticism due to apocalyptic expectations, radical Pentecostals and charismatics associated with Kingdom Now theology have little or nothing to say about the literal, bodily return of Jesus Christ and the future kingdom of God on earth or in a new heaven and new earth. Their hope is entirely and exclusively for present blessings that often include financial prosperity, total physical healing (sometimes including ability to skip death) and supernatural powers that may even enable them to control the social world and turn it into Christ's domain. The writings of these radical Pentecostals and charismatics are normally found only in specialized Christian bookstores and are available from television and radio evangelists. Exclusively realized eschatology is antithetical to Christianity because it explicitly or implicitly denies a major element of both divine revelation and Christian tradition: the promise and hope of Christ's bodily return to the world for judgment and redemption and establishment of God's rule and reign over everything and every-

---

[11]See Rudolf Bultmann, *Jesus Christ and Mythology* (New York: Charles Scribner's Sons, 1958).

one. This aspect of Christian belief cannot be spiritualized or existentialized into the present; it is what provides Christians with their restlessness about the present and prophetic expectation of something better.

The second alternative to Christian universal eschatology is *extreme adventism and millennialism*. This heresy is the opposite of the first one; it identifies the kingdom of God—God's rule and reign—as exclusively future and pits that future when Christ returns in catastrophic mode against the past and present which are viewed as devoid of God's kingdom. Many churches and denominations have the word *Adventist* in their names. The largest and best known is the General Conference of Seventh-day Adventist Churches, but there are others, and some adventist groups do not even use that term. "Extreme adventism" is not necessarily embraced or promoted by all of these self-identified adventist movements and organizations. In order to qualify as "extreme adventism" the eschatology must go beyond merely emphasizing Bible prophecy and "the signs of the times" to attempting to identify the year of Christ's return and emphasizing dogmatically a detailed set of extra-biblical concepts about the end of the world. Adventism becomes heretical when it goes the next step and portrays the present age of world history and the present creation as godless such that God is not Lord and sovereign ruler now but only in the future.

Like the Kingdom Now form of radically realized eschatology, extreme adventism seldom appears in a formal statement that expressly denies God's present lordship; it normally appears in such obsessive, one-sided focus on the futurity of God's kingdom that the world in which we now live (nature, history) is naturally viewed as not only fallen under a curse but pervasively evil. The first alternative belief—radically realized eschatology—emphasized *continuity* between God's kingdom and present reality (inward, spiritual, churchly), whereas extreme adventism emphasizes *discontinuity* to the point of totally neglecting all continuity. This heresy (or serious error of belief) may be found in certain offshoots of the Adventist movement that are sects or cults of Christianity. Some of them peddle their extreme emphasis on the future kingdom of God and extremely negative views of the present world and even the church via television and radio programs and door-to-door witnessing with colorful brochures and booklets about the future kingdom and how to survive the destruction of this world and live forever in God's earthly paradise.

Extreme adventism is mistaken and represents an alternative to the Christian consensus of belief because it neglects or denies the present reality of God's kingdom and focuses so much on future events and conditions that concern for this world drops away. It also falls into conflict with Christian belief in God's sovereignty now as well as in the future. It has a tendency to focus more on future redemption than on the cross and resurrection of Jesus Christ as God's crucial redeeming works. Extreme adventism devalues the church of Jesus Christ except as a spiritual lifeboat for those who want to be ready when Christ returns. All in all, we must reluctantly criticize both radically realized eschatology in all its forms and extreme adventism in all its forms as sub-Christian at best and antithetical to true Christianity at worst.

### Diversity Within Christian Belief About Universal Eschatology

Very few official divisions have taken place among Christians solely over disagreements about eschatology. And yet there exist within Christianity several significant models of the kingdom of God and its relationship with the second coming of Christ and the re-creation of heaven and earth. Occasionally branches and groups of Christians have felt strongly enough about a particular vision of the kingdom of God and the end times that they have elevated it to the status of doctrine for that group. Very few Christians have ever treated one of these models as essential Christian belief even when they have promoted it vigorously. Before examining the models themselves it will be helpful to understand divergent approaches to interpreting Scripture's apocalyptic literature—those portions of Scripture that deal with the kingdom of God and the return of Jesus Christ symbolically and heavily emphasize conflict, catastrophe and extremes of good and evil pitted against one another. The best known example is the book of Revelation, which is also known as the Apocalypse of John. Portions of Daniel and Matthew and other books of the Bible are also of the apocalyptic genre. Much Christian belief about the end of the world as we know it derives from these apocalyptic passages of Scripture. Fortunately we are not totally dependent on them, because they are notoriously difficult to understand. Differences of opinion about universal eschatology often arise from different hermeneutical approaches to apocalyptic literature.

Three main Christian approaches to understanding apocalyptic literature are *futurism, preterism* and *historicism*. A quick glance at definitions of these terms in theological dictionaries will only confuse most readers. Especially *futurism* and *historicism* also have other meanings unrelated to eschatology and apocalyptic literature. Here they refer to beliefs about the time and history references of the symbols used in apocalyptic books and passages. For example, when the book of Revelation uses the image of the antichrist is it referring to someone or something that existed when the book was written (or vision experienced)? Or is it referring to an exclusively future person or entity? Or is it perhaps referring to a reality that was future when the book was written but appeared afterwards and is now, to contemporary readers, past or already present and no longer future? There is no consensus among biblical scholars about these matters.

Futurism is the mode of interpretation that assumes most or all of the symbols and images of biblical apocalyptic literature refer to realities still in the future. Preterism regards all or most as already fulfilled for us even if the fulfillment was future for the visionary and his first readers. Historicism sees the symbols and images as codes for persons, entities and events contemporary with the apocalypticists. Thus for a futurist the antichrist is yet to appear. For a preterist, the antichrist has already appeared and may be an office or a kind of person or political entity rather than a specific person. For a historicist, the antichrist was (for the seer of Revelation) the Roman emperor or simply Rome itself. It is easy to see, then, that how one views the kingdom of God and Christ's return and the new heaven and new earth promised in divine revelation may depend somewhat or very much on which approach to interpreting apocalyptic literature one follows (or vice versa).

The three main models of Christian belief about universal eschatology are *premillennialism, postmillennialism* and *amillennialism*.[12] *Millennialism* refers simply to any belief in an earthly, visible rule and reign of Christ within world history. It is sometimes even used for belief in Christ's invisible rule and reign through the church if or when it results in a true Christianization of all the nations. Such a Christianization of the world would be a millennium if it is immediately preceded or followed by Christ's return. (Here *millennium* refers to a specific earthly historical, and political order over which Christ rules. Such a world order led by Christ during which Satan is "bound" is found in Revelation 20.)

*Premillennialism* is any belief that Christ will return visibly to the earth at

---

[12]These models are well described in the following volumes: Doyle, *Eschatology;* Stanley J. Grenz, *The Millennial Maze: Sorting Out Evangelical Options* (Downers Grove, Ill.: InterVarsity Press, 1992); and Robert G. Clouse, ed., *The Meaning of the Millennium: Four Views* (Downers Grove, Ill.: InterVarsity Press, 1977).

the end of this present age of world history and establish his kingdom—the kingdom of God in its fullness—over all the world. In order for a model of the end to be truly premillennial it does not have to include a literal one thousand years, but it must include some earthly, socio-political (not merely spiritual), historical reign of God through Jesus Christ *after* the parousia and *before* the new heaven and new earth. For premillennialists, Christ's return will be accompanied by the sounding of the "trumpet of the Lord" (that is, it will be very public), but time will *not* be "no more." Rather, history will continue—probably for a thousand years. During that millennium Christ himself will rule and reign as Messiah and Lord and he will enforce peace and justice. This interim period between this present age and the new heaven and new earth ("New Jerusalem" mentioned in Rev 21) will be the fulfillment and manifestation of the kingdom of God.

Premillennialists come up with all kinds of diverse interpretations of what will happen just before Christ returns and during the millennium, but they all agree that Christ will reign on earth and every knee shall bow and every tongue confess that he is Lord unto the glory of God the Father. Some premillennialists believe in a two-stage parousia of Christ including a "secret rapture" of true believers before Christ returns bodily to destroy the antichrist and usher in his earthly kingdom. Many do not. Premillennialism enjoyed popularity among Christians primarily in the early church and the late modern church. It was almost unheard of for fifteen hundred years except among a few marginal individuals and groups. Early church fathers Irenaeus and Tertullian were premillennialists, as are twentieth-century evangelical Christian theologians George Eldon Ladd and Millard Erickson. Most popularizers of Christian eschatology, including the vast majority of writers of Christian fiction dealing with the end times (Tim LaHaye), and most television evangelists (Jerry Falwell) are premillennialists.

Premillennialists appeal to many different passages of Scripture scattered throughout the Bible to support their belief in an earthly kingdom of God led by Jesus Christ after his return. They view Old Testament prophecies of a fulfilled and perfected Davidic kingdom and of an earthly paradise as evidence of and support for premillennialism. One such passage is Isaiah 11, which anticipates a righteous descendent of King David ("shoot . . . from the stump of Jesse") ruling the earth during a time when "the wolf will live with the lamb, the leopard will lie down with the goat, the calf and the lion and the yearling together; and a little child will lead them. . . . The earth will be full of the knowledge of the LORD as the waters cover the sea" (Is 11:6-9). Premillenialists especially look to Revelation 20, which three times mentions a one-thousand-year period during which Satan will be bound and Christ will reign over the nations with his martyred, resurrected saints.

When asked the purpose of this interim kingdom of God—the millennium—premillennialists suggest that it will be God's way of demonstrating righteousness and showing humanity (and possibly heavenly beings as well) what he intended the world to be like—especially if people had accepted Jesus Christ as their Messiah and Lord when he came the first time. Critics argue that premillennialists are too literalistic in their interpretations of biblical prophecies and apocalyptic literature. Some critics also believe that premillennialism inevitably detracts from Christian concern for the environment and social justice now. If Christ will come to straighten everything out, they ask, why feel urgency to work for the kingdom now?

The second main Christian model of universal eschatology is *postmillennialism*. It is belief in an actual kingdom of God on earth *before* Christ's second coming. In order to count as true postmillennialism the model of the kingdom of God must include a Christianization of the world order prior to the parousia. It does not have to include belief in everyone's salvation. In fact, most postmillennialists have not embraced universalism of salvation even during the millennium. Postmillennialism is an optimistic view of history and the kingdom of God. According to it, "Jesus shall reign where e're the sun does its successive courses run," and the story Christians tell to the nations will "turn their hearts to the right" and "the darkness shall turn to dawning, the dawning to noonday bright, and Christ's great kingdom shall come on earth, the kingdom of love and light" (Isaac Watts 1719)—all without any visible return of Christ until afterwards.

Two prominent and influential postmillennialists were Daniel Whitby, late-seventeenth- and early-eighteenth-century Anglican theologian, and eighteenth-century New England Puritan preacher and theologian Jonathan Edwards. Postmillennialism became very popular in the New World (North America) under the influence of the Puritans. It suffered a severe setback in the world wars and genocidal atrocities of the twentieth century. Things no longer seemed to be evolving into the kingdom of God. Premillennialism largely replaced postmillennialism as the most popular and influential Christian form of millennialism. However, a few postmillennialists have pressed its cause throughout the century. Reformed theologians Lorraine Boettner

(United States) and Hendrikus Berkhof (Netherlands) have championed it, as have a few Lutheran theologians. If there is any prooftext to support post-millennialism it would be Matthew 13:31-33:

> He [Jesus] told them another parable: "The kingdom of heaven is like a mustard seed, which a man took and planted in his field. Though it is the smallest of all your seeds, yet when it grows, it is the largest of garden plants and becomes a tree, so that the birds of the air come and perch in its branches."
>
> He told them still another parable: "The kingdom of heaven is like yeast that a woman took and mixed into a large amount of flour until it worked all through the dough."

Critics of postmillennialism consider its biblical support too thin and point out that nobody in church history seems to have embraced it before the late seventeenth century (Daniel Whitby). They also view it as hopelessly optimistic about the upward direction of history. Was the twentieth century—touted as the "Christian Century" at its beginning—any better than the calamitous fourteenth century? Perhaps it was worse. Postmillennialists, however, view the kingdom of God as a social order that will come with ups and downs, and they defend their model as a powerful motive for Christian involvement in social justice and evangelism.

The third Christian model of universal eschatology is *amillennialism*—denial of any sociopolitical, historical kingdom of God before or after Christ's return. The vast majority of Christian theologians and church leaders since the church father Augustine have been amillennialists. Augustine's *City of God* identified the kingdom of God with the church and with God's hidden rule and reign within the world generally. That is, Augustine tended to spiritualize the kingdom of God without in any way denying the future return of Christ. What would come after Christ's parousia would be the judgment and then the new heaven and new earth (and, of course, hell). For Augustine, the millennium or one-thousand-year period mentioned in Revelation 20 was the time between Christ's incarnation and his return—the age of the church. Of course, even for Augustine, the city of God, the great kingdom of God, continues for eternity. The new heaven and new earth created by God after Christ's return will be a new form of God's glorious rule and reign over creation. But for him, as for all amillennialists, the primary form of the kingdom of God *within history* is not a utopian social order in which all the nations of the earth are Christianized or under Christ's political dominion (as in millennialisms), but God's spiritual presence through Christ and the Holy Spirit in the church and in heaven. The only essential difference between amillennialism and millennialism of both kinds (post- and pre-) is that the former does not believe in a literal kingdom of God within history and on this earth as a "new world order" under the dominion of Christ himself or Christian principles. Amillennialists simply interpret the apparent biblical references to such an earthly, historical kingdom of God spiritually or else as referring to the post-parousia new heaven and new earth. They see no need for a literal millennium within history.

Christian millennialists are not satisfied with amillennial interpretation of Revelation 20 and other biblical passages that seem clearly to point toward a time on earth and within history when Satan will be bound and Christ will rule and reign over all the nations. If one is allowed to spiritualize such passages, they wonder, what else in Scripture might be spiritualized? They fear that amillennialism may lead to radically realized eschatology. Also, Christian millennialists and especially premillennialists point to the fact that most of the earliest church fathers who touched on eschatology in their writings were premillennialists and argued against allegorizing or spiritualizing New Testament references to the historical kingdom of God during which Satan will literally be bound and after which the judgment and new heaven and new earth will take place. Only with Augustine did amillennialism replace premillennialism as the most widely accepted model of universal eschatology among Christians. Many premillennialists wonder if that could possibly have anything to do with the so-called Christianizing of the Roman Empire or Constantinianism in which the lines between the church, empire and kingdom of God became blurred.

Amillennialists, on the other hand, argue that it is perfectly legitimate to interpret Revelation 20's references to a thousand-year rule and reign of Christ allegorically or spiritually because so much of Revelation and apocalyptic literature in general is symbolic. Furthermore, they argue, there is simply no need for a literal millennium. Every biblical reference to the kingdom of God can be understand adequately without that. The kingdom of God is one reality in several manifestations—the church, God's presence in Christian hearts and lives, whenever and wherever God's revealed will is being done, paradise, the future new heaven and new earth.

Debates among Christians over these eschatological models used to consume a great deal of time, energy and attention. Some denominations of

Christians took firm positions on one side or another. The Roman Catholic Church has always tended to assume amillennialism. Most Lutheran and Reformed Protestants are amillennialists as are most traditional Baptists, Methodists and members of the Churches of Christ. In the twentieth century many conservative Baptists and some fundamentalist Presbyterians adopted premillennialism. The vast majority of Pentecostals embrace premillennialism. No denomination is officially postmillennial. That dying eschatological model is found primarily among certain Lutheran and Reformed theologians, although it is enjoying a small renaissance among Kingdom Now Pentecostals and charismatics.

## A Unitive Christian Vision of Universal Eschatology

Two dangers face Christian reflection about universal eschatology and the issue of what beliefs Christians ought and even must hold regarding the ultimate future of the world and humanity. First, there is the danger of minimizing Christian truth and belief about these future events and states of affairs. Some Christians would like to leave the entire subject in a cloudy realm of unknowing—sheer mystery—because they are afraid that teaching and preaching about the future and what has been revealed about it will somehow detract from interest and involvement in the present. Many churches and Christian organizations never touch on the subject; some positively avoid it. The phenomenon of eschatological fever that has occasionally gripped certain sectors of Christianity especially in North America since the mid-nineteenth century is often used as an excuse to neglect Christian discussion of the end times entirely. One frequently hears the claim to "panmillennialism"—"It will all pan out in the end"—as a discussion-stopper when questions and issues of the kingdom of God arise.

The second danger is as great if not greater than the first. It is the danger of eschatological fanaticism and obsession. Beginning at least with the rise of the Adventist movement in New York and New England in the 1830s, wave after wave of intense focus on the "signs of the times" and speculation about the year of Christ's return and meanings of symbols in biblical apocalyptic literature have rolled through North American Protestant Christianity. Some churches, denominations and religious organizations have responded to this eschatological fervor with lengthy doctrinal statements requiring their adherents to affirm a detailed set of beliefs about the end of the world. Books with titles such as "Eighty-eight reasons why Christ will return in

1988" have appeared in Christian bookstores, and entire ministries have been devoted to frightening people into repentance and faith by means of lurid accounts of the antichrist and his sidekick the Great Beast and the terrible havoc they will wreak on those who miss the secret rapture at the beginning of the great tribulation period. Many Christians have come to equate this kind of highly speculative, detailed, frightening belief about the end times with biblical eschatology in general. Others have rushed away from that so quickly and so far that they do not want even to touch the subject of universal eschatology. The few moderate, balanced books published about this area of Christian belief go out of print quickly due to lack of interest.

Christians need to realize that God's revelation of the future is *good news.* It is not meant to frighten people with visions of their doom and destruction should they happen to miss some secret rapture event that comes like a thief in the night. Instead, we need to recapture the notes of great promise and high hopes that infuse the biblical message about the future. That message is, in a nutshell, *God wins in the end.* And if God is both perfectly good and great, there is nothing for those who trust in him to fear. The biblical message and therefore the essence of Christian belief about the future is that every corruption of creation will be healed and God will be all in all or everything to everyone. Christian belief in the future should focus on the promise of peace and reconciliation, love and justice, abundant life and fulfillment. These are not legitimate hopes, however, without some basic, core beliefs about what happens to bring them about. Christians need to learn how to revel in Christian hope for the future without wallowing in sensationalism and fear-mongering. We need to realize that the great kingdom of God inaugurated by Jesus Christ in his first coming will be completed and fulfilled by the same Jesus Christ in his second coming. One Savior and Lord; one great kingdom in different modes of manifestation.

Christians can embrace one another as equally Christian in spite of differences of opinion about world eschatology. Postmillennialists, amillennialists, premillennialists can agree on the more important beliefs that have united Christians for two thousand years: that Jesus Christ will return to the world he left on the day of his ascension, that God's rule and reign of love and justice will be finally realized and made manifest to all so that God's will shall be done "on earth as in heaven," and that God will renovate this creation and unite it with heaven so that his people will dwell with him in a new heaven and new earth for eternity. We cannot expect to know much about "the furniture of heaven" or the "temperature of hell," but we can hold fast to the distinctively Christian hope (confident expectation) that the ultimate resolution to the intractable problems of nature and history lies not in failing human devices, plans and schemes but in the one who is coming; the Christian does not live in despair over "what this world is coming to" but in hope because of "who is coming to this world."

# Names Index

# Subject Index

adiaphora, 44-45
adoptionism, 142, 143, 225, 233-34, 237
adventism, adventist, 327-29, 338, 339, 340, 348-49
Albigensians. *See* Cathari
Alexandria, Alexandrian school, 235, 237
amillennialism, amillennialists, 333, 350, 353-55, 356
Anabaptist(s), 118, 139, 231, 250, 272, 299, 300, 302, 303, 313, 314, 333
animal rights, 167
annihilationism, annihilationists, 321, 328-29, 330
antichrist, 333, 337, 339, 350, 356
antinomian, 283
Antioch, Antiochian school, 235-37
apartheid, 192
apocalyptic literature, 333, 339, 340, 342, 349-50, 352
   futurist interpretation, 349-50
   historicist interpretation, 349-50
   preterist interpretation, 349-50
Apocrypha, 90, 91
*apokatastasis,* universalism, 273, 275-76, 329, 342, 352
Apollinarianism, 236
apologetics, 73, 221
apostles, 289-90, 291-92, 295, 305, 312, 336, 341
Apostles' Creed, 37, 54, 55,

64, 157
Arian controversy, Arianism, 137, 142, 144, 234-35
Arminianism, Arminians, 14, 196, 272, 277-78, 280-85
Athanasian Creed, 55, 245
atonement, 244-63, 265, 276, 278
   Christus Victor theory, 259, 261
   governmental theory, 261
   limited, 278-79
   moral example theory, 252-53
   moral influence theory, 258-59
   objective, 256, 262
   penal substitution theory, 260
   propitiation, 262
   ransom theory, 256-57
   satisfaction theory, 257-58
   subjective, 256, 262
   vicarious penitent theory, 260
Augsburg Confession, 38, 296, 313, 339
baptism, 220, 282-85, 289, 292-94, 296, 299-303
   of the Holy Spirit, 285, 294
   baptismal regeneration, 219
Baptists, 134, 219, 226, 261, 284, 285, 299, 302, 303, 355
belief, 20-21
big bang, 167, 188
bishops, 291-92, 295, 298, 305
Book of Common Prayer, 298
Calvinism, 277-85
Carthage, Council of, 91
Cathari (Albigensians), 166
cessationism, cessationists,

85, 88
Chalcedon, Council of, 226-28, 238
Chalcedonian Definition, 38, 55, 226-27, 230-32, 245
Christian Reformed Church, 285, 298-99, 313, 355
Christomonism, 125
*Christus Victor* theme, 250, 259, 261. *See also* atonement
church, 287-306, 333, 339, 341, 344
Church of Christ, 299, 355
Church of England (Anglican), 230, 272, 284, 285, 296, 297, 298, 300, 325, 329, 352
classical theism, 129
congregationalism, congregational, 297, 299
Constantinople, First Council of, 137, 289, 290
Constantinople, Second Council of, 275
consubstantiation, 40-41, 301
Coptic Church, 232
cosmological argument, 82
creation, 155-75
   out of nothing *(creatio ex nihilo)*, 159, 160, 165, 166, 167, 172, 196
Creation Research Institute, 169
creationism, 155, 168
   progressive, 171-72, 175
   young earth (scientific), 169-70, 172, 175
creeds, 38, 200, 245
Darwinianism, Neo-Darwinianism, 170, 172
death, 308, 317, 320, 325, 326
Deism, Deists, 60-61, 65,

# Scripture Index

Hegel p.24

Great Tradition:
- Trinity
- Hypostatic Union
- Resurrection, ascention and
  session of Christ.